Mass Communications in the Caribbean

Mass Communications in the Caribbean

J O H N   A.   L E N T

Iowa State University Press / Ames

For my father, John Lent,
who set an unselfish example

For my mother, Rose Marie Lent,
who provided the discipline and encouragement

JOHN A. LENT is director of Third World Media Associates, 669 Ferne Blvd., Drexel Hill, Pennsylvania 19026.

Manufactured in the United States of America
♾ This book is printed on acid-free paper.

First edition, 1990

Library of Congress Cataloging-in-Publication Data

Lent, John A.
    Mass communications in the Caribbean / John A. Lent. — 1st ed.
        p.   cm.
    Includes bibliographical references (p.   ).
    ISBN 0–8138–1182–1 (alk. paper)
    1. Mass media — Caribbean Area.   I. Title.
P92.C33L46   1990
302.23′09729 — dc20   90–33583
                                                         CIP

CONTENTS

v

II. Topical Perspectives

INTRODUCTION

Variety characterizes the Caribbean, where cultural remnants from nearly every continent blend and create a patchwork effect — Danish street names in St. Croix, Amsterdamesque building facades in Willemstad, Indian curry restaurants in Trinidad, Latin American rhythms in the Dominican Republic, Eastern European tinned foods in Cuba, and African folktales and linguistic roots almost everywhere.

The diversity of the Caribbean represents a microcosmic picture of the history of Western exploration. Before the first mainland colonies of the United States were fully organized, flourishing appendages of England, France, the Netherlands, and Spain had been set up in the Caribbean. Other European countries also left their imprint — Denmark in the Virgin Islands and Sweden in St. Bartholomew (see Appendix). Even two noncountries exerted a powerful influence; the Dukes of Courland ruled in Tobago and the Order of St. John of Jerusalem, under its Grand Masters in Malta, in St. Croix.

Some islands were moved about as pawns in European wars. St. Lucia changed flags on thirteen occasions, and St. Croix did so seven times. This factor, along with the extermination of the native Arawaks and Caribs by the Europeans and the many migration flows, left islands without stable institutions or indigenous cultures and peoples. For example, Martinique had a succession of populations that included Caribs, Arawaks, French, Africans, East Indians, other Europeans, and French-speaking immigrants from North Africa and Southeast Asia.

Colonial political groupings often did not match up with cultural ones. Thus, Guadeloupe, Martinique, Dominica, and St. Lucia (the first two under French rule, the last two under British) formed a linguistic unit where the people now speak mutually understood Creoles, similar to the language of Haiti. On the other hand, the politically severed island of St. Maarten (under French and Dutch occupancy) has used mainly English and Papiamento, the latter a Creole of the Netherlands Antilles.

The long colonial periods were marked by forces that shaped the

Caribbean—slavery, the plantation system, sugar, and emancipation. Known from the days of Columbus, who enslaved Arawak Indians, slavery in the Caribbean was closely tied to the plantation system and the harvesting of sugar. Before emancipation, more than ten million Africans were shipped to the Caribbean and the mainland United States to carry out European imperialistic designs. In the process, they were thoroughly dehumanized and stripped of their cultures.

When slavery was abolished in the British West Indies in 1838, and later in Cuba in 1886, other sources of manpower were sought. Within a century, 500,000 East Indians and 135,000 Chinese were brought to the region. Workers from other islands were also tapped, and between 1912 and 1924 alone, 250,000 Jamaicans and Haitians moved to Cuba to work the sugar fields under North American tutelage.

Many characteristics of the contemporary West Indies have been attributed to these historical experiences. First, the Caribbean societies are among the most Westernized in the world; having been retained as the oldest colonial sphere of European expansionism, they were imbued with Western education, languages, values, and mass communications. Second, Caribbean peoples, despite regional organizations and interisland migrations, remain isolated from one another. French- and Dutch-speaking islanders are largely unaware of each others' doings and of those of their British Commonwealth Caribbean neighbors, and the reverse also holds true. The policies of colonial powers encouraged communication with European cities, such as London, Paris, or Amsterdam, rather than with other islands. Third, as Caribbean people were denied their cultural heritage and forced to depend upon others psychologically and economically, they lost confidence in themselves, opting to imitate European ways. Fourth, national integration and identity efforts have been less than totally successful in some countries because of their pluralistic natures, brought about by slavery flows and interisland migration.

Virtually all the Caribbean islands, the three Guianas of South America, and British Honduras of Central America remained colonies until after 1958. The only independent countries were Haiti (since its 1803 revolution), the Dominican Republic, and Cuba. The last two were only nominally independent, as they were under U.S. domination for much of the twentieth century. Haiti was under U.S. control for a shorter period.

In 1958–1959, two events changed this political configuration—the formation of the West Indies Federation of British territories and the Castro revolution. The federation, doomed after only four years, lasted long enough to spur Commonwealth Caribbean countries toward independence. By 1966, Jamaica, Trinidad, Barbados, and Guyana declared themselves free of the British, as did the Bahamas in 1973, Grenada in 1974, and six others between 1978 and 1983. The contribution of the second event — Castro's revolution — was to rid Cuba of the twentieth century bane of the Third World — economic dominance by metropolitan countries.

By 1989, Montserrat and the British Virgin Islands remained the only colonies of the British. French Guiana, Guadeloupe, and Martinique had been given departmental status as parts of metropolitan France. Puerto Rico and the U.S. Virgin Islands were still territories of the United States. The Netherlands Antilles functioned as autonomous states of the kingdom of the Netherlands.

Since the 1960s, other political and military upheavals have affected the Caribbean. Cheddi Jagan assumed Guyana's presidency at the advent of the 1960s as the first elected Marxist leader in the hemisphere; he was followed in office by Forbes Burnham, who kept his power despite accusations of rigged elections and other political and human rights violations. In 1965, U.S. troops invaded the Dominican Republic, as they were to do in Grenada nearly two decades later after the murder of Maurice Bishop. Curaçao suffered devastating riots in 1969 that made the Netherlands Antilles somewhat more autonomous, and Jamaica was hit with a number of disturbances in the 1970s during the socialist-leaning government of Michael Manley. In 1980, Suriname experienced a military takeover that changed the status of that country. Haiti, after removing the Duvaliers in 1986, went through a succession of governments, including military ones.

The political economy of the Caribbean made a sharp turn to the right in the 1980s as governments, such as those of Jamaica, Belize, (formerly British Honduras), Dominica, and Antigua, among others, followed the lead of the Reagan administration in the United States. Puerto Rico, Jamaica, Barbados, and Trinidad adopted conservative development models, which resulted in token prosperity amid masses of poverty, and in some cases tourism and offshore banking replaced sugar and other products as economic resources in what would have to be temporary recovery measures. Many countries joined the Reagan administration–created Caribbean Basin Initiative, which promised trade concessions and financial assistance to foster free enterprise and to deter the spread of communism. The latter goal was obsessively on the agenda of the U.S. government and had much to do with the invasion of Grenada and the creation of Radio Martí and, later, Television Martí.

Besides these factors, geography has been responsible for the region's development. The Caribbean region, after all, stretches over great distances. It reaches north to Bermuda, off the coast of South Carolina, and south to Trinidad and the Netherlands Antilles, very near the coast of Venezuela. At its heart are Cuba and the Cayman Islands in the west and the Leewards and Windwards in the east. Added to that are French Guiana, Guyana, and Suriname, all on the northeast coast of South America, and Belize, squeezed between Mexico and Guatemala in Central America. The islands alone make up about fifty inhabited units and span twenty-five hundred miles of sea between Mexico's Yucatan Peninsula and the north coast of South America.

The distances create insularity and often result in little contact among countries with common characteristics. For example, the Commonwealth Caribbean territories of Jamaica and the Eastern Caribbean are separated by one thousand miles of water. In other cases, regional unity and communications have been stymied by the relative sizes of the islands, since the larger ones opted to stay removed from much smaller neighbors. A country such as Jamaica is many times larger than Montserrat, yet Jamaica has only one-tenth the land area of Cuba, which is forty-four thousand square miles. The largest land areas are the mainland units of Guyana, Suriname, Belize, and French Guiana and the islands of Cuba, Hispaniola (the Dominican Republic and Haiti), and Jamaica.

Most Caribbean nations, however, are tiny, actually "island ecosystems," with correspondingly small populations. Cuba is the most populous with about 10 million people. On the other hand, the total population of the thirteen Commonwealth Caribbean nations is about 5.5 million, and that includes a combined total of 3.5 million for Jamaica and Trinidad and Tobago.

All of these geographical, political, and socioeconomic factors have surely fostered the types of communications infrastructures and practices one finds in the Caribbean. Normally, population sizes of countries have determined the degree of development of mass communications channels, and relative proximity to the United States has led most of the region to adopt the U.S. television technological standard and thus its programming. On the other hand, geographical distances between islands have resulted in very little interisland communication and, therefore, insular prejudice and ignorance.

Although most islands have fulfilled their independence goals (many in the past generation), the media in the Caribbean reflect European and U.S. influences. There are newspapers in English, Dutch, French, and Spanish, some using formats or features that are common in London, Amsterdam, or Paris. Episodes of "Dynasty," British dramas, and novellas regularly fill television schedules. Media operations are just as varied economically, ranging from ultramodern newspaper plants, such as those of Jamaica's *Gleaner* or the Puerto Rican dailies, to an apartment converted into a radio studio, such as Guadeloupe's Radyo Tanbou.

Since my first research trip to the Caribbean in 1968, I have tried to capture some of this diversity and also to document the changes in mass communications, of which there have been many. Telecommunications infrastructures have definitely improved, using digitalization, fiber optics, and satellites now in contrast to cable and telephony a generation ago. Still other changes are the increased availability of television through more domestic and satellite-relayed overseas channels; the strengthened regional news flows through Prensa Latina and the Caribbean News Agency (CANA); the diminished role of foreign media owners, such as Rediffusion, King, or Thomson; the greatly augmented dependence upon outsiders for equipment and programming; the tightened governmental control of the media in countries such as Guyana, Antigua, Grenada, and Haiti, among others; and the increase in training activities and professionalization.

All of these and other aspects of change are covered in this book. Unlike the few similar works, *Mass Communications in the Caribbean* employs both historical and contemporary approaches as well as overviews and case studies of the print and electronic media in all countries of the region. Additionally, topical perspectives are provided on technology, national development, research, training and education, and popular culture.

Originally, *Mass Communications in the Caribbean* was to be a collection of some of the more than fifty articles I have written on the region's media. However, as I began to edit and update, I created virtually new chapters. Five chapters (chapters 13, 15, 18, 19, and 26) were written specifically for this volume, four others (chapters 6, 12, 20, and 22) had not been published elsewhere when the book was completed, seven others (chapters 1, 4, 5, 7, 14, 24, and 25) have been reworked and updated so that they constitute new work, and the other ten, although they have not changed much structurally, have been updated. All contemporary media chapters reflect 1980s data, and most are updated to 1987–1988.

For the most part, my emphasis is on the media of those countries where I conducted original research; thus, I have devoted six chapters to the British Commonwealth Caribbean, three to Cuba, and two each to the U.S. Virgin Islands and the Netherlands Antilles. Besides being my main area of research, the Commonwealth Caribbean deserves more attention because of the number of countries involved and the geographical space they cover. The archipelago of British and former British territories strings out from Bermuda off the coast of South Carolina in North America, to Belize in Central America, and to Guyana in South America. The islands alone — Antigua, Barbados, the British Virgin Islands, the Bahamas, Dominica, Grenada, Jamaica, Bermuda, Montserrat, St. Kitts–Nevis, Anguilla, St. Lucia, St. Vincent, and Trinidad and Tobago — have about 13,500 square miles, or about one-seventh the total land area of the Caribbean.

I did interviews and library work in Martinique, Guadeloupe, Cuba, the Dominican Republic, Aruba, Curaçao, St. Croix, St. Thomas, the British Virgin Islands, Belize, the Bahamas, Montserrat, Anguilla, St. Kitts, Antigua, Jamaica, Barbados, Dominica, Grenada, St. Lucia, St. Vincent, and Trinidad. In my fifteen trips to the region, I interviewed more than 130 editors, broadcast managers, other media personnel, government officials (including three prime ministers), and educators. Additionally, I used scores of archives and libraries in the United States and the Caribbean. The complete list is too large to present here, but some of the main ones are the Library Company (Philadelphia); the American Antiquarian Society; the Library of Congress; the Institute of Jamaica; the University of the West Indies; the national archives of Martinique, Cuba, and the Dominican Republic; national and other public libraries in Tortola, St. Croix, St. Thomas, Martinique, Cuba, the Dominican Republic, Anguilla, St. Kitts, Montserrat, Dominica, St. Lucia, St. Vincent, Grenada, Barbados, Trinidad, Jamaica, the Bahamas, and Belize; and the *Trinidad Guardian* library, since destroyed by fire.

In most chapters, I provide a general picture of the mass media in a region or country. However, I have also employed case studies in an effort to hone in on particular issues and problems. The chapter on the Stockdale sisters and Bermuda printing brings to light a little-known story about early women editors in the Caribbean, while the chapter on Rickey Singh's plight exemplifies the problems some press people experienced with West Indian governments. The 1971 portrayal of a small Dominican weekly is given as a real example of the difficulties faced by newspapers in microstates; at the time, that paper, *The Star,* represented one-third of the national press of Dominica. Similar press operations still survive throughout the region. Other case studies focus on Grenadian press-government relationships and the use of U.S. television programming in the Leewards and Windwards and in Belize.

The book is organized into two main parts — regional and country perspectives and topical perspectives. The regions are divided according to their ties to a metropolitan power — the British Commonwealth Caribbean, the French Caribbean, the Netherlands Antilles, and the U.S. Caribbean. Cuba and the Dominican Republic, both independent Spanish-speaking countries, are in a section together.

I would like to thank a number of people for helping me with this study of Caribbean media. Among these are the many librarians, editors, broadcast managers, other media personnel, government officials, and educators who provided information or consented to be interviewed; James W. Carty, who mailed part of his library to me at various times; other Caribbean scholars who shared views in their writings or at conferences; and the publishers and editors of *Gazette, Journalism Quarterly, Printing History, IPI Report, Studies in Latin American Popular Culture, Publishing History, Journalism Educator,* and *Revista interamericana* for permitting the reprinting of parts or the whole of my articles.

I would also like to thank the following for generously granting me permission to reprint photographs and illustrations: the American Antiquarian Society, *Nobo,* the *Island Sun, Extra Aruba,* Spice Islands Printers, Ltd. (publishers of the *Grenadian Voice*), *Haiti Progrès,* Cheddi Jagan, the *Mirror,* the *Outlet,* and Emory King.

Others were supportive in a personal way, especially my children, Laura, Andrea, John, Lisa, and Shahnon; my parents, John and Rose Lent; my relatives and friends, Russ Lent, Mary Ann and Harry Furlong, Roseanna and John Kozup, John and Darlene Caperelli, Marie Wexler, Don and Adrah Payne, Jane Meadows, Irene Dent, Gerald Sussman, Dan Regan, Donna Vesci, Lee Carl, Dave Murta, Ed Barrett, Rick and Kitty Finizio, Jill and Scott Gilbert, Joe and Ruth Carter, and especially Peter Sandwell, whose anecdotes, advice, and analogies showed me alternatives.

But most of all, I want to thank Roseanne Kueny, who, besides typing this manuscript amid the flurry of planning and making arrangements for our wedding, continued to be my best friend.

I

Regional Perspectives

1

Commonwealth Caribbean Mass Media: History and Development

Mass media development had a relatively late start in the Commonwealth Caribbean. For example, the first British settlement in the Caribbean, named St. Christopher and commonly called St. Kitts, was occupied in 1623 and had its first press in 1746 or 1747 (Thomas 1874, 190). In 1624, John Powell landed at Barbados and the second British colony in the region was established; about 1730, the island had its first press. Among other examples, Nevis was claimed by the British in 1628 (Sherlock 1966, 23), and available records show that the island was without a newspaper until 1871. Antigua and Montserrat, settled in 1632, did not issue their first newspapers until about 1748 and 1876, respectively (Thomas 1874, 182; Eames 1928, 308). Bermuda and the Bahamas had their first presses in the mid-1870s, hundreds of years after these islands were discovered.

In the Leewards, Thomas Howe started the first newspaper, the *St. Christopher Gazette,* in 1747. The *Gazette* survived for more than a century and a half. At least sixteen other newspapers were published in St. Kitts before the twentieth century. A copy of the 6 March 1780 *Gazette* showed that it was then printed by Edward Low and contained mainly London datelines, a "Poet's Corner," and an "Essay on the Duty and Qualifications of a Sea Officer."

Antigua's first newspaper was part of one of Benjamin Franklin's printing arrangements in the Caribbean. The arrangement may have formed the first international media agreement, as well as one of the first instances of media imperialism. In 1748, Franklin sent Thomas Smith,

NUME. XLVII

THE WEEKLY
Jamaica Courant.
With News Foreign and Domestick.

Publish'd by Authority.

Wednesday, April 15. 1719.

GREAT BRITAIN.
London, January 14.

HIS Day his Grace the Archbishop of York preach'd a Charity Sermon at the Parish Church of St. Paul Covent-Garden, for the Benefit of the British Charity School, lately erected by Subscription, for the pious Education of poor Children descended of Welch Parents, in and about the Cities of London and Westminster, and for providing them all necessary Apparel, and placing them (when qualify'd) to useful Trades.

Yesterday His Majesty was pleased to confer the Honour of Knighthood upon John Askew of Liddiard Millicent Esq; High Sheriff of the County of Wilts for this present Year, being introduc'd to His Majesty by his Grace the Duke of Kingston, Custos Rotulorum of the said County, and the Right Honourable the Lord Viscount St. John.

Madrid, January 3. N. S. The King grows better and better, having been purged several times with Success, and recover'd his Sleep and Stomach; so that there is grounds to hope his Majesty's Health will soon be entirely re-establish'd.

Paris, January 18. N. S. The Marshal de Villeroy is very ill of the Gout. The Duke of Chartres, the Regent's Eldest Son, is made President of the Council of Regency. Mr. Law hath bought the fine Palace of Nevers, which hath a long Gallery painted by Rubens; and is going to employ Two hundred Workmen to repair the House and Gardens. [*The following is more fully express'd than in our last.*]

Paris, January 11. N. S. On the 16th Instant, the Parliament made an Arret, which orders the Suppression of a Printed Paper, Entitled, A Declaration made by the Catholick King, December 25. 1718. The King's Advocates represented, that that Paper, which bears so awful a Name, being fill'd not only with the most injurious Terms and Expressions, but also with Maxims directly contrary to the Principles of the Government, they were far from thinking it was the Work of a Prince instructed in the Rights of Sovereigns, and educated in the Kingdom: That the Authors seem'd to design to excite Division and Revolt, having advanced their Temerity against the most Sacred Laws of the Land, and disown'd the Lawful Authority by which we are govern'd. The Court of Parliament hath order'd that Paper to be suppress'd as Seditious, tending to Revolt, and impugning the Royal Authority; enjoining all such as have Copies thereof, to bring them to the Registry, and forbiding all Persons to print, ... otherwise distribute it, upon pain of being prosecuted as Disturbers of the

---

1.1   First newspaper in the British islands, the *Jamaica Courant,* 15 April 1719.

1.2 *St. Christopher Gazette,* 6 March 1780.

whom he called at that time a "very sober, honest and diligent young man," to Antigua to develop both a press and, that same year, the *Antigua Gazette.* When Smith died in mid-1752, Franklin asked his own twenty-year-old nephew, Benjamin Mecom, to continue the newspaper. Writing to his sister on 14 September 1752, Franklin expressed a revised opinion of Smith, claiming he had grown "careless and got to sitting up late in Taverns, which I have caution'd Benny to avoid." The terms of the arrangement stipulated that Mecom was to pay his mother a yearly sum and to provide Franklin with "Sugar and Rum for my Family use"; for this, Mecom could then "enjoy all the Rest himself." Apparently, Mecom also sent Franklin money, for a bill of shipment in the Historical Society of Pennsylvania shows that on 27 January 1755, Mecom sent to "B. Franklin" some "42 pounds, 8 shillings and 5 pence half penny with 10 Spanish dollars." By 1756, Mecom sought an agreement entitling him to own the press; when there was no immediate response from Franklin, Mecom decided to leave. By the end of 1756, Franklin wrote to his sister that Mecom had arrived home safely, had paid his accounts with Franklin, had purchased the Antigua press equipment and had moved it to Boston. The *Antigua Gazette* continued publication twice weekly on another press (Eames 1928, 303–48; see Swan 1956; McMurtrie 1943a). At least nine other newspapers existed on Antigua in the next century.

In the British Windward Islands, press development was also late. Dominica came under British sovereignty by cession from France in 1763; the first newspaper appeared two years later. In St. Vincent, the

1.3   Bill of shipment indicating that Benjamin Mecom shipped profits from his Antiguan printery to his uncle, Benjamin Franklin, 27 January 1755.

ST. JOHN'S, April 25. 1753.

For the Entertainment of the Curious,

There is Now to be EXHIBITED at the House of Messrs. *Alleyn & Williams*, in *Newgate-Street*, and to be continued for a few Weeks;

A COURSE of EXPERIMENTS

On the newly-discovered

ELECTRIC FIRE,

CONTAINING, not only the most curious of those that have been made and published in *Europe*, but a considerable Number of new Ones lately made in *Philadelphia*; to be accompanied with methodical LECTURES on the Nature and Properties of that wonderful Element.

By EBENEZER KINNERSLEY.

LECTURE I.

I. OF Electricity in General, giving some Account of the Discovery of it.

II. That the Electric Fire is a real Element, and different from those heretofore known and named, and *collected* out of other Matter (not created) by the Friction of Glass, &c.

III. That it is an extremely subtile Fluid.

IV. That it doth not take up any perceptible Time in passing thro' large Portions of Space.

V. That it is intimately mixed with the Substance of all the other Fluids and Solids of the Globe we live on.

VI. That our Bodies at all Times contain enough of it to set a House on Fire.

VII. That tho' it will fire inflammable Matters, itself has no sensible Heat.

VIII. That it differs from common Matter in this: Its Parts do not mutually attract, but mutually repel each other.

IX. That it is strongly attracted by all other Matter.

X. An artificial Spider, animated by the Electric Fire, so as to act like a live One.

XI. A Shower of Sand, which rises again as fast as it falls.

XII. That common Matter in the Form of Points, attracts this Fire more strongly than in any other Form.

XIII. A Leaf of the most weighty of Metals suspended in the Air, as is said of *Mahomet's* Tomb.

XIV. An Appearance like Fishes swimming in the Air.

XV. That this Fire will live in Water, a River not being sufficient to quench the smallest Spark of it.

XVI. A Representation of the Sensitive Plant.

XVII. A Representation of the seven Planets, shewing a probable Cause of their keeping their due Distances from each other, and from the Sun in the Center.

XVIII. The Salute repulsed by the Ladies Fire; or, Fire darting from a Lady's Lips, so that she may defy any Person to salute her.

XIX. Eight musical Bells rung by an electrified Phial of Water.

XX. A Battery of eleven Guns discharged by Fire issuing out of a Person's Finger.

IV. Electrified Money, which scarce any Body will take when offer'd to them.

V. A Piece of Money drawn out of a Person's Mouth in spite of his Teeth; yet without touching the Money or the Person.

VI. Spirits kindled by Fire darting from a Lady's Eyes (without a Metaphor.)

VII. The Electric Fire shewn to be the same with Lightning.

VIII. A bright Flash of real Lightning darting from a Cloud in a painted Thunder-Storm.

IX. The Force of a small Quantity of it making a fair Hole thro' a Quire of Paper.

X. Metal melted by it (tho' without any Heat) in less than a Thousandth-Part of a Minute.

XI. Animals killed by it instantaneously.

XII. Air issuing out of a Bladder, set on Fire by a Spark from a Person's Finger, and burning like a Volcano.

XIII. A few Drops of cold Water impregnated with Lightning, and let fall on a Person's Hand, supplying him with Fire sufficient to kindle a burning Flame with one of the Finger's of his other Hand.

XIV. A sulphureous Vapour kindled into Flame by Lightning issuing out of a cold Apple, a Lime, or an Orange.

XV. The Cause and Effects of Lightning explained by a more probable Hypothesis than has hitherto appeared.

XVI. An Experiment shewing why Clouds charged with Lightning, fly nearer the Earth than other Clouds; and why Eminences are most frequently struck by Lightning.

XVII. Another Flash of Lightning from the painted Thunder-Storm.

XVIII. An Experiment shewing how Lightning, when it strikes a House or Ship, &c. may be conducted to the Earth, or Water, without doing the least Damage.

XIX. A Flash of Lightning made to strike a small House, and dart towards a little Lady sitting on a Chair, who will, notwithstanding, be preserved from being hurt; whilst the Image of a Negro standing by, and seeming to be further out of Danger, will be remarkably affected by it.

XX. An Experiment, shewing how to preserve Houses, Ships, &c. from being ever *struck* by Lightning.

XXI. The endeavouring to guard against Lightning, shewn to be not chargeable with Presumption, nor inconsistent with any of the Principles either of natural or revealed Religion.

XXII. A Wheel of a curious Machine turned round by Lightning, and playing Variety of Tunes on eight musical Bells.

XXIII. A Battery of eleven Guns discharged by Lightning, after it has darted thro' ten Foot of Water.

LECTURE II.

I. A Description and Explanation of Mr. *Muschenbroeck's* wonderful Bottle.

II. The amazing Force of the Electric Fire, in passing thro' a Number of Bodies at the same Instant.

III. An Electric Mine sprung.

As the Knowledge of Nature tends to enlarge the human Mind, and give us more Noble, more Grand and Exalted Ideas of the Author of Nature, and if well pursued, seldom fails producing something useful to Man, 'tis hop'd these Lectures may be thought worthy of Regard and Encouragement.

☞ TICKETS to be had at Mr. John Lindsay's, at the *Printing-Office*, and of Mr. Kinnersley, from 10 to 12 o'Clock, at the Room where the Experiments are to be exhibited.——PRICE a Piece for each Lecture. The First Lecture to be on Mondays, Wednesdays, and Fridays; the Second Lecture, on Tuesdays, Thursdays, and Saturdays, beginning precisely at 5 o'Clock in the Afternoon, provided the Weather be suitable, and Tickets enough sold to make up a sufficient Company.——As the best Season for exhibiting these Experiments is almost over, and Mr. Kinnersley's Stay here is intended to be very short; those Gentlemen and Ladies who design to be Spectators of these Entertaining and astonishing WONDERS of Nature, are desired to be expeditious, or they will certainly be disappointed——It may, perhaps, be quite equal to some Persons which Lecture they begin with; BUT the Experiments of the Second Lecture may be much better understood by those who have well attended to the Experiments of the First, the One being a proper Introduction to the Other.——Note, *The Experiments succeed best in fair dry Weather.*

1.4 Broadside from Antigua, 25 April 1753, about an exhibition of "electric fire" for the "entertaining of the curious."

first newspaper was published in 1817, in St. Lucia in 1788, and in Grenada about 1765.

A number of reasons might be postulated for the lateness of media development. Among them are (1) a press was not needed to disseminate information on islands so small and intrapersonal in nature, (2) the colonizers felt that the islanders, mostly slaves, were not important or intelligent enough to have use for the printed word, (3) the unstable nature of the islands did not allow for the establishment of permanent institutions, and (4) governments feared the impact of the presses and thus did not encourage their development. One Caribbean historian offered this very plausible explanation.

> This long period may partly be explained by the fact that a large number of those who came over in the army of occupation merely looked for plunder and not towards settlement, and that later the chains of buccaneering appealed to many, including those in high places, and that it was probably only when it became apparent that the printing of reports of legislative enactments and commercial intelligence and the like was a crying necessity, that a press was established (Cundall 1916, 290).

Available evidence supports this statement. The first printing in the British Caribbean was used to issue and make known the latest laws and proclamations. This was so on at least St. Christopher, Dominica, Trinidad, Tobago, Barbados, and Jamaica.

Because the British government was usually the initiator of press development, the mantle of government ownership and control was there from the outset. In Jamaica, a number of the first editor-pressmen were "printers to the House of Assembly," "to the Corporation of Kingston," or "to the Honorable Council in Harbour Street" (Thomas 1874, 185). When John Wells started the first newspaper in the Bahamas, the *Bahama Gazette,* he automatically assumed the position of government printer. Linkage of the press and the Crown was also evident in the first newspapers in Dominica and Grenada, which used logotypes bearing the word "Royal" or a line drawing of the king's arms.

In another instance, the first six newspapers of St. Lucia were "printed under contract at the Government Printery." In fact, some of these periodicals were so government dominated that they printed only administrative news and advertisements. When St. Lucia did have an independent press, the *News,* its editor, Charles Wells, was rewarded for his press-freedom stands with jail sentences on at least two occasions. In fact, Wells, along with friends on the outside, edited his second newspaper, the *Palladium and St. Lucia Free Press,* from a jail cell, where he spent a year for libeling the chief justice (Devaux ca. 1970, 7).

Wells's difficulties with the officials were neither unusual nor unexpected. From the outset, island governments made it known that they would not tolerate press criticism. For example, one learns of the first newspaper on Trinidad when reading that the island's governor had deported Jean Viloux, editor of the weekly *Gazeta.* Viloux was accused of printing "various articles from the foreign newspapers about the present revolution in France, which were published items calculated to spread discussion, corrupt the true faith, and disturb the good order of our rule" (McMurtrie 1943b, 1). Discussing press freedom in colonial Trinidad, one author wrote: "The British Governors or officials exercised a strict control over the Press. Governor Woodford, when annoyed by any articles published, would send a polite note to the editor asking for the loan of the handle of the printing press, thus virtually suspending publication until its return" (Carmichael 1961, 88).

Methods of harassing editors were not always executed as subtly as borrowing a press handle. For example, the aforementioned St. Lucian editor, Charles Wells, was tried without a jury and found guilty by the judge he supposedly libeled. Samuel Keimer was presented with defamatory libel charges by a member of the King's Council of Barbados, and even though the attorney general ruled that there was nothing libelous in Keimer's paper, the *Barbados Gazette,* he was still bound to "keep the peace during six months" (Thomas 1874, 189).

Besides government control, there were also perceptible ties between politics, literature, and journalism. Moreover, newspaper audiences tended to be somewhat elitist in nature. Because of a shortage of educated intellectuals, a characteristic endemic to most colonial societies, it was not unusual in the islands to find an individual wearing the hats of politician, journalist, poet, and man of letters. Some newspapers, such as *L'Impartial journal politique, commercial et litteraire de Ste. Lucie,* displayed in their nameplates the close liaison between journalism, literature, and politics. The elitist nature of newspaper audiences in colonial times resulted mainly from limited purchasing power. Usually, only the colonialists had enough money to advertise in and subscribe to a newspaper or magazine; the poor, illiterate slaves and Caribs and Arawaks had to be content with the traditional oral news systems. For example, the *Royal Gazette and Bahama Advertiser,* published twice weekly, cost its subscribers $7.50 Bahamian annually at a time when a slave in that colony, depending on his age and strength, could be purchased for $200 to $300.

The smallness of this elitist community forced newspapers to take up other projects to keep solvent. Thus, some editors were storekeepers, peddling merchandise ranging from liquor to ox tongues, while many others became government printers. The editor of the *Barbados Gazette* in 1787 was bottling spirituous drinks for sale at his shop, for he advertised in the 17–21 November issue: "Four bitts a doz. will be given, for 50 or 60 dozen of empty Quart Bottles. Apply to the Printer. Who wants to hire, an honest, sober negro man who can attend in a family; if he has been used to a liquor store, he will be more acceptable." A few weeks later, the same editor was selling "London particular and London market wines by the gallon. Port wine by the dozen, ale by the dozen . . . a few bottles of genuine muccadau snuff, etc., etc." (Shilstone 1958).

Collecting subscription money was a difficult chore, and editors' pleas that customers pay up dot many newspaper pages. Samuel Keimer, in his *Barbados Gazette* of 4 May 1734, resorted to poetry in an attempt to embarrass delinquent subscribers. A few lines from the "Sorrowful Lamentation of Samuel Keimer, Printer of the Barbados Gazette" follow.

> What a pity it is that *some* modern Bravadoes,
> Who dub themselves Gentlemen here in Barbadoes,
> Should, Time after Time, run in Debt to their Printer,
> And care not to pay him in Summer and Winter! (Thomas 1874, 189).

By the start of the nineteenth century, the West Indies had seen the birth of at least forty-four newspapers, including at least two dailies, the *Daily Advertiser* and the *Kingston Morning Post,* both published in Jamaica. In addition, at least four magazines commenced publication in Jamaica during the eighteenth century. Probably the first magazine of the Commonwealth Caribbean was *Jamaica Magazine or Monthly Chronicle,* which appeared in 1781.

CRISES AND THE NEWSPAPERS

Newspaper growth was stimulated during times of crisis in the islands. Two such crises revolved around the year 1834, when the British Parliament enforced the Act of Emancipation and ended slavery in the islands, and the period from 1938 to 1944, which marked the establishment of popular governments through universal adult suffrage, with independence and nationhood as accepted goals. Most newspaper growth was quantitative, not qualitative. However, some of the foremost

THE BARBADOS-GAZETTE.

From Saturday April the 14th, to Wednesday April the 18th, 1733.

BARBADOS.

AT a Meeting of His EXCELLENCY in Council at *Pilgrim* on *Tuesday* the 17th Day of *April*, 1733 being the Day inCourse.

PRESENT,

His EXCELLENCY the Right Honourable the Lord Viscount HOWE.

The HONOURABLE

James Dottin,
William Terrill,
Ralph Weekes,
John Frere,
Joseph Pilgrim,   Esqrs;
William Leslie,
Thomas Maxwell,
John Abel,
Othniel Haggat, and
Thomas Applewhaite

Then His EXCELLENCY was pleased to order the Assembly to be called in, and made the following Speech to the Council and said Assembly, viz.

Gentlemen,

WHEN His Majesty did me the Honour to appoint me Governour of this Island, I was in Hopes I should have been able to have attended the Service of it immediately, but the setling my Affairs took up a much greater Time than I expected, which was the Reason I had not the Satisfaction of seeing you sooner; but even during that Delay, I endeavour'd to make my self as useful to you as I cou'd, by representing the many Hardships and Disadvantages the Trade of this Island now labours under, and by soliciting for a speedy Redress. How fortunate I may have been in my earnest Endeavours for obtaining it, I can't say. Cou'd the Success be equal to the Desire I have to serve you, you would soon have all your Expectations answer'd, and all your Wishes granted. But this with Pleasure I can assure you, several Resolutions have already been agreed to in your Favour, and I do not in the least doubt, from the known Goodness of our most gracious King, and from the Assistance you may expect from the Justice of the British Parliament, you will have a considerable Relief in a very short Time.

Gentlemen of the Assembly,

ALtho' it may have been a Custom for some Governours upon their first coming to call a New Assembly, the Confidence I have in your Wisdom and Care for the Publick Good, and the Desire I have that the necessary Business of this Island shou'd have all imaginable Dispatch, determin'd me not to follow their Example, but call you together the first Opportunity, (I am sure this Island will find the Good Effects of it) I fix'd upon the Day to which you stood adjourn'd, it being the most agreeable to me because I thought it would be the most convenient to you.

I have Orders from His MAJESTY to lay before you several Instructions tending to the Honour, Security and Advantage of this Island; All these at proper Times shall be communicated to you.

I have also receiv'd an Additional Instruction relating to me, and the Support of the Dignity of this Government, but being unwilling to enlarge upon an Affair which in so great a Measure, relates to my self, and relying wholly upon you, you shall now have a Copy of it.

I believe you will all agree that the present State of the Fortifications of this Island requires your utmost Attention; your own Security depending so much upon their being put and kept in good Repair, I need not make Use of any Arguments to enforce the Necessity of it.

Gentlemen of the Council, and Gentlemen of the Assembly,

I Have nothing more at Heart than the Prosperity of this Island, my Hopes

1.5 Second newspaper in the Commonwealth Caribbean, Samuel Keimer's *Barbados Gazette,* 18 April 1733.

journalists and best-remembered newspapers came out of the emancipation movement of the 1830s. For example, during the four years leading
up to emancipation in 1834, Jamaica was saturated with as many as
twenty newspapers and journals. At least one paper of that era, the
Watchman, and two journalists, *Watchman* editors Robert Osborn and
Edward Jordan, are remembered today as significant contributors to
Jamaican history. The *Watchman* was a lone voice in the 1830s, a newspaper for the "coloureds" and definitely antislavery. A more typical
newspaper of the era was the *Jamaica Courant,* which on 6 January 1831
expressed what it passed off as the opinion of Jamaicans on antislavery
advocates: "Shooting is . . . too honourable a death for men whose conduct has occasioned so much bloodshed, and the loss of so much property. There are fine hanging woods in St. James and Trelawney, and we
so sincerely hope that the bodies of all Methodist preachers who may be
convicted of sedition, may diversify the scene."

From the same emancipation period, historians recognized the *New
Times* and the *Liberal,* both edited by Samuel Prescod, as newspaper
champions of human rights on Barbados. Prescod served as editor
without pay for eight months before being relieved of his duties because
he was considered too outspoken for conservative Bridgetown (Vaughan
1966–1967). As emancipation and, later, colonial status sparked heated
debate, the press exploded onto the scene in Commonwealth Caribbean
territories, to the extent that the 104 newspapers in the first half of the
nineteenth century more than doubled the total 44 of the eighteenth
century. Some islands had more newspapers in those crises-laden times
than they do today.

Frustrations caused by the crown colony system also stimulated the
accelerated growth of newspapers, especially in Trinidad and St. Lucia.
Some of the crusades of these newspapers were quite effective. For example, Trinidadian newspapers took credit for the recall of a governor in
1880, the dismissal of an attorney general in 1870, and the censure of a
chief justice in 1892 (Wood 1968, 305).

But most of these newspapers did not receive much acclaim and
died quickly. Partly because of this factor, only a few newspapers that
predate the twentieth century still exist in the islands today. They are the
Nassau Guardian (1844), the *Barbados Advocate* (1895), the *Jamaica
Daily Gleaner* (1834), the *Royal Gazette* of Bermuda (1828), and the
Voice of St. Lucia (1885). Two Catholic organs, the *Catholic Opinion*
(1896) of Jamaica and the *Catholic News* (1892) of Trinidad, might be
included except that they never had to depend solely upon circulation
and advertising to survive.

NASSAU The GUARDIAN

AND COLONIAL ADVERTISER;

A SEMI-WEEKLY PAPER, ESTABLISHED FOR THE PROMOTION OF USEFUL KNOWLEDGE AND THE FURTHERANCE OF COMMERCE.

BE AT PEACE WITH ALL MANKIND, BUT AT WAR WITH THEIR VICES.

VOL. V.   NASSAU, NEW PROVIDENCE, SATURDAY, MARCH 3, 1849.   NO. 30

WEEKLY CALENDAR.

POLICE OFFICE.

SITTING MAGISTRATES FOR THE ENSUING WEEK,

W. H. Doyle, Esq., J.P.   H. McCartney, Esq., J.P.
Acting Police Magistrate—J. S. Rhina, Esq., J.P.

CONVICTIONS, &c.

GOVERNMENT NOTICE.

SALE OF CROWN LAND.

AN EDITOR'S COUNTRY VISIT.

1.6   March 1849 issue of the *Nassau Guardian,* the third-oldest surviving newspaper of the Commonwealth Caribbean.

Many of these early newspapers provided the islands with lively and competitive journalism. For example, in 1886 four dailies competed for subscriptions and advertisements in Jamaica. Today, of all the islands, only Trinidad has as many as three dailies.

Although newspapers seemed to be prospering during the nineteenth century, they did not do much to alleviate the interisland and intraisland communication problems of the British West Indies. Most newspapers were published in the island capital and oftentimes never reached outlying areas, let alone neighboring islands.

It was the telegraph, and later broadcasting, that helped to link each island to the others as well as to the rest of the world. Nevertheless, telecommunication machinery was accepted on some islands with the greatest reluctance. When Grenada was being connected telegraphically with the world in 1871, the House of Assembly was so unimpressed that it debated giving the telegraph act a telling name — "Act to tax the whole community and to benefit only a few interested parties" (Kay 1966, 21). Telegraph service in Jamaica was opposed by the propertied class, whose members observed that foreign news was uninteresting. A telegraph act was not passed in the Bahamas until 1891.

To make sure that more than just "a few interested parties" benefited from the telegraph, the West Indian and Panama Telegraph Company, and in one case an island government, supplied a free daily bulletin of world news, posted outside their offices.

On Dominica, a newspaper resulted from the daily posting of news items by the telegraph company. In 1902, when the elite residents of Roseau tired of walking to the wireless office to read overseas news, they persuaded the Roman Catholic bishop, who had a print shop, to issue a newspaper. The paper, the *Cable News,* virtually reproduced the wireless items (Interview, Boyd 1971).

PERSONAL JOURNALISM

By the end of the nineteenth century, personal journalism had grown so rampant in the region that newspapers on an island such as Barbados seemed more bent on destroying each other than the evils of society. Until the *Barbados Advocate* changed the tide in 1895, it was not uncommon to read of one Barbadian paper labeling another as a "dirty son of Ananias" or a "filthy excrescence on responsible journalism" (Cozier 1970).

At the dawn of the new century, the issues of concern to Commonwealth Caribbean editors included questioning the status of crown government, developing trade and labor unions and political parties, and pushing toward nationalism. Among these crusading editors were Etienne Dupuch of the *Nassau Tribune,* Clennel Wickham and Clement Inniss of the *Barbados Herald,* Valence Gale and Charles Lynch Chenery of the *Barbados Advocate,* and T. A. Marryshow of the *West Indian* of Grenada.

Even in Jamaica, where the *Gleaner* perpetuated a tradition of conservatism, changes toward a more activist press were developing (McFarlane 1963). At the forefront of the activist press movement on Jamaica was Marcus Garvey, internationally known leader of black nationalism, who used journalism to promote his values, his ideas, and his own image. The first of a series of periodicals Garvey was to sponsor was *Garvey's Watchman,* started while he was employed at the Jamaica government printing office in 1910. Although he supported a series of short-lived periodicals, his only other Jamaica-based publication was a political fortnightly, *Our Own.* His Jamaican, Costa Rican, and U.S. periodicals were designed to promote Garvey's goals of a Black House

1.7 Crusading editors of the Caribbean: (*from left to right*) Valence Gale of the *Barbados Advocate,* and Clement Inniss and Clennel Wickham of the *Barbados Herald.*

(instead of the White House), black legislators, black generals, and a black-based economy.

Two Barbadian idealists, Clennel Wickham and Clement Inniss, were responsible for publishing the *Barbados Herald* from 1919 to 1930. Both were unselfish in their devotion to the causes of the masses and expected neither material nor prestigious rewards for their services. One writer said that this concern for the common man and his suffering was unique in Barbados, where people did not care much about changing societal ills (Hoyos 1953, 142–43).

On several occasions, when advertisers boycotted the *Herald,* Inniss and Wickham tightened their budget and kept right on, usually saved by generous donations from the more liberal businessmen of Barbados. The *Herald* folded in 1930, not able to withstand the vindictive judgment of the Barbados Grand Jury, which awarded staggering damages to the paper's opponents in a libel suit. Next to Prescod's *Liberal,* the *Herald* has been called by many the "greatest radical journal" in the island's history.

The newspaper in the Bahamas that usually pitted itself against government was the *Tribune,* edited by Sir Etienne Dupuch. Because of its incessant fight to break the color lines of that colony (which it succeeded in doing by the 1950s), the paper suffered a number of deprivations, some of which were captured by Dupuch: "All kinds of things happened. Most of the time I locked horns with the all-powerful financial and political interests in the town, or I was facing a ruinous libel suit brought on me by an excess of enthusiasm for a cause that *Tribune* had espoused, or all my property was being wrecked by a hurricane" (Dupuch, 1967, 32).

Still other editors motivated by something besides the pound note were Valence Gale and his brother-in-law, Charles Lynch Chenery, on Barbados and T. A. Marryshow on Grenada. In 1895, when the Barbados economy was at one of its lowest points, Gale was dissatisfied with the politically oriented personal scandal sheets and started his *Advocate.* One of his first goals was to hinder the government's plan to federate; he did not want Barbados to lose its long tradition of representative government.

At about the same time, Grenadian statesman and politician T. A. Marryshow was fired up about West Indian nationalism, a subject quite unpopular then. He used the *West Indian,* which he founded in 1915, and his public offices to push his paper's motto, "West Indies must be West Indian," and to pioneer the labor movement in the region.

NATIONALISM AND IDENTITY

A number of writers would agree with Sherlock that "in 1938 the West Indies moved out of the nineteenth century into the twentieth century" (Sherlock 1966, 82). In that year, at the cost of forty-seven dead and hundreds injured, the West Indian masses decided that the road to equality was through active protest.

The popular movements for trade unionism and nationalism, like the emancipation cause of the 1830s, were stimulators of media development in the Commonwealth Caribbean. In Jamaica, at least thirty-two publications appeared between the 1920s, when unionism and nationalism sparks were struck, and the 1940s, when the movements were conflagrant in nature.

During the same time, the first labor or union newspapers were established. They are significant because their spirit was contrary to that of their predecessors, which had represented the "conservative sugar-owning interests" or the primarily personal desires of editors (Hallett 1957). To trace the origins of the labor press in the Commonwealth Caribbean, one must return to the post–World War I era, when unions and their newspapers were organized somewhat clandestinely because of prohibitory laws. For example, on St. Kitts–Nevis, a union was organized as a friendship society. To carry out its propagandistic work, the society started a monthly periodical in 1921, the *Union Messenger.* The paper became so popular that it eventually became a daily (Procope n.d., 3). By 1942, when the unions were much more acceptable, another St. Kitts labor paper, the *Workers Weekly,* an organ of the St. Kitts Workers League, was issued.

In Antigua, the labor press emerged in 1943 when Edward Mathurin, a printer and former officer of the Antigua Trades and Labour Union, printed a newspaper in pamphlet form (Richards 1964, 32–33). The following year, the same organization established the *Workers Voice,* which still survives.

The strikes and riots of 1938 and their aftermath have been credited with developing a West Indian cultural identity, which found outlets in various new media, such as the trade and labor newspapers, newsmagazines, and radio stations.

An interpretative newsmagazine first appeared with Jamaica's *Spotlight* in 1939. Years later it was followed by the Barbadian *Bajan* (1953) and by *Newday* (1957) and *West Indian Review: Magazine of the Caribbean,* both of Jamaica. *Spotlight* appeared when a newspaper writer, Evon Blake, realized he could not say what he wanted in someone else's paper. Fired by the *Jamaica Gleaner,* Blake borrowed one pound and lived on it for a month until he sold his first advertisement for *Spotlight*. He ran the magazine single-handedly for eighteen and one-half years (*Spotlight* 1964).

Radio came to the islands in the 1930s. Its relative lateness might be explained by (1) the financially insecure position of the people, who were unable to afford the media, (2) the insularity of the islands, (3) the merchants' lack of awareness of the benefits of advertising, and (4) the lack of extensive electrification on most islands. An amateur radio operator who wanted to develop a radio station on Barbados to announce the 1935 cricket matches gave still another reason: "The legislators and advisors failed to recognize the power of the modern media at their disposal and adamantly refused to grant any applications for licenses which were submitted. . . . Numerous applications for stations were turned down by government because broadcasting 'supported by sponsored programs is not in the interests of the people' " (Archer 1964).

Broadcasting in the British West Indies owes its inception to the experimental station, VIBAX in the Bahamas, that was on the air during the winter of 1930–1931. VIBAX was started by C. Ravenhill-Smith, recently arrived in the Bahamas from Florida (Pactor 1988, 1002).

Individual islands received local radio service at various times: British Guiana in 1934, Barbados in 1934–1935, Trinidad in 1935, Jamaica in 1939, Bermuda in 1943, Montserrat in 1952, Antigua in 1955, and the Windward Islands in 1954–1955 (Information Department of Colonial Office 1956, 4–167). Anguilla, which did not have a newspaper until 1967, entered the broadcasting field latest among the islands. In March 1969, that island had its first radio service when a limited broadcast took place from HMS *Rhys,* a British ship anchored offshore during Anguilla's revolt against St. Kitts. The shipboard station was successful enough that the British Foreign Office established a more permanent station on Anguillan soil (Interview, Dunlop 1971).

Many of the first broadcasting stations were rediffusion services, and until midcentury, most Commonwealth Caribbean radio was through wired systems. In 1934, Commander Mansfield Robinson, Royal Navy (retired) formed the first station on Barbados, but subscribers were not connected until the following year. Amateur operators developed the first broadcasting stations on other islands, such as St. Vincent and Jamaica. World War II spurred the development of Commonwealth Caribbean broadcasting, and the medium was used to relay war news and hurricane warnings to isolated British West Indians.

Britain's impact on broadcasting was apparent. Overseas Rediffusion Ltd. of London, through local subsidiaries, took control of the Jamaican and Barbadian sole outlets in 1950 and 1951, respectively. On

Trinidad and Bermuda, Broadcast Relay Services (Overseas) Ltd. of London was granted radio franchises in 1947. Two years after its creation in 1961, as an offshore unit for Martinique and Guadeloupe, Radio Caribbean International on St. Lucia was also associated with London Rediffusion. For a stretch of time in the 1960s, press lord Roy Thomson of Fleet Street owned numerous broadcasting interests in the region before selling them to island governments.

During the 1950s, as local governments and national leaders came onto the scene, so did government radio. By 1958, the Jamaican government had established a public broadcasting corporation. It took the name Jamaica Broadcasting Corporation, while the original JBC turned into Radio Jamaica Ltd., still a rediffusion station. From the outset, ZNS in the Bahamas was government operated, as was the Windward Islands Broadcasting Service in Grenada, started in 1955 to serve St. Lucia, St. Vincent, Dominica, and Grenada. Other local government-owned stations existed on Antigua after 1956, on St. Kitts after 1961, on Barbados after 1963, on Trinidad after 1969, and on Dominica after

1.8 Windward Islands Broadcasting Service headquarters in Grenada before network's dissolution in early 1970s. (*Photo by John A. Lent*)

1971. Radio Montserrat, owned and maintained by a voluntary broadcasting committee, also has become a semiofficial station.

By 1970, approximately sixty newspapers, a scattering of magazines and government journals, nineteen radio systems, and seven television stations served the Commonwealth Caribbean. The estimated circulation of the newspapers was 550,000 in a population of approximately 3.9 million. Thirteen dailies were published, eight of which accounted for two-thirds of the total circulation. In nearly every instance, the mass media were concentrated solely in the capital city because secondary cities were too small to support media operations.

The thirteen dailies included the *Antigua Workers Voice;* the *Nassau Guardian,* the *Tribune,* and the *Grand Bahama Tribune,* all of the Bahamas; the *Barbados Advocate-News;* the *Bermuda Royal Gazette;* the *West Indian* of Grenada; the *Jamaica Daily Gleaner* and the *Star,* both of Jamaica; the *Labour Spokesman* of St. Kitts–Nevis, and the *Trinidad Guardian,* the *Evening News,* and the *Express,* all of Trinidad. Only in Trinidad and the Bahamas were dailies owned by different corporations competing with each other.

In 1970, the Gleaner publications had the largest circulations in the region—the *Star* with 64,037 and the *Daily Gleaner* with 59,349. They were followed by the *Trinidad Guardian* with 52,717, its sister, the *Evening News,* with 53,793, and the *Express,* also of Trinidad, with 35,000. Relatively large circulations also were maintained by weekend editions. The Friday *Weekend Star* had a circulation of 75,853. On Sundays, the *Guardian* reached 87,796 readers; the *Gleaner,* 83,674; the *Express,* 54,000; and the *Advocate-News,* 30,321. A Trinidadian editor explained that Sunday was a "big day for rural readership as many people buy one paper [the Sunday edition] for the week and read it then" (Interview, Chongsing 1970).

As the editor of the *Evening News* of Trinidad pointed out, the *Guardian*'s Sunday circulation of 87,796 ranked proportionately among the top in the world, as almost one-tenth of the total population of Trinidad and Tobago purchased the paper (Interview, Delph 1970). In the early 1960s, Bermuda had more copies of newspapers available per one hundred people (41.9) than did most nations of the world. On Barbados, the *Advocate-News* was sold to one in ten of the 250,000 population. With an average household of five people, the paper may have been read by every other Barbadian (Interview, Grosvenor 1970).

Besides the dailies, a plethora of political nondailies were published in Jamaica, Trinidad, Barbados, the Bahamas, and the Leeward and Windward Islands. As is the case today, it was a wonder that presses existed at all in the smaller islands (see chapter 3). Economic and political pressures, the heavy influx of foreign media, and the regionalization of Barbadian and Trinidadian dailies all dictated against them. Yet newspapers and radio and television systems functioned, as they do now, in these mini-islands. In 1970, St. Lucia had a very competitive media apparatus, with a television station, two radio services, a literary magazine, and five nondailies for a population of less than 100,000. Dominica, with approximately 60,000 people, had three weeklies and a national radio system; Grenada (90,000) had three newspapers and a radio network; Antigua (60,000) had three newspapers, two radio stations, and a television channel; and St. Kitts (57,000) had two newspapers and its own radio station. St. Vincent (92,000), Montserrat (13,000), the Cayman Islands (10,000), and Anguilla (6,000) each had one newspaper. Montserrat had two radio stations, and Anguilla, one.

In at least St. Kitts and Antigua, the number of newspapers in 1970 matched the number of political parties. In Dominica, two of the three papers were opposition party supporters, and the third was a Roman Catholic organ. In Grenada, all three papers were antigovernment; one was the organ of the opposition party. In St. Lucia, three of the papers were politically oriented, and a fourth was a Catholic paper. The *Crusader* was an organ of a radical group called the Forum (Interview, Reid 1971). Concentrated, as they were (and still are), in one city in each island, the newspapers were extremely competitive.

Magazines seldom survived on most islands, mainly because they were too expensive, lacked advertising markets, and competed with an abundance of United States and British periodicals. Newsmagazines ran the risk of not being newsy by the time they could be published. Because of insufficient advertising and circulation money, they did not come out more frequently than monthly. At least three newsmagazines were published in 1970: the *Bajan* in Barbados, *Spotlight* in Jamaica, and *Bahamian Review* in the Bahamas.

Literary magazines long played a key role in the development of local writing talent. *Bim,* published in Barbados, has been an outlet for Caribbean writers from the early 1940s (Interview, Collymore 1971), and *Link* was edited in St. Lucia by the editor of the weekly *Crusader.*

In 1970, as now, comparatively large electronic media systems operated in the Commonwealth Caribbean, especially the Jamaica Broadcasting Corporation and Radio Jamaica, with eight and four transmitters, respectively. Others included Radio Antilles, 200-250 KW on Montserrat; the old Windward Islands Broadcasting Service, with substations on each Windward Island; Radio Caribbean, with English and French broadcasts directed to St. Lucia, Martinique, and Guadeloupe; both Radio Trinidad and the Trinidad and Tobago National Broadcasting System; ZNS of the Bahamas; and the Caribbean Broadcasting Corporation. Radio operations were also carried out by the Antigua Broadcasting Service and ZDK in Antigua, Radio Anguilla, Barbados Rediffusion (also Radio Barbados), ZBM 1 and 2 and ZFBI in Bermuda, Radio Montserrat, ZIZ in St. Kitts, and ZBVI in Tortola, British Virgin Islands.

Bermuda, Barbados, Antigua, Trinidad, Jamaica, and St. Lucia had television systems in 1970. The Caribbean Broadcasting Corporation in Barbados had a television relay station in St. Lucia from 1966, and the Leeward Islands Television Services of Antigua maintained translator stations in Montserrat and St. Maarten. Two different television companies operated in Bermuda, the Capital Broadcasting Company Ltd. and Bermuda Radio and Television Ltd. Color television existed in Bermuda and Barbados. Television's development was impressive, since local service was unknown in the Commonwealth Caribbean, except for Bermuda, until the independence era of the 1960s.

2

Early Women Journalists:
The Stockdales of Bermuda

Three sisters who edited a newspaper in Bermuda from 1803 to 1816 should be considered among the pioneer women printer-editors in the world. Priscilla, Frances, and Sarah Stockdale, perhaps with some help from their mother Frances, edited and printed the *Bermuda Gazette and Weekly Advertiser,* the colony's first newspaper, which had been started 17 January 1784 by their father, Joseph.

Despite the island's early settlement in 1612, printing came to Bermuda rather slowly. Not until 1771 was the introduction of printing seriously broached, when the House of Assembly passed a resolution calling for a "capable person to come out from England and establish a proper press" (Lincoln 1925, 3). The following year, the famous American printer, Isaiah Thomas, who was disturbed because in his native Massachusetts a printer had to be "either of one party or the other," wrote to his father-in-law in Bermuda about the possibility of establishing a press there. Thomas ended that letter with, "If Sir, you and the gentlemen of your Island are still willing to encourage me I beg you would favor me once more with a Line . . . that I may settle my affairs here so as to come over in the fall" (McMurtrie 1928, 5).

Nothing came of this plea, nor of a subscription started in the House of Assembly in 1781 to start a press. Although the documentation is not readily available, this may have resulted because there was not a printer willing to leave England or the American colonies to come to Bermuda, or because of the British slowness in starting presses in other parts of the Caribbean. Finally, on 28 March 1783, money was subscribed to start a press and to bring Joseph Stockdale, brother of the printer to the House of Commons, from England (Simmonds 1841, 123).

Stockdale's *Gazette* was the normal size for that time—four pages, three columns to a page—but during paper shortages, it was reduced in size. It was published every Saturday and was numbered consecutively. The first number carried front-page stories under the headline "The Definitive Treaty between Great Britain and the United States of America." The other pages featured London news, verse, Bermuda news (assembly meeting and shipping information), advertisements for arrival of ships, and goods and slaves for sale. Like other printers of the period, Stockdale also printed other materials, including a 1794 imprint, "Plan for the Establishment of a Marine Academy in the Islands of Bermuda"; an oath of 1784; the *Bermuda Almanac* as early as 1789; acts to establish a militia (1789); and acts of the General Assembly (1799).

By issue no. 921 on 3 October 1801, Stockdale began crediting his daughters' contributions with the statement "Printed for and by Jos. Stockdale and Daughters." Except for occasional lapses, this statement was carried until Stockdale's death at age forty-nine on 10 October 1803. His death was announced in the *Gazette* on 15 October 1803, along with the daughters' plans to keep the paper alive. Actually, as they paid homage to their father, they also admonished advertisers to pay up.

> Monday last died, at St. George's, Mr. Joseph Stockdale, Printer, after a long and painfull illness which he bore with christian fortitude.
>
> The Miss Stockdales beg leave to inform their customers and the Public at large that they propose to continue the publication of the Bermuda Gazette in the usual manner; and that their best efforts will be used to give satisfaction. Obliged to conduct the Press under many disadvantages, they will be extremely thankful for every assistance, and they trust that their attention to their business will sufficiently evince their gratitude for the favors they may receive. At the same time a proper attention to their own interests obliges them to say that it will not be in their power to publish any advertisements (except from their customers) unless accompanied by the Money. No advertisement can appear in the Gazette which is not sent to the Office before ten o'clock of the Saturday it is meant to appear. — They have farther to apologize to their Customers, and the Public, for the omission of last week's Gazette. They trust their late domestic misfortune will be a sufficient excuse.

That issue was printed for F. Stockdale. Issue no. 1045, 18 February 1804, was "Printed by F. P. and S. Stockdale," and it was not until Issue

Bermuda Gazette,
And WEEKLY ADVERTISER.

No. 1162. SATURDAY, MAY 17, 1806.

THE Subscribers wish to Charter immediately, a Vessel capable of carrying 5 or 600 Barrels, to go to one Port in the West Indies.

NATHANIEL BASCOME & Co.
St. George's, May 3, 1806.

To be Sold at Public Vendue,

On Tuesday next, the 20th instant, At eleven o'clock in the forenoon, In St. George's,

THE Cargo of the Schooner Thorne, just arrived from Philadelphia, Consisting of

50 whole barrels of Superfine Flour,
40 half ditto ditto,
10 barrels Rye ditto,
10 ditto Pork,
10 ditto Bread,
30 kegs Crackers,
6 casks Hams, and
A few boxes of best brown Soap.

B. S. HAYWARD,
Vendue Master.
St. George's, May 17, 1806.

To be Sold at Public Vendue,

On Wednesday, the 4th of June, At ten o'clock in the forenoon, In St. George's,

THE Dwelling HOUSE, Out-houses, Cistern, Garden, &c. (now in the occupation of Mr. George Brown) the Property of the late Reverend Alexander Richardson, deceased.

JOHN SMITH,
Public Vendue Master.
St. George's, May 17, 1806.

For SALE,

At low prices for Cash, On board the Sloop Betsey, laying at the Long-house Wharf,

CONNECTICUT Prime PORK and BEEF,
Mess Beef in half barrels,
Potatoes in barrels, Oats,
Indian Corn,
Superfine Flour,
Hams, smoak'd Beef,
Soap, Candles,
Butter, &c. &c.

Apply to the Master on board, or to John Musson.
St. George's, May 3, 1806.

THE Persons who borrowed, Piozzi's Anecdotes of Doctor Johnson; Travels of St. Leon, vol. 2d; Novelist's Magazine, vol. 16th containing Avellaneda's Quixote and the virtuous Orphan, are desired to return them to

J. M'LACHLAN.

For SALE,
On reasonable terms by
RICHARD FISHER, viz.

SUPERFINE FLOUR, in whole and half barrels,
Pilot Bread,
Crackers in kegs and half barrels,
Black eyed Pease, by the bushel or barrel,
A few lots of Rigging, a little worn,
Two Cables, (7 and 9 inch) ditto,
One Anchor about 250lb. nearly new.
St. George's, April 26, 1806.

NATHANIEL BASCOME & Co.

HAVE received for Sale on reasonable terms, per the Enterprise, from New York.

Mould Candles, 4, 5 and 6 to the pound,
Dipt ditto, 6 to the pound,
Superfine Flour,
Prime Pork,
Navy Bread,
Rye Flour,
Black eyed Pease,
Mess Beef and Tongues, in half barrels,
Hams and Cheese,
Soap, Indian Corn, and
Albany Boards.
May 3, 1806.

NOTICE is hereby given, to all parties concerned, that a distribution of the net proceeds of the Spanish Polacre, Nuestra Senora del Carmen, and Cargo, captured by his Majesty's Ship Unicorn, L. F. Hardyman, Esq. Commander, October 19th 1805, and condemned in the Court of Vice Admiralty of these Islands, November 19th following, will commence at the Compting House of the Subscriber, in St. George's, the 26th instant; and notice is hereby further given to all parties concerned that, in case they should not then be upon the spot, the Subscriber will attend at his Compting House, in St. George's, from 9 to 12 o'clock each Monday and Thursday following, until the 26th of August next, for the purpose of continuing the same distribution, unless it should be finally made by him previous to that day.

HENRY TUCKER, Jun. Agent.
St. George's, May 15, 1806.

For sale, at the Printing-Office, and at Captain Tuzo's, Hamilton,

Powers of Attorney,
Sterling Bills of Exchange,
Bills of Exchange for Dollars and Cents,
Bills of Lading, &c. &c.

NOTICE to Negroes, Mulattoes or Mustees whether Bond or Free.

WHEREAS information has been given me by several of the Inhabitants of the Town of St. George, that in and about the said Town, the vending or retailing of Goods, Wares or Merchandize, as also the exercising the Trade or Business of a Butcher, is daily practiced by Negroes, Mulattoes or Mustees, contrary to an Act of the Legislature of these Islands, entitled " An Act to prevent vending or retail- " ing Goods, Wares or Merchandize " by Negroes, Mulattoes or Mustees, " whether bond or free, wandering up " and down throughout these Islands; " and also the Sale of Goods, Wares " and Merchandize by Lottery, Dice, " Cards or Raffling, and to prevent Ne- " groes, Mulattoes or Mustees in these " Islands, whether bond or free, from " exercising the Trade or Business of a " Butcher," as well as in violation of an Act of the Mayor, Aldermen and Common Council of said Town, entitled " An Act for the regulating and " well governing of the Negroes within " the limits of the Town of Saint " George." I have therefore thought fit, as well to prevent any farther infringement of said Acts, as to render to the Inhabitants of the Town of St. George that justice, which from my situation they have a right to expect from me, to give Public Notice that, upon a regular Complaint being made to me or either of the Aldermen of the Town of St. George aforesaid, of any offence committed against the said Acts, duly supported to conviction, the said Acts will be rigidly put in force against the offender.

J. V. NORDEN,
Mayor of the Town of St. George.

NOTICE.

ALL Persons having legal demands against the Estates of Martha Forster and Sarah Forster, both of Sandy's Tribe, deceased, are hereby desired to render attested Accounts of the same, in thirty days from the date hereof, to the subscriber for a settlement; and all Persons indebted thereto are hereby requested to make payment, as a final settlement of the said Estates is about to be immediately effected.

Benjamin Gibbs,
Administrator to the Estate of Sarah Forster.
Somerset, May 10, 1806.

For Sale at the Printing-Office,
The BERMUDA ALMANACK,

---

been seriously imposed on by Captains of foreign vessels, who have frequently detained their letters, subsequent to their arrival, from fraudulent motives, and for the purpose of extorting sums of money. While this measure is to be strictly enforced, we are glad to learn that the Post Office has adopted, and will adopt such expedients, at their own expence, as will greatly facilitate these dispatches, without any delay whatever beyond the sailing of any ships from any of the ports of the United Kingdom. It must even be a subject of surprize, that such a culpable negligence in this department of revenue should so long have escaped official observation.

July 26.

A few days since, a most admirable bust of the late Marquis Cornwallis, by Turnerelli, was put in the liberary of the East-India House.

July 30.

Yesterday a telegraphic dispatch was received at the Admiralty from Plymouth, announcing that the Eurydice frigate had captured a French vessel, with dispatches on board for Buenos Ayres, and a large quantity of arms and ammunition. The prize, with the dispatches, are on their way to Portsmouth.

August 1.

On Saturday, while out for a field day, the 2d brigade of Guards, consisting of the 1st battalion of the Coldstream, and Third Regiment, received an express, ordering them to be in readiness to embark for foreign service on the shortest notice, they will immediately be compleated from the 2d battalion of their respective regiments in London to 1300 rank and file each. On the order being communicated to the men, they testified their satisfaction by loud and repeated huzzas. We understand, that a similar order was, at the same time, sent to the 1st brigade at Deal, consisting of the 1st and 3d battalions of the Duke of York's regiment.

FASHIONS.

Description of the prevailing Fashions for the Month, as taken from minute observation by a Lady of distinguished taste from real dresses; extracted from "La Belle Assemblee; or, Bell's Court and Fashionable Magazine," for the present month.

The yellow and pink pelisse of shawl-muslin, and imperial cambric, is now become so very general, that though an enlivening and attractive habit, we cannot any longer rank it amidst a fashionable selection. They are now worn by every description of females, and the tired eye turns from their oppressive glare to rest on the cool and refreshing shade of pea-green, primrose, celestial blue, silver grey, and pale lilac. In pelisses, scarfs, robes, and mantles, these colours are very distinguishable; and they are composed of the most light and transparent textures. There is little

novelty in their construction, and they are generally formed and disposed in so varied and fanciful a style as to preclude the possibility of any regular or decided delineation. The *Spanish Mantle*, and *Patriotic Bonnet*, are lately become a favourite appendage to the outdoor costume, and are at once both interesting and elegant. The former article differs little from the Spanish cloak, so long in fashionable request, except that it is shorter than they are usually worn; has square ends, finished with tassels; and a deep cape formed in sharp points, or scollops. It is composed of clear muslin, or crape, and bordered with chenille. The bonnet is constructed with a round crown, somewhat like the jockey-cap, but has a deep front, which is turned up so as to appear like a Spanish hat, and ornamented with the *Union border* in chenille. At the *dejeuné*, or in public parties, they are decorated with the ostrich or willow feather; but on less particular occasions are worn plain, or with a simple rose or cockade in front. The Patuski bonnet and Sardinian mantle are also worthy of adoption, from their graceful construction, and adaption to the form; and the compact and ingenious composition of the *honey-comb tippet*, must render it a favourite summer ornament, and well worthy a place in a select wardrobe. The straw hat and bonnet are now entirely confined to the walking and morning dress. In carriages, and on the evening parade, the hair with flowers, jewellery, small French caps and veils, small half handkerchiefs of figured net, edged with scolloped lace, placed towards one side of the head, the point fastened nearly in the front, with a broach of silver, pearl, diamonds, &c. the ends brought under the chin, exposing the hair on one side, in full curls, is by far the most fashionable style of decoration for the head. The Persian braid, or cable twist, with the ends curled full on the crown of the head, or on one side, fastened with a gold filligree vine-leaf, with an animated butter fly in the centre, is often adopted by those females, the luxuriance and beauty of whose tresses induce them wisely to reject a redundance of ornament.

The style of gowns and robes offer little novelty since our last communication, except that the *long waist* is becoming universal. It extends behind to the commencement of the fall in the back; taking in its regular circumference a portion of the small of the waist.

No lady of fashion now appears in public without a ridicule—which contains her handkerchief, fan, card-money, and essence-bottle. They are at this season usually composed of rich figured sarsnet, plain satin or silver tissue, with correspondent strings and tassels—their colours appropriated to the robes with which they are worn. The stomacher

antique, and laced cottage front; the simple wrap front bordered to suit the dress; with short sash, tied either behind or in front, are conspicuous amidst the gored and round bosoms, which are still very general.

Silver filligree ornaments have not had so great a claim to fashionable distinction, as from their novelty we might have expected. In this instance our females have evinced their judgment and taste.

In the article of gloves we have observed the pea green and pale olive, of French kid, to unite with those recommended in our last. Shoes of painted kid, checked at the toes, jean wrought in a leaf, together with plain colours, are now worn even by the pedestrian fair. In full dress we scarcely see any thing but white satin, French silk, and kid, variously trimmed. The most fashionable colours for the season will be found at the commencement of these marks.

We have only to add, that the short sleeve begins to renew its advances in full dress, although the long sleeve of the most transparent texture retains the majority.

Trains of any remarkable length are now seldom seen; but some few females have lately appeared in parties, with their robes resting about a quarter of a yard on the ground. This we hope is approaching to that graceful and distinguishing style which should mark the several degrees of personal attire.

BERMUDA, October 15.

By the schooner Porpoise, Captain Bassett, which arrived this week, from St. Croix, we learn, that a vessel arrived the 23d of Sept. from Porto Rico, which informs, that a vessel arrived there from Cadiz, (which place she left the 20th of August) a few days previous to her sailing, and brought the following intelligence: " that the Senate and People of France had declared Ferdinand VIIth King of Spain—the Prince of Peace was killed, and Buonaparte attempted to put an end to his existence but failed in the attempt."

His Majesty's ship Milan, Capt. Sir Robert Laurie, came off these Islands on Tuesday last.

Thursday sailed on a Cruize, His Majesty's sloop of war Indian, Captain Austen, and schooner Vesta, Lieut. Mins; and Observateur, Capt. Lawrence, for Halifax.

SHIP NEWS.

ENTERED, From
Schooner Porpoise, J. G. Bassett, St. Croix
CLEARED, For
Brig Juno, A. Rutherford, New Orleans
Schooner Lord Nelson, John Philpot, Turk's Islands
Sloop Bellerophon, B. R. Dill, Ditto
Sloop Phoenix, T. J. Burrows, Newfoundland

For the rest of the news see the first page.

BERMUDA: Printed by F. P. & S. STOCKDALE.
Where Advertisements, Intelligence, &c. &c. will be thankfully received.

2.2   Back page of *Bermuda Gazette* showing F. P. & S. Stockdale as printers. (*Photo courtesy of the American Antiquarian Society*) no. 1405, 12 January 1811, that Frances, Priscilla, and Sarah printed their names in full. Starting with the 8 October 1814 issue, the paper was printed only by Priscilla and Sarah (Hallett 1985, 158), as Frances had been married to John B. Tucker in June of that year.

Apparently, the Stockdales thought a newspaper should also appeal to women, for on page four of the 15 October 1808 issue, they carried a two-column article titled "FASHIONS," which described the "prevailing fashion" for the month as gleaned from *La Belle Assemblee, or, Bell's Court and Fashionable Magazine*.

Although they were the licensed printers, the sisters apparently found reason to attack and question the British authorities. In 1809, when difficulties erupted between Governor Hodgson and the public, the *Gazette* carried what were called "libellous attacks" upon the governor, leading him that year to bring Edmund Ward from Halifax to be "King's Printer" and start a rival newspaper, the *Royal Gazette* (Lincoln 1924, 139). For the next seven years, the two newspapers engaged in a competition that the sisters mentioned in their farewell issue as having led to "times of peculiar difficulty." Ward also had quarrels with the government, and in 1816 he discontinued his *Royal Gazette* and returned to Halifax (Lincoln 1925, 5).

The Stockdales were apparently exhausted by the ordeal of the previous seven years. On 14 September 1816, Priscilla and Sarah told their readers that they would, at the end of the month, "relinquish the arduous duties they have performed since the ever-lamented death of their Father" to Charles Rollin Beach, whose marriage to Sarah is mentioned two issues later. At the same time, they requested "all demands against them may be sent in for payment—and hope every person indebted to them will be in readiness to settle their accounts without delay."

The last issue the Stockdale sisters published was dated 28 September 1816. In it they recognized that they had perhaps been pioneers.

> With this week's publication, the Proprietors of this Paper relinquished their Editorial labors—and, with mingled emotions of regret, take leave of their Patrons. For more than thirteen tedious years, they have exerted themselves unceasingly to give every possible satisfaction to the Public; and are happy, on the close of their concerns, to feel an assurance that their efforts to please have not been unavailing. Perhaps the whole history of the pursuits of business cannot furnish another example, where females have thus assiduously applied themselves to the fatigues of a profession so wearisome and laborious. They can truly say, that the whole time that has elapsed since the much-lamented death of their Father in 1803, has been comparatively speaking, a succession of days of fatigue and nights of sleepless anxiety.

In the same issue, after thanking those patrons who stood by them in those "times of peculiar difficulty," they pointed out that though they had been "enjoined to *forgive*" those who forsook them, "it may not always be in their power to *forget.*" The Stockdales also printed a poem of eight verses emphasizing how the printer helps the public, ending with these lines:

> Ye politicians, too, can tell
> Who makes you understand so well
> Th' affairs on which you love to dwell?
> THE PRINTER
> Than, in no case, should you delay,
> (Tho' many do, from day to day),
> With punctuality to pay,'
> THE PRINTER

It is interesting that their father, Joseph, had inaugurated the *Gazette* on 17 January 1784 with a verse concerning the printer:

> The PRINTER thus earnestly tunes up his Pipe,
> And begs you'll attend to his FIGURE and TYPE;
> With ardent affection he zealously pants,
> And hopes to supply your several Wants.

When Beach took over with the 5 October 1816 issue, he changed the paper's name, format, and place of publication. Called the *Bermuda Gazette and Hamilton and St. George's Weekly Advertiser,* the paper had the motto "Free and Loyal." Since the *Royal Gazette* had quit publishing, Beach began his career as "Printer to the Colony," and as such, he had to move his press and newspaper to Hamilton to be where the seat of government had moved the previous year. The move upset some St. George residents, who canceled their subscriptions and threatened to start a rival newspaper, which they did, called the *Bermudian.*

In his inaugural issue of 5 October, Beach gave a brief history of the *Gazette,* paying tribute to his wife and sisters-in-law:

who have been very justly applauded for their unexampled industry and exertions, in an occupation of all others the most anxious and laborious, as in almost every department it calls for the united and unceasing exertions both of the faculties of the mind and the muscular [*sic*] activity of the body. Although these deserving females have the satisfaction to find themselves, and their aged mother, above the pressure of immediate or anticipated want, it is most certainly an unpleasant truth, that what little they may have gained is by no

means commensurate to their unwearied assiduity and care, which
have been highly aggravated by the numerous difficulties they have
often had to encounter, from secret enemies as well as from opposition.

What is clear from the writings of both Beach and the sisters is that they
considered printing in Bermuda a laborious, difficult, and, perhaps,
thankless profession. What is not so clear was the identity of the "secret
enemies," although it may be assumed that they were government personnel.

In his first issue, Beach promised his readers an "enlarged" and
"much improved" paper, claiming "some advantage may likewise accrue
from its being under the management of a man, whose stronger exertions and facilities of association with society may be productive of more
general satisfaction." He set the terms for subscribers and advertisers,
informing those who lived in outlying areas that they would have to pay
an additional dollar per year for delivery. Apparently, Priscilla Stockdale
stayed with the *Gazette,* because job-printing customers and advertisers
were told to leave their orders with her.

Frances Stockdale, the mother, died at age seventy in September
1818. Beach, who from 1817 had also been printing a weekly entitled
The Ladies Library, used this periodical to honor his mother-in-law:

> Although the industrious prosecution of the printing business by the
> family in this Colony since the year 1784, had not enabled them to
> accumulate any considerable property, the revered and venerable
> matron whose loss we now deplore, had, by the blessing of God,
> been enabled to enjoy the satisfaction of regular and agreeable
> meals, decent apparel, and a house managed with order and
> economy, ready for the reception of a friend or the hospitable enter-
> tainment of a stranger. — GAZETTE (Davies 1984).

Beach stayed with the *Bermuda Gazette* (the title was shortened
again with the 6 October 1821 issue) until 22 May 1824, when he sold it
to a group of merchants who published it until August 1824. The paper
was later revived in a new series in 1826. In his last issue (22 May 1824),
Beach gave as reasons for quitting the paper "the general depression of
business — the 'badness of the times' — the deteriorated state of health of
'ourself' and that of our 'better half' — together with the yet unsettled
state of political differences in the country."

The "political differences" he mentioned were understated. Hallett
points out that Beach was "scathing in his editorials on the despotic
activities of Governor William Lumley who eventually prosecuted him

and, in effect, had him deported" (Hallett 1985, 158). Also, in the last issue, an advertisement was carried for the sale of the Beaches' domestic belongings. Beach then left for the United States, where he died in Buffalo in 1826 at age thirty-eight. Sarah Stockdale Beach probably emigrated to the United States with her husband; Beach seemed to speak for them both in his final issue when he said, "we have come to the resolution of immediately closing our concerns here, to seek our fortunes elsewhere."

The more general histories of printing and the few specific works on Bermuda printing fail to tell us much about the pioneer Stockdale sisters after their years in printing. There is little doubt, though, that they were among the first woman printer-editors in the islands that surround the continental United States. Except for the few women in eighteenth-century England and the United States who printed newspapers when their spouses or fathers died or who started their own periodicals, usually of a specialized nature, the Stockdale sisters are unique in the history of journalism.

3

A Typical Day for a Small Island Newspaper in 1971

It was Thursday, and Thursday was press day for Dominica's three Saturday newspapers. All three are Saturday papers because that is market day. The editors of one of the weeklies, the *Star,* did not have time to sit down for an interview and so took this author on their rounds instead.

Robert and Phyllis Allfrey, editors of the *Star,* came to the journalistic profession with outstanding credentials, having accomplished a great deal in many fields and a little in journalism. Robert, a British mechanical engineer, came to the islands on holiday and has never returned to England. Phyllis, whose grandfather was the famous Sir Henry Nicholls, was born and raised on Dominica. At various times in her career, she has been the minister of labor and social affairs and holder of six portfolios in the West Indies Federation cabinet, the founder and leader of two political parties on Dominica, a novelist, a poet, a housewife, and the mother of five children, three of whom were adopted.

The *Star* was founded by the Allfreys in 1965. Its production is unusual, since it is printed in two different offices and uses two types of printing processes. The editors cut stencils for the paper at their converted millhouse home on the fringes of Roseau and shuttle them to their Roseau "depot," a twelve-by-fifteen-foot dining room in a friend's home, lent to the Allfreys for production and distribution purposes. The paper employs a combination of mimeograph and lithograph. The front page and all advertisements are done by pasteup, and the other pages are stenciled. Headlines are hand set. The result, according to Robert, is a "poor newspaper for people with bad eyes." He added that the most frequent criticism of the *Star* is that its print is too small and dull. "People here cannot afford eyeglasses, and without them they cannot see what we write." The total equipment used to publish the *Star* are a Roneo 795 mimeograph machine located in the middle of the former dining room, some hand-set type for advertisements, a photoengraver, and a typewriter, both of the latter kept at the millhouse home where Robert said he can keep them "under my eye."

On this particular press day, the routine took this form:

Phyllis had just brought a stencil to the "depot" to be duplicated. She gave the boy operating the Roneo meticulous instructions and then phoned a couple of reporters who had failed to cover their stories. All the time, a young employee was pondering what twelve-point type was. She showed him from a past issue. Before we could get out of the depot, a man came in to sell raffles; Phyllis took time out to buy a couple and asked about the raffle-seller's wife and father.

We got into the Allfreys' green dune buggy for a trip across town to pick up a picture of a girl who had won a beauty contest the week before. After spending a few moments with the girl's mother, Phyllis returned to the vehicle. The picture was too small to use. On the way back to the depot, Phyllis told me, between stops and honks to greet neighbors, about her printer. "He makes at least one or two mistakes in every heading, and if I ask him to correct them, he makes more. So I just say forget it," she explained, shrugging her shoulders. "He's a member of the Black Power group here, and we expect any day for the whole paper to go up. Just last week, our writers went to the Black Power meeting at deadline time, and we didn't get the paper out on time. We lost sales of one thousand copies because of that." It is extremely important to get newspapers out early in Dominica, even though they are weeklies, because the paperboys go to the newspaper office that has its issues ready and they start selling. When they tire themselves out, they do not return to circulate newspapers that have the later pressruns.

Back at the depot, Phyllis called a government communications official to apologize because her reporter had failed to cover a meeting. Hanging up the phone, she sighed, "I get into enough trouble with the government; I don't want them to accuse me of not holding to what I say I'll do."

Finally, we were on our way, over extremely bumpy roads, to the millhouse home-office-plant. Although the distance between the two offices can be covered in "seven minutes flat" under normal weather conditions, Dominica doesn't have much of the latter. Frequent slides and an occasional bridge washout hamper the shuttle service employed by the

Allfreys. On the way, Phyllis remembered that the first issues of the *Star* had not gone over well; only three hundred copies were sold. "The people didn't like the paper because it was stapled" and prestige newspapers are not stapled, she explained. Once the paper quit stapling and began running off issues on a new Roneo obtained from England, circulation went up. "But we almost needed an engineer to run the machine at first." Today, the circulation of the *Star* is two thousand on good weeks, and when there is nothing exciting happening, sixteen hundred. If it rains on the day of issue, the paperboys and papers get sopped and circulation falls off tremendously.

Noticing a stalled vehicle on the side of the road, Phyllis stopped to see if she could be of help. "Haven't seen you for a long time. How's the family?" she greeted the driver. And at that point, I made the connection: these greetings were more than just casual remarks; they were also questions to gather information for next week's issue.

At the former millhouse, a table was set up on the patio, and there,

3.1   Phyllis and Robert Allfrey at their millhouse office
of *Dominica Star,* 1971. (*Photo by John A. Lent*)

in the outdoors with lush foliage and a clear stream only inches away, Robert and Phyllis Allfrey typed stencils, answered correspondence, laid out advertisements, fed their adopted Carib Indian children, and talked about the *Star* and island politics. Robert recounted how the paper came about. "Phyllis and I were running the *Herald* (another Dominican weekly) for a while for an old blind man who was easily influenced on most matters. In the *Herald* building, the blind man also had a drinking place where he imbibed quite a bit. I split with him after an argument and as people began asking about getting duplicating jobs done, we set up this operation." The *Star* does not pay for itself, so these job-printing chores help make up the deficit.

Over a lunch of fish and breadfruit, the conversation turned to politics. The Allfreys are still in politics "more or less," with Phyllis on the executive board of the Freedom party. "Oh yes, we support the Freedom party openly," she said, giving the reason why they support that group and not the Labour party, of which she was president at one time. "When the Federation collapsed, my political teammate [premier of Dominica in 1971] was afraid I'd return to Dominica and stand for election as premier. He chucked me out of the party although I was president. His excuse was that I criticized my own land."

How has the *Star* survived with an expatriate as editor? Phyllis answered. "They'd like to get Robert out but it would be like chucking the prince out of Buckingham. I'm one of the few white people here who is indigenous and I have held some powerful positions. They'd like to get Robert out and then shut down the *Star*. Robert runs the paper really and I'm the strength because they cannot get the *Star* out of the way as long as I'm behind it."

At that point, another stencil was finished, and the editors were soon back in the dune buggy, making another one of their very regular jaunts to the dining room office in Roseau.

The Allfreys struggled with the *Star* until 1982 when Phyllis closed it. She died on 6 February 1986 in penury and virtually unheralded for her many accomplishments. During her final years, she took care of Robert, who had become ill. He died in 1988 (Haniff 1988).

4

Cultural and Media Dependency:
The Price of Modernity

Unlike Asian and African colonies, the English-speaking West Indies, upon receiving independence, had no previous culture with which they could identify. When the European explorers came to the islands, they superimposed their institutions and values on those of the Caribs and Arawaks. Later, as the plantation system developed in the islands, millions of Africans were taken out of their societies and shipped to the British West Indies as slaves (Ayeast 1960, 14; Sherlock 1966, 13). In the process, they too were stripped of their cultural identities. The result, as Lewis (1968, 393) made clear, is that the West Indian is a "schizoid person . . . *peau noir, masque blanc* [a little black, white mask], the possessor of a pseudo-European culture in an Afro-Asian environment."

The confusion and contradiction of such an existence have afflicted institutions and individuals alike in the islands. In the schools, children learned about Gladstone and the queen, rarely about sugar and calypso. In the libraries, the litterateur read novels set in London, not in Kingston or Port of Spain; in fact, there was not much West Indian literature until the second third of the twentieth century.

The Commonwealth Caribbean cultural background is further complicated by the fact that the French and Spanish had left their marks before the English arrived. This was especially so linguistically. Some would argue that the influence of French and Spanish languages on the region added to the complexities of fragmentation and separatism inherent in the British West Indies; others would claim that the result was beneficial in that the masses were given their distinct languages. In the Windwards, the Creole language is French *patois;* in Trinidad and Tobago, the Creole takes on both Spanish and French accents. The result has been that the many people of the Windwards who still speak French *patois* can communicate with residents of the French islands of Martinique and Guadeloupe but not with residents of Antigua or Barbados, who speak a Creole based on English. Dependence on the Creole varies but has been most intense in Dominica and St. Lucia, where an estimated 95 percent of the inhabitants use *patois* as their mother tongue; not more than one-third of these can express themselves in English (Taylor 1970, 613).

The degree of Creole use can be related to the social status attached to the language. In Jamaica, for example, Creole has been considered "just bad English"; on other islands, teachers and parents have discouraged its use. The low social status attributed to the language produced problems for children who, having heard the vernacular in their homes, mixed it with the English they learned in school; the resultant mixture often inhibited any kind of creative expression. Comprehension of the broadcast media by the masses has also been hindered as a result (Alleyne n.d., 28), and even more so when editors and broadcasters not only refused to use the Creole but insisted upon writing and speaking "English English."

There have been a few instances of media use of Creole, especially in St. Lucia, but media personnel elsewhere in the islands explained that the use of the dialect is either too expensive, too limiting, or too unpopular. All in all, the islands have found themselves in the perplexing situation of many new nations; having no national language, they must carry out the business of modernization in the metropolitan tongue.

Whereas in colonial times Caribbean media were designed with the colonists in mind, by the mid-1970s, in many islands, they were aimed at the tourists. For example, *Bajan,* a newsmagazine published on Barbados, was printed for the white tourist, not the black Barbadian. "It proclaims the white beaches of the island, pushes the products of hotels, airports and duty-free shops," according to one of the magazine's editors (Interview, Wickham 1971). Bahamian magazines, such as *Bahamas* or *The Visitor,* also were aimed at the tourists, as were the two dailies of Nassau, which regularly used interviews and photographs of visiting entertainment personalities appearing at the hotels and casinos, as well as bathing beauties. Finally, the Caribbean Broadcasting Corporation, during peak tourist months, televised a preponderance of United States, Canadian, and European fare for the benefit of tourists who represented the buying power to which advertisers directed their messages.

OUTSIDE OWNERS

Among Commonwealth Caribbean broadcasting systems, it was indeed rare for a station to be both locally and privately owned. On islands with competing stations, the pattern traditionally was that one station was owned by the government and the second by Rediffusion or another foreign enterprise.

By the mid-1970s, the picture was somewhat different for newspapers. Although two-thirds of the island newspapers — seven of the thirteen dailies and thirty-three of the forty-six nondailies — were owned or significantly controlled by outside entrepreneurs and local political and church interests, the majority of the region's circulation was in the hands of local, privately owned papers. The six dailies under local private owners had a combined circulation of 184,319, or over 56 percent of the total daily circulation. Four dailies owned by foreign groups had a total circulation of 134,715, 41 percent of the total, and three political party dailies circulated to 6,700, or 2 percent.

It was never difficult to get foreign conglomerates to invest in the islands' media, especially radio and television. All that the Commonwealth Caribbean nations had to do was flirt with the idea of television, and foreign investors came courting. As a result, all of the television stations in the region were developed with generous amounts of U.S. dollars and British pounds. Even in the 1970s, as the smaller islands contemplated television of their own, they found that their first big decision was to decide which foreign offer of assistance they should accept.

Besides the U.S. and British media concerns, the Canadian government was more than mildly interested in developing electronic media in the islands. In the mid-1960s, at the request of the Canadian government, the Canadian Broadcasting Corporation conducted a feasibility study on the possibility of establishing a radio network to service the Commonwealth islands. After studying the report, the Canadian government made an offer of U.S. $4 million to create a Canada-Caribbean Broadcasting Center and a string of stations in the British West Indies. The offer was not accepted, partly because it came from outside the region (*Advertising Age,* 31 October 1966, 94).

Without doubt the three most persistent outside owners involved in Commonwealth Caribbean media have been British entrepreneurs Roy Thomson and Cecil King and the British company, Rediffusion Ltd. In the 1960s and early 1970s, Thomson was active in radio, television, and newspaper ownership in the islands, maintaining control over two of the few region-oriented dailies, the *Barbados Advocate-News* and the *Trini-*

dad Guardian, as well as the latter's mass circulation sister, the *Evening News.* Together, Thomson's three papers represented 39 percent of the total daily circulation in the islands. He also owned part of Capital Broadcasting in Bermuda. But his interests in the region have dwindled since the mid-1970s. In 1975, the *Trinidad Guardian* and the *Evening News* were sold to a Caribbean conglomerate, McEnearney-Alstons Group. At various times, Thomson was involved financially with the *Voice of St. Lucia,* the *Antigua Star,* the *Trinidad Mirror,* and the *Barbados Daily News,* and with broadcasting units on Trinidad, Jamaica, Barbados, and Bermuda. His Thomson Television International (TTI) usually acted as a partner to a consortium of investors. For example, in Trinidad and Tobago, the consortium partners of TTI were Rediffusion, the Columbia Broadcasting System, and the Trinidad and Tobago government. Thomson's name also came up occasionally in discussions of Bahamian media; at different times, he tried to purchase the *Nassau Tribune* (Dupuch 1967, 116), the *Nassau Guardian,* and Radio Station ZNS of Nassau. And in 1960, he made an unsuccessful bid for the *Jamaica Daily Gleaner,* a decade after his rival, Cecil King, had surveyed Kingston as to the possibility of developing a third daily there.

Rivaling Thomson in the Commonwealth Caribbean was Cecil King, also of Fleet Street. In the mid-1960s, when Thomson seemed in an invulnerable position in Trinidad—owning both daily newspapers, half of the radio stations, and shares in the only television system—King established another newspaper there, the *Mirror,* with a Sunday edition. Within a few months, King's International Publishing Corporation, in conjunction with the Liverpool Post and Echo, Ltd., also succeeded in acquiring the *Barbados Advocate* and its subsidiaries, the *Voice of St. Lucia* and the *Antigua Star.* (The *Advocate* became the *Advocate-News* in 1968 when Thomson bought and merged it with the rival *Daily News;* it has since reverted to its former name and has become a tabloid.)

However, by 1966, King, realizing his profit margin was being sliced (Hunt 1967, 53), sold all his Caribbean interests to Thomson, who as a result owned all three dailies in Trinidad, the only daily in Barbados, and the chief newspapers of St. Lucia and Antigua. Thomson's subsequent sale of the *Mirror* plant and equipment to a Canadian firm led to the paper's death. He did not hang on to the *Voice of St. Lucia* or the *Antigua Star* very long, selling them both by 1970.

The third big outside owner, Rediffusion, controlled broadcast rights in the Commonwealth Caribbean from the outset. By the early 1950s, the London-based organization controlled radio stations in the three most populated islands, Jamaica, Barbados, and Trinidad and Tobago. By the mid-1970s, radio companies in Jamaica, Barbados, Trinidad and Tobago, St. Lucia, Bermuda, and Tortola (in the British Virgin Islands) were owned by Rediffusion. Rediffusion was also a partner in the consortia that owned Trinidad and Tobago Television and Leeward Islands Television Services of Antigua (Central Rediffusion 1956, 14–15).

Because London- or New York–owned media in the islands were there only at the beck and call of local governments, they exhibited much caution during controversial situations, especially those of a political nature. This criticism was leveled at the Thomson newspapers of Trinidad by the general manager of the *Express* in that island. He said that during the Black Power campaigns of early 1970, the *Guardian* was mute, not saying anything editorially for ten days about the riots and the state of emergency. On the other hand, he said his *Express* editorialized daily (Interview, Gordon 1970).

There is a continuing debate about foreign ownership of most media in the Third World. On the one hand, many believe that developing regions such as the Commonwealth Caribbean, obsessed with collecting electronic media as part of the paraphernalia of nationhood, would not be able to raise necessary investment and equipment capital, produce their own programs, or provide required training without resorting to foreign ownership. Others argue that foreign-owned media are commercially oriented and depend on mass sales and advertising volume that developing nations are not prepared to provide (Ainslie 1968, 242). Additionally the urge for profits leads the media to stress the entertainment aspects of journalism rather than the educational, developmental, or informational issues desperately important in developing countries.

Proponents of developmental issues explain that reliance upon the ledger book as the sole indication of a medium's success is not conducive to the needs of a developing nation, where sacrifices must be encouraged for longer-term goals. For example, a UNESCO team surveying West Indian mass media in 1968 felt Thomson could do more sacrificing financially to ensure that the smaller newspapers in the region survived. The UNESCO team criticized Thomson's relinquishing of the *Voice of St. Lucia* because of its poor financial showing. The team noted that Thomson had already established a preponderance in the region with his Trinidad and Barbados dailies and no longer needed the smaller *Voice*. Such behavior by outsiders, UNESCO feared, would destroy small island media (Roppa and Clarke 1969, 12).

The foreign-owned media of Trinidad regularly felt the pressure of the criticism that they did not represent the people's interests. As a reaction, the *Guardian* and the *Evening News* periodically ran editorials and stories boasting of the public services they provided, proclaiming that their "roots are deeply sunk in the community," and explaining that the expatriate owner of the *Evening News* was "not here to peddle the propaganda of the country of which he is a citizen."

As would be expected, the foreign influences seriously affected news flow and media content in the region. Commonwealth Caribbean media users depended upon foreign agencies for information both from abroad and from neighboring islands; the chief sources in the mid-1970s were Reuters (fourteen subscribers), Associated Press (nine), United Press International (four), and foreign broadcasting services, such as the BBC, CBS, the Voice of America, the Canadian Broadcasting Corporation, Visnews, and the Central Office of Information in London. At the time, only Reuters attempted regionalization of news through its Caribbean Desk in Barbados. The Reuters operation included re-editing the London-to–South America Editing Service for Caribbean consumption and reception as well as editing and retransmitting messages from stringers in thirteen island territories. AP and UPI both transmitted their news for the Caribbean by radio teletype from New York, neither service providing regional bureaus. The seriousness of this potential wire service imperialism was pointed out in a 1968 survey, which found that 40 percent of all news presentations on island radio stations originated from studios abroad (Roppa and Clarke 1969, 12). Even if a BBC news show was beamed directly to the Caribbean, it contained numerous items of little or no significance to West Indians.

Part of the problem of foreign news sources was solved in 1976, when, on the basis of an idea from the Caribbean Heads of Government seven years before, the Caribbean News Agency (CANA) was set up. CANA was considered a model regional news agency in that, among other things, it was not government dominated. Of its shares, 54 percent were held by privately owned media and 46 percent by public media. After five years, CANA was described as a success, having expanded its daily output of Caribbean and world stories, maintained its independence, and survived financially (Cuthbert 1981, 3).

Even if they were not made in the United States or Great Britain, radio and television shows in the region have at least been patterned after prototypes in those nations. Thus, sitting in a Barbadian guest house in the 1970s, I could view a TV quiz show that not only copied an American format but even used questions about the United States rather than about Barbados. The reward for winning the quiz—a trip to the United States. All television stations, with the exception of Trinidad and Tobago Television, relied upon foreign sources for 60 to 80 percent of their content. For example, approximately 39 of Jamaica Broadcasting Corporation's 58½ weekly broadcast hours were foreign-originated programs, while 34 of Leeward Islands Television's (Antigua) 42 hours and 45 of Caribbean Broadcasting Corporation's 56 hours were in the same category.

The Trinidad and Tobago station, however, quickly approached an equal ratio of local to foreign shows. It was also an exception because its locally produced shows included formats in addition to the news, sports, panel, and government-information types that Commonwealth Caribbean TV stations rely on as their only homemade products. Part of the reason TTT—and also TTNBS radio—created more domestic programming is rooted in the Trinidad Third Five-Year Plan. To offset the costliness of local program production, the drafters of the plan recommended that immediate attempts be made to substitute "high quality canned" programs for the traditional "low quality canned" material, and that, gradually, a higher proportion of local-oriented programs be introduced.

But Trinidad was unique. In the 1970s, a typical day's format of a Commonwealth Caribbean television station (in this case, that of Jamaica Broadcasting Corporation) looked something like this: the first one and one-half hours of children's shows ("Sesame Street" and a local "Romper Room") were followed by adventure and light comedy ("Daniel Boone," "Joe 90," "Gentle Ben," "Daktari," "I Dream of Jeannie," "Bewitched," "Flying Nun," or "Real McCoys") until news and sports at 7 P.M. From 8 P.M. to 10 P.M., shows were designed for adult audiences and included panels, mystery and intrigue shows, light comedy, and variety. Typical programs during this period included "Name of the Game," "The Val Doonican Show," "Mod Squad," "Love American Style," "Lancer," "Hawaii Five-O," "Ben Casey," and "Adam-12." After a ten-minute newscast, the late evening format began at 10:10 P.M. with shows such as "Peyton Place," "Alfred Hitchcock Presents," "The FBI," "The Saint," "Dragnet," and movies. "Late, Late News" ended the JBC day.

Very little television drama has been produced in the islands, mainly because of high costs and lack of expertise. Any regional dramas, such as soap operas, would also have faced the obstacle of cross-cultural interpretations, but the most obvious reason for the heavy dependence upon foreign shows was their relative inexpensiveness. In the 1970s, there was insufficient advertising support for domestic programming. Moreover, there were strong cultural ties with both England and the United States. The proximity of most Commonwealth Caribbean islands to the United States facilitated travel between the two areas, and a large number of West Indians resided in the United States. For these reasons, broadcasting fare was often patterned after U.S. radio and television.

As indicated elsewhere (see Chapters 5, 6, and 22), foreign programming had become even more pervasive in the 1980s. Calling it "cultural displacement by invitation," Wilson said it affects the people's "perception of self, inflates the kind of material return expected from national economies, and in a real sense, questions the legitimacy of some of our cultural traditions and values" (1987). Citing figures from a study done by Aggrey Brown in 1987, he showed that imported content on four national television services in Jamaica, Barbados, Antigua, and Trinidad and Tobago jumped from an average 77 percent in 1976 to 87 percent a decade later. Trinidad's television service had a 17 percent increase in foreign programs over the ten years. Most Commonwealth Caribbean national television services used 86 to 92 percent foreign shows (quoted in Wilson 1987, 10–11). In a survey of Trinidadian media, Skinner concluded that there was a strong relationship between foreign media dependency and producer nation dependency (1987).

Some attempts have been made in recent years to change television programming, but their effect has been minuscule in relationship to the problem. Trinidad's Banyan Group has done local programs, including a popular arts magazine show, "Gayelle," and Barbados' Caribbean Broadcasting Corporation (CaBC) has increased its local productions. CaBC has a one-half-hour local show nightly and others throughout the day, including one game show, "Bust Yuh Brain." The station director revealed the entrenchment of foreign programming, however, when he said that his hope was to get local programming up to 30 percent of the schedule (Taitt 1987, 31).

Radio, like television, has used a large proportion of foreign programming over the years. In the mid-1970s, Radio Trinidad still obtained over 70 percent of its materials from overseas, while at smaller stations, such as the Antigua Broadcasting Service and Radio Anguilla, the percentages were 75 and 95 percent, respectively. The Jamaica Broadcasting Authority, a governmental body that appraises broadcasting performance, in its yearly reports in the 1950s and 1960s decried the use of U.S., British, and Australian shows. In one such report, the authority characterized the majority of Jamaican listeners and viewers as "non-whites watching white faces and white mores and white attitudes"; at another time, it chastised Jamaican announcers for mimicking the voices of U.S. and Canadian colleagues (see Maxwell 1958; *Daily Gleaner* 23 September 1964: 18, 6 November 1962: 8, 25 January 1966: 5).

It has always been difficult to determine what West Indian radio station managers have meant by local content. When personnel at Antigua's ZDK boasted in the 1970s that 99.9 percent of the programs were local, they were saying that because Antiguan disc jockeys spun the records and read the news, then the station was predominantly domestic. They did not take into account the origins of the music and news.

Since the late 1950s, efforts have been made to localize larger portions of Commonwealth Caribbean radio content, especially in Trinidad and Tobago, Jamaica, Barbados, the Bahamas, and St. Lucia. After its takeover by the government in 1969, TTNBS in Trinidad and Tobago increased its local fare to 40 percent. Radio Barbados took a similar step; only one in six hours of its shows was of foreign origin.

Of much concern in the 1980s was the onslaught of evangelical radio and television from the United States. In early 1988, some Caribbean churchmen denounced the U.S. tele-evangelists and their impact in the Caribbean. They singled out Jimmy Swaggart, describing him as presenting God as "a rich wealthy North American with a colonial mentality" (*Caribbean Contact* 1988, 1). The churchmen said that the broadcasting evangelists had hidden agendas of becoming rich and of promoting the New Right of the United States.

In 1988, Helen Television Service of St. Lucia was considering a proposal of the Trinity Broadcasting Network (TBN) in the United States calling for TBN to provide the expertise and Helen Television an extra channel for the sole broadcast of TBN. The twenty-four-hour channel, relayed by satellite, would broadcast through Helen Television Service to St. Lucia, St. Vincent, and Barbados.

Obviously, mass media of the Commonwealth Caribbean are still very heavily dependent upon outside factors in the areas of ownership, programming, and technology. A number of the mass media problems in the region are those of emerging nations in a hurry to become modernized. Basically, these problems relate to one central point: developing areas need those resources that they can least afford and that are, oftentimes, least indigenous to their cultures. In the 1980s, with Reagan's Caribbean Basin Initiative, the foreign media resources flowed into the region virtually uninhibited.

5

U.S. Broadcast Programming Use
in the Small Islands

A s already noted in the previous chapter, other cultures have been transplanted to the Leeward and Windward islands for centuries and have been blamed for decimating indigenous artifacts. The outside influences of language and education persist to this day. They have been strengthened by the influence of modern information technology and by the identification of the region as convenient for religious proselytizing, military surveillance, and the training of foreign medical students.

Once primarily the domain of the British, the Caribbean has become important to the United States in recent years. Religious organizations based in the United States have gospel stations in at least Anguilla (Radio Beacon), St. Kitts (Radio Paradise), Nevis (Trinity Broadcasting Network), and Antigua (Radio Lighthouse). The Voice of America maintains a strong outlet on Antigua, and the U.S. Navy and Air Force keep bases there. Medical colleges, backed by U.S. money and used almost exclusively for the training of U.S. students, function on Montserrat, St. Kitts, Grenada, and Antigua. Obviously, all of these leave cultural imprints.

From the beginning, when the English and Americans established the first presses, the mass media relied and became dependent upon these outside forces. Broadcasting was most seriously affected, as programming, staff, training, and equipment were imported, often as parts of packages of groups, usually from Great Britain but also from the United States. More recently, in the 1980s, the impact has been extremely pronounced, especially in smaller countries in the Leewards and Windwards, and the country most responsible for these impacts now is the United States. In fact, government-owned stations in the English-speaking Caribbean have been so anxious to carry live U.S. television programs that the U.S. government, according to one source, "has been able to put pressure of possible exclusion from its Caribbean Basin Initiative (CBI) on a number of nations, including Jamaica, to accept restrictions and pay fees for the 'privilege' of retransmitting U.S. television programmes that in no way cater to the particular interests or priorities of the Caribbean region" (*Caribbean Contact* 1984).

TELEVISION

U.S. television programs, received by satellite and retransmitted live by local TV stations and cable systems, now dominate the screens of

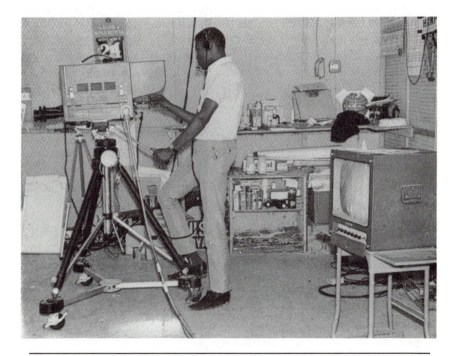

5.1   Early production work at Leeward Islands Television Service, now Antigua Broadcasting Service.

Leeward and Windward islanders. The deals worked out to enable these small territories to benefit from the use of modern carriers of this programming (satellite and cable) threaten the very existence of national broadcasting systems. Ivor Bird, whose family owns Antigua's cable, predicted that, once fully implemented, cable will "wipe out" the audience of the national television service, the Antigua Broadcasting Service (ABS-TV). To survive, ABS-TV became one of the ten channels offered by the cable service (Interview, Bird 1984). Antigua's CTV, handled by a "U.S. representative company," brings in via satellite U.S. movie, sports, and other channels. Antiguans, according to Bird, watch the island's station only for local news. Cable services cost viewers U.S. $13 monthly.

Cable television's establishment in St. Kitts in mid-1984 created a controversy that fed into the national election campaign being held at that time. According to the Labour party, as reported in the *Labour Spokesman* of 5 May, an agreement to introduce cable television was worked out in a letter of intent from the premier to the home affairs minister on 22 July 1983. Cable's introduction was to be processed through St. Kitts–Nevis Cable Ltd., and Ridgewood Investments (whose equity was to come from a "U.S. source") would own 60 percent of the equity and the St. Kitts–Nevis government, with private shareholders, 40 percent. An article in the oppositionist *Labour Spokesman* revealed that the cable franchise had been sold to St. Kitts–Nevis Cable Ltd. for U.S. $625,000 with stipulations that the cable system could use ZIZ-TV facilities if it upgraded the station's equipment by a value of U.S. $60,000 by 31 December 1983. The deal further called for providing an access channel to the government's ZIZ-TV and for allowing all channels to simultaneously carry subjects of significant national importance. The cable company was to pay for pole attachments at about U.S. $.40 per pole per year and for the franchise at 3 percent of gross profits.

The opposition accused Premier Kennedy Simmonds of entering into joint ownership of cable television without public disclosure, an act of "arrogance," according to the *Labour Spokesman*. An editorial of 16 May 1984 asked how a system such as ZIZ-TV could be sold or transferred without public disclosure and why majority control over an area as sensitive as national communications had been given to foreigners (*Labour Spokesman* 1984). Only shortly after, according to J. N. France, Secretary of both the Labour party and the Trades and Labour Union, did the premier explain that the government had secured 20 percent of the shares in the cable company in exchange for the use of its television premises, facilities, and duty-free concessions. The government had also received 20 percent equity to be made available to the public (Interview, France 1984).

ZIZ-TV General Manager G. O. Caines called the *Labour Spokesman* accusations examples of "irresponsible journalism," claiming that the joint venture guidelines were clear from the beginning. He emphasized that Ridgewood Investments owned 60 percent of the cable system but had no equity in either ZIZ television or radio. Caines justified the need for upgrading ZIZ-TV, saying, "If cable brings in good shows from the United States, then the cable company must help us to put out something that does not make us look bad. When cable comes, we at ZIZ-TV could not compete, if we did not upgrade" (Interview, Caines 1984). According to Caines, the deal was beneficial to the government, which shared in the cable television profits without putting up capital. Instead of pledging 20 percent capital, the government lent the use of ZIZ-TV equipment to the cable operator. Caines said that the 20 percent public shares will be put on the market when cable is nearly profitable, thus safeguarding the public; those shares will not be sold to the government or to foreigners but only to the St. Kitts public (Interview, Caines 1984).

In the mid-1980s, St. Kitts' cable television used twelve channels, with a capacity for thirty-six. Of the twelve, two were allocated to ZIZ-TV, one to Antigua's ABS-TV, and the other nine to U.S. stations. Caines was not threatened by cable's impact upon his station, saying, "We at ZIZ will keep existing as we are, plus we'll be on cable. Cable cannot completely compete with ZIZ. Some people will receive us on cable, while others will get our direct signal" (Interview, Caines 1984). One ZIZ-TV cable channel featured information (flight announcements, parliamentary proceedings, etc.) and could be used like a telex system, while the other carried the regular program schedule, made up of 60 to 65 percent U.S.-originated shows. Caines said he hoped to bring the foreign content down to 40 percent because he believed the St. Kitts culture had been hurt as a result of foreign TV. He said there was a big drive to produce local shows, mainly of a cultural and educational level. According to Caines, ZIZ-TV would offer shows that "tell the people about where they live, what is happening around them and what makes the country run. We will produce shows to motivate people to produce more local food. We could be a movie house, but TV in a developing country to too expensive to have that" (Interview, Caines 1984).

Efforts were made to avoid duplication of programs on the cable channel of ZIZ-TV and the nine U.S. program channels. Cable television costs St. Kittitians U.S. $10 per month; for an extra U.S. $4, subscribers obtain two additional channels, one devoted to movies.

Satellite TV Montserrat Ltd., serving part of the 13,000 population of Montserrat, has offered six cable channels since about 1983. The cable service is limited to the capital of Plymouth, although plans call for coverage of the southern part of the island. Of course, almost all shows are from the U.S. An issue of *Montserrat Cable TV Guide* in 1984 listed movies such as *Tootsie, A Streetcar Named Desire, Guys and Dolls, Friday the 13th, Shampoo, Brainstorm, Henry Fonda Tribute, Still of the Night, Marx Brothers Go West, Rocky III, The Deep,* and *Heidi,* among others. Most were listed as PG (parental guidance), although a few were rated R (restricted). The explicit content and language of a number of these movies brought some adverse reactions from the audience.

Operated by a Puerto Rican firm, the cable system has been granted a fifteen-year duty- and tax-free franchise. According to Howell Bramble, son and brother of former island premiers and editor of the *Montserrat Times,* the government made this concession because it believed cable television was an aid to island tourism. He said, "We attract older tourists who need something to do, not the young ones looking for beaches" (Interview, Bramble 1984). Bramble also believed "someone in government is benefitting from cable"; he stated that tax-shelter industries require employment of local people, yet the cable service was handled solely by a Canadian. Cable services cost U.S. $16 per month.

Montserrat's locally registered television station, Antilles Television (ATV-7), is "financed out of Europe" (Interview, White 1984) and uses mostly U.S. programs relayed by satellite from WGN in Chicago, from Cable Network News, and from other cable stations. ATV-7 is on the air from 6:00 to 8:00 A.M. and from 4:00 to 11:30 P.M. seven days a week. In an evening, one is apt to see CNN News, followed by a Michael Jackson video, "The Jeffersons," or "Solid Gold." ATV-7 relays WGN, complete with Chicago news, reports on its non-Caribbean type weather, and even advertisements for "Chuck's Chicken" and other distinctly Chicago products; on alternate nights, viewers see a New York station's local news, weather, and commercials.

The Windward Islands have been similarly affected by foreign television. In St. Lucia, since at least 1984, the locally owned Helen Television Service (HTS) has transmitted, free of charge, U.S. satellite television. Originally, the service was twenty-four hours daily. As one writer reported, "No one paid for this. You purchased your TV, put up your antenna, and viewed. HTS had not yet a full license to operate" (Bousquet 1986). Two other companies, Soufriere Community Television and Southern TV, also picked up U.S. satellite-relayed programs and transmitted them to St. Lucians.

The usual complaints surfaced about the U.S. television: that performance of students at school suffered; that there were negative effects on the outlook of Caribbean people; that political perceptions were formed by the constant diet of U.S. news and the American line on international affairs; and that the commercials caused a frustrating situation for viewers. After Prime Minister John Compton and cabinet members criticized satellite television, legal action was taken. The hours of television transmission were reduced, and the medium was regulated after November 1986. Almost simultaneously, HTS announced that it had the capacity to institute pay television, and Cable and Wireless also planned to launch cable television. Both HTS and Cable and Wireless decided not to offer a local program, either for economic reasons or for lack of desire. Cable and Wireless planned only to tape from other British and U.S. channels and to relay at a cost. Summing up the changed situation in St. Lucia, one critic wrote, "What many have not yet recognized is that after every factor is considered, St. Lucia has moved from a period when US cultural penetration and invasion of cultural sovereignty by satellite took place on a 24-hour uninterrupted basis, to a period when the penetration is now regulated, with the victim drinking the poison in smaller doses. Worst of all, the victim now has to pay for the canned cultural poison" (Bousquet 1986, 7).

RADIO

Besides the foreign ownership of Radio Antilles in Montserrat, of the gospel stations, and of VOA and BBC outlets, the dominant outside influence upon radio in the Leeward and Windward islands is in music programming. Although the situation has changed in recent years to allow more Caribbean music, most stations still spend a great amount of time functioning as pop music jukeboxes. Radio Montserrat, for example, uses a "'Top 40' in the United States format," with the difference that "instead of all Michael Jackson, we use some reggae" (Interview, White 1984). Actually, the station manager said that the ratio of Caribbean to western music is three to one. He added that less BBC programming is used, even though the people "grew up with BBC" (Interview, White 1984). ZDK on Antigua is popular because of its U.S. and British pop music; it plays *Billboard*'s "Top 50" chart weekly, as well as the "Top 50 of the Caribbean." The station caters to U.S. Navy personnel stationed in Antigua by providing an hour of news and sports every evening (Interview, Bird 1984). St. Kitts' ZIZ is also mainly music (60 percent of total time), 35 percent of which is Caribbean, the other 65 percent U.S. and European (Interview, Caines 1984).

Although one source said Radio Antilles plays U.S. top hits "to death" (Stivers 1981), station managers claimed the main music is Caribbean. Of all programming on Radio Antilles, 60 percent is music, including a "Top 70" list that mixes Caribbean and western pop. The station also broadcasts educational programs relevant to the region (sent by CARICOM), a Caribbean children's hour, and regular newscasts (Interview, Willock 1984). [The station ceased broadcasting in 1990.]

Despite efforts to change, the predominant type of broadcasting in the Leeward Islands is either from the United States or is patterned after that country's programming. As one writer observed, "Antiguans have shamelessly accepted the immoral penetration of warped and misleading news carried by the media. They have accepted the penetration of Voice of America and related instruments of propaganda (and they have accepted) dis-jockeyism [*sic*]" (Lett 1982).

Changes in the future are likely to make broadcast media even more dependent upon foreign multination concerns on the one hand and national governments and political parties on the other. As these two controlling interests continue to link up, further Americanization of Leeward and Windward mass media and cultures can be expected, leading to bastardization of indigenous cultural forms, further commercialization of the societies to the benefit mainly of elite foreign and national residents, and obliteration of the few independent media voices. A writer in *Caribbean Contact* (1984) voiced this lament.

> To accept, pay for, and retransmit to Caribbean audiences on a regular basis programming which at best treats the region as a silent and passive eavesdropper on a communication process in the developed world, and at worst instills in viewers a sense of the irrelevance of events and actions within their own cultural milieu, is a dehumanising process. . . . Uncritical, unsupervised retransmission of satellite television through local Caribbean stations should be reined in before it becomes established as a vehicle for a new colonisation of the minds and hopes of the people of the region.

6

Belize since Television: Country of No Return

In the ever-occurring deliberations about possible effects of mass communications, certain countries surface as archetypal examples — each is almost a "country of the moment." In the 1950s and 1960s, when radio (especially through forums) and television were believed to be development catalysts, India, American Samoa, and one or two other territories were at center stage. In the 1970s, Brunei, with its gigantic and accelerated leap into color television, and Indonesia and India, with their PALAPA and S.I.T.E. satellites, became focal points, followed by the Middle East, with its overall rapid advancement in use of new information technology.

In the 1980s, the "country of the moment" seemed to be Belize. For various reasons, this multiethnic, independent nation sandwiched between Mexico and Guatemala drew the attention of outside communication scholars. The country has an interesting and unusual mass communications history. First, television was introduced chaotically by private entrepreneurs who pirated via satellite. Second, Belizeans are exposed to programs from stations in two different cultures, the United States and Mexico. Third, the medium's development began without a national television service in operation and still lacks, even today, even 1 percent local programming. Fourth, Belize was rather backward in mass communications before television, with only one radio service and a handful of weekly newspapers.

PRESS AND RADIO

From the beginning, the mass media in British Honduras (the former name of Belize) were dependent upon outsiders. For example, in the 1820s, when settlers reacted in print to an ex-superintendent of the British settlement (who had called it the "most detestable spot on the face of the globe"), their protest, which became the first printed material, had to be sent to Jamaica to be set in type. By December 1825, the magistrates ordered that a "printing apparatus" be obtained, and the following March *The Honduras Almanack* appeared. Its printer, James Cruikshank, also brought out a weekly newspaper, the *Honduras Gazette and Commercial Advertiser,* on 1 July 1826. The first thirty-eight issues were edited by the magistrates; for the next eight months, the printer edited the paper until "intemperance" (in his outspokenness) forced him to turn it over to a Legislative Assembly committee (Cave 1974–1975, 3).

Cave (1974–1975, 8–11) listed eighteen other newspapers published during the nineteenth century in British Honduras, including the *Colonist,* published in 1864 by the Colonist Office; the *Central American Telegraph* and the *Times of Central America,* both intended for regional audiences and both short-lived; and the *Clarion,* started in 1879 as a weekly and converted in 1935 to a daily, which it remained until its demise in 1961. Most newspapers lasted only a year or two, mainly because of the smallness of Belize City, whose population hovered between four thousand and nine thousand throughout the century (see Leslie 1978). The newspapers contained mainly advertisements and descriptions of social events among the colonialists, but the *Colonial Guardian,* published from 1882 to 1913 by Frederick Gahné, had definite political views in its weekly editorials (Dobson 1973, 326).

In more recent times, a significant newspaper was the *Belize Billboard,* started in 1946 and used as an important organ of the labor movement and the oppositionist National Independence party. Labor Minister Philip Goldson, who was *Billboard* managing editor in its early days, described how he ran into difficulties with the colonial government in 1951 when he wrote a story suggesting that there were two ways to self-government—evolution or revolution. The British government, assuming he favored the latter, jailed him and news editor Leigh Richardson for eight months on sedition charges. Goldson said that the dice were loaded against them by a jury handpicked by the government. While in jail, Richardson wrote articles on toilet paper, which Goldson smuggled out to his brother, who was editing the paper during his absence (*Belize Today* 1987a).

With the intensification of the drive toward independence, other outspoken newspapers incurred the wrath of the authorities or mobs. For example, the *Sentinel* in 1978 unleashed what one source called a "vicious and vulgar attack" upon various public and private figures. The governor was called the "asshole [later modified to "ass"] of the month," after which he ordered the arrest of the editors. The rumor reported in the *Belizean Review* was that the *Sentinel* attack was done with the backing of the Belizean government, which was upset with Britain's handling of the colony. At the time of independence, the *Belize Times* plant was destroyed by fire, and a contemporary editor suspected it had been started by parties opposed to independence (Interview, Mai 1987).

Belizean newspapers, for the most part, still serve political purposes. The *Belize Times,* started in 1959, is the organ of the People's United party (PUP), and *Beacon, Amandala,* and the *Reporter,* to varying degrees, support the ruling United Democratic party. The leanings of the *Voice,* owned by two previous ministers in the PUP government, are not quite clear.

All except the *Voice* are weeklies that claim circulations of thirty-five hundred to five thousand and are distributed nationally. As in the case in other small territories of the Caribbean, they suffer problems of lack of staff, adequate equipment and supplies, and advertising revenue. The *Times* editor voiced an objection heard from oppositionist newspapers elsewhere, that supplies, advertising, news and information — all tied to government — are denied (Interview, Mai 1987).

Radio broadcasting started in 1937 with a 200-watt telecommunications transmitter modified for part-time broadcasting use. One source said that ZIK2 (the station's call signal) was not "even a station, just transmitting around Belize City" (Interview, York 1987). A British grant almost fifteen years after this inauspicious beginning provided equipment and seconded personnel from the BBC, enabling the development of British Honduras Broadcasting.

A number of things happened in the early 1960s to change the status of broadcasting. In 1961, after Hurricane Hattie had destroyed much of the facility, new equipment was obtained, and by the following year local staff had replaced most foreigners. In 1963, the station was removed from the Information Services and given autonomous status with its own chief broadcasting officer. The following year, Radio Belize, as it was then known, became semicommercial. In 1965, schools broadcasting began at the initiative of William Faux.

Describing radio in the mid-1970s, Faux said it was an AM-only service, broadcasting a large amount of imported programming from 6 A.M. to 11 P.M. daily. He added that it was regulated by an advisory council under the Ministry of Broadcasting, Information, and Health, with no specific broadcasting laws. The council, made up of nonbroadcasting professionals, had been created in 1971 to advise on programs. The most popular programming in 1976, according to Faux, was Western pop music, with some reggae and calypso. Because of the affordability of radio receivers and the availability of a number of signals—BBC, VOA, and stations from Mexico, Guatemala, and Honduras—nearly everyone listened to the medium. Faux said the problems at that time related to the need for an emergency energy supply and staff training and expansion. Radio Belize had a huge personnel turnover because of the limited budget of about U.S. $100,000, which was allocated by the government (Interview, Faux 1976).

At the time of independence in 1981, more expansion occurred with the introduction of FM and, in some areas, stereo. The FM service was funded by the European Development Fund and the British Development Aid Programme. Of the U.S. $1 million cost of FM, the Belizean government put up U.S. $150,000; UNESCO and Cable and Wireless also helped. Simultaneously, the service was made into a national system with two new 10kw transmitters.

Today known as Radio One, the station and its sister, Friends FM, are the only radio service in the country, except for an internal station of British Forces Radio, which has some spillover in Belize City. Radio One and Friends FM follow the "guidelines of the law of the country concerning broadcasting," that is, the "General Orders for the Public Service, Belize 1982."

Program organizer Ed York said the strengths of government ownership are that the station has more access to officials, especially since the 1984 change of government, and does not have to depend on commercial revenue alone for its survival. However, he thought the weaknesses were more prominent, among which were lack of latitude in working conditions and dependence upon government-issued funds. As York said, "We can't make final decisions on our own for the public good. We have to get permission and this hurts us internally in hiring employees. It affects the speed in which to pass information because of the bureaucracy involved. Having to depend on government-issued funds, we are not able to execute to the maximum our projects. Total funding is by government. All our advertising money goes to the government treasury, which redistributes to us" (Interview, York 1987).

Because of competition from television and videocassette recorders, Radio One has changed its policy to reflect local culture. Of all its shows, 75 percent are local. Of the music, which makes up 30 percent of all programming, at least 60 percent must be Central American and Caribbean. Other local shows are specially prepared by cultural associations representing the Maya, Ketchie, or Garifuna and are presented in those languages. Thirty percent of all radio programs in Belize are in Spanish, while most of the rest are in English. An in-house drama club produces radio plays.

There are three major newscasts of one hour total duration, and two of them are bilingual. Four news summaries of five minutes each are also provided. Other shows are of social interest, featuring various youth- or government-oriented agencies; two one-hour phone-in programs are aired — one an open microphone format, the other an "ask-your-doctor" format.

Radio's main problems did not change much between 1967 and 1987. York claimed the biggest difficulty is lack of resources, such as enough modern equipment and properly trained personnel (Interview, York 1987).

TELEVISION

History

Obviously, radio and newspaper development was not very advanced in the mid-1970s when Belizeans living near the borders erected large antennas to pick up Mexican or Guatemalan television. At the time, Belize itself was considered too small to justify investment in a television service by an entrepreneur or by the colonial government. However, with the worldwide popularization of videocassette recorders and satellite television, the circumstances changed for Belize. The first move toward television came after an American, Robert Landis, introduced commercial video to the country in 1978. He sold VCRs to ten Belizeans and supplied them with tapes by mail from Miami. Within a few months, Giovanni Smith, a Belizean flight engineer based in Miami, provided improved VCRs and a local system of tape rentals. By Christmas 1979, VCRs had become a popular gift among the wealthy. The video business had become lucrative enough that Smith returned to Belize to operate his Nibble and Co. Efrain Aguilar became a competitor in the rental business, and the rental price of cassettes was lowered by nearly one-half (Krohn 1981, 16). However, Nibble and Aguilar depended upon contacts in the United States to tape and air freight cassettes to them, which was a slow and costly venture.

On 23 December 1980, television entered its second phase when local entrepreneurs Emory King and Nestor Vásquez introduced the first commercial earth station to Belize. Calling their company Tropical Vision, King and Vásquez taped television shows transmitted via satellite from the United States and made copies for rental to VCR owners. Describing his experience, King said, "Vásquez and I decided that with an earth station, we could have television twenty-four hours a day and we could make money. We researched companies and bought a Harris earth station. In October 1980, I went to Texas, bought the station, and we set it up. The business went very, very well. We rented tapes for U.S. $2 a night, and in ten months, were making U.S. $5,000 gross income per month. There were enough VCRs to support all three companies very well" (Interview, King 1987).

Neither King nor his partner has admitted that what they were doing was piracy. King said he was "completely innocent" and believed satellite-fed television was a "good service of the United States to provide American views to the region." He added

> In 1980, I wrote a letter to every channel that was on the satellite we were using, such as WTBS, HBO, WGN, ESPN, Cinemax, Showtime, etc. I said, "Look, we bought this earth station, and we are renting tapes to the public that we do of your shows. And we want to know what your royalty is." I received two responses only, both saying they could not charge anything because of an international

6.1   Emory King, developer of video, satellite, and television in Belize. (*Photo by John A. Lent*)

treaty, which the US is a signatory to, that allows each government
to put up a satellite for its own domestic service, but which it cannot
sell beyond its national borders (Interview, King 1987).

Vásquez likened satellite reception to receiving a "foreign station on
radio, getting it from our backyard" (Interview, Vásquez 1987).

The third stage in television development involved over-the-air
broadcasting of television signals. From the time it established an earth
station, Tropical Vision applied for a license to telecast but was repeatedly turned down; so was Nibble and Co. Yet, in mid-1981 another
Belizean, Arthur Hoare, was allowed to erect a second earth station, to
establish his Coordinated Electronics Ltd., and to rebroadcast satellite
programs live to twenty-four individuals who paid him U.S. $2,000 each
for a special decoding antenna to receive the signal. Coordinated Electronics operated without the license required by the Belize Telecommunication Authority (BTA) Ordinance of 1972. A number of explanations
have been postulated about the exception made for Hoare. First, he had
government friends who allowed the illegal activity; moreover, his wife
was a top official in a PUP division (Interview, Vásquez 1987). Other
reasons were attributed to bureaucratic inefficiency, especially at that
hectic period of Belizean independence; uncertainty of officials as to
whether satellite transmission fell within Belizean broadcast law; and
government apathy about a situation that initially involved only a small
number of rich Belizeans (Krohn 1981, 19).

But the limited audience changed when a local technician found a
way to tune into Hoare's signals free of charge, and this complicated
matters for the government. Vásquez commented about the government's reaction to the large audience for over-the-air, illegal television.

> Not wanting a head-on confrontation with the public that quickly
> grew used to the television Hoare started, the government closed its
> eyes to the illegal activity, which killed our cassette rentals. At the
> time, I said to King that we would broadcast too without a license.
> King refused, saying he was a friend of government, and sold his
> Tropical Vision shares to me. I knew the government could not close
> Tropical Vision because it would have to close Hoare as well. He
> was progovernment (Interview, Vásquez 1987).

Vásquez brought in transmitters and converted his operation into
Channel 7, and he was followed by others. King said that broadcasting
stations "sprung up like mushrooms once they knew Hoare got away
with it" (Interview, King 1987). Despite the establishment of the Belize
Broadcasting Authority (BBA) and a broadcasting act in 1983, on-the-

air television and cable stations appeared without seeking government permission. Not until late 1986 did the BBA license nine television stations (two each in Belize City and Orange Walk and one each in Corozal, Punta Gorda, Belmopan, St. Ignacio, and Stann Creek) (Interview, Ewing 1987).

The proliferation of television definitely placed Prime Minister George Price and his government in a delicate situation. Price was notable for keeping out Western paraphernalia of modernity and was sensitive to the dependency relationships that inevitably result from technology. He feared that U.S. television, with its portrayal of first-class lifestyles, posed a threat to his party's thirty-year domination in Belize. His government also was concerned about Belizeans' monitoring television from Guatemala, which was considered an enemy that would telecast propaganda to Belize. Thus, he favored one national television system, organized along public lines. Such a system, he believed, would not sap many national resources in the trouble-laden, agriculture-based economy, nor would it bring in the large number of foreign programs that numerous stations would be capable of broadcasting. He was hamstrung, however, because the first illegal on-air television was owned by Hoare, whose wife was a leading politician in his party, and because television had become so popular that to rein it in was tantamount to political suicide (Lapper 1984, 16).

The opposition, United Democratic Front, which supported the United States and big business interests, exploited the situation, identifying with television entrepreneurs who favored multiple stations. In November 1982, a government bill to legalize a sole station was soundly defeated in Parliament when seven of twelve deputies defected to the opposition UDF for the vote (Barry 1984, 18).

Within two years, the situation in Belize changed considerably. The national election of 1984 was won by Manuel Esquivel, marking the first change of government in three decades. As a result, the "small-is-beautiful" thinking of Price was abandoned in favor of a free-market philosophy with the aim of attracting outside investment. Esquivel's right-of-center government is pro-Western politically and very friendly with the United States.

Although legislation was enacted in 1983 to bring some order to cable and television, more than three years elapsed before action was taken. King believed the government inaction from 1980 onwards resulted because no one had ever defied the authorities as blatantly as Hoare and others had. As a result, he said the government "dithered, wrung its hands and made admonitory statements, saying the public be advised that it is illegal to broadcast television shows like this. When the law was established in 1982–1983, it was too late to do anything about the chaotic situation" (Interview, King 1987).

By 1987, the number of earth stations pirating U.S. television had reached at least twelve. In a country of 166,000 people, with a per capita income of U.S. $977 and only one city with a population of more than 10,000, at least nine licensed television stations and probably nine cable companies function. Belize City, the largest town with 40,000 people, has two television and four cable services; other towns with television— some with populations as low as 1,500, and none exceeding 7,000—are Belmopan (the capital), St. Ignacio, Orange Walk, San Pedro, Corozal, Dangriga, and Punta Gorda. Placentia and Caye Caulker expected to receive service by 1988. As King said, "we'll have more television here than in the whole of Britain" (Interview, King 1987).

A recent estimate claimed that there are 14,000 to 15,000 television receivers and 2,500 VCRs in Belize. In the Western Hemisphere, only the United States, Canada, Panama, and Venezuela have more widespread use of VCRs than does Belize, where there is one machine for every 14.8 people. Fifty percent of all households and 80 percent of all household electricity consumers have television sets. One television exists for every 10.8 Belizeans (Petch 1987, 12–13).

Television and cable companies survive in this cutthroat arena because they have no production costs and very little overhead. As Vásquez said of his Channel 7, "I take from the satellite. I don't pay as they don't charge and don't scramble. If I had to, I'd pay on the rate of a small, poor country. There is not much complaint from the United States on copyright infringement. It doesn't mean much to them—a drop in the bucket. I use network shows because the networks don't scramble and they have the best shows" (Interview, Vásquez 1987).

Cable companies charge customers an installation fee of about U.S. $75 to U.S. $125 and a monthly service rate of U.S. $10 to U.S. $15. Broadcasters sell advertising in addition to their other means of gaining revenue. Channel 7 charges U.S. $6 for a thirty-second spot, which Vásquez said was such a low rate that to be financially successful he would have to get all Belizeans "drunk and fat from drinking Beliken [a local beer that is one of his accounts]" (Interview, Vásquez 1987). Thus, hundreds of spots, some merely card announcements, are used daily. During one twenty-five-minute, prime-time period in May 1987, at least sixteen commercials interrupted Channel 7 programming, seemingly without any interval schedule.

Also, broadcasters canvas door to door for donations, while others sell their television program schedules for U.S. $2.50. One enterprising Corozal broadcaster numbers the guides and has a monthly lottery, offering a television set or case of liquor to the holder of the guide with the winning number (Interview, King 1987).

Governance

After much opposition and many amendments, the Broadcasting and Television Act was passed in July 1983. It included stipulations dealing with station licensing and operation. Stations seek licenses by applying to the BBA, which in turn submits applications to the minister of communications. The minister has the final authority on the issuance of a license and its duration. In consultation with the BBA, the minister may regulate advertising, program content, and standards and may proportion time for advertising, for matters of religious, political, or industrial controversy, and for "ensuring of the preservation of due impartiality in programmes relating to such matters," and for educational, cultural, sporting, or scientific matters. Licensees must certify yearly that they are complying with the regulations. Violators of licensing requirements can be fined U.S. $2,500 or imprisoned for twelve months, or both (Broadcasting and Television Act 1983).

When the broadcast authority finally licensed stations in 1986, it issued a mimeographed sheet titled "Conditions of Licence" that gave more specific guidelines. Television stations are required to log all commercials, to not use more than one-fourth of their time for advertising, and to notify the BBA three days in advance ("or as soon as possible") when program changes are anticipated. Additionally, each station must present local news in conjunction with that of international origin, must provide at least three educational programs weekly, and must allocate 1 percent of all time for local shows other than news and commercials. R-rated shows can be shown after midnight and X-rated are prohibited on the air. Cable operators are required to seek all permission from the competent authorities to use their facilities. A second mimeographed sheet, almost as an afterthought, specified that programs should be of high quality and not in violation of Belizean law on defamation, obscenity, privacy, respect for the rule of law, or due process of law. Nothing can be telecast that is detrimental to national defense, security, public safety, public order, public morality, or public health or that is discriminatory on the grounds of sex, race, place of origin, political opinion, color, or creed.

The 1983 act created the Belize Broadcasting Authority to advise the minister on licensing matters, to maintain radio-TV services, to supervise proper maintenance of equipment, and to monitor stations concerning license requirements. The BBA can determine the hours of broadcast, conditions for the use of advertising, and types of programs. Agnes Ewing, BBA secretary, said that the BBA has been effective, especially in collecting the license fees of U.S. $2,000 for Belize City stations and U.S. $1,000 for other districts. She said that board members planned to make stricter laws, including the licensing of cable operators (Interview, Ewing 1987). The seven-member board is appointed for renewable one-year terms by the minister of communications. One member is the permanent secretary to the minister responsible for broadcasting, while two represent the television industry.

Vásquez, one of the industry representatives, who also chairs the Belize Telecommunication Authority (BTA), said that the BBA's job is to manage all national and international broadcasting services in Belize. The minister of communications, on the other hand, since March 1987 has been in charge of administering frequency allocations, including broadcasting. The BTA handles all domestic and international telephony (Interview, Vásquez 1987).

As of January 1988, the BTA ceased to exist and was replaced by Belize Telecommunications Ltd. (BTL), a private company whose shares initially are being held by the government. The BTL manager-designate for international services, Ernesto Torres, gave the thinking behind the changeover, saying, "BTA now is a statutory board and as such, it cannot be run as efficiently as BTL will be. As a statutory board, BTA was not free to act as a private group. The new company will work on a commercial basis in the hope its efficiency and revenue-drawing capacity will be enhanced" (Interview, Torres 1987).

BTL will be heavily committed to the modernization of telecommunications services, including a U.S. $10 million program to establish digital exchanges throughout the country. Torres said digitalization should be advantageous both to the economy as a whole, since it is heavily dependent upon exports, and to individual businessmen (Interview, Torres 1987).

Programming

As already indicated, Belizean television stations use dishes to intercept satellite-relayed programs, mainly from the United States, and to retransmit them either over the air or via cable systems. As a result, local programming is nearly nonexistent.

The stations present a five-minute, local, "talking-head" news show daily supplied by the Curriculum Development Unit of the government. The unit was able to enter production after receiving a gift of U.S. $25,000 in equipment from the Japanese government (Interview, Krohn

1987). One Belize City channel claims to air agriculture shows, government press conferences, and national sporting events, but these are on very rare occasions.

The BBA requirement that 1 percent of programming be produced locally has not been enforced; in fact, the present government seems to be taking the same posture as the former government on illegal broadcasting — turning its head on the matter. In 1987, the deputy minister in charge of television actually said that the 1 percent figure was very high, "if one looks at the amount of hours we transmit during a twenty-four hour period. Unfortunately at the moment we have no production unit in the country which could produce particularly news items or programmes that could be aired countrywide" (*Belize Today* 1987b, 13). He added that the government planned to create a miniature television unit to produce national programs, but until then one could not expect local shows.

Conveniently, he ignored the existence of Belizean production units with supplies of shows. One such unit, Great Belize Productions, started in 1982 by Emory King, when he sold his Tropical Vision shares, and by Stewart Krohn, has produced mainly promotional documentaries for tourist agencies and business investors. Education films and commercials have been produced, but for a large amount of its revenue, the company relies on feature film management carried out for foreign producers shooting on location in Belize. Krohn said that the "very strange system" of free television via satellite was "very stacked against local television production," adding, "When broadcasters get all their programming free from satellite, there is absolutely no incentive to do local programs. The situation will not change. We thought it would with the BBA 1 percent ruling, but the government has gone on record that it will not enforce the rule" (Interview, Krohn 1987).

Krohn said that in August 1986, immediately after the rule was created, he wrote to all broadcasters to inform them that from the existing stock of Great Belize there were enough programs to meet the 1 percent ruling for three months. "If all eleven or twelve broadcasters paid the U.S. $475 for the package of nineteen shows available (ranging from twenty minutes to one hour), we'd be in business," he said. But that did not happen, and only one broadcaster responded "nonnegatively." In a May 1987 letter to the minister of home affairs, Krohn reacted to the above-cited deputy minister's remarks, calling them "both false and detrimental to the development of a viable system of local programming" and claiming broadcasters had become accustomed to borrowing, as they know the ministry will not enforce the law (Krohn letter to Curt Thompson, 28 May 1987).

Great Belize Productions continues to make programs with the hope that local broadcasters will eventually buy them. A magazine show, designed along the lines of "60 Minutes," was produced in 1987. Called "Belize All Over," the show's thirteen segments were each divided into culture, profiles, and socioeconomic issues; a new show was scheduled for every two weeks. Expecting the show to be a "money loser," Krohn said it was produced to "fight the stupidity of the ministry." Great Belize also makes four commercials monthly for television (Interview, Krohn 1987).

Radio One, already involved in television production, plans to increase its output. According to Ed York, the government's broadcasting department has purchased television equipment and with permission of the BBA will produce shows. Plans have also proceeded for a separate government television station (Interview, York 1987).

The major difficulty of television production in Belize, according to Krohn, is purchasing and maintaining equipment. Recently the company had to sell shares to the public because of a U.S. $150,000 equipment investment. Often equipment must be sent to Miami for repairs, the process taking as long as a month. The duty of 57 percent on television equipment and insufficient advertising revenue have been debilitating to producers. In fact, Krohn has stated that the demographics of Belize do not allow for local programming and that the solution rests with regional efforts (Interview, Krohn 1987). On the other hand, regional programming is difficult to mount because it requires outside funding, either from the United States, which under Reagan was more inclined to binational rather than to regional agreements, or from supranational agencies.

Impact of U.S. Television

A number of consequences have been suggested regarding the effects of U.S. television in Belize. Most are based on anecdotal or impressionistic evidence, but, unlike in most countries, some are backed by scientific research.

Early on, warnings about television were sounded. For example, in a 1979 article in *Brukdown,* a local magazine, Krohn predicted that the programs would be U.S. reruns and that some necessities of life would be given lower priorities as limited financial resources went into television receivers. Krohn thought that the prime beneficiaries would be those with the motivation and resources to purchase time and produce their own shows, "those same wonderful folks who presently bring us 'Back to the Bible,' 'Hour of Decision,' and 'Showers of Blessing'" (Krohn 1979, 11).

Lamenting the "far more important social costs," he foresaw what

Belizeans now experience, virtually empty streets at night and a diminishment of social chatter. He wrote that Belize was "a place where strangers greeted each other on the street; where children grew up spinning tops, flying kites and shooting marbles, not heroin, and that their parents could walk anywhere at any time without fear. . . . [in Belize, these qualities] survive despite the rapid-fire onslaught of Bruce Lee, Donna Summer, Night Train Express and disco dancing contests. Television, however, might just be the straw that broke Belize's back" (Krohn 1979, 13).

That the debate still flourishes is evidenced by a commencement address by the Belizean Roman Catholic bishop who, in the 14 June 1987 *Belize Times,* accused the "lifeless one-eyed monster situated in our living rooms" of "incredible manipulation" of minds. He hit upon an impact other Belizeans are concerned about, namely that in Belize, "we are quickly losing our identity, self-respect and our capacity for self-determination. We are brainwashed to such an extent that we are beginning to think, speak, and act as though everything Belizean is no good."

No doubt Belizeans have absorbed parts of the U.S. way of life. American products, sports, fashions, and slang have become popular. Football and baseball compete strongly with sports such as soccer or cricket that the British left behind. For example, Belize has a mania for the Chicago Cubs, whose baseball games are telecast by Channel 7. Bumper stickers with "WGN – Cubs" adorn automobiles; fans display "Belizeans Love Cubs" at games; and Cubs players and coaches have gone to Belize to donate baseball equipment, to operate clinics, and to start Little League. Hoare's Channel 9 carries New York Yankees baseball.

Some Belizeans, Vásquez and King prominent among them, see the absorption of U.S. lifestyles via television as beneficial propaganda. Vásquez said that showing the U.S. way of life fights communism (Interview, Vásquez 1987), while King thought Americans would be "crazy to enforce antipiracy law." He added that "the U.S. is getting its point of view across to the Third World with Reagan and John Wayne on the television sets. In fact, Latin Americans are upset as hell about this, saying TV is creating desires for things we can't afford and selling us U.S. foreign policy. The U.S. Congress would be wise to provide taxpayer money to film companies as royalty to keep pushing this type of TV fare out to the world" (Interview, King 1987).

Specifically, U.S. television viewing has been associated with changes in Belizean politics and elections. Claiming Belizean politicians are adopting U.S. views on foreign policy, King quoted a "leftist" as saying that the medium not only brainwashes the public, but also officials, who see "Reagan doing things on TV and they want to do them also" (Interview, King 1987). Vásquez went so far as to postulate that the 1984 election went against the incumbent government because of television. According to him,

> Television broadcasting helped Belize tremendously. For years, the PUP government had a complete monopoly of the airwaves with Radio Belize dishing out government propaganda. Then people saw television and saw that it was okay to criticize the government. In the world news we gave them daily, they saw democratic systems working in other places. Then in 1984, both parties used television for campaigning. Hoare and I did what we could for the parties we supported. Television drew the people away from Radio Belize; as more preferred TV, no one was listening to radio. A different mentality was at work and we changed the government for the first time in thirty years, peaceably, without one drop of blood shed. That is a big accomplishment (Interview, Vásquez 1987).

Contrary views have been expressed on the impact of television viewing upon consumer habits. In the only scientific study on the subject, Oliveira (1986b) compared viewing and purchasing habits of Belizeans living in the Corozal district, who have available daily eighteen hours of Mexican and nineteen hours of U.S. television. In his conclusions, Oliveira said that exposure to U.S. television was positively associated with U.S. product preference and Mexican viewing with Central American product preference. He concluded that his findings "provide grounds for the view that U.S. programming encourages consumption of U.S. products, and at the same time discourages the use of Third World–made items" (Oliveira 1986b, 142). In reporting his results elsewhere, he also linked traditionalism with Mexican, but not U.S., television viewing (Oliveria [*sic*] 1986a, 46–47).

King said Belizean dress codes have changed because of television; for example, young people prefer jeans, and at high school graduations, tuxedos and corsages, seen on U.S. television shows, are in vogue for the first time. King explained, "We have always been pro-American, but, for many years, American television has certainly reenforced this. Thousands upon thousands of Belizeans live in the U.S. and send back TVs, shoes, VCRs, etc. Eventually, local stores start importing them as the demand increases" (Interview, King 1987).

Agnes Ewing of the BBA agreed that Belizeans have changed their buying patterns because of television. She said that Belizeans "see something on television today, and within weeks it is in the local stores and people buy it at four or five times its original price. TV is making people buy things they cannot afford. Belize has fresh fruits and other local products but our markets are importing stuff we don't need and should not import" (Interview, Ewing 1987).

Vásquez did not agree that television was the main impetus for changes in cultural and consumer values. He contended that it was inevitable that seeing U.S. products would whet the public's appetite for them, but that it would have happened without television because merchants work at promoting these goods. He said those who claim U.S. television has that impact are "anti-American" (Interview, Vásquez 1987).

Roser, Snyder, and Chaffee (1986, 23), attempting to correlate U.S. television viewing with emigration patterns, concluded that of the 54 percent of those willing to emigrate, 86 percent chose the United States as a new location. They said that U.S. entertainment programs did not seem to act as a pull for emigration, but that "while news media are not as strongly related to desire to emigrate as is interpersonal communication, those who watch U.S. news broadcasts are more likely to want to emigrate."[1]

Other changes in Belizean lifestyles are said to have occurred since television, such as lower achievements of school children, different eating and sleeping habits, and more relaxed moral standards. A teacher member of the BBA related that students' grades have dropped in the past few years, and Ewing said, "Definitely there are fewer people on the streets at night. People used to go to the movies or out to chat, but when TV came in, they stayed home rather than risk being robbed on the street" (Interview, Ewing 1987).

A direct impact of television upon eating habits was related by King. Apparently when "Santa Barbara" was being shown at noon by Channel 7, irate husbands complained to the station that they could not get their lunches as their wives were immersed in the soap opera. As a result, Channel 7 taped the show and aired it at 1:30 P.M. (Interview, King 1987).

Shows featuring nudity and obscenity that appear on cable at all hours, and on broadcast stations later at night, have been criticized as having unhealthy effects upon the audience. However, the BBA has not yet taken a firm stand on the issue.

The audience pull of television has seriously hurt other media, such as radio and movie theaters. York stated that Radio One drastically altered its format and style because of VCR and television viewing. He added

VCRs had a lot of impact on radio listening, causing us to change our programming somewhat. We did it not just to compete with TV but also to go on our own and get as much local input in programming as possible. When TV was a novelty, that is, when VCRs brought in TV, our listening plummeted. It is surging upward now because of the 60 percent Caribbean music and local program emphasis. Instead of ranting and raving about VCRs and television, we in radio changed our programming, realizing that TV was here to stay (Interview, York 1987).

The few movie theaters in Belize have felt television's effects. Of four Belize City theaters, two have closed and one has been converted into a video palace with a twenty-foot screen, on which satellite-gathered movies, sports, and other fare are shown. Theaters have also folded in St. Ignacio and Dangriga, and the Corozal cinema opens only on weekends.

Apparently, local newspaper sales have not changed. *Times* Editor Amalia Mai attributed this to the near nonexistence of local fare on television. She added that "TV only has five minutes of government-represented news. So it does not affect readers who just see U.S. television. Belizeans will always want to read about Belize, so they turn to newspapers. Radio is government propaganda repeated over and over every twenty-four hours" (Interview, Mai 1987).

CONCLUSION

Belize represents to a heightened degree a new nation that adopted television without first establishing a national policy concerning the medium. Actually, not even basic guidelines were set. The result has been that television has sprouted everywhere in Belize, yet nowhere is there a service that can be called Belizean. Virtually all programming is imported — perhaps more appropriately, stolen via satellite — with possible consequences to politics, elections, lifestyles, leisure time, and consumerism.

What started out as simply renting cassettes to a few wealthy Belizeans has been magnified to a complex, problem-riddled situation that befuddles the government and others involved with television. With viewers devoted to U.S. shows and broadcasters and cable operators accustomed to free programming, efforts to present local fare meet with lackadaisical attitudes. Governmental reforms are not expected to be very remedial. The momentum of television development may be such that it is no longer possible to return to a stage where national betterment changes can be made.

7

Freedom of Expression: An Overview

The former British colonies in the Caribbean have been among the territories of the world in the process of redefining the concepts of press freedom inherited from their mother countries. Because of the transitional nature of these societies, government leaders rationalize such modifications of traditional press concepts and maintain that they are in order. They claim that in emerging nations, unusual powers are sometimes necessary to force decisions that will benefit the people. Acting as benevolent dictators, they ask the mass media to show restraint in criticizing government and at the same time to promote national goals and identities. The leaders emphasize concepts such as government-media dialogue, as if the two institutions were not on speaking terms under libertarian systems.

Leaders of such new governments tend to have authoritarian personalities, even though they are often the same individuals who rebelled against colonial oppression. In the Commonwealth Caribbean, although the two-party system of government predominates, many islands are controlled by strong, charismatic executives, some of whom have been in office over a decade. Over the past two decades, one-man rule has been particularly evident in Belize, Guyana, Grenada, St. Kitts–Nevis, Antigua, St. Lucia, and Trinidad and Tobago. Opposition parties have existed, but because of pressures from the ruling parties the opposition always finds it extremely difficult to make itself heard.

The opposition press in the Commonwealth Caribbean is equally maligned so that at varying times dissenting media in the region have been hindered by the tightening of licensing regulations, the misuse of libel and sedition acts, economic restrictions, government monitoring of radio and television and clipping of newspapers, denial of air time on government-owned broadcasting outlets, or the drying up of traditional news sources.

The governments of the region say that they have reason to be sensitive to oppositionist press outpourings. First of all, they feel that some of the newspapers are too destructive in their criticism. Second, the governments say that because of the small size of the political units in the Commonwealth Caribbean, internal problems tend to be magnified; even a whispering campaign does not go unnoticed.

Possibly for these reasons, governments in the area have made concerted efforts to own and control as many media as possible or to make them become part of big business concerns tied to, or dependent upon, government.

LEEWARDS AND WINDWARDS

Newspapers in these island-states have been extremely political; they are owned by the parties to serve their purposes, much in the tradition of the late eighteenth century partisan press of the United States. A difference is that there were scores — and later hundreds — from which to choose in the latter, while each Leeward and Windward island has only a couple of weeklies.

The two regularly published newspapers in St. Kitts are the nearly forty-year-old *Democrat,* a Saturday tabloid of the People's Action Movement, and the twenty-eight-year-old *Labour Spokesman,* a tabloid published on Wednesday and Saturday by the St. Kitts Labour party. A third, the *Opron Star,* is a mimeographed bimonthly published by the Organization of Progressive Nationals. The *Star,* classifying itself as a political sheet for intellectuals, was started in 1981 (Interview, Browne 1984).

Antigua has three tabloids, with other newspapers appearing from time to time, usually around elections. The *Workers Voice* of the Antigua Labour party (ALP) is the oldest, dating to 1943; also supportive of the ALP is the *Nation's Voice,* edited by an official of the Government Public Information Department. The oppositionist voice is the *Outlet,* published in one form or another by the Afro-Caribbean Liberation Movement (ACLM) since 1968. Started in time for the 1984 elections was the *Standard,* an organ of the Progressive Labour Movement. Since 1981, Montserrat has had a weekly tabloid, the *Montserrat Times,* and more recently, the *Montserrat Reporter* and the *Montserrat Mirror.*

7.1   Politically owned and motivated weeklies of the Leewards—the *Labour Spokesman* of St. Kitts–Nevis, the *Workers Voice* of Antigua, and the *Montserrat Times.*

In the Windwards, Dominica has the *New Chronicle,* a privately owned weekly whose majority shares are held by the Roman Catholic Church. St. Vincent continues to support the *Vincentian,* a weekly owned by the Metrocint General Insurance Company, while political papers flourish. Among these weeklies are the *Newtimes,* New Democratic party; the *Justice,* United Peoples Movement; the *Star,* St. Vincent Labour party; and the *Unity,* Movement for National Unity. The St. Lucian and Grenadian presses also have been very political party–oriented (see chapter 9 for analysis of the Grenadian press).

In the Leewards and Windwards, it is difficult to take opposition editors seriously when they complain about press freedom restrictions. Regularly, but especially during elections, their newspapers carry vituperative and scurrilous material, defamatory enough, if published elsewhere, to keep a team of lawyers scurrying to and from court. Yet, there are instances—through ownership and party affiliation, legislation, arrests and harassments, and denial of space and time to opposing views—where freedom of expression is constrained.

Because politics plays such an important role in the culture of the region, much of the rumor-mongering, gossip and innuendos, double meanings, and libelous name-calling seems to be natural to the newspaper pages. It would appear that many of the stories are read for their fun-evoking characteristics rather than for their credulity. For example, columns in St. Kitts papers ("Is It True?" in the *Democrat* and "Dem Say Dat" in the *Labour Spokesman*) ask questions and share gossip in potentially libelous language that seems to come from fertile but mischievous minds rather from reality. The *Democrat* column discusses the opposition as "Misleaders of the defeated Labour Party," "De Pig," "sadistic woman-beater," "The Mace Tief," or "Chinee" and refers to the opposition newspaper as "The Labour Latrine." A statement in the *Labour Spokesman* column will read like this one in a May 1984 edition: "He know who tief gold chain—he know everything—he even does know who kill dis and who kill dat but now de finger pointing on he, dey quick to say no foul play in that."

The charges and exchanges between parties can become extremely vitriolic and sensationally readable. For example, in 1982 the *Democrat* showed a picture of the former premier and leader of the opposition, Lee Moore, sprawled on the floor, with the caption that he was "knocked out with the liquor that he vomited like a whale, urinated like a dog, exposed himself like a jackass and wallowed in his muck like a pig." The response from Moore, also published in the *Democrat* (29 May 1982, 12), must have been just as delightful to readers.

> Let us start from the assumption that I was drunk—so if I was drunk who it is drunk? Is me drunk—me drunk ain't trouble you. Who money I drunk wid? Is my money. So why I have to explain to anybody if I drunk. Now if I drunk in the street and you see me behaving in a disorderly manner you might have a problem—but you hear them talk about dat? So comrades, if I drunk out of my money I don't have to explain to anybody. If you drunk off a you own money, you don't have to give me an explanation. If you drunk you drunk and if I drunk I drunk.

When Moore threatened a libel suit, the *Democrat* reprinted the offending photograph and carried letters written by attorneys for both sides. Vowing not to retract or apologize, the *Democrat* lawyer, in the 10 July issue, said his client's reaction to the demands was one of "amazement and disgust at the audacity of your outrageous request for a 'withdrawal and apology.'" The *Democrat,* of course, then said that the threatened lawsuit was an attempt at gagging. Editors do not allow readers to forget these incidences. In February 1984, more than eighteen months later, the *Democrat* had occasion to resurrect the Moore affair when commenting on another leader of the opposition: "When the man talks he ain't even got an excuse like Lee Moore. Because the man don't drink hard. The man don't be drunk; the man ain't suffering from delirium tremens." In another story, the editor, discussing Moore, said his "head comes and goes."

The St. Kitts *Labour Spokesman* also spouts much venom against politicians, often in anonymous letters to the editor. In the 2 June 1984 issue, when new elections were announced, a boxed item declared, "19 more Days of Corruption, Oppression, victimisation, mismanagement, the give-away of St. Kitts, increased electricity rates, increased house and land tax, taking advantage of sugar workers, Civil servants, young people, sick patients in the hospital." It is as if the newspapers in St. Kitts are expected to provide a constant sideshow using their political counterparts as the "freaks."

In Antigua, the same pattern exists, but the ruling party paper is more subdued than the St. Kitts *Democrat*. This is because the Antigua government, headed by the oldest elected leader in the Caribbean, Vere Bird, is very secure, having swept the 1984 elections, and enjoys the support of the U.S. government. The *Workers Voice* and the *Nation's Voice* of the ruling party take on opposition elements, especially Tim Hector, his socialist-oriented Afro-Caribbean Liberation Movement (ACLM), and its weekly, the *Outlet*. The *Worker's Voice* has carried statements such as, "Antiguans imagined tiny Tim being brutally murdered by lonely lovely," while the *Nation's Voice* has not been above running a picture of dead people with the caption that the ACLM supports Cuban-Russian killings in Nicaragua.

Both the *Outlet* and another opposition paper, the *Standard,* of the Progressive Labour party counter by emphasizing the absolute rule and "victimisation" of the Bird government, or "birdism," as the *Outlet* terms it. Hector's "Fan the Flame" column, which is rather intellectual as well as political, regularly criticizes the government, calling it "drunk with the heady wine of a one-party state." The column carries titles such as "The Ruin of Antigua's Economy by Bird," "The U.S., the Caribbean, the Cold War," or "The Rise and Fall of the PLM." Editorials in the *Outlet* point an accusatory finger at Bird's mispractices and question the government's credibility.

In the Windwards, politically oriented newspapers have been known to be less than responsible at the same time that they claimed they were victimized by government. Grenadian and Dominican papers, for example, have called national leaders "Hitlerites" or "Gestapo imitators." In 1976, a Dominican paper asked how the premier's wife can love the country when she cannot make love to any man (Interview, Scobie 1976).

All newspapers in the Leeward islands are either owned or strongly affiliated with the government or the opposition political party, while all broadcasting stations in the Leewards and Windwards, with a few rare exceptions, are government affiliated or owned. In the context of small islands such as these, where there is not a plethora of outlets for expression, this factor can be debilitating.

The island in which government ownership, control, and influence over media are most pronounced is Antigua. The ruling Bird family (Vere Bird is premier; his son, Vere, Jr., is a member of Parliament, deputy premier, and minister of communications) owns the only cable service (CTV) and Radio Station ZDK, which was founded by the family and is managed by Ivor Bird, another son of the premier. ABS, which includes the only television system and the island's other radio station, is owned by the Bird-controlled government. Two of the three regular newspapers, the *Workers Voice* and the *Nation's Voice,* are part of the ruling Antigua Labour party.

For decades, newspapers in St. Kitts have been owned or aligned with the trade unions and their political parties. The *Democrat* is owned by a group, PAM Pubco, which bought 51 percent of the shares in 1981. PAM Pubco is part of the People's Action Movement party. Editor Fitzroy Jones, a realtor who in 1984 was a candidate for Parliament, said that the paper was dying for lack of machinery and circulation when Pam rescued it. He said that the other shares are owned by four St. Kittitians whom he would not identify (Interview, Jones 1984). The broadcasting stations, ZIZ radio and television, are government owned; the sole cable system is 60 percent owned by a U.S. firm, Ridgewood, 20 percent by government, and 20 percent by the public.

On Montserrat, the tradition has been to have government or political-party ownership of or affiliation with newspapers. The *Mirror,* which folded in 1981, had government ministers as chief shareholders. Its replacement, the *Times,* is edited by Howell Bramble, son of one former chief minister and brother of another. Bramble maintains that his brother has kept the paper out of political ownership because he was "sickened by the political papers of St. Kitts and Antigua" (Interview, Bramble 1984).

Obviously, benefits accrue to the mass media owned by ruling political parties or governments. In some instances, economic amenities are given to these media and denied to those of the opposition. The *Outlet* on Antigua, for example, does not share lucrative government advertisements, nor, according to Hector, those of the big businesses, most of

Outlet ♥

The weekly voice of
LIBERATION

$1:00

ACLM Publication   Vol. 12   No 10   March 9,   1984

"OUTLET MUST BE CLOSED" – LESTER

Speaking at a poorly attended meeting in the Point on Tuesday February 6, Deputy Prime Minister Lester Bird said that he has spoken to P.M Bird about "bringing" more charges against Outlet, and continued the Deputy Prime Minister, "And if this won't work then something else must be done to the Outlet."

Lester Bird who huffed and puffed throughout his speech did not reveal what other sinister plans the administration had for Outlet which he confessed was the main thorn in the administration's side. Lester Bird said that P.M Bird's approach to Outlet was "too soft" an a stronger line would have to be taken against Outlet.

One observer pointed out that once Lester is not "recitin, a speech written by Ron Sanders he sounds scratchy and incoherent, even stupid."

A foreign correspondent who listened to Lester Bird said that he was

LESTER BIRD, misleader of the Young Turks.

"appalled by Lester's low level, his assault on Press Freedom and his mean anti-communist diatribe". Lester labelled former Premier George Walter as "a Communist" and thereby revealed that his party's only defence against charges of corruption, squandermania and incompetence, is to label every major opposition force, especially ACLM, as "Communist".

Lester Bird has been particularly angry about revelations in Outlet, which showed him to be opposed to keeping Antiguan troops in Grenada, and opposed to the U.S military training schemes still on-going in Antigua. The U.S. is upset about his charges against them for militarising the region, especially the revelation, that in these U.S. military exercises the U.S. acted without the prior consent of host governments in the region.

Meanwhile old charges against Outlet Editor Tim Hector arising out of

Continued on page 2

WHAT A MESS!

The 1983 Sugar Crop, and the Bird government's approach to the Sugar Industry was a complete disaster, characterised by wilful and woeful abuse of public funds.

This was revealed in the Report of the General Manager of the Antigua Sugar Industry Corporation, Herman G. Rohlehr, who resigned in disgust and recently returned to Guyana.

In his report on the sugar crop of 1983, General Manager Rohlehr, pointed out that the yield was not only poor, but disastrously low. It took 22.23 tons of cane to produce a single ton of sugar. So that from a harvest of 5029 tons of cane the Antigua Sugar factory got only 211 tons of sugar!

General Manager' Rohlehr replied that this woeful performance was

the result of the Bird administration insisting on a crop at any cost and at the wrong time of the year. Public funds were just poured down the drain. The General Manager's report showed that the poor yield of sugar from the canes was the result of "low sucrose content, which is characteristic of Antiguan canes at this time of the year."

The Bird government insisted on a crop last year, which lost money, and which commenced at the late date of 20th June 1983 when the sucrose content of the cane was known to be very low.

This pitifully small crop of 211 tons cost the huge sum of $568,239 to produce.

The loss in sugar was reflected in

$1.18 per pound when Antiguan wholesalers can supply sugar at 52 cents per pound. That is more than a 100% cheaper than Bird's expensively produced local sugar. The Bird government was been resisting wholesalers who want to provide sugar at a low price to the public.

Every aspect of the 1983 crop was poor. The frustrated General Manager before his resignation said in his report "cane supplies to the factory were disastrously inadequate and the over-all, average, daily delivery was 110 tons, compared to a minimum requirement of 320 tons a day". Continuing, Mr Rohlehr a highly trained and qualified chemical engineer, said "Such poor performance was reflected in a 46 per cent loss of net grinding time,

Continued on page 8

MASS ACLM PUBLIC MEETING
AT THWAITES CORNER
THURSDAY   MARCH 15, 1984

7.2   The oppositionist *Outlet* of Antigua lets readers
know the government attitude about the weekly.

which are foreign controlled and, out of fear or patronage, give their allegiance to the government (Interview, Hector 1984). A similar situation is said to exist in other islands in the Leewards and Windwards.

In most cases, the media not owned by or supportive of government have difficulty getting access to national officials. The director of Montserrat's Government Information Unit said officials do not often have press conferences; but he explained that in a small island such as Montserrat they are unnecessary, as the public has easy access to leaders (Interview, White 1984). The opposition editor in St. Kitts said that the government often declines to provide him with news, and so he "mentions things" (probably in the gossip column) that the authorities then deny. He added, "Then the story comes out when the government can't keep it covered any longer" (Interview, France 1984).

A persistent complaint of opposition parties generally in the Caribbean is that they are denied fair and equal time on the predominantly government-owned radio and television stations. On Montserrat, the opposition can have as much commercial time as it can afford, but it is denied participation in discussion, news, and other types of shows. Government projects and views are aired on at least the Government Information Unit programs for five minutes daily and for one-half hour weekly (Interview, White 1984).

On St. Kitts, ZIZ claims it does not give political time, including paid commercials, to either party. The general manager said that a politician will appear on broadcast media only in his role as a government minister or as a participant in Parliament proceedings, which are broadcast live (Interview, Caines 1984).

Legislative actions or considerations potentially punitive to the press include required annual licensing fees in Montserrat and Antigua; misuse of official secrets and libel laws in Antigua; and a revision of the penal code in Montserrat, which would have allowed the government more leeway in deciding seditious material. Actually, both Montserrat's licensing act and revision of the penal code were withdrawn. The licensing stipulated a prohibitively high E.C. $50,000 bond for publication; it failed to win the consent of the British Foreign Secretary.

In Antigua, there have been a number of legal and extralegal incidences aimed at the press, at the *Outlet* in particular. When Vere Bird resumed office in 1976, he honored an election pledge to repeal the Newspaper Surety Act that had been in force during the previous government of George Walter. The act required newspapers to deposit a E.C. $60,000 surety bond in case of libel and a E.C. $600 license fee. However, the Bird government has since amended the Public Order Act of 1968 with a sweeping statement that made virtually any criticism of government a criminal act:

> Any person who in any public place or at any public meeting makes any false statement concerning any public official which is calculated or is likely to bring any such person into ridicule, odium or contempt or undermine public confidence in the conduct of public affairs by such official shall be guilty of an offence. . . . any person — [who] (a) in any public place or at any public meeting makes any false statement; or (b) prints or distributes any false statement, which is likely to cause fear or alarm in or to the public or to disturb the public peace, or to undermine public confidence in the conduct of public affairs shall be guilty of an offence . . . (*Caribbean Contact* 1985).

The main victim of this law has been Tim Hector. An outspoken critic of the Antiguan government, which has termed him and his paper as communist, Hector sees himself and his ACLM as "socialist oriented" and involved in consciousness raising. He believes there is a need to modify the traditional party vanguard and to organize and link community-oriented groups to proceed with their activities to bring about social change. Hector said the group's policies include "discussing the paper, the *Outlet;* to state its disagreement; to raise issues in the community; and to have raised in the paper those issues related specifically to a locale" (Interview, Hector 1984).

By late 1985, Hector and his *Outlet* had been put on trial for the third time in two years for violations of the Public Order Act. *Outlet* stories that provoked these actions claimed that the Space Research Corporation was testing artillery in Antigua for the South African military, that a cabinet minister had been picked up in Miami by United States Intelligence with two million dollars in his possession, and that the Ministry of Economic Development was engaged in illegal activities.

Hector has faced an assortment of government-inspired harassments, including arrests and jailings, libel threats, seizure of copies of his paper, closure threats, and a raid of his office. In June 1978, the Antigua Printing and Publishing Company stopped printing the *Outlet,* using as an excuse that it was concerned that the paper might be sued for libel. Hector pointed out that his paper had never been sued for libel, while the government party's *Workers Voice* was defending three such suits at the time. In August 1982, the *Outlet* challenged in the Antigua High Court the government's denial of its "constitutional right" to publish. The case came about after the paper had charged government corruption and the Bird authorities had claimed that the *Outlet* lacked a surety bond and thus was not legally registered. After a new application for another bond of E.C. $960 was made, the *Outlet* office was raided and E.C. $8,000 in equipment was stolen. The police then seized copies of the 21 August issue. Troubles continued in September 1982 when an ACLM member was arrested (and later freed) for possessing and distributing an illegal document, the *Outlet*.

Hector recalled the 1982 conflicts.

> In July 1982, in daytime, our premises were submitted to police search without warrant. The official reason was to search for a UNESCO report on education in Antigua which we published. The Official Secrets Act was used as the basis for the search. They took copy off the press and a whole host of documents were never returned to us. We did not prefer charges. We don't do so because we are cautious of legal charges as the government won't pay even if it lost. So litigation is too expensive for us and nothing is to be had except a moral victory. Also in 1982 our publication bond of E.C. $960 mysteriously disappeared from the courthouse, yet we published a mimeographed, magazine-type publication since 1968. The government said we could not have published fifteen years without being legally bonded. Our lawyers said we had had a bond; the magistrate said the bond money was not there. Before the case began, we filed a motion in the High Court. We had applied for a new bond and had been refused. Then the authorities granted a new bond when they knew we were determined to take the action all the way through (Interview, Hector 1984).

In May 1986, Hector was acquitted of having uttered a false statement undermining confidence in government ministers. The incident occurred in November 1985, at which time he was arrested and imprisoned for four days (*Caribbean Contact* 1986a).

JAMAICA

In Jamaica, what is interesting is that both the socialist Michael Manley and the conservative Edward Seaga governments, almost as equally and as loudly, were accused of tampering with freedom of expression in the 1970s and 1980s. Throughout the first Manley administration (1972–1980), and especially during the 1980 election, the conservative, independently owned *Daily Gleaner* was the center of the controversy. Under the Seaga rule, at issue were the roles of journalists within the government-owned media (the Jamaica Broadcasting Corporation, the *Jamaica Daily News,* and the Agency for Public Information) and the restructuring of broadcasting.

Manley believed that freedom of the press should be tied to social responsibility and, correspondingly, that the national interest should be the overriding concern of the mass media. If privately owned media were incapable of self-discipline, according to Manley, then society should be free to redress the imbalance by creating additional press organizations under "people control" or ownership—that is, by trade unions, agriculture societies, or the like (Cuthbert 1976, 54). Freedom of the press, therefore, should entail freedom from governmental control and freedom from the economic control of groups not representative of society. Former Prime Minister Manley said, "I am very concerned with the way press freedom is misused. It is used by a given class to promote a given class, linking together the interests of multinational corporations, etc. Such freedom is not reflective of others. Jamaica has a tradition of press freedom, and I have had it drilled into me so I believe in it. But freedom of the press for whom? The press is often used to manipulate" (Interview, Manley 1981).

Initially, Manley and the *Gleaner* saw eye to eye; however, as Manley's People's National party (PNP) moved steadily to the left, and in the process alienated the business class, the *Gleaner* became increasingly critical, expressing a strong editorial bias against the brand of social and cultural transformation Manley sought (Cuthbert 1976, 54).

When Manley declared a state of emergency in the mid-1970s, the press definitely feared its potential impact, especially the possibility of censorship and detention without warrant. However, for the most part Manley did not use emergency powers against the media; instead, his government usually resorted to warnings.

But from the beginning of emergency, the press was in an ambivalent position. When the emergency was declared, Manley called editors and broadcasting managers together for an off-the-record meeting. Following that, what censorship existed was self-imposed, and editors such as Hector Wynter of the *Gleaner* thought this even worse than government censorship.

Wynter felt that the possibility of detention without warrant under Section 35 of the regulations cowed the press. "If any of us writes articles which the government does not like, over a period of time we can be 'controlled,' " he said. A Jamaica Broadcasting Corporation official said his station practiced self-censorship regularly. "If we buried Manley in the news, we'd worry about a phone call from him, although we have never had one," he said (Interview, Whylie 1976).

To protect journalists, the newspapers dropped bylines and informed their staffs of five self-imposed rules. The result was that the few attacks on government policy were very mild, and reports of security forces' activities usually were to their credit. Twice daily the security forces issued bulletins that all newspapers were obliged to print; they could not be edited or appended to other stories. At least the *Gleaner* also published eyewitness accounts of incidents reported by the security forces, resulting in contradictory statements.

The *Gleaner* and the *Star* carried daily notices to their readers that the papers' contents were affected by emergency regulations, and Radio Jamaica Rediffusion used spot announcements to inform the public about the emergency—what it was, how long it might last, and its effects on freedom of expression.

The foreign press—meaning the U.S. and Canadian press—was criticized frequently in both government and private sectors for its gloomy reports on Jamaica. In 1976, the favorite song in Jamaica was called "Foreign Press," the first lines of which were

> They are trying their best
> To stop our progress
> With bad propaganda . . .

The song was played often as background music for the government's nightly thirty-minute television program of public information, and Manley even used it at election rallies (Lent 1977c).

However, foreign correspondents were not mistreated during this emergency or during later periods. Laws such as those on the submission of cables to proper authorities and the banning of undesirable publications existed but were very rarely enforced.

The turning point in the *Gleaner*-Manley affairs coincided with the period when the paper was in financial difficulties and had floated a $4 million public bond issue. Oversubscribed by more than twenty-three hundred applications, mainly by individuals, the bond issue gave the *Gleaner* some financial independence. Newspaper officials said that the bond was to pay off short-term loans and to liquidate all foreign commitments (Neita, 1979). The government and the Manley-supporting Press Association of Jamaica (PAJ) believed that the *Gleaner* drastically changed after the bond issue, mainly because the Central Intelligence Agency (CIA) of the United States pumped a great deal of money into the paper in an effort to overthrow Manley. In 1980, Fred Landis, a critic of the CIA brought to Jamaica by the PAJ, testified that the CIA had played a role with the *Gleaner* similar to their role with *El mercurio* in

Allende's Chile. A pamphlet Landis issued charged that the *Gleaner's* "language style and unblinking coverage of violence and economic woes are the handiwork of the CIA" (Huey 1980). The language of *Gleaner* columnists was termed seditious because it called "for the overthrow of the government and the disobedience of lawful government decrees" and told police and soldiers to "disobey any order that is illegal [meaning government decrees]." Some writers said that the *Gleaner* was obsessed with Cuba, that the paper believed just about every Cuban diplomat was an agent of Cuban intelligence, or that the *Gleaner* distorted news frequently to hurt Manley's image (Ray and Schaap 1980).

Throughout 1978, despite the bond issue, the paper continued to worry both about an alleged threat that it would lose its license to import paper and about dwindling advertising in then-socialist Jamaica. The staff was cut by 25 percent and the number of pages by one-half. In eight months, the *Gleaner* laid off 188 people, which the PAJ said was the paper's way to strike back after the 1976 election. Called "voluntary redundancy," the layoffs allowed the *Gleaner* to gain total control over its workers in the fight against Manley, the *PAJ News* of February 1978 charged. The PAJ later said that the *Gleaner* had, since a 1974 strike, been very opposed to the Union of Journalists and Allied Employees and had made things very difficult for union workers (*PAJ News* 1978). The two sides traded charges and threats throughout the 1970s.

After 1978, the Gleaner Company (with two dailies and three weeklies) was the only independently owned media company. The *Daily News,* the new paper that Manley had promised when he came into office, was started in 1973. In 1978, the *Daily News,* in deep financial trouble, was taken over by the government to ensure its continuance. The paper had been owned privately, by the pro-PNP section of the same rich, minority class that controlled the *Gleaner* (Dunn 1978, 5). The *Daily News* worked under charter from the government, which stated that the paper "must not support reaction; must promote egalitarianism, not elitism; must support the Third World in the North-South dialogue; and must support a 'mixed' economy of state-owned and private firms" (Huey 1980). Also in 1978, the government assumed ownership of Radio Jamaica Rediffusion (RJR) in the name of the people, allegedly to counterbalance the oppositionist *Gleaner.* Actually, the RJR shares were to be split among the government, 24 percent; the workers, 25 percent; and the "people" (twenty-three organizations such as trade unions, councils of churches, etc., with no single organization owning more than 10 percent), 51 percent. The government was to own RJR for an interim year.

By late 1979, Manley and the *Gleaner* were at opposite poles — the *Gleaner* standing for capitalist enterprise, alliance with the West, and a conservative sensibility; and Manley standing for socialist development, Third World alignment, and an insurgent spirit (Kopkind 1980). By September, Manley himself had resorted to calling the paper "the brothel of North Street," "harlot," and "Call girl," and its editors, "pimps for imperialism." He accused the paper of "mendacity, lack of patriotism, and subversion." Also, according to Manley, the paper stirred up matters and then reported them, and the editors created many of the problems attributed to the leadership. The *Gleaner* charged Manley with moving toward communism, creating the nation's economic problems, and preparing to stifle the press by political and economic means (Kopkind 1980). In September, exasperated with an edition of the *Gleaner* that called Manley a "Judas," the prime minister angrily adjourned a cabinet meeting and marched his ministers to a protest demonstration at the *Gleaner.* During his denunciation at the protest rally, he said, "next time, next time," which the *Gleaner* and some Western media called a veiled threat to press freedom. In October, a PNP delegation, including five cabinet ministers and the party general secretary, marched into the *Gleaner* to answer charges and to make countercharges. The PAJ called for a public inquiry about the paper's "unethical and improper journalism". Manley himself brought two libel suits against the *Gleaner,* and Jamaica Broadcasting Corporation (JBC) News filed one as well (Ross 1979; *PAJ News* 1979a).

When national elections were held in 1980, the *Gleaner* had become one of the key campaign issues. To some, the *Gleaner* had more clout than the opposition party; it *was* the opposition. Huey thought the *Gleaner* election coverage was very biased, quoting an editor as saying that one columnist seemed to become unhinged in his criticism of Manley (Huey, 1980). Through all this, the PNP limited itself to replying with libel suits, verbal attacks in interviews, press conferences, and ministerial meetings. After Manley's defeat in 1980, the *Gleaner* seemed to rub salt into the wounds. For example, a headline on 22 December gloated, "Seaga Stuns Them with Elegance"; others were as laudatory.

Shortly after the election, popular television shows were dropped, especially those that were public affairs programs. An interim board for JBC was formed and charged with reorganization; it included no media personnel. At the same time, *Daily News* columnists encountered difficulties with the government, and the *Daily News* editor, also president of PAJ, was suspended for one week on the charge that he passed confidential information to the PAJ. Seaga, who kept the Ministry of Information, Broadcasting and Culture portfolio for himself, meant to seek revenge on the government media he felt had done him an injustice (*Caribbean Contact* 1981b).

Between November 1980 and January 1981, four API staff members were fired without cause, and six others, including some supervisory staff, were transferred to other sections of public service not related to journalism. The new API director said that they all were troublemakers not willing to accept the change. At JBC, journalists were called to account for what the government termed "inaccurate and distorted" stories, and three members of the public affairs department were dismissed. When the deputy general manager, Claude Robinson, objected to submitting a program to review, he was fired. In early 1981, sixteen others were fired at JBC, bringing the total of public media employees fired, suspended, or transferred to thirty-three. PAJ President Ben Brodie predicted that ninety-five others were due to be cut (Letter to JBC staff, 9 March 1981). Many were key officials of PAJ. As the PAJ stated, the issue was not communism or communist domination, as the government charged, nor were the dismissals for economic reasons; rather, they were meant to rid the media of ideologically committed people. Simultaneously, the JBC board said it was considering closing the news department and completely rebuilding it. It did as much by firing thirteen of the fifteen people on the news staff without giving disciplinary reasons. Earlier, the JBC board had ordered the suspension of all TV discussion programs normally produced by the Current Affairs Department (Bennett to deputy general manager, 11 December 1980).

In the print media, a government-appointed board of the *Daily News* demanded a J. $50,000 security deposit in cash from the *Struggle,* the paper of the Workers Party of Jamaica, before allowing the *Daily News* to print it. The board claimed that the security deposit was protection against libel, but the PAJ pointed out that the *Daily News* had printed the *Struggle* since 1977 without any instances of libel. The authorities also increased the printing costs of the *Struggle* by 300 percent and required a press run of sixteen thousand as a condition for publication (Brodie to interested groups, 1 March 1981).

By April 1981, the PAJ campaign to expose Seaga's harassment of critical journalists had attracted the attention of the European Parliament (at a time when Jamaica was seeking EEC aid). Also, a Jamaican court prevented JBC from filling the vacancies created by the dismissals until the matter was settled by arbitration. The government was also sharply criticized for its attempt to financially freeze out the *Struggle.* In April 1983, the *Daily News* folded when the government collected the half-million dollars owed it.

As a reaction to the closing of the *Daily News,* a number of small newspapers sprang up by the mid-1980s. In 1987, the president of the Press Association of Jamaica attributed the growth and resilience of the small papers to the people's need for sources other than the *Gleaner.* However, the small newspapers fared very poorly in capturing part of the island's $100 million–dollar annual advertising budget, much of it locked into the *Gleaner.* Also, government policies, such as high interest rates and prohibitive taxes, did not help them (Nation 1987).

The dominance of the *Gleaner* has been pointed to as a problem of freedom of expression. In 1986, the chairman of the Jamaica Council for Human Rights (JCHR) said that although the *Gleaner* had used its dominant position a bit more responsibly of late, it still deprived a "significant section of the population of the means of publicly expressing their ideas and opinions" (*Caribbean Contact* 1986b). The following year, JCHR asked Americas Watch to study the *Gleaner* and its sister, the *Star,* and their handling of police killings of suspects, which averaged 217 per year from 1979 through 1985. JCHR said that the newspapers normally used police accounts that described "shoot-outs," "ambushes," or criminals firing at police. Americas Watch reported that eyewitness accounts differed from those reported by the press (*Index on Censorship* 1987).

Perhaps the most concern should have been directed to Seaga's restructuring of Jamaican broadcasting. From the beginning of his administration, Seaga favored private over public ownership. In 1986, when he told Parliament that JBC was losing money, he said that the government should divest itself of the company. A year later, the prime minister announced the divestment of the JBC-AM station and 40 percent of Radio Jamaica, at the same time giving his approval for the creation of seven additional broadcasting stations (including a religion-oriented TV station and a similarly oriented radio station, a new public and a new private TV station, and a private regional station) (Royes 1987).

Thus, under this plan, privatization of broadcasting would shut the government out of much broadcasting (*COMBROAD* 1986; Malik 1987). What was not broached was who the private leasees were to be. One media critic thought it ironical that the Seaga government divested some areas of media, since it also had amassed more media entities over the years than had any previous government (Wilson 1987).

GUYANA

In the 1970s, the government of the late Forbes Burnham virtually took over Guyanese mass media, purchasing newspapers, nationalizing broadcasting, and harassing the opposition with legislative, economic, and physical sanctions. By the end of the decade, the government, which by then was socialist, owned both dailies — the *Guyana Chronicle* and the *Citizen* — both radio stations, and the new television service.

Governmental policy, usually enunciated by Christopher Nascimento, minister of state in the prime minister's office, stated explicitly that media were national resources whose ownership could not be left to chance. Burnham himself publicly declared that the press must be an agency of the state to support development (Lent 1977a). In 1974, the prime minister declared that the government had a right to own parts of the media and to form a policy for communications to mobilize the country for development (Nascimento 1974, 7). Cheddi Jagan, former prime minister and leader of the opposition People's Progressive party, questioned the government's rationale for owning media in the name of development communication. He wondered for whom the development was meant and thought that development communication had been misused (Interview, Jagan 1980).

Government ownership started in 1971 when one of the four dailies, the *Guyana Chronicle,* was purchased, leaving the *Mirror,* the *Guyana Graphic,* and the *Evening Post* independently owned. Over the next two years, the government bought and merged the *Graphic* with the *Chronicle* and nationalized the Guyana Broadcasting Service. The *Evening Post* died for financial reasons.

The early 1970s also saw the implementation of a number of other regulations and policies that affected mass media. Sanders pointed out that a number of government policies had had adverse effects upon broadcasting, perhaps not anticipated by the authorities (Sanders 1978b). Among these were the development of a central importing agency that imported only one brand in each product field, thus reducing product competition and cutting advertising revenue, and the setting of quotas on imported raw materials needed for local industry, meaning that local companies sold everything they produced and did not need advertising.

In 1972, the Publications and Newspapers Act forced printers and publishers of newspapers and pamphlets to post G. $5,000 bond with the registrar and to provide two sureties who would post similar sums. All parties concerned had to agree that the printer or publisher would pay all fines that might result from a libel suit. When one paper, the *Dayclean,* refused to comply with the law, a controversial court case resulted.

Among the most stringent rules of 1971–1972, however, were those requiring licenses for the importation of printing equipment and newsprint. The opposition *Mirror,* the intended victim from the outset, suffered the most from these regulations over the next decade. When newsprint came under license control after 31 December 1971, the *Mirror* certainly was the victim, plagued by what became known as M.A.D. (Maximum Administrative Delay). *Mirror* applications for newsprint were not answered; thus, the paper was forced to limit its size or to suspend operations, the latter of which it did four times between June 1972 and May 1973. The *Mirror* filed a motion against the government in 1973, asserting infringement of press freedom by newsprint denial. In 1976, the High Court, ruling in the *Mirror*'s favor, found a "gross delay" in granting newsprint allocations, struck down the 1971 and 1972 orders as unconstitutional, and awarded special damages to the *Mirror* of G. $10,650 plus legal costs. Nevertheless, the decision was reversed on appeal in March 1979, at which time the *Mirror* was taxed G. $24,119 (*Democratic Journalist* 1978).

In 1975, the government again initiated a number of actions that affected the media. First, a gradual and systematic erosion of civil and political rights resulted because of the "paramountcy of party" statements in the Declaration of Sophia enacted that year. A strong executive

7.3 Guyana's *Mirror* cartoon calling attention to the plight of the press.

president and party-nominated government were to rule Guyana; henceforth, all organs of state, including the government, would be considered agencies of the ruling party and subject to its control. Second, the government declared itself socialist. Sanders observed that as companies were merged and nationalized under socialism, more monopolies were formed, lessening the need for advertising and thus adversely affecting broadcasting revenue (Sanders 1978b, 7). Third, the government wholeheartedly embraced the concept of development communications, thus giving it more control over content, at the expense of heavily taxing the government treasury because of the need for subsidies.

With all state agencies under party control, Burnham and his PNC rode roughshod over any opposition during the next six years. The order of October 1974 allowed the government to ban any literature that in the opinion of the minister was "prejudicial to the defence of Guyana, public safety or to public order." First to be affected was the *Dayclean.* Copies of the paper were seized and burned, duplicating machines and other equipment were confiscated, and lengthy legal proceedings were commenced against its publishers, who were accused of publishing without posting bond (Jagan and Nagamootoo 1980, 15).

The *Mirror* continued having difficulties concerning newsprint since the authorities refused to respond to requests. Between 29 August and 3 November 1977, thirty-five unanswered calls were made to the authorities concerning newsprint (Persaud to author, 1 November 1977). The government-owned Guyana National Newspapers Ltd. (GNNL), publishers of the *Chronicle,* quit lending the *Mirror* newsprint after 1977 and in 1978 informed the *Catholic Standard* that it would no longer print that paper (Persaud to Blackman, 20 October 1977). By that time, GNNL had a virtual monopoly on imported newsprint. After 1977, the government denied the *Mirror* all rights to import newsprint, and the *Mirror* had to purchase its paper on a week-to-week basis from GNNL at a price and quantity dictated by the latter.

By the end of the 1970s, the *Mirror,* which at one time had published 17,000 copies on weekdays and 32,000 on Sundays, was down to only 12,000 copies of a four-page Sunday edition printed on expensive bond paper (Interview, Jagan 1980). The newspaper's fate was precarious a number of times when it could not carry advertisements with its limited space or had to close for lack of paper. Foreign papers were not allowed to present gifts of newsprint to the *Mirror,* since the authorities claimed that this would interfere with the government policy of conservation.

Also affected by the newsprint policy was the weekly *Catholic Standard,* an eight-page tabloid, which by 1978 was reduced to a smaller format and four pages. An editor reported in late 1980 that the government refused to sell him newsprint because he reported on human rights violations in Guyana (*Action* 1980). The newspaper suspended publication temporarily in mid-1981 at the same time the *Chronicle* introduced a Sunday supplement. The *Standard* also faced other government harassment. Its offices were searched by police who claimed they were looking for weapons and ammunition. In 1979, a Jesuit priest who supplied photographs to the *Standard* was beaten and stabbed to death. The murder was attributed to Burnham's PNC (*IPI Report* 1979).

With its purchase of Radio Demerara in January 1979, the government completed its control over all major media. After nationalization of Radio Demerara and the Guyana Broadcasting Service, both experienced financial problems. In 1979, a government committee was created to formulate a broadcasting structure under which the two stations could operate effectively.

The government received severe criticism in 1980 after a national election was called fraudulent by international observers. In short order, international and regional groups publicly condemned human rights violations in Guyana. The upshot was that Burnham intensified his campaign against foreign media, especially those from other parts of the Caribbean. The Caribbean News Agency (CANA), *Caribbean Contact,* and press and radio stations of the region were blamed for the deteriorating image of Guyana. In 1980–1981, the Guyanese government and its media organs decided to sever relationships with CANA. In CANA's place, the Guyana News Service was formed.

By 1982–1983, the government increased its pressures on the opposition press with added newsprint controls and a series of libel suits. All three opposition papers, the *Mirror,* the *Open Word* (aligned slightly with Working People's Alliance), and the *Catholic Standard,* had newsprint shortages; the *Mirror* and the *Standard* appeared as weekly single sheets on end-roll newsprint or bond paper. Probably more threatening however, were seven or more libel suits filed in mid-1982 by government ministers, including Burnham, against the *Catholic Standard,* the *Open Word,* and the *Dayclean.* The targeted *Catholic Standard* was served with five libel suits, and some observers believed the suits were brought to force the paper out of existence (*Caribbean Contact* 1982). In 1983, the *Standard* lost the first of the suits when the court ruled that libel suits brought by politicians were not governed by constitutional clauses on freedom of expression. The public paid the fines through public subscription.

The type of journalism left in Guyana was described by the committee that investigated human rights in Guyana. It said that the *Chronicle* read like an "election broadsheet for the PNC," while the government radio "relentlessly churned out the PNC party line, ignoring all facts unfavourable to the PNC or its agents, distorting or inventing stories with a view to discrediting opponents of the regime" (*Caribbean Contact* 1981a). The cult of personality was heavily emphasized on radio as well, the committee said, pointing out that a daily phone-in program was "heavily and obviously rigged"; that "any breath of criticism" was "entirely absent," and that censorship occurred even in religious sermons.

Burnham's death in 1985 did not bring the relief expected in some circles. Opposition newspapers continued to face newsprint shortages. By early 1988, after celebrating its twenty-fifth year of publication, the *Mirror* was still reduced to four pages on Sunday. The *Catholic Standard* did not fare that well. After its 16 August 1987 issue, the paper's supply of newsprint ran out. An attempt by the *Trinidad Express* to donate newsprint was blocked by the government, which stated that the *Standard* did not have the required import license (Pritchard 1987, 22).

The *Standard*'s problems continued throughout 1988. In February the paper lost two libel suits instituted by President Desmond Hoyte. Later in the year, the judge in those cases was elevated to attorney general and minister of justice. Meanwhile, the *Standard* faced even more lawsuits brought by Hoyte.

The government maintained its ownership of the only daily, the *Chronicle,* and the sole radio station, Guyana Broadcasting Service (GBS). In 1986–1987, both of these media were involved in dismissing staff members for conflict of interest or refusal to reveal a source. A cricket commentator at GBS was fired for writing an article in an American-funded and Guyanese government–approved weekly, the *Stabroek News,* and a *Chronicle* reporter was dismissed for refusing to disclose a source in a controversial story about a government decision. Others had been dismissed or reassigned, including the GBS general manager, prompting the opposition Working People's Alliance to state, "If the ruling party has to intervene between the news and the listener and the reader as often as it does, then perhaps it does not need journalists at all" (*Caribbean Contact* 1987a).

TRINIDAD AND BARBADOS

Not much has been heard from Trinidad and Tobago or from Barbados about recent infringements of press freedom. Trinidad's dailies (the *Guardian* and the *Express*) and broadcasting outlets (Trinidad and

Tobago Television, Radio Guardian, and Radio Trinidad) are guaranteed freedom of expression under the constitution.

The Trinidad government frequently complains of press irresponsibility but does not take punitive legislative or political action. Between 1983 and 1988, no press-government skirmishes were reported. One 1983 incident involved the firing of the director of television because of his refusal to dismiss a reporter opposed to the ruling People's National party (Morales and Ballard 1985, 65).

In fact, what is probably more responsible than the government for shutting out free expression is the partisanship of the dailies. Like Jamaica's *Gleaner,* the *Trinidad Guardian* is criticized for its very biased favoritism toward established business interests. One source wrote, "An entirely disproportionate amount of space is devoted to upper class minority events, while matters that concern the mass of the population are ignored" (Brown and Sanatan 1987, 194).

The *Express,* owned by the newer business class, is less rigid than the *Guardian* but maintains similar political and labor policies. For example, it campaigns strongly against regional incidences of socialist rule. One source wrote of the Trinidad dailies

> Both newspapers make regular claims to be defenders of the sacred principle of freedom of the press. How genuine their concern is, is very doubtful. . . . But [professional standards and ethics] are practised only as far as they avoid treading on the interests of the business people who own and control the newspapers. As a result of the system of interlocking directorates in business in the country, the Boards of the two dailies are full of persons who run other enterprises in the banking and commercial sector and they do not fail to exert pressure on the editorial departments of the newspaper they control (Brown and Sanatan 1987, 194).

Thus, the daily press is owned and controlled by the business community to serve its purposes, while television and one of the two radio stations are government entities. The latter, as well as the *Guardian,* were purchased from the Thomson group in the 1960s and 1970s. The government bought Trinidad and Tobago Television and 610 Radio in the 1960s and welcomed, if not helped to arrange, the 1975 sale of two-thirds of the Trinidad Publishing Company (publishers of the *Guardian* and the *Evening News*) to local businessman, Charles McEnearney. Thomson retained 33.5 percent of the papers' stock until 1976, when he sold 10 percent to the company's employees.

Shortly after, the *Trinidad Sunday Guardian* editor said that the government had brought about the sale in an indirect fashion. "We were very critical of government [under Thomson] and management felt we might get into trouble so they sold their interests," he said (Interview, Ince 1977). The general manager of the Trinidad Publishing Company said that Thomson knew of the regional feeling that mass media should be owned locally, and so he had sold out. He said there was no government interference or pressure in the transaction and that the government did not own any of the newspapers' stock (Interview, Conyers 1977).

If the relationship between government and the media was a quiet one in the late 1980s, this was not always the case in Trinidad. Under the longtime prime minister, Eric Williams, a number of clashes occurred. Williams was known for lashing out at the media, even at those owned by government. But normally that was the extent of the fighting; Williams did not issue restrictive directives or otherwise interfere in the affairs of media. The publisher of the *Express* appreciated Williams's noninterference and gave the Trinidad government good marks for the way it allowed abuse of press freedom, referring to two gossip weeklies published in the country (Interview, Gordon 1970). On the other hand, Williams was not above acting spitefully against the media that attacked him. The *Express* publisher and others said that Williams admitted publicly in the 1970s that he had turned down a request from the *Express* to establish a second television channel, after first "tearing apart sentence by sentence" a critical editorial in that paper. Williams later said he had denied the request because the *Express* wanted to install color television, which he said was not compatible with government policy. But this was not the truth, for in another context, the head of the government Trinidad and Tobago Television said, "When the *Express* put in their bid for color television, the prime minister said this was ridiculous. I told him we can't keep black and white television as we cannot get the spare parts. The prime minister sent me a private note saying go ahead with color television" (Interview, Bain 1977).

Barbados has had very few difficulties between government and the media. The two dailies, the *Advocate* and the *Nation,* and the radio station, Voice of Barbados, are privately owned. The Caribbean Broadcasting Corporation is state owned, but independently operated.

The criticism of business class ownership is equally applicable to the press of Barbados. The *Advocate* and its sensational weekly, *Investigator,* are owned by McEnearney-Alstons, a conglomerate involved in many businesses, including car/truck dealerships, finance, and import. The *Nation* has also become a huge corporation, publishing the *Nation,* the *Sun, EC News* (oriented to the Eastern Caribbean), *Bajan* Magazine, and *Barbados Tele-Direct* (yellow pages), in addition to owning the Voice of Barbados and travel agencies.

Free expression is guaranteed in the Barbados 1966 Independence Order. In 1983, however, the prime minister, the late Tom Adams, put a blemish on Barbados's defense of press freedom when he expelled *Caribbean Contact* editor Rickey Singh for his articles critical of the U.S. invasion of Grenada (see chapter 8).

CONCLUSION

In the 1980s, media practitioners and scholars met in various venues to discuss the problems of the Caribbean mass media, including those dealing with freedom of expression. What was unusual at some of these meetings was that freedom of expression no longer was narrowly confined to state-media relationships. Other more subtle forms of suppression made up the discussion agendas—topics such as ownership of the media by conglomerates or by other big business interests, the smothering of Caribbean forms of expression by outside cultural and media fare (especially television), and the domination of news flows by other than Caribbean interests.

Perhaps also unusual was the recognition that governments had become more sophisticated in their manipulation of the media. Increasingly they dispensed with arrests, suspensions, and censorship and relied instead on building up their public relations arms, manipulating development communications, and generally guiding the media.

8

Rickey Singh: Man without a Country

When the Barbados prime minister revoked Rickey Singh's work permit twenty months prematurely in November 1983, it was the third time in a decade that the *Caribbean Contact* editor had to search for a new country because of his writing. He had been forced out of his native Guyana in 1973 and out of Trinidad in 1978.

In mid-1984, he was denied a work permit by the pro-Reagan government of Jamaica, after the *Gleaner* sought authorization for him to remain as Caribbean and international news editor.

Singh's 1983 expulsion occurred when the Barbados prime minister, the late Tom Adams, took strong exception to his articles published in the *Nation,* a Barbados daily, and reprinted in *Caribbean Contact,* the monthly organ of the ecumenical Caribbean Conference of Churches (CCC). Singh wrote that the U.S. invasion of Grenada could not be justified on any legal or moral grounds and that it set a dangerous precedent for the region. The November 1983 *Caribbean Contact* also carried a CCC statement strongly condemning the invasion. Two days after the magazine appeared, Singh was given one day to leave Barbados.

Although no official reason was given for the work-permit revocation, Singh said that Adams, who had obtained regional support for the invasion, objected to the articles because they challenged his government's version of events. Subsequently, Singh's stay was extended pending negotiations, but these soon broke down in a meeting of Adams, Singh, and Singh's attorney. Singh said that he was asked to sign a letter disclaiming many of the allegations he had made in the articles and saying he had been treated well since his arrival in 1978. When he would not comply and claimed that to sign was equivalent to getting "down on my knees [to] beg pardon," Adams promised a new draft of the letter. However, before this was done, Adams publicly stated that he would not rescind the order.

In a statement issued 15 November 1983, Singh said that he had not set out to "deliberately question the honesty or veracity of statements by Mr. Adams" and that he had given the prime minister the right to reply, an offer that was refused. He emphasized that his leaving the island was not to be construed as acknowledgement of wrongdoing or a change in his position on Grenada. He was quoted as saying, "It is better for me to join, if I must, the unfortunate suffering masses in Guyana today under the Forbes Burnham administration than to genuflect to the local politician directorate by compromising my self-respect in order to be allowed to remain and work here."

Numerous groups deplored Adams's actions, including the Barbados Association of Journalists, the Caribbean Press Council, various Jamaican and Barbadian publishers, the Committee to Protect Journalists, and the American Newspaper Guild. Because of such reactions, Adams was moved in mid-1984 to accuse Singh in the *Caribbean Impulse* of having close contacts with foreign spies, presumably Cuban. In a statement to the Caribbean News Agency, Singh said that the accusations were totally untrue and were "serious enough to warrant legal advice" because they were "highly offensive and prejudicial" to his integrity.

After Singh left as editor, *Caribbean Contact* was in transition from the liberal stance Singh had maintained to one that would be more responsive to the concerns of its sponsoring churches. The December 1983 issue was abbreviated to twelve pages, mostly filled with copy already on hand. The interim editors put the logotype on a black background and allowed many blotches of white space to remain where stories were omitted, including the editorial space normally filled by Singh.

The next *Caribbean Contact,* a combined January-February 1984 edition, discussed its new policy in a page-one story, "Voice for the Region's Powerless." It also carried an advertisement seeking a new editor and an editorial warning about Eric Gairy's possible return to power in Grenada.

The front-page policy statement said that the magazine was putting into effect measures agreed upon at a September 1983 CCC meeting. *Caribbean Contact*'s editorial policy was to be examined to "bring about certain other reforms" and to make the periodical more responsive to the concerns of the churches. A committee of review, made up of three ministers and the editor of the *Barbados Nation,* had met for four months before reporting in September. Additionally, a Barbados-based editorial advisory committee was established "to monitor" the magazine and to give it a "distinctively Christian orientation." However, *Contact* was to continue to be the voice for the voiceless and powerless in the region and for justice and peace.

    Caribbean Contact, started by the CCC in 1972, initially struggled to stay afloat, partly because it was distributed free, mainly to the churches. Singh became *Contact*'s third editor in 1974, accepting the position on the conditions that he be given editorial independence and that the magazine convert to paid circulation. He was somewhat adrift himself, having been transferred to a British paper by his boss, Roy Thomson, after reporting about graft by the ruling party in the 1973 elections in Guyana. In early 1977, Singh told how he lost both his position as editor and political reporter of the Guyana *Graphic* and eventually his homeland: "The Guyana government had enough of us [Singh and colleague, Ulric Mentus]," he said, adding, "We were cleverly maneuvered out of the *Graphic;* Thomson was maneuvered out of the *Graphic* and the *Chronicle* was started. Mentus was let go. I was forced to resign, as the government was going to take over the *Graphic*" (Interview, Singh 1977).

    Almost immediately, Singh changed the direction and policy of *Caribbean Contact,* making it a liberal and independent voice on numerous issues affecting the region. For his efforts, he said he received threats on his life from government supporters and was actually assaulted by a cabinet minister. In 1978, the Trinidad government, upset over his editorial stances, refused to renew Singh's work permit, and he and *Carib-*

8.1   Expelled from three countries because of his writings, Rickey Singh continues his *Caribbean Contact* column.

bean Contact moved to Barbados (Interview, Singh 1977).

As early as January 1977, Singh said in an interview that he received a "lot or criticism from the churches and governments of the region," which thought his publication was "subversive or communist." Grenada's Prime Minister Gairy, coming from the right, was against *Contact,* as were socialist politicians. Discussing the latter, Singh said

> Politicians with socialist views are saying we are asking for too much — for press freedom of an unrestricted type. No one is asking for that. We say the people have the right to be informed. No one is asking to be able to be irresponsible. No editor is trying to fight against revolution or for capitalism and against socialism. Private enterprise media are full of ads and don't allow their own interests to be criticized. So, I don't buy the argument that government control is the end of freedom of the press (Interview, Singh 1977).

Singh's independent stance was displayed later when he supported Maurice Bishop's government in Grenada and at the same time criticized the People's Revolutionary Government for its postponement of elections and press suppression. Earlier, he showed this independent streak in two remarks he made to me. Discussing government propagandists, he said, "Everyone wants to tell the editor how to do his job. Yet they don't tell other professionals how to do their jobs." On the dangers of self-censorship, so prevalent in the Caribbean, Singh said, "We editors can be our worst enemies. I won't censor myself and that's why I left Guyana" (Interview, Singh 1977). Perhaps that is why he also left Barbados.

In 1984–1985, Singh freelanced for various media in and out of the Caribbean, while his children continued their schooling in Barbados. In January 1984, he started writing for the *Nation* in Barbados, at which time he also asked to be allowed to write for the government-owned daily, the *Chronicle,* in his homeland of Guyana. He never received a response to that request.

Later, in the summer of 1984, when he accepted an offer from *Caribbean Contact* to write a monthly column emanating "from where I choose to operate," Singh said that he faced a "convergence of interests among some CARICOM governments" to prevent him from earning a living "through their abuse of immigration and work-permit regulations." He let it be known that although he preferred to go home to Guyana, he could not abandon his morals. Singh wrote, "I know it is not a question of simply moving from one Caribbean country, where I have been suddenly dislocated, back to one's own country. But, like a mother, everyone has only one country. Mine remains Guyana" (Singh 1984b, 5).

It is interesting that Rickey Singh, until 1987, remained a man without a country, despite the fact that the three leaders who took expulsion actions against him were deceased.

With a change of government in Barbados in 1987, Singh was given immigrant status there (*Caribbean Contact* 1987c). He continued writing columns for the *EC News* and for *Caribbean Contact,* and in November 1986, he established the Caribbean Association of Media Workers (CAMWORK). Presiding over CAMWORK, Singh hopes to make the association a facilitator for discussion of issues dealing with mass media, including press freedom, professionalism, high standards, exchange of information, and support of public welfare (Wilson 1987, 4).

9

Grenada: Three Lives in a Decade

The Windward island of Grenada, "discovered" for news purposes during the 1983 U.S. invasion, has had a stormy government-press relationship since the advent of the 1970s. At that time, the three Grenada newspapers practiced a rather subdued opposition to the autocratic—and at times brutal and frivolous—government of Eric Gairy; the other medium, Windward Islands Broadcasting Service, was under strict government control. Gradually, by middecade, the *New Jewel,* published by a movement by that name, seriously challenged Gairy's rule. This led to the government's passage of a very strict newspaper act, seizure of unauthorized publications, and arrests and beatings of news reporters. After Maurice Bishop halted Gairy's reign in 1979, the media were eventually reorganized along Marxist lines; in the process, the government forced the closure of newspapers not conforming to that doctrine.

Thus, in the course of about a dozen years, Grenada experienced a media metamorphosis that saw newspapers and broadcast stations operating under an authoritarian premier and "democracy," a Marxist government, and the occupation forces of a superpower.

GAIRY AND THE MEDIA

Premier Eric Gairy's long tenure in office, including three elected five-year terms, did not bode well for human rights, including that of freedom of the press. Numerous media people suffered the wrath of his policies and regulations.

In the early 1970s, Grenada had three newspapers and was the head-quarters for a regional radio service. The oldest paper was the five-times-weekly *West Indian,* founded in 1915 by nationalist hero, T. A. Marryshow. It and the twice-weekly *Torchlight* were locally and privately owned with circulations of a mere one thousand. The third paper was the weekly *Vanguard,* supported by the Grenada National party (GNP) and edited by a lawyer, who in 1962 had carried his campaign door to door in an effort to unseat Gairy. The *West Indian* was a shoddy affair with very little meaningful content, while the other two papers devoted most of their space to local politics. The *Vanguard* was very emotional about what it termed "Gairyism," likening the premier to Hitler (Lent 1977b, 133).

The island had its first radio service in 1955, when the Windward Islands Broadcasting Service (WIBS) was set up for St. Lucia, St. Vincent, Dominica, and Grenada. WIBS was administered by the West Indies Broadcasting Council, made up of the premiers of the islands. Between council meetings, the premier of Grenada acted on the council's behalf. That left enormous power in Gairy's hands, according to the chief program officer of WIBS in the early 1970s (Interview, Theobalds 1971).

In fact, broadcasting in Grenada was so unfair that during parliamentary debate only the government arguments were aired, and opposition party advertisements and announcements were not permitted on radio. After considerable criticism, the government allowed the opposition party one-half hour of time during legislative broadcasts (Interview, Smith 1971). WIBS was discontinued in 1971, and on 1 January 1972, Radio Grenada, a government station, was inaugurated.

Grenada Television Company Ltd. was incorporated as a private company on 27 May 1974 with 1,000 shares, each worth E.C. $250. Of the 420 shares issued by 1977, 268 were held by the family of station manager Joseph Pitt, 80 by Ralph Alves of St. Vincent, and 72 by Glenn Evans of Grenada. The government planned to purchase 30 percent of the shares (*Caribbean Monthly Bulletin* 1977). Most programs were relays from Trinidad and Tobago Television. Despite the lack of sufficient advertising revenue, the station survived from receiver sales; the government had given Grenada Television the monopoly on set importation.

In addition, there was the Government Information Service, better staffed and more active than neighboring island services and used strictly as a propaganda outlet for Gairy. After assuming office, Gairy had decided that the government did not need an information chief and instead appointed a public relations official directly responsible to him. In 1971, all editors agreed that Gairy was attempting to rule by news releases, all

9.1 The controversial *Torchlight* and the *Vanguard*, both published during the repressive Gairy era.

of which dealt with him. The *Vanguard* editor said that all releases were "ego-centered for Gairy" and oftentimes were libelous and personal. Gairy would choose an enemy and then attack him through releases read over WIBS (Interview, Cruickshank 1971). Prior censorship existed in that all press releases had to be signed by Gairy or by his cabinet secretary; once signed, they could not be amended or corrected in any way (Interview, Seon 1971).

Fear and distrust permeated government-media relationships. One editor who had been a victim of Gairy said that the premier gave himself "God-like characteristics" and that the people, through fear, reinforced his behavior by rushing to WIBS to outdo their neighbors in saying good things about him (Interview, Cruickshank 1971). Gairy regularly lambasted the press, leaving the impression with audiences that Grenada papers did not count (Interview, Clyne 1971). He also used libel laws to intimidate domestic and foreign media. Between 1969 and 1971, he threatened or brought suit against *Look,* some London media, the *Torchlight,* and the *Vanguard.* The editor of the *Torchlight* said that Gairy had instituted a libel suit against him two years previously but didn't "bring it forth" (Interview, Mason 1971), and the *Vanguard* editor said that four libel suits against him in two years were intended "to cripple us financially" (Interview, Cruickshank 1971).

The *Vanguard* editor discussed what he called indirect pressures from the authorities.

> The government does threaten people connected with the paper. Anonymous letters are sent to us saying we will be burned out in our cars. People are therefore afraid to attach their names to letters to the editor; they are afraid of mayhem and victimizing by the Gairy government. Only a few people will come to our office to pick up copies of the paper. Downtown, if a person buys a *Vanguard,* he hides it inside a *Trinidad Express* or *Trinidad Guardian,* so no one will know he bought it. Civil servants are not allowed to read *Vanguard* in public or in their offices. The paper is not allowed in the libraries. If you're seen with *Vanguard,* you're automatically blackballed. If we get a letter from a reader, we take it downstairs, rewrite it so the government boys cannot trace the handwriting. Then we burn the original copy and set the letter in type. Government gangs have threatened members of our staff with beatings and rape (Interview, Cruickshank 1971).

In 1975, Gairy's government passed the Newspaper (Amendment) Act, stipulating that it was illegal to print or to publish any newspaper unless an annual payment of E.C. $5000 was made for a license, as well as a bond of E.C. $960 and a cash deposit of E.C. $20,000. Of five newspapers in Grenada then, only the *West Indian* published within the context of this law; the rest had to suspend publication or to go underground. Later in 1975, at the suggestion of the Caribbean Publishers and Broadcasters Association, the law was amended to allow the papers to purchase E.C. $20,000 in libel insurance rather than to deposit that amount in cash.

Unauthorized publications were seized, and persons caught selling, purchasing, or reading any paper not meeting the stipulations of the act were arrested. Even photographers caught taking pictures of the police seizing papers and arresting people, or of armed police and defense forces in the streets, had their cameras smashed; in some cases, the photographers were beaten with ax handles and pieces of wood. On 18 July 1975, Kenrick Radix, a leader with Maurice Bishop of the oppositionist New Jewel Movement whose paper had angered Gairy into passing the Newspaper Act, was beaten and shot while trying to photograph the scenes of near riot. The occasion was a confrontation between police and *New Jewel* vendors. Nine New Jewel members were arrested and charged with distributing the *New Jewel,* which then went underground. The New Jewel Movement had avoided a government ban on "unauthorized publication of periodicals issued more frequently than 100 days apart, by changing the publication's name with each issue. A new publication appeared each week with Volume 1, Number 1" (Mydans 1984).

Throughout the remainder of the 1970s, the New Jewel Movement continued to attack Gairy's policies and to harp on its own 1976 principles, which included freedom of expression and religion. The Gairy government, in turn, continued to censor, threaten, and fine the media, and it took over the *West Indian.*

BISHOP AND THE MEDIA

Shortly after the 13 March 1979 coup that brought Maurice Bishop to power, the media began experiencing still another set of changes. The oppositionist weekly, the *Torchlight,* began having run-ins with the authorities. Publication of the *Torchlight* was finally suspended, and reorganization occurred among other media.

Closing the Oppositionist Voices

Bishop blamed the *Torchlight* for jumping on the bandwagon to discredit the revolution. He cited the 6 May issue as carrying a number of "malicious and distorted articles," some of which were potentially dangerous to national security. He also claimed that some *Torchlight* stories contained "classical CIA planted anti-Communist propaganda" (*Caribbean Monthly Bulletin* 1979).

The New Jewel Movement, which supported Bishop, and the *Torch-*

light continued to trade barbs, and on 20 August the *New Jewel* called upon Grenadians to put the *Torchlight* under "heavy, heavy manners" (discipline and control). The movement objected to the paper's reprinting of anti–People's Revolutionary Government (PRG) articles from abroad, some of which were unsubstantiated. At a September press con-

The Revolution Must Be Respected

ON March 13, 1979, the people of Grenada, led by the NJM, boldly seized power from the Gairy Dictatorship. Our aim was not only to remove Gairy, but also to build a new and just society where all our people, not just a privileged few, could be masters in our own country, and gain the benefit of progress and development.

Certain Big estate-owners and Big-business people, who are accustomed to exploiting the people for many years, mistakenly believed that the NJM would allow them to continue to wield power and abuse the people. When they saw that this would not be permitted, they began a campaign to get back power for themselves.

* They, and the CIA together used Winston White and De Raviniere to try to overthrow the revolution in November 1979.
* They used the Torchlight, The Catholic Focus, and various pamphlets to destabilize the revolution, by spreading lies and propaganda, and revealing national security information, which endangered the Revolution
* Now, they have published a new newspaper called "The Grenadian Voice".

No Newpapers Are Permitted

After the last attempt to publish a newspaper, the PRG announced that no more newspapers are to be published until after a media policy was issued to give guidelines which would prevent counter-revolutionary newspapers from being published.

The PRG clearly said "no more newspapers" and all Grenada knows this.

The NJM says, this is a revolutionary country, and this bold-faced contempt for the revolution cannot be accepted. Those who refuse to respect the revolution must feel its full weight.

9.2   Statement, issued during Maurice Bishop's period, proclaiming newspapers had to respect the Grenadian revolution.

ference, Bishop, in outlining a PRG press policy, said, "We do not accept the right of the *Torchlight* to reprint scurrilous materials from overseas," and he accused the paper of representing minority and foreign interests.

On 13 October, the *Torchlight* was closed by the government, which ordered its publishers not to bring out other newspapers. Apparently what triggered the closure was a story in the 10 October issue that alleged government discrimination against the Rastafarian sect, which the *Torchlight* predicted would go to the streets to demonstrate. The front-page headline implied that "one of the PRG's grass-roots support groups was turning against the revolution" (EPICA 1982, 59). The "Rastas" actually demonstrated in front of the *Torchlight* against both the paper and government, and on 13 October, PRG "civilian supporters" demonstrated against the *Torchlight,* after which it was closed (Smikle 1979; Hughes 1980).

Obviously the Bishop administration and the *Torchlight* editors had conflicting views on press freedom. The *Torchlight*'s position was that the publisher alone has the right to determine the type of paper and its editorial position, while the PRG maintained that the press has a national responsibility beyond the interests of a particular sector, class, or group. A quote from Bishop at the time clearly brings out the latter point.

> The job of the media is to inform and educate. . . . If the government is involved in programmes, and we are, a national, not a sectarian, newspaper must publish those programmes. . . . We have no objection to any one individual putting their views out in writing, but if their views are really one individual, call it that. Don't try to fool anybody with "national" and "free" and "responsible" and "independent." If one man owns and controls the *Torchlight* newspaper . . . it should be called "The Cromwellite" and you publish under that, so nobody is fooled. . . . We cannot afford a situation in our country where minorities are allowed to peddle their views and their news under the guise of nationalism (*Grenada Newsletter* 1979).

The fear that the paper would attempt to destabilize Grenada through CIA help came at a time when the U.S. president, Jimmy Carter, described the country as a threat to U.S. national interests. One analyst claimed, "The *Torchlight* conflict might not have ended in such extreme measures had it not been for the mounting possibility of interference by the U.S." (EPICA 1982, 60). The government feared that the CIA would use the *Torchlight* for destabilization, much as it was accused of using the newspapers in Chile and Jamaica (EPICA 1982, 60).

Among other concerns, Bishop thought that the paper's ownership was ideologically tied to Grenada's ruling class, which was "opposed to structural economic change" (EPICA 1982, 60). Also at issue was the 13 percent ownership of the *Torchlight* by the *Trinidad Express*. The *Express* was a foreign company with economic ties throughout the region, and it influenced public opinion against threats to its own economic power in the socialist states of the Caribbean. In fact, in a later speech, Bishop revealed the results of a study that showed the economic reach of Trinidad's newspapers, the *Express* and the *Guardian*. Ten of the eighteen members of the boards of the two dailies accounted for forty-seven other directorships within the Trinidad economy alone, and the *Express* interlocked with the Neal and Massey Group, one of the two largest manufacturing conglomerates in Trinidad, which in the late 1970s had fifty-one subsidiaries in nine Caribbean countries (Bishop 1982).

After the closing of the *Torchlight,* the authorities said that it would eventually reopen but not until the PRG had had time to create ownership rules to make the media more democratic. The result was People's Law 81, which excluded aliens as shareholders of any company that is a proprietor, printer, or publisher of a paper and which prohibited any Grenadian from holding more than 4 percent of the shares in any such company. This had dramatic consequences for the main shareholders of the *Torchlight,* automatically transferring to the government the 13 percent owned by the *Trinidad Express* and most of the 22 percent owned by Grenadian businessman D. M. B. Cromwell (*PAJ News* 1979b).

In August 1981, the government felt that the private owners of Grenada Publishers Ltd., former publishers of the *Torchlight,* were sabotaging and abandoning the printery, at which time the employees took over the company, renamed it Grenada Co-operative Publishing Society, and sought help from the National Co-operative Development Agency. Employees said that the company slowed down on commercial jobs that brought in revenue and refused to honor wage agreements after the *Torchlight*'s closing. The owners said that they had no money to pay employees after the newspaper was closed (*Media Worker* 1982; "*Torchlight Workers*" 1981; *New Jewel* 1981).

Some sources, including those favorable to Bishop, have said that the closing of the *Torchlight* dealt a damaging blow to the revolution's image abroad. For example, the Caribbean Conference of Churches cabled Bishop, asking for an immediate resumption of the paper (*Caribbean Contact* 1979). Writing in December 1983, after he had lost his work permit on Barbados for writing against the U.S. invasion of Grenada, former *Caribbean Contact* editor Rickey Singh maintained:

Had there been in Grenada a media system capable of permitting dissent, however restrained, given the siege mentality prevailing in St. George's, then Maurice Bishop himself may have had a vehicle to transmit to the Grenadian masses some of the problems his once loyal comrades insisted on concealing from the people. . . . The closure of the newspaper [*Torchlight*] was an overkill. As editor of the *Caribbean Contact,* I editorially criticised this action and warned Bishop that his government might be playing into the hands of its enemies (Singh 1984a; see also Singh 1981).

In February 1980, the PRG closed the *Catholic Focus* after its first issue, although, as a church property, it did not fall under the aegis of PL 81. Bishop explained its banning: "The publication of that paper [the *Catholic Focus*] was illegal as it was printed by the 'Torchlight' newspaper Company in defiance of People's Law 81 which forbids a newspaper Company from publishing a newspaper if there are individuals in the Company who own more than 4% of the shares" (Hughes 1980, 5).

The third instance of suppression of a newspaper concerned the *Grenadian Voice,* published in 1981 by what was termed "the Group of 26" — businessmen, lawyers, and large landowners, including the former manager-director and leading shareholders of the *Torchlight.* The first issue of this sixteen-page, stenciled paper said that it had no counter-revolutionary intent, that it would conform to all laws, and that, at least at the start, it would be "deliberately innocuous" (Mydans 1984). The second issue was printed on 18 June and loaded into four automobiles for distribution when the police seized the cars, all copies of the newspaper, the typewriters, and the duplicating machines and arrested four people, including Leslie Pierre.

Obviously showing concern about the *Voice,* the New Jewel Movement had distributed a four-page flyer in which it warned that some big estate owners and business people were trying to regain power through the *Voice;* that the publication of the paper demonstrated "bold-faced contempt for the revolution"; that when these "exploiters" were in control, the people suffered; and that just as the CIA had destabilized Jamaica through the *Gleaner,* it was attempting to do the same on Grenada. The flyer said that seven of the twenty-six owners had shares in the *Torchlight* and that thirteen had been big businessmen and managers. In very strong language, the New Jewel Movement described some of these owners. For example, editor Leslie Pierre was characterized as "famous before the Revolution for forcing women workers to sleep with him, and even for raising women employees' dresses on the pretext of looking for stolen goods. He himself was fired from being manager of

Buy Rite for stealing a large sum of money, including workers [*sic*] Christmas bonuses" (New Jewel Movement 1981).

In a speech the day after the closing of the *Grenadian Voice,* Bishop told a rally that the paper was part of an international plot to destabilize the government and to create chaos and that the twenty-six publishers were CIA connected and engaged in counterrevolutionary activities. The PRG claimed that *Voice* shareholders had met with the first secretary in the U.S. embassy in Barbados, Ashley Wills, who earlier had been heard boasting that Grenada would soon have an oppositionist newspaper. Alister Hughes said that if CIA money was used for the paper, he never saw it; "Each of us put up E.C. $100 to start the Voice," he added (Interview, Hughes 1984).

The charges were summarized in a 20 June PRG statement: (1) the paper's owners included the manager-director of the *Torchlight;* (2) the paper violated the clear ruling by the PRG that no more papers could be published until the government had formed a code of media policy; (3) the group, under the name of the GNP for Reconstruction and Libera-tion, had issued five counterrevolutionary pamphlets during the previous six months, some calling for violence; (4) one of the twenty-six owners was actively involved in a plot to attack militiamen; (5) the Group of 26 was closely linked to the CIA through agents in Barbados; and (6) "this is a revolution, that Grenadians live in a revolutionary society; that there is revolutionary legality; and that they will have to abide by the laws of the revolution" (*Caribbean Contact* 1981c). Writing in the same year, one source claimed that if the group's "links to the United States were not overt, they were certainly credible" (EPICA 1982, 120). The same publi-cation claimed that whether or not the United States was involved with the *Voice,* its interests were served, for if the paper continued, "reac-tionary interests" had a foothold to challenge the revolution; if it was closed, the PRG would be blamed for violating press freedom (EPICA 1982, 120).

In his speech, Bishop made explicitly clear what had been stated previously: "No newspaper, or other paper, pamphlet, or other publica-tion containing any public news, intelligence or report of any occurrence or any remarks or observations thereon upon any political matter, pub-lished for sale, distribution, or other purpose, shall be produced, printed, published or distributed in Grenada" (*People's Law No. 18*).

The ruling would be in effect until a national media policy could be formulated. Violators would receive a fine of E.C. $10,000 and/or a prison term of not more than three years. In implementing the law, government authorities had the power to search and seize property and equipment. "This afternoon, comrades, we have passed another law to keep them (the 'counterrevolutionaries') happy. Under this law, it is again made clear, this time in the kind of form that they like, that no newspaper is to be printed for the period of the next year until the media policy is formulated" (Bohning 1981).

Reorganization of Media

The PRG gradually changed mass communications along socialist lines, reorganizing and renaming older media as well as developing new ones related to unions, workers' organizations, and mass movements. In a speech in 1982, Bishop could point to eleven papers, the chief of which were the *New Jewel* and the *Free West Indian*. Others were the *Fight,* the *Women's Voice,* the *Pioneers Voice,* the *Cutlass,* the *Fork,* the *Media Workers Voice,* the *Workers Voice,* and the Armed Forces' *Fedon.*

In the first two years of the revolution, the *Free West Indian* did not appear regularly because of inadequate equipment. The result was that the tabloid *New Jewel* came closer to acting as the national daily. The six legal-sized, mimeographed pages of the *New Jewel* were topped by numerous mottoes over the nameplate, such as "Not Just Another Society, but a Just Society," "New Jewel for a United People!" "Let Those Who Labour Hold the Reins," and "Year of Education and Production." The stories contained very emotional writing, condemning, urging, chastising, and calling names. Slogans and opinions filled the news items and editorials, which denounced special favors, rumors, and, in the 26 April 1980 edition, a marijuana industry that supported Seaga's government in Jamaica. The *Free West Indian* appeared on a regular timetable in early 1981, and after receiving new press equipment as a gift of the East German government in 1982, expected to appear twice weekly (*Media Worker* 1982). The paper also received a government subsidy that provided 40 percent of its budget; the other 60 percent came from advertisers and subscribers.

Television Free Grenada, which grew out of Grenada Television, was purchased by the PRG in 1981. Before then, the station was poorly equipped, had a weak signal, and was almost devoid of local programming. In January 1981, fifteen youths began a training course to upgrade television; in April of that year, a series of local programs commenced, the first of which was a documentary (Ross 1982). Television Free Grenada was on the air from 6 to 10 P.M. Wednesday and Sunday and continuously during special events. The goals in 1982–1983 were to bring Television Free Grenada to all parts of the three islands of Grenada, Carriacou, and Petit Martinique by installing better transmitters and video screens in villages; to link Grenada to the Soviet Intersputnik system; and to arrange for the Soviet Union to provide films, radio tapes, documentaries, and a TASS, English-language news service on a daily basis.

Radio Free Grenada, on the air eighteen hours daily (another three hours on shortwave), also added equipment in 1982, opening a new 50-kw transmitter at Beausejour, which assured that the station's messages could reach all rural areas. The upgrading of the radio signal also was designed to transmit news of Grenada regionally and at the same time, to react to Caribbean press attacks upon Grenada (David 1982).

Two significant events in 1981–1982 launched by the Grenadian media were designed to have far-reaching effects upon internal and external media organization. On 11 July 1981, Radio Free Grenada, Television Free Grenada, the *Free West Indian,* and the Government Information Service set up the Media Workers Association of Free Grenada (MWAFG) to better working conditions, upgrade skills, and seek training (*Media Worker* 1981).

In launching the organization, Bishop, who seemed very prepared with a fifteen-page speech, discussed the need to stop the negative flow of information into Grenada, the "information monopoly" by the West, and the CIA timetable for the overthrow of the revolution. He warned that counterrevolutionaries among journalists would meet the same fate as four of the *Voice* editors (detained by authorities that morning) and that the road ahead for Grenadian journalists would be difficult as they countered lies from abroad, made messages relevant for the people, reflected grass-roots needs, and expressed news topics ignored by the other Caribbean media (Bishop 1981).

The proposed constitution of the MWAFG stated that the group (1) supports the revolutionary process started 13 March 1979; (2) firmly supports publicly owned media that reflect the interests and aspirations of the people; (3) strongly opposes the use of media by minority interests; and (4) condemns the monopoly of international flow of information by imperialism and multinational corporations and strongly supports moves towards the establishment of the New International Information Order. The MWAFG constitution also stated that "The Association condemns Imperialism, racism, apartheid, zionism, fascism and all forms of exploitation, and fully supports the national liberation movements of all the oppressed peoples of Africa, Asia, Latin America and the Caribbean."

Dedicated to the best interests of "progressive" media, the MWAFG aimed to foster high standards of professional and technical competence by improving members' abilities and by offering incentives such as scholarships and awards; to show recognition for meritorious work with the

Marryshow Prize and other awards; to promote unity, cooperation, goodwill, and activities in the public welfare; to seek "all avenues for training for its members" at home and abroad; to join with other forces in the struggle for the New International Information Order; and to encourage internal socialization through social activity. Membership was open to all media personnel, including foreign correspondents resident in Grenada. All officers were elected annually, and all members paid a "monthly subscription fee of 1 percent of gross salary" ("Draft Proposal for a Constitution" 1981).

The second important event occurred in April 1982, when the MWAFG, with support from the International Organization of Journalists (IOJ) and the Latin American Federation of Journalists (LAFJ), called together the "First Conference of Journalists from the Caribbean Area." It was attended by fifty-six journalists representing forty-one publications and seven "media organizations" from twenty-two countries. The conference considered the information flow in the Caribbean region; the social, economic, and political situation of Caribbean journalists; and the goal of creating national associations of journalists linked to LAFJ and IOJ. In another long speech (twenty-six legal pages), Bishop hit the falsehoods spread about Grenada through the Western media, blamed the existing world media structure, and called for a new order. He said that "propaganda destabilization" had been practiced on Grenada, and that Grenadians were exposed to a dozen radio stations and many newspapers that disseminated "blatant lies and disinformation as to create the screenplay for the most fantastic and vulgar of Hollywood melodramas, notwithstanding the remarkable record ex–Hollywood actors have sometimes seemed to demonstrate in that particular field of endeavour. . . . In fact, the absurdity of the propaganda caricature of Grenada has reached such a point of high farce and such levels of hallucination and absurdity as to have completely refuted itself" (Bishop 1982, 8).

The prime minister wondered why the big U.S. media spent so much space on tiny Grenada. He related how, after Caribbean editors had been invited to the United States by the U.S. International Communication Agency (USICA) in 1981, papers in the region had carried identical editorials negative to Grenada. He denounced USICA and the Inter American Press Association as twin enemies of democracy and the Trinidad newspapers as parts of big business enterprises spreading negative information about Grenada. Bishop called on the region's journalists to democratize their media in their own ways, to work for peace, to expose examples of imperialists threatening the area, and to fight concentration and monopoly ownership of Caribbean media (Bishop 1982, 8).

The conference declaration condemned U.S. military maneuvers in the region and information flow imbalances, adding, "There are also limitations at the national level where governments in some of our territories, through victimization, dismissals, censorship and other forms of pressure, inhibit journalists from making their full contribution to the development process." As examples of governments that took action against such victimization, racism, and censorship, the declaration commended Cuba and Grenada, as well as IOJ and LAFJ for their pursuit of peace, truth, and progress. The conference urged journalist organizations of the Caribbean to join IOJ and LAFJ and to "democraticize media," removing them from the control of private interests and placing them in "the hands and the service of our peoples." Additionally, the declaration supported the role UNESCO played in the establishment of the New International Information Order and recognized the "serious financial constraints" on nontraditional news services (CANA, Prensa Latina, and IPS) brought about by increasing telex feed (*Democratic Journalist* 1982).

U.S. OCCUPATION

After the United States invaded Grenada in October 1983, the Bishop mass media apparatus was disbanded and gradually replaced by the U.S.–supported *Grenadian Voice* and Spice Island Radio. Governor-General Sir Paul Scoon claimed the power to censor the media, and all freedoms of speech, press, and assembly were limited by the emergency declaration in effect for an unspecified time. The government strictly applied an old Gairy press law involving bonding and registration, but according to one Grenadian editor, it was not the restrictive law that Gairy had instituted—the posting of E.C. $20,000 (Interview, Hughes 1984). Rather, the 1984 law required the posting of a bond of E.C. $1,000 (U.S. $370) to cover libel damages and the registration of all publications with the Supreme Court. Some Grenadians believed that the law was aimed at the *Indies Times,* published by the Maurice Bishop Martyrs' Foundation. The government ordered seizure of any paper not registered by 1 May 1984.

The *Indies Times* registered and paid its bond but was stopped when the government-owned West Indies Publishing Company refused to print its 5 May issue. The following week, the paper used a private firm for its printing. Other papers with political views similar to those of the government continued to be printed by the state-owned company (*CPJ Update* 1984).

THE GRENADIAN

VOL. 3 NO. 27 Week ending Saturday July 14, 1984   PRICE $1.00

Reagan to visit Grenada?

SPECULATION has been rife in Grenada for sometime now on the subject of whether or not President Ronald Reagan would visit Grenada and the most likely date mooted has been October 25 which has been tipped as the date for the opening of the International Airport at Point Saline. Enquiries of American officials on the island have all elicited negative responses.

Now a Washington Times Editorial of Wednesday July 11 has indicated that a pre-election visit by the President is a possibility. The full editorial titled, "Remembering Grenada" is reprinted here by kind permission of

the Washington Times.

Being among the first to recommend a Presidential visit to Grenada, we are especially gratified to learn that Ronald Reagan may yet include it in his pre-election itinerary. Such a visit would be a powerful reminder of the first time in history that consolidated Marxist-Leninist regime was dislodged and its captive people liberated.

Mr. Reagan would be sure of an enthusiastic reception that would, among other things, give the lie to the canard-sedulously spread by Jesse Jackson and others -- that his administration is "anti-black".

American voters would be reminded that nearly the entire leadership of the Democratic Party condemned the Grenada mission while most Americans were applauding it -- the loudest applause coming from the hundreds of medical

PRESIDENT RONALD REAGAN

students rescued from the island. (A poll taken at the time revealed that 92 percent of the students felt the President did "the right thing".)

Gary Hart wailed that the Liberation of Grenada "invokes in the

minds of the world and the region a checkered history of US involvement and gunboat diplomacy." Walter Mondale denounced the President for acting "in violation of the most fundamental of all principles" and in such a way as to undermine "our ability to effectively criticize what the Soviets have done in... Afghanistan, in Poland, and elsewhere." But what Americans saw on television were American medical students kissing the ground in gratitude, and what they heard were excited crowds shouting, "God Bless America". If the President's schedulers

are looking for an appropriate date for the visit, we would suggest Oct. 25 the first anniversary of the mission. St. George's University School of Medicine, its "parent network," and the students themselves plan to unveil a permanent memorial that day, dedicated to the servicemen who died liberating Grenada. It will replace a hand-lettered marker reading, "in memory of the American soldiers who lost their lives here."

Our soldiers, Mr. President. Your soldiers, politics to one side, most Grenadians and most Americans would appreciate your being there.

Attempt to halt inquiry dismissed

MR JUSTICE Nedd Chief Justice of Grenada dismissed the application of Counsel for Bernard and Phyllis Coard which sought to halt the preliminary inquiry into murder charges against them while certain Constitutional questions were referred for judgement of the High Court.

Counsel for the Coards, Mr Clarence Hughes of Guyana made the submission under section 102 sub-section 1 of the Grenada Constitution which states that: "where any question as to the interpretation of this Constitution arises in any court of law ... and the Court is of the opinion

that the question involves a substantial question of law, the court shall refer the question to the High Court.

The application was for Writs of Mandamus and Prohibition against Magistrate Lyle St. Paul and DPP Velma Hylton who were represented by Mr. Karl Hud-

son-Phillips Q.C. Hudson-Phillips described the Application as a "fishing expedition" and argued that the appellants were "approbating and reprobating" and in effect using the Constitution to question its own validity and existence.

The Chief Justice dismissed the case on the grounds

that none of the 7 questions before him raised for which an interpretation of the Constitution was necessary before continuing with the preliminary inquiry into the murder charges against the Coards. He noted that, "It may well be that the applicants are entitled to receiving from

the High Court answers to the questions posed but not in the circumstances and not by adopting the procedure as adopted in the present case.

"This, he said amounted to an abuse of the Court and an attempt to stop the wheels of Justice turning, even temporarily.

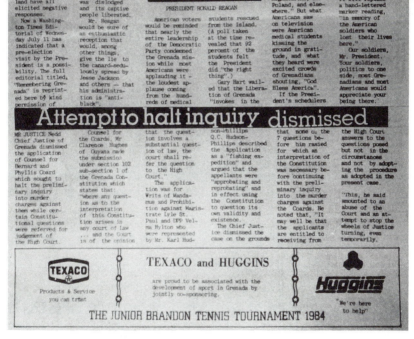
9.3 Pro–United States *Grenadian Voice,* which attempted publication under Bishop rule.

9.4 The *Indies Times,* a post-Bishop paper of the Maurice Bishop Martyrs' Foundation; the *Grenada Newsletter,* an anti-Bishop periodical that still survives; and the *New Jewel,* organ of the group that helped bring Bishop to power in Grenada.

Under the new government backed by the United States, the press accused of being CIA agents and exploiters of the people before were publicized as heroes. Such was the situation of Alister Hughes, for years editor of the mimeographed *Grenada Newsletter,* and Leslie Pierre, who along with Hughes and others published two issues of the *Grenadian Voice* in 1981. Both men had been imprisoned and were released at the time of the invasion. Hughes said that he had broken out of prison (Interview, Hughes 1984). Pierre revived the *Grenadian Voice* on 20 November 1983.

The low-budget weekly of sixteen pages—three devoted to letters—left no doubt at first as to its stance. It carried headlines such as "God Bless America, May the U.S. Heroes Rest in Peace" and stories discussing the "tyranical rule of Bishop." Gradually, the *Voice* returned to less emotional fare (Mydans 1984), although Pierre's views have remained decidedly pro–United States. He unsuccessfully campaigned for a Puerto Rico status for Grenada and for postponement of elections on the grounds that the people were not used to voting. The paper received support from the *Barbados Nation* and the *Trinidad Express.* The type of help included printing at low cost and the short-term loan of copy editors and business managers.

By 1987, the press of Grenada had seen the birth of the aforementioned *Voice,* the *Indies Times,* and the *Grenada Newsletter.* Other new papers included the *Informer,* a weekly operated by a private businessman; the *National,* owned by the ruling New National party and published weekly; the *Grenada Guardian,* a weekly owned by private individuals sympathetic to Gairy's Grenada United Labour party; the *New Guardian,* a Christian Democratic Labour party organ; the *Newsline,* a government official gazette; and the *New Grenadian,* started by a political activist who had been imprisoned by the Bishop government (Morales and Ballard 1985, 36). Both the *Informer* and the *Guardian* are published in Trinidad (Brown and Sanatan 1987).

Radio Grenada, controlled by the United States for some time, is the only broadcaster and is on the air nine hours daily. The postinvasion name, Spice Island Radio, was not popular, and the name was changed in January 1984. Transmission was the responsibility of the U.S. Army, the reason given being that spare parts could not otherwise be obtained for the 50-watt Soviet transmitter, damaged slightly in the 1983 invasion. Television, which under Gairy and Bishop included local programming, depends on a direct relay from Trinidad.

CONCLUSION

The period since Grenada became an independent nation has been turbulent and unsettling for political and social institutions, especially those of the mass media. Service under three different types of governments and philosophies and the many legislative and other infringements have left their imprint upon newspapers and broadcasting stations. The mass media had seemed to be on the verge of their most systematic organization in the two years before the U.S. occupation. Equipment had been slightly updated for better coverage, training had commenced, and media personnel had been organized under MWAFG. After 1982, Grenadian journalists had increasingly looked outward, attempting to unify other Caribbean media in much the same way Cuba had done earlier with cinema, seeking closer ties and aid from East European countries. These latter efforts were probably feared by other Caribbean governments and the United States as further evidence of the growth of communism in the area.

As for the claim that the revolution was hurt seriously by the government's procrastination to acknowledge the legitimacy of an opposition and to institute a promised constitution, some evidence shows that within a few months of the coup, Caribbean papers such as the *Jamaica Gleaner* and the *Trinidad Express* were already attacking Grenada in a way that echoed U.S. mass media. By May 1980, and escalating with Reagan's election, the U.S. coverage became "hostile and hysterical," using unsubstantiated reports, according to one source (EPICA 1982, 119). Perhaps Bishop's wondering why there was so much attention on tiny Grenada is the most important question, given that a more prolonged, probably more brutal, and almost unreported suppression of media had occurred under his predecessor, Eric Gairy.

10

Cuban Mass Media, 1723–1973

COLONIZATION

Compared with Spanish colonies elsewhere, Cuba was relatively late in developing a printing press, but compared with the rest of the Caribbean and Central America, it was early. As the seat of the captain-general, and through the efforts of Carlos Habré, Cuba had printing at least by 1723. The dominant printing house in Havana through the early nineteenth century was Imprenta de la Capitanía General, established in 1781. The following year, this shop published Cuba's newspaper, *Gazeta de la Habana* (the *Havana Gazette*), edited first by Diego de la Barrera and later by Francisco Seguí.[1] In 1790, the shop issued the first Cuban magazine, *Papel periódico de la Habana* (*Periodical Paper of Havana*). These early publications came into being under Spanish press laws that had been in place for Spanish America since about 1584 (Quesada 1917).

Among Cuban journalists in the nineteenth century, at least for five or six decades beginning in the 1830s, were the *costumbristas,* editorial essayists who wrote about Cuban customs and manners. Calling the essays "curious," "delightful," and "festive," Suárez-Murias (1980, 375) said that they were published in newspapers and literary magazines in both Havana and the provinces and appealed mostly to the middle classes, although they related to the society at large. She added that the essays, probably developed by José Victoriano Betancourt "expressed a strong civic concern about educating the *pueblo,* society at large." Betancourt's son, Luis, is credited with best portraying mid-nineteenth-century customs of Havana. Others prominent in this genre were Anselmo Suárez y Romero and Gaspar Betancourt Cisneros, the latter writing in *La gaceta de Puerto Príncipe* between 1838 and 1940.

During the same period, Havana's longest-lived and perhaps most conservative newspaper, *Diario de la marina* (the *Coast Daily*), was established in 1832. From its beginnings, *Diario* spoke for Spain and against revolution. Ferguson (1946, 18–19) said that the paper committed many unforgivable sins in its 128-year history: it denounced national hero José Martí as a foolish dreamer and Cuban generals Máximo Gómez and Antonio Macéo as bandits; it impugned the motives of the United States in declaring war against Germany in World War I; and it supported Mussolini as a bulwark against communism and also supported Franco in the Spanish civil war.

Contemporary Cuban press historians spend a great deal of time discussing the nationalist press of the latter nineteenth century because of its revolutionary nature. Looking at "clandestine working-class and revolutionary publications" in Cuba, an International Organization of Journalists (1976, 159) publication placed the history of Cuban media into four periods: the Ten Years' War from 1868 to 1878; the War of 1895; the Pseudo-Republican Era from 1902 to 1959; and the War of Liberation from 1952 to 1958. In 1869, during the first war of independence, the colonial government issued a press-freedom decree with the aim of winning over the reformist circles. In the succeeding months, however, a number of reformist periodicals sprang up. The most important was *El cubano libre* (the *Free Cuban*), edited by Carlos Manuel de Céspedes, which appeared on the first day of the war. Others were *La estrella solitaria* (the *Lone Star*), *El mambi,* and *El boletín de la guerra* (the *War Bulletin*) (see Rodríguez-Betancourt 1980, 18). Opposing these organs was *La voz de Cuba* (the *Voice of Cuba*), founded in 1870 as the paper of the *voluntarios* ("white man's terror league"). *La voz* printed diatribes against the patriots, including scurrilous attacks against women. An outraged Cuban killed the editor, Gonzalo Castañon, in a duel. An incident concerning Castañon after his death led to a threatening controversy at the time. A group of young people was overheard making derogatory remarks about the editor at his tomb. All forty-three were tried and acquitted, but, according to Ferguson (1946, 152), the *voluntarios* held a second trial, after which eight of the youth were shot and the rest imprisoned at hard labor.

In 1895, during the second war of independence, still other newspapers of *los reformistas* (the reformers) were prominent, the most significant being *Patria* (*Fatherland*), started in New York in 1892. José Martí, who had written for numerous newspapers and magazines, including *La nación* (the *Nation*) of Buenos Aires and the *New York Sun,* was the spark behind *Patria.* Ferguson (1946, 188) said of Martí's writing: "All Martí's prose was journalism, but according to Pedro Enríquez-Urena, it was 'journalism raised to an artistic level that has never been equaled in Spanish or probably in any other language. . . . The style he achieved was entirely new to the language . . . he shuns pedantic words, his syntax is full of unexpected but racy constructions.' "

After Martí's death in 1895, Enrique José Varona took over *Patria*. In 1895, *El cubano libre* was revived under General Antonio Macéo; still other patriot papers were *El productor* (the *Producer*), *La verdad* (the *Truth*), *La república* (the *Republic*), *Patria y libertad* (*Fatherland and Liberty*), *Alcance de la república* (*Latest News of the Republic*), *La libertad* (*Liberty*), and *Las villas* (The *Villages*) (International Organization of Journalists 1976, 159).

THE REPUBLIC

From the time of the establishment of the Republic of Cuba on 20 May 1902 until the early days of Castro's Revolution, the Cuban press was rich in number of titles. At least a dozen dailies existed in Havana at

10.1   Cuban national hero, José Martí, the spark behind *Patria,* a pro-independence paper begun in 1892.

any given time; often the number was more like twenty-one or twenty-two. Jorge Martí (1946, 124) attributed this large number to the ease of starting a newspaper, the existence of political parties as sponsors, and a strong economy. Perhaps another reason can be given for press prosperity, especially after 1928. In that year, the dictator, President Gerardo Machado, in an effort to subdue the press, issued subsidies in exchange for support. In addition, he also instituted censorship. After the economic crisis of 1929, Cuban newspapers did not fare well financially and many had to seek the government money. The situation deteriorated further when Machado was overthrown in 1933, leading to even more political instability. In the next two years, the papers suffered as strikes and lockouts forced most to close for brief periods and as government subsidies alternated with censorship as forms of control. Press professionalism reached a low point as underpaid journalists moonlighted for government agencies, and this, along with the subsidies, assured favorable coverage of the authorities. Martí (1946, 126–28) said that efforts were made in the early 1940s to upgrade the press. For example, after *El mundo* (the *World*), a morally and financially bankrupt daily, was taken over by Empresa Editorial El Mundo, S.A., the new publishers' first act was to refuse the government subsidy. Later, in 1943, *El mundo* informed its staff that they could not be officials in the government. In 1941, the Asociación de Reporters de la Habana (Reporters' Association of Havana) pulled together all press associations to discuss the state of journalism and called the first National Journalists' Congress in Havana. As a result, the journalists established a professional guild named Colegio Nacional de Periodistas (the National College of Journalists), a school of journalism, and a plan to reform retirement benefits. The school of journalism, created by presidential decree in April 1942, was in operation the next year under the Ministry of Education. It was funded entirely by the government. The guild, also set up by a presidential decree of 1942, began functioning in 1944. Prospective members of the guild had to have a certificate of competency from the school of journalism and had to swear to uphold eight rules of professional conduct (Martí 1946, 127). Although these actions seem laudatory on paper, it is doubtful that they did much to change media-government relationships, since they came about through presidential decree and received government funding.

During the presidencies of Ramón Grau San Martín and Carlos Prío (1944 to 1952), some criticism by the oppositionist party, Ortodoxo, was allowed, even though the government purchased a considerable amount of favorable press and broadcasting coverage. The leader of Ortodoxo, Senator Eduardo Chibás, exercised this right to criticize the government over CMO Radio Network and CMQ-TV until he killed himself in 1951. Alisky (1981, 156) claimed that the years 1949 to 1951 represented the nearest approach to a high point in press freedom after the republic was formed in 1902; given the less professional era before 1949, however, another writer claimed that the period had sensationalism of the worst type. García (1967), reporting on a content analysis of Cuban newspapers in 1950, 1955, 1960, and 1965, showed how the press progressively moved from a sensationalistic to a more informational and cultural state. In 1950, the six largest Havana dailies carried 17 percent national news, 7.2 percent international news, 25.5 percent advertising, 9.6 percent society news, and 40.7 percent sports and political propaganda.[2] In a 1960 sample of *Revolucíon* (*Revolution*), *Hoy* (*Today*), *Combate* (*Combat*), and *La calle* (the *Street*), national news and international news received the most coverage, 33 and 12.3 percent respectively. Sensationalism and advertising space were waning by 1960. In 1965, a study of *Granma, Juventud rebelde* (*Rebellious Youth*), and *El mundo* revealed that 40 percent was devoted to national news, 28 percent to international news, 22.3 percent to sports, and 9.7 percent to culture and ideology.

Countering the progovernment press during the republican era were some left-wing newspapers. As early as 1905, *La voz obrera* (*Labor's Voice*) appeared as an organ of the working class party. The first Marxist-Leninist paper was *Lucha de clases* (*Class Struggle*), started in 1924 and later renamed *Justicia* (*Justice*). The main paper of the Marxist-Leninist party became *El trabajadore* (the *Worker*), a clandestine organ started in 1931 and replaced by *Bandera roja* (the *Red Banner*). One of the longest lived was *Noticias de hoy* (*Today's News*), a daily begun in 1938, and closed at times by the government until it was suppressed in 1951. The paper reappeared after the 1959 Revolution (Vera 1979, 13); between 1953 and 1959, it was replaced by another underground paper, *La carta semanal* (the *Weekly Letter*). Still others were *El sentinela* (the *Sentinel*) (1934), intended for Communist cells in the army and navy; *Mella* (*Dent*) (1934), published by the International Workers' Defence; the daily *La palabra* (the *Promise*) and the periodicals *Mediodía* (*Midday*) and *Masas* (*Masses*). Underground publications had a high mortality rate because of government suppression.

Radio broadcasting in Cuba was introduced in September 1922 when Luis Casas Romero operated his amateur station, 2LC. The following month, RWX broadcasts were beamed to Cuba; the station was owned by the Telephone Company, a subsidiary of ITT. Radio developed quickly, and the stations of the 1930s were known to have good technical and production capacity. By the early 1940s, Cuban musical and serial dramas were distributed to other parts of Latin America, and later in the decade, large networks based on the North American model became prominent. One Cuban broadcasting analyst said that the peak of radio's golden age in Cuba was 1948, two years before television went on the air (Interview, Coro Antich 1982).

PRE-REVOLUTION, 1952–1959

Perhaps two different histories are required to describe Cuban mass media of the 1950s. One pertains to the very competitive newspapers and stations, most of which accepted bribes and subsidies of the government. The other concerns the guerrilla media that supported the aims of Fidel Castro.

No doubt exists about the competitiveness of the already established mass media. Zimmerman (1961, 97) reported that in 1953 Cuba had 559 periodicals and newspapers, while Alisky (1981, 157) described the Havana media of 1952 to 1958 as the most competitive market in the world, with twenty-one dailies of more than one million total circulation,[3] thirty-two commercial standard-band radio stations, and five television stations. Such stiff competition meant that all newspapers and broadcast stations were limited in growth, as any one medium could not grow huge enough to command large advertising budgets. The result fit into Fulgenicio Batista's plans once he resumed the presidency in a March 1952 coup. Batista preferred issuing bribes and subsidies to the media rather than using censorship. All twenty-one dailies in Havana reportedly received subsidies of varying amounts; fourteen small dailies existed on government subsidies; two dailies each in English and Chinese received some help, while the largest three, *Diario de la marina, El mundo,* and *Información* (*Information*), obtained support in the name of culture. Government subsidy helped *Información* to publish rotogravure sections and to maintain fine arts critics. Of fifty-eight Cuban newspapers in 1959, only six did not have government subsidies or advertising. Black (1976, 318) reported that in the last years of Batista, the government paid 200,000 pesos monthly to newspapers and 22,000 pesos monthly to individual journalists. Those papers of journalists who would not take bribes were pushed out by trumped-up taxes or by restrictions on necessary imports such as newsprint. In some cases, the media were owned outright by Batista. Alisky (1981, 157) wrote, "No press censorship was needed, for Batista had substituted the big carrot for the big stick."[4]

Yet, there were instances where Batista had to wield the big stick.

When he took power, Batista announced he would not tolerate the printing of "inflammatory material," and for the first time in Cuban history, he established a Ministry of Propaganda to watch over the media and to issue regular government news releases. Within a few months, the agency was renamed the Ministry of Information, and Batista, perhaps seeing the advantages of using positive reinforcements, said that the proceeds of two national lotteries would go for the benefit of the press association. Until 1957, he had imposed censorship at least three times — in 1955 against *La calle* for being "insolent" and in both April and June 1956 against the press generally after a weekend civilian revolt and unsuccessful attack on a military barracks. But as the Castro forces made some successful attacks in 1957, censorship became more regular and harsher. From 15 January to 27 February 1957, all newspapers were censored, and in June 1957, the *New York Times* was censored for carrying stories about Castro and his predictions of revolt. In mid-1957, as a general strike spread against his rule, Batista suspended civil rights, in the process muzzling the mass media, including foreign newsreels and TV film. Media portraying Castro were seized. In January 1958, twenty-five thousand copies of *Bohemia* featuring the rebel leader were picked up, some actually taken from customers' hands. The weekly magazine *Zig Zag* also was seized for carrying a Castro article. In February 1958, Batista lifted the severe censorship that had been in effect for six months. Censorship continued in Oriente Province, where rebel fighting continued. However, the following month, the jittery Batista suspended all constitutional rights, including freedom of expression (*Editor and Publisher,* 2 July 1955).

Similar generalizations can be made about broadcasting during the last seven-year reign of Batista. In some areas, however, broadcasting continued as a thriving institution, independent and even pioneering.

Cuba had been known for taking independent and innovative stands since 1937, when, during a frequency dispute, an allotment of North American broadcasting channels by the North American Regional Broadcasting Conference omitted the island republic. As a result, Cuba went its own way, causing claims of interference to be made by six hundred standard-band U.S. stations (Jordan 1952, 362). On 9 August 1950, a presidential decree made Cuba the world's first country to have a right-to-reply-to-radio law. The targets of the legislation were the radio commentators — favorites of listeners — whose shows were known as "radio newspapers" or "newspapers on the air" and who often made violent accusations against individuals (Jordan 1952, 358).

Cuba was also one of the first four Latin American countries to have television. Experimental television was on the air in November

1949, and regular programming started the following January under the Unión Radio y Televisión. By 1958, the country had four stations in Havana and one in the province of Camagüey (Otero 1980), with twenty-seven transmitters and a total 150.5kw power. The stations, like those of radio, were predominantly owned privately; they broadcast an average of 9.56 hours daily on three national channels. The number of television sets was estimated at 365,000 in early 1959 (Vera 1979, 15).

During Batista's administration, the broadcast stations often had ties to the leadership through bribes or ownership. For example, one radio station, Circuito Nacional Cubano, was owned by Batista's son-in-law. Many broadcasters smoldered under the "petty repressions" of Batista censors (Redding 1971, 36).

Despite Batista's heavy hand, the opposition press (in some cases, underground) consisted of an assortment of publications ranging from a stenciled-page newssheet to full-sized newspapers. Some of the early newspapers were student organs. In 1952, a cyclostyled paper, *Son los mismos* (*They Are the Same Ones*), and *El acusador* (the *Accuser*) were started and used by Castro to denounce Batista's government. After an unsuccessful coup in early 1953, the Federation of University Students reissued *Alma Mater;* the federation was also responsible for *Boletín 13 de marzo* (March 13 Bulletin), issued in Havana, Tampa, New York, and Sierra del Escambray. Still other oppositionist publications were *Mella,* a magazine of the Socialist youth since 1944, which went underground during Batista's reign; *La carta semanal,* which became the illegal paper of the militants of the Popular Socialist Party after *Hoy* was shut down as a reprisal for the attack on the military barracks of Moncada; and *La calle.* These publications helped to air Castro's views until his exile to Mexico in 1955.

When Castro and eighty-two followers landed in Cuba again on 2 December 1956, they already had organs to represent their viewpoints. The Revolutionary Movement of the 26th of July had published since 30 November its official organ, *Boletín informativo* (*Information Bulletin*), which was later issued as *Ultimas noticias* (*Latest News*) and then as *Sierra Maestra.* Immediately upon the landing of Castro's boat, the *Granma,* the movement started *Revolución,* which appeared as its national paper. The Movement of the 26th of July also published *Vanguardia obrera* (the *Workers' Vanguard*), which directed organizational and propaganda work among workers, and *Surco* (the *Furrow*), started by the Frank País Second Front (International Organization of Journalists, 1976, 161). Still other papers were *Aldabonazo* (*Knocker's Stroke*), *Sujo,* and *El cubano libre,* resurrected in the Sierra Maestra by Ernesto (Ché) Guevara, who wrote for it under the pseudonym of

10.2   Cyclostyled *Son los mismos* and *El acusador,* employed by Castro in 1952 to oppose the Batista government.

Franco Tirado. *El cubano libre* had the same patriotic fervor that characterized it in earlier lives in 1868 and 1895. Also under Guevara's guidance was *Patria,* the official organ of the Revolutionary Army in Las Villas, and *Milicianos* (*Militiamen*), the periodical of the militiamen of the Movement of the 26th of July in Las Villas. Both were printed in the offices of the Commander of Unit No. 8 Ciro Redondo in Caballete de Casa, Las Villas (International Organization of Journalists 1976, 161).

The rebel forces understood the need for a radio transmission to acquaint the population about their aims and accomplishments. On 24 February 1958, Ché Guevara started Radio Rebelde (7RR) in the mountains of Sierra Maestra (see Radio Havana Cuba 1982; Martínez Victores 1978); soon the modest, clandestine station became the keystone of Castro's propaganda efforts. Although the transmitter was small and dilapilated, the studio a grass shack, and the signal barely audible, Radio Rebelde became important enough to be monitored by U.S. news organizations, Cuban citizens, and guerrilla units. Besides informing the citizenry of actions fought by rebel forces, the station also denied Batista information and was used as a link and a rallying force for guerrilla

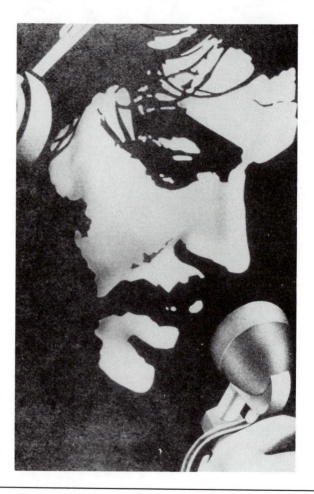

10.3   Ché Guevara started Radio Rebelde in February 1958 as a clandestine station of the revolution.

units. In battle, Radio Rebelde used loudspeakers to demoralize Batista soldiers (Internation Organization of Journalists 1976, 161). At other times, when rebels suffered losses, announcers appealed to doctors to come to the mountains to render medical aid. When military units were separated, 7RR (and later, other clandestine stations) kept them appraised of one another's activities. The station was also used to transmit personal messages from guerrillas to families: "Mama, this is Pepita. Don't worry, I'm fine" (Nichols 1979, 6).

As Batista's censorship became harsher, more people tuned to Radio Rebelde to hear the suppressed news, and it became one of the most listened-to stations in the Caribbean. As Nichols noted, "Each night, a growing number of Cubans would tune in to the station and hear a barrage of reports of guerrilla victories, manifestos, patriotic poems and music. Castro frequently polished his oratorical skills over the air, and by the time the revolutionaries took control of the government he had refined his ability to the point that many analysts considered him the world's greatest political speaker of the era" (1982a, 258). Others followed the lead of Radio Rebelde, and within a few months, twenty other clandestine stations operated (Vera 1978, 19).

THE REVOLUTION

Upon his triumph, Fidel Castro quickly restructured, and otherwise used, the mass media to promote the aims of the Revolution. In January 1959, an assembly of Latin American journalists was held in Havana, at which time Prensa Latina was established as a news agency to counter the messages of the international news services (Carty 1981, 26). The same year, the Cuban government created Casa de las Américas to promote and consolidate book publishing and Cuban literature, the Cuban Institute of Cinematographic Art and Industry (ICAIC) to initiate the development of a culturally organized, high-quality film industry to serve the purposes of mass education and mobilization, and a Cuban broadcast institute.

Initially, most editors and publishers hailed Castro's victory. Rather soon, however, some editors began to disagree with the new government, and mildly outspoken papers, such as *Prensa libre* (*Free Press*), *Diario de la Marina,* and *Avance* (*Advance*), became targets of Castro's invective (usually during his television appearances). They were pressured by threats that they would be killed with anemia through a boycott of their advertisers (Szulc 1959). Although there was no overt censorship in 1959 and the few privately owned newspapers had considerable latitude to criticize Castro (Nichols 1982a, 257), there was government reaction. Castro had learned from the previous government that an effective means of dealing with the media was to tie their purse strings. Thus, through expropriation, discontinuance of subsidies, withholding of government advertising, and encouraging independent advertisers to do the same, Castro began to starve out the opposition. Immediately upon assuming power, Castro stopped all press subsidies except those to *Revolución*. In his first month in power, he expropriated under the Law for the Recovery of Illegally Acquired (Stolen) Property, the newspapers *Alerta* (*Alert*), *Mañana* (*Tomorrow*), *Tiempo* (*Times*), *Ataja* (*Intercept*), and *Pueblo* (*People*). The grounds for takeovers were that these papers had been subsidized by Batista. The *Alerta* plant was used to publish *Revolución,* while the other four papers were renamed *Noticias de hoy, La calle, Combate,* and *Diario libre* (*Free Daily*) (Black 1976, 319). Periodicals sympathetic to Castro were allowed to thrive. For example, although the Popular Socialist party (PSP) was not Castro's party, its daily, *Hoy,* began to publish larger issues in a new plant after May 1959. In August of that year, PSP's youth magazine, *Mella,* also acquired its own printing shop and by April 1960 claimed a circulation of thirty thousand (Farber 1983, 70).[5]

In its first year in power, the Castro government attempted to innovate in control mechanisms. For example, a law was proposed to tax individuals mentioned in society news. The tax would have levied one dollar on any person mentioned, to be increased proportionately for every adjective used to describe the person. Photographs would be taxed five dollars per column inch. The government said that such a tax would drastically reduce other taxes, but it withdrew the proposal when there was opposition (Phillips 1959b; 1959c). In November 1959, La Habana Province Journalists' Guild passed a resolution that in effect allowed printers to edit as well as to set type. The resolution authorized postscript comments (*coletillas*) to be appended to any article or broadcast considered unfriendly to the government. Thus, an editorial might carry a postscript: "The contents of this article do not conform to the truth, nor to the most elemental journalistic ethics" (Black 1976, 318). Alisky (1981, 158) said that the pro-Castro printers' unions kept up the offensive against the anti-Castro staffs of *Diario de la marina, Avance,* and others until the Ministry for the Recovery of Illegally Acquired Property could confiscate them. Describing the *coletilla,* another author wrote:

> [Critical papers] invariably add a "coletilla" or clarifying footnote disclaimer, which has been imposed with complete government concurrence by government-controlled unions. That disclaimer states in

effect that the article is being published to prove that Cuba has a free press but that the unions, also in the exercise of "freedom of the press" declare that the article is factually incorrect, is a violation of journalistic ethics, an attack, and forms a part of a plot, against the Cuban revolution (Brown 1960).

Eventually, the National Collegium of Journalists and trade unions refused to print anti-Castro editorials (Szulc 1960).

The existing press in 1959 suffered from lack of access as Castro spent more time with television. Newspapers were given little or no information during times of crises, and when they picked up news through secondary sources, they were criticized for being unprofessional. The foreign press was continually attacked, and from 1959 to 1961, a number of foreign newsmen were jailed or expelled (Phillips 1959a).

By mid-1961, the privately owned press of Cuba ceased to exist. One source claimed that the number of papers was cut because they all represented the same national interests, and after the U.S. economic blockade, they could not survive for lack of supplies (Vera 1978, 21). *El mundo* was seized and operated by the government; in May 1960, *Diario de la marina* was taken over by two labor unions. By February 1961, six papers remained in Havana: *Revolución, El mundo, La calle, Combate,* and *Prensa libre,* all semiofficial papers, and *Noticias de hoy,* the PSP paper. But the press situation was to tighten even more in November when *La calle, Combate,* and *Prensa libre* merged to become *Diario de la tarde* (the *Afternoon Daily*). Later in 1965, *Revolución* and *Noticias de hoy* also merged to become *Granma,* the official organ of the Central Committee of the Cuban Communist party, and *Diario de la tarde* was converted into *Juventud rebelde,* an organ of the Union of Communist Youth. *Revolución*'s demise had far-reaching implications for the Cuban media; perhaps one of the most important was that some writers who wrote for the paper, such as Carlos Franqui and Guillermo Cabrera Infante, left Cuba. *El mundo,* which claimed autonomy in the mid-1960s and until 1967 carried classified advertising, was used as part of the University of Havana journalism course in 1968 and the following year was merged with *Granma* (Black 1976, 319).

In the early 1960s, then, the revolutionary government, through "intimidation, expropriation and increased economic pressure," gained control or ownership over print and broadcast media and introduced the Marxist media philosophy. Castro's dictum — "for those within the Revolution, complete freedom; for those against the Revolution, no freedom" — guided media contents. Yet, as Nichols (1982a, 258) and others have pointed out, considerable debate existed in the Cuban press, especially between *Hoy* and *Revolución,* over the future direction of the Revolution (see Alisky 1981, 158).

The role of broadcasting in the initial stages of the Revolution cannot be overstated.[6] Because of their advanced development and pervasiveness, and Castro's awareness of their preciousness from his guerrilla days, radio and television were used constantly to exhort people to produce more, to rail against "Yankee imperialism," to build the cult of personality of the leadership, and to forge an alliance between the urban middle class and rural poor (Nichols 1979, 8). One writer in 1961, reporting that Castro used to broadcast at least three times weekly to the people, said that if he lost his voice, the Revolution would fail in two months (Phillips 1961a). Others termed Castro's rule "government by television," as he mesmerized audiences for four to six hours at a time, describing all details, no matter how insignificant, of the Revolution. Other analysts believed that Castro's broadcasts may have helped prevent bloodshed in the early days of the Revolution by "letting people stay at home and watch the revolution on television instead of going out in the streets" (Redding 1971, 36).

In the early days of the Revolution, punitive reprisals were taken against stations with ties to Batista; thus, Circuito Nacional Cubano (Cuban National Circuit), which was owned by Batista's son-in-law, Union Radio Network, and Reloj de Cuba (Clock of Cuba) were expropriated. Initially, the Communications Ministry assured that expropriated stations would be sold at public auction, that a new broadcast law would be written, that the rest of the radio and television stations would be retained by their original owners, and that there were no plans to nationalize broadcasting. The government expressed a concern for the need for educational broadcasting as Castro continued to use the media to indoctrinate, reaching as much as 95 percent of the population by August 1959.

But as Castro began to accuse the media of being enemies of the Revolution in the last quarter of 1959 and in early 1960, the final phase of the takeover of broadcasting started. In February 1960, Cuba-Telemundo Network was seized and renamed Televisión Revolución; this was followed by a takeover of Channel 12 (renamed Revolutionary Channel) and, in September, another takeover of Goar and Abel Mestre's CMQ-TV, the largest network, with stations in five cities. CMQ-TV reportedly was worth U.S. $12 million when it was confiscated. Phillips (1961b) said that there was no compensation paid to the original owners. All television outlets were incorporated into an organization called Televisora Nacional. By August 1960, the government controlled 43 of the 88 independent and 75 network-affiliated AM stations, 18 of the 24 FM stations, and 23 of the 24 television outlets. All stations were incorporated into a new network, the Independent Federation of Free Radios (FIEL), for the purpose of consolidating the Revolution and orienting the public. Eventually, Televisora Nacional and FIEL were put directly under Communist control.

Control also came in other forms. After May 1960, a regular TV program on Friday, "The Fidel Show," was broadcast, and in 1960, policies were set concerning other content. Earlier, commercial time had been curtailed and sexual overtones eliminated, and in 1961 the numerous soap operas were reduced to just two, "both pure in indoctrination" (Phillips 1961b). Films showed revolutionary progress, and critical commentaries had to carry *coletillas* similar to those in the press. Foreign shows, such as "Donald Duck" and some others, were used on television as the government beefed up plans to produce more domestic programs.[7] However, certain foreign content was banned, such as "cowboy and Indian" westerns and shows depicting blacks as primitive Africans. In both cases, Castro said that the people were stereotyped as savages. Many broadcasters were fired in the early 1960s as a security witch-hunt escalated after a former CMQ news department employee, accused of being a CIA agent, was executed in March 1964. Trials of many Cubans indicted as enemies of the Revolution were carried live on radio and television.

In February 1961, Cuba began international broadcasts to counter the anti-Communist propaganda beamed to the island from many sources. For example, from mid-1960, the CIA's Radio Swan was on the air with anti-Castro materials. The Cuban government purchased several 120-kw transmitters from a Swiss firm and inaugurated Radio Habana Cuba on 1 May 1961; part of its purpose was to urge Latin American people to overthrow their pro-U.S. governments. By 1963, Cuba was fourth among Communist international broadcasters, and by mid-1965, the country beamed more than 150 hours a week in six languages to Latin America alone (Redding 1971, 41). A director of Radio Habana Cuba said that the emphasis on Latin America was to enable Cubans to share their reality with their neighbors (Interview, Prado 1982). Others, especially Radio Progreso, began overseas broadcasts; Radio Progreso broadcast to the black population of the southern United States with an English-language program, "Radio Free Dixie." After 1963, Cuba also responded to U.S. interference by starting electronic jamming of U.S. stations (Frederick 1982).

Along with its other achievements, the government promoted professionalization of media personnel, and the Unión de Periodistas de Cuba (UPEC) was formed in July 1963 for the improvement of journalists politically, ideologically, culturally, and technically. The first journalism school was started the same year at the University of Havana;[8] in 1969, another school was started at the University of Oriente. UPEC's goals were set in 1966 when the Second Congress of Cuban Journalists charged the organization with systematizing both the general education of journalists and their specialized training on fundamental aspects of Cuban economic production; teaching each journalist a second language by 1970; structuring the education of correspondents in the interior; promoting interchange among reporters on certain aspects of professional practice; allowing journalists to attend university courses and setting up correspondence schools for them; and providing better cultural and ideological facilities. By 1967, UPEC developed a Seminary of Professional Education with twenty-two sessions in six months for any active journalist (*Democratic Journalist* 1967, 80).

After resolving the ideological conflict between the revolutionary Ché Guevara and the old-line, Soviet-style Communists, Cuba entered a five-year period of "international isolation, economic hardship and considerable repression," from which it emerged in 1975 (Nichols 1982a, 259). The move from isolationism was evident in broadcasting when, in 1975, Cuban stations decided to lift the 1973 ban on American and British pop music, recognizing the futility of this policy with Miami stations so near.

The contemporary era that resulted saw numerous social gains based on *poder popular* (people's power) that were intended to communicate the needs of masses to higher echelons of government. The media were to serve as channels for citizens' complaints about the tactical operation of government. Perhaps an indication of this press role-change was *Granma*'s initiation of the letters-to-the-editor column ("A vuelta de corréo") on 24 June 1974. Studying the first two years of those letters, Rodríguez (1978) found that they rarely were printed verbatim; instead, they were excerpted, explained, and reported by an editor who usually gave the writer's name and address. Editors reported the subjects of the letters with a "wide margin of rhetorical interpretive freedom" (Rodríguez 1978, 53). Of 389 topics covered in 166 columns between 1974 and 1976, 141 (36 percent) dealt with negative items in society, 38 (10 percent) with positive, and 210 (54 percent) with information or service/favor-demanding items. The first few columns gave *Granma* suggestions for stories, and throughout 1974 and January 1975, readers wrote about irregularity in pricing, availability of services, and bureaucratic processes. Editors responded by consulting appropriate authorities, printing their recommendations, and doing some investigative work of their own. Rodríguez concluded that "the column can be useful . . . as an instrument of transmission for 'revolutionary themes' and values to be internalized, and as an effective component of the government's strategy to capitalize on and sustain manifested degrees of revolutionary 'climate' and orientation from below."

The emphasis on *poder popular* emanated from the First Congress of the Communist Party in 1975, which drew up the Cuban constitution. Delegates challenged the mass media to criticize certain aspects of society, adding the limitation that "criticism through mass media must strictly observe the constructive and fraternal nature which is the overriding characteristic of criticism under socialism" (Carty 1978a). Another congress resolution said that journalists should "devote special attention to the development of a truly revolutionary and socialist style in the use of the various forms and techniques of expression. It should be free from sensationalism, superficialities, tendencies to find easy ways out, imitation of decadent trends of the capitalist world, and concessions to bad taste and vulgarity" (quoted in Carty 1978a). Later in the decade, the Central Committee of the Communist party again called for self-evaluation of all individuals and groups in a 3,500-word document published in *Granma,* "About the Strengthening of the Exercise of Criticism in the Medium of Mass Communications." The document accused the press of not providing adequate evaluation of society because staff members do not have the subject-specialization knowledge needed to be critics. Party and government officials were told to provide documents to journalists and to answer their questions frankly and fully; party organizations were reminded they are the most important sources of exposés of deficiencies and of orienting the press about problems; and individuals were encouraged to express their knowledge of personnel deficiencies in letters to the editors of *Granma, Juventud rebelde,* and *Bohemia* (Carty 1980).

To provide the qualified journalists, another push at upgrading professional standards was made in the mid-1970s. For example, in 1973, UPEC established an annual congress at which awards were given for reporting achievements; at the third UPEC congress in 1975, 2,300 journalists were honored. In broadcasting, an interesting training scheme resulted from the establishment of Radio Victoria de Girón (RVG) in September 1977. RVG, developed to unite isolated rural areas, was staffed by young people selected from "circles of interest." Staff selection, which started in seventh grade, allowed students six years of experience; however, they had to achieve "consistently satisfactory results" to stay in broadcasting. Fifty-six "circles of interest" (similar to staffs) were set up, one for each educational institution in the area, and the students worked under the guidance of professional broadcasters. RVG monitored and reported on the progress of the citrus cultivation plan of the region, stimulated enthusiasm and competition among brigades in harvesting and plant care, and offered criticism as an incentive to improve quality and output (Urivazo 1982, 388–93).

There were a few remaining structural changes in the 1970s. *Los trabajadores,* the organ of the working people's trade union, was converted to daily status, and five additional Cuban provinces developed newspapers. Two television stations merged to form the Telerebelde network, and color television compatible with NTSC, SECAM, and PAL systems came into being. After these changes, the mass media in Cuba settled down to the situation of today.

11

Contemporary Media of Cuba

STRUCTURE AND FUNCTION

By the time the Revolution celebrated its quarter century in the early 1980s, the mass media structure had evolved into three national dailies (*Granma, Juventud rebelde,* and *Los trabajadores*), a daily for each of Cuba's fourteen provinces, and a number of periodicals to serve specific needs and audiences. In broadcasting, there are now fifty-four radio stations and three television-originating stations, plus fifteen provincial, program-originating centers, all under the supervision of the Instituto Cubano de Radio y Televisión (ICRT) (Interview, Coro Antich 1982). A prolific film industry, under the aegis of Instituto Cubano del Arte e Industria Cinematográficos (ICAIC), has produced yearly eight to ten features, forty-five documentaries, fifty-two newsreels, and ten animated films (Address, Alvarez 1982). Additionally, Cuba has a news service, Prensa Latina, serving about one thousand clients with articles in three languages; a number of external media, topped by Radio Habana Cuba, broadcasting sixty hours daily in eight languages over twenty frequencies (Interview, Prado 1982); and a thriving book publishing industry, which, epitomized by Casa de las Américas, has produced 11,800 titles and more than 360 million copies since the early 1960s. Professionalism, training, and research are promoted by the Unión de Periodistas de Cuba (UPEC), a body of more than twenty-seven hundred member journalists, and its arm, Centro Estudios Medios Difusión Massivos (CEMEDIM); by the Union of Writers and Artists of Cuba (UNEAC); and by the journalism school at the University of Havana.

Functionally, the Cuban mass media have been affected by occasional shifts in the ideology and philosophy of the Revolution and by guidance statements by Fidel and other ministers. Throughout the Revolution, cultural policy and the role of the mass media have been closely entwined. For example, Fidel Castro's statement at a cultural seminar in 1961 — "For those within the Revolution, complete freedom; for those against the Revolution, no freedom" — was meant to apply equally to all parts of the intellectual community, including the mass media. At other times, the mass media have been specifically mentioned; for example, at the 1971 National Congress on Education and Culture, it was declared that "radio, television, cinema and press are precious instruments for ideological formation and for creation of a collective conscience. The mass media cannot be left to chance or be used without directives" (Black 1976, 320). Later, when the state defined cultural policy at the aforementioned First Congress of the Cuban Communist Party in 1975, the first paragraph of the resolution included the mass media, stating that they should become an "organic part of the assembly of institutions, responsible with [*sic*] the political-ideological, moral and aesthetic education of the people and carry on the mission of complementing the process of direct communication with the masses" (González-Manet 1982, 7). The same congress adopted a constitution, article 52 of which guaranteed that "Citizens have freedom of speech and of the press in keeping with the objectives of socialist society. Material conditions for the exercise of that right are provided by the fact that the press, radio, television, movies and other organs of the mass media are state or social property and can never be private property. This assures their use at the exclusive service of the working people and the interest of society" (*Constitution,* n.d.).

The First Congress called on the media to popularize Marxist-Leninist ideology, party lines, aims of socialism, and activities of mass organizations and to criticize all areas of social development (see chapter 10). As indicated previously, the ideal type of journalism should be "free from sensationalism, superficialities, tendencies to find easy ways out, imitation of decadent trends of the capitalist world, and concessions to bad taste and vulgarity" (Communist Party, Cuba 1981; also, Carty 1978a).

At various congresses of UNEAC, Culture Minister Armando Hart Dávalos, outlining the expected development of the culture industry, has also elaborated upon the role of the mass media. At the 1982 congress, for example, he reiterated that "artistic creativity is free as long as its content is not contrary to the Revolution"; he called for a closer relationship of writers to the working class and said that radio and television play a large role in shaping the artistic tastes of the masses (Hart 1982, 5).

Some of the tasks of the Cuban mass media are to state and advance government policies, objectives, and official positions; to report news, information, and entertainment; and to mobilize and influence behavior by featuring exemplary individuals or mass organizations (Milner 1979). Alisky (1981, 156) said that another function is to help the government make its foreign positions known internationally and to be understood by specific governments.

The functions have been carried out effectively because of a symbiosis between the media and officials and because of mass organization support. Nichols explained that media policymakers are aligned with the goals of the Revolution partly because at least a third of them have "at least one significant affiliation with the Cuban power structure" (Nichols 1982b, 11). He also reported that 41.6 percent of Cuban journalists belong to either the Communist party or the Communist Youth Union; only the armed forces officers have a higher percentage of membership (Nichols 1982b, 13). The main organization support that aids and complements the mass media comes through the Committees for the Defense of the Revolution (CDRs) and voluntary correspondents. The CDRs, called a "capillary" system organized by blocks in cities and by groups of homes in rural areas, were initiated in September 1960. By 1980, five million Cubans, or more than 80 percent of those over fourteen years of age, were organized into CDRs (Fagen 1969). The editor of *Granma Weekly Review* called the CDRs the "main means of getting communications in and out of mobilizing the people." He said that if the "newspapers went away, Cuba would still have strong communications" and gave an example: "Let's say we're going to have an anti-mosquito campaign. The national authorities through public health would go to the CDRs to get the campaign going. Within twelve hours, all the CDRs would be killing mosquitos" (Interview, Benitez 1982).

A chief information officer in the Central Committee of the Communist party, claiming Cuba's goal is the "real participation of the masses in the revolutionary process," showed how CDRs exemplify this goal while complementing the mass media: "The propaganda, for example, says you must save bottles for the Revolution. The CDRs help do this at local levels. TV supports the campaign to recycle with a spot announcement. We ask a government minister to go to a TV program to talk about bottle saving. Then, we send a reporter to interview the CDR who saved the most bottles and run that in the press" (Interview Margolles Villanueva 1982). Nichols (1982b) showed how CDRs have been effective in audience research, stating that they can reach the homes of 170,000 Cubans fifteen minutes after a broadcast to find out listenership.

Voluntary correspondents also play an important media role. They are recruited, organized, and trained by members of the Unión de Periodistas de Cuba (UPEC). Throughout the country, about ten thousand individuals submit news items to the media "about where they work or the town where they live" (Interview, Benitez 1982).

PRINT MEDIA

Newspapers

Cuba's three national dailies have a combined circulation of more than 1.2 million and represent national-level policy. Together they overwhelm the rest of the press. Of the dailies in the provinces in the late 1970s, the largest, *Sierra Maestra,* had a circulation of 43,000, and the smallest, *Venceremos,* 3,500; the total circulation of the provincial papers was about 150,000 (Carty 1978a; International Organization of Journalists 1976, 162). Published by party committees of the provinces, these dailies are closely modeled after *Granma,* although they are given greater leeway to comment on local affairs than the national papers have to comment on national issues (Nichols 1982a, 260).

Of the national dailies, *Granma* is the largest and most important. The official organ of the Central Committee of the Communist party of Cuba, *Granma* has a circulation of 700,000. The eighty journalists of *Granma* are divided into six departments—national news, international news, sports, economics, culture, and ideology; additionally, there are fourteen correspondents (one per province) and hundreds of volunteers. At 3 P.M. daily, the heads of the departments meet to decide which of about two hundred news dispatches will make up the news for the following day's editions. They are guided partly by the yearly objectives prescribed for the media by the congress of the Communist party; in 1982, the goals were to increase educational incentives and to provide the masses with "more opportunity to rise" (Interview, Benitez 1982). The six-page daily normally includes two and one-half pages of national news (including page one); one and one-half pages of international news; and one-half page each of sports, culture, ideology, and economics. Citizen feedback, self-criticism, and societal criticism are important functions of *Granma* and other dailies, according to José Benitez, a *Granma* editor. He said that the feedback comes from letters to the editor, instituted in mid-1974 (see Rodríguez 1978) as a type of consumer column, and from the CDRs, adding, "We send reporters to places where readers complain about something. Also, the CDRs at the local level listen to the people and pass this information up to us" (Interview, Benitez 1982). Although being a self-critic (along with agitator, propagandizer, and organizer) is part of the ideology, Cuban newspapers were slow in accepting this role, prompting First Vice President Raúl Castro in March 1980 to call for more press criticism (Nichols 1982c, 9). Later that year, Fidel Castro also showed the need for criticism and self-criticism. Alisky (1981, 163) believed there is a hidden reason for the criticism: "By allowing some critical aspects of local government to be reported, the national administration can divert frustrations that might otherwise be felt towards the central government to the local level."

Besides the daily, *Granma* has a rural paper, *Granma campesino,* and weekly editions in Spanish (100,000 circulation), English (60,000), and French (50,000) for overseas audiences. A Portuguese edition is planned.

Juventud rebelde, the lively organ of the Cuban youth, has an evening circulation of 260,000 and 300,000 on Sunday. The paper traces its history to 1965, when at a mass youth rally Fidel promised young people their own newspaper. The name was decided at the same assembly. The problems *Juventud rebelde* faced were those common to Cuban journalism then and, in at least the first case, now: lack of supplies because of the U.S. embargo, especially newsprint and spare parts for the predominantly North American equipment; inadequately trained staff; and low literacy and cultural levels of the population (Interview, Grande 1982).

Delineating the difference between *Juventud rebelde* and *Granma,* the director of the youth daily said that his paper was more interesting because it can publish jokes or pictures of beautiful actresses, which the party daily does not do. *Juventud rebelde* publishes three issues a week of four pages, two issues of six pages, and the Sunday edition of eight pages. A typical issue has international news on page one and devotes one-half page each to sports and culture on the second page. The other pages include stories of young people studying, letters from youth, economic development news, comics, and humor. In fact, the paper issues a weekly humor supplement, *De De Té,* of biting political cartoons. Other features include a section on sexual education published on Sunday, "Hello Girl" for young women, a debate column, and popular music stories. The paper includes on its staff both a psychologist and a sociologist, whose jobs it is to survey the readership for story ideas (Interview, Grande 1982).

The third daily is *Los trabajadores,* organ of the Confederación de Trabajadores de Cuba, which, by contrast, has a very bland appearance.

Magazines and Books

Most mass organizations and divisions of the party and government publish their own periodicals, and it is estimated at least one hundred such publications exist. Among some of the more important national periodicals are the weekly *Verde olivo,* an organ of the Revolutionary Armed Forces, with a circulation of 100,000; *Revista Bohemia,* the oldest periodical (since 1908), with one of the largest circulations (257,000); *Mujeres,* a monthly organ of the Cuban Women's Federation and the largest, with 273,000 circulation; and *Pionero,* an organ of the José Martí Pioneer Organization, with a circulation of 225,000. Still others are devoted to youth, *El caimán barbudo* (The *Bearded Crocodile*) and *Somos jóvenes* (*We Are Young*); to humor, *Palante* (*Forward!*), 225,000 circulation, and *De De Té;* to farmers, *Revista ANAP;* to CDRs, *Con la guardia en alto* (*With the Guard Above*); to the Ministry of the Interior, *Revista moncada;* to women, *Romances;* to sports, *El deporte;* to the Ministry of Foreign Affairs, *Política internacional;* and to the Ministry of the Sugar Industry, *Cuba azúcar.* In each case, the sponsoring organization is responsible for staffing, editorial policy, and operation (Vera 1979). Nichols (1982b, 7) reported that because of the diversification of control of the periodical press and its insulation from direct supervision, most magazines enjoy "greater latitude to comment on political issues."

The book industry is organized under the Ministry of Culture with ten publishing houses sharing printing, editorial, and distribution responsibilities. The largest and most prestigious of the publishing houses is Casa de las Américas; it is technically independent of official ties to either the government or party.

A number of organizations have been responsible for the growth of the book publishing trade. In 1962, Editorial Nacional de Cuba (the Cuban National Publishing Company) was set up under the Council of Ministers to coordinate publishing. Three years later, Edición Revolucionaria (Revolutionary Edition) was begun to cope with the growing demand for textbooks. In 1967, the first organization to deal with all aspects of publishing, Instituto del Libro (the Book Institute), was started with an immediate mandate to publish textbooks.

Speaking before the second meeting on printing techniques in 1982, Minister of Culture Hart reported that 49.7 million copies of 1,500 book titles were published in 1981, up from 19.8 million copies of 883 titles a decade before. The 1981 titles were broken down into 60 percent education, 22 percent art and literature, 10 percent social sciences, and 8 percent science and technology. He said that originally more copies of fewer titles had been necessary but that at present the goal is to have more titles and to limit the press run to about 50 million copies yearly. Hart also called for more titles dealing with industrial and technical development, business administration, management, and cadre training (*Granma Weekly Review* 1982, 13).

BROADCASTING

Radio

Media officials proudly claim that Cuba is the first Third World country with nationwide coverage in press, radio, and television (Interview, González-Manet 1982). The widest-ranging medium is radio, with a total of fifty-four stations. Five are national networks, and there are also fourteen provincial and thirty-five regional stations. Their total output is 900 kilowatts, and they are reportedly capable of covering 99 percent of the island. All the stations combined broadcast about one thousand hours daily. The networks are Radio Reloj, which features twenty-four-hour news, information, and sports, with a half-hour repetition rate; Radio Rebelde, with news, sports, and some programs of historical importance but not dramatized; Radio Progreso, with popular music, magazine shows, and some news; Radio Liberación, with cultural shows and dramas, including soap operas dramatizing the classics; and Radio Musicale Nacional, with classical music. One broadcasting official was critical of the latter, claiming it lacked educational value, was made up of foreign music, and is meant for "debutantes, not everyday people" (Interview, Coro Antich 1982).

The other forty-nine stations are used as the party's arm at the local level; they cater to the needs of smaller communities with stratification of programs, differentiating among municipal, provincial, and national levels. The smallest stations have six to eight hours of their own programs, after which they link up with the provincial stations that are most closely allied to them. Citing the audience interaction possible with the local stations, Coro Antich said that some shows allow for participation without the "silly talk shows of the United States." For example, "Radio 1590" discusses water supply, effective use of available resources, vocational topics, and vaccination, using local artists and volunteer broadcasters. The small stations also are used as telephones, relaying messages to isolated people. Coro Antich said, "For example, when a mother and baby are ready to leave the local hospital, the radio will broadcast to the family messages such as, 'Baby is nine pounds; please come get mother and baby and bring diapers'" (Interview, Coro Antich 1982).

Ninety-nine percent of radio shows are national productions. A partial breakdown of radio content shows 39 percent devoted to music; 22 percent to information and information-related topics; 7 percent to juvenile topics; 4.5 percent to education; 2.5 percent to children, and 1 percent each to drama, history, and humor (González-Manet 1982).

Improvements are considered necessary in a few areas of domestic radio broadcasting. These include the use of more high-quality links to help AM; the development of FM on a nationwide basis; the further upgrading of content to include more programs for specialized audiences; and at the local level, continued efforts to make broadcasting relate to the masses (Interview, Coro Antich 1982).

Radio Habana Cuba, the nation's external broadcasting service, is divided into sections of information, programming, and international correspondence and relations. Like other media, Radio Habana Cuba follows the orientations of the national informational policy, but, according to one official, not slavishly.

> We are not robots. We share a political line interpreted in a creative way. No one has to tell us exactly what to write. For example, in the case of the Falklands war, our sources are political parties, trade unions, government, or the liberation front of Argentina. We get their information and interpret it. They don't have to come and tell us to write this or that. There is a group of journalists who participate in editorials (Interview, Martínez Pirez 1982; also see Browne 1982, 259–61 and Alisky 1981, 161).

Television

Cuba was at the forefront of television development in Latin America, since it was one of the first four countries to introduce the medium and probably the first to build a nationwide microwave system. When Castro marched victoriously into Havana in 1959, the country had six channels, which he readily realized could be used as his link to the people. The outcome was what became known as "government by television," with Castro regularly speaking for long periods (four to six hours nonstop) during prime time (Green 1972, 53–69).

Two networks have served the country since the only provincial channel in Santiago de Cuba was merged with Telerebelde during a media centralization campaign of the late 1970s. However, during the same time, the number of repeaters for the two national networks has more than doubled. The networks broadcast 132½ hours weekly, about seven each weekday and fourteen each on Saturday and Sunday (Prida 1980). Six of the seven daily hours are in color. The weekly breakdown of programming includes 22.7 percent news-related information, with great emphasis on foreign affairs; 20.8 percent films; 12.5 percent children's shows; 11.7 percent music and variety; 10.9 percent sports; 6.4 percent public service and educational spots; and 5.6 percent soap operas, teleplays, and dramas (Prida 1980).

Among some of the more popular shows are those in which bureaucrats are called upon to answer questions sent in by viewers (such as "Información pública"), "Cocina al minuto" (Cooking in a Minute), which provides nutritional information for housewives facing food shortages; films, both domestic and foreign; cultural programs; and "24 por segundo" (24 Frames a Second), which describes current films, shows clips, and discusses their history and structure (Prida 1980; Aufderheide 1984, 32). Because of the expenses of local programming, the networks rely on exchanges, especially with Mexico but also with Spain and Nicaragua. Soviet programs are occasionally received via satellite and translated (Interview Coro Antich 1982). The *noticieros* (newscasts), which, according to Prida (1980, 11), viewers thought were too frequent, are presented in more interesting formats than those of many Third World countries and use expressive newscasters interspersed with film of actual events. The topics seem to be developmental, patriotic, and supportive of Cuba's friends. On the days I monitored programming, 2 and 3 May 1982, they included stories about visits of foreign dignitaries, conferences, exemplary workers, and foreign events tied to Cuba's policies. From 7 to 10 A.M. daily (7:00 to 11:30 A.M. on Saturday), a magazine-type program is shown, including live music, sports, news, and personality sketches. The hostess for the show also does translations and spot assignments, reviews books, broadcasts baseball games, and acts in other TV dramas, including "San Nícolas del Peladera" (Interview, Ramírez-Corría 1982), a satire on local life before the Revolution that uses all the stock characters, music, and slapstick of another era. (I was able to observe the twentieth anniversary performance live, 3 May 1982.) In summary, television programs are described as having "themes emerging from an adequate appraisal of reality from the educational, economic, political, social, and cultural standpoints" (Vera 1979, 15).

In addition to popular fare, Cuban television has been providing educational programs since 1959, when an experimental project was launched for primary school children. At various times, educational television has been intensified, especially during the 1961 literacy campaign, the 1966 "Schools to the Countryside" movement (an effort to reduce differences between the city and rural sectors), and the 1969 strain on the secondary school system. During the First National Forum on ETV in 1973, it was recommended that television be used to carry out pedagogical principles of the Revolution and that ETV should contribute to pedagogical, ideological, and political training of students. By the late 1970s, there were twelve weekly teleclasses, a total of four hours, devoted to junior high and preuniversity courses; seven teleclasses, three hours, for teacher training; and four teleclasses, two hours, for university level (Wertheim 1977, 132).

González-Manet, discussing television, generalized that broadcasting in Cuba still has problems of needing more public participation, more technical and scientific programs, youth debates, broader economic information, more drama based on "national actualities," better children's shows, and "further exploitation of the possibilities of orienting the population concerning the use of free time" (Interview, González-Manet 1982).

In the 1980s, state and party officials had probably been more critical of television than of the other media. Raúl Castro in 1980 charged television with mediocrity, emphasizing the need for better training, while Culture Minister Hart seldom missed an opportunity to implore that television's role must be as an educational and cultural bridge to the masses.

Some of the problems that have hindered television from gaining its expected status relate to economical and technological constraints—allocation of scarce foreign exchange to import receiving and transmitting equipment; lack of technical compatibility between the existing U.S.–built television system and those of the Soviet Union and Eastern Europe; outdated equipment kept operative by repairs and "cannibalization" because of the U.S. trade embargo on replacement parts; inadequately trained technical staff; and greater dependence upon less expensive foreign programs than is desirable in a Third World socialist country (Prida 1980, 11; Nichols 1982c, 11–12). Officials are caught in a quandary; although they would like to depend more heavily upon television to reach the masses with relevant information, they cannot afford to release the funds and time from other sectors of the country that are struggling to develop economically.

PROSPECTS FOR THE FUTURE

Efforts are being made to alleviate problems, especially the technological problems, facing the mass media. Discussing communications in the national assembly, delegates called for an increase, up to 95 percent, of equipment imported from socialist countries, thus decreasing dependence upon capitalist markets for spare parts. The Soviets already make two different radio receivers (Juvenil 80 and Ciboney) and a television set (Caribe) especially for Cuba, and parts are shipped to the island for local assemblage.

In the mid-1980s, Cuba was working to become one of the first nations in the world to operate a national coaxial cable network, extending the full length of the island. Supported by the Soviet Union, the project is expected to satisfy every type of long-wire requirement, including facsimile, and will allow national newspapers to be published simultaneously throughout Cuba. Newspapers now face distribution problems because of the limited number of vehicles and their poor condition. The coaxial cable will have a potential capacity of ten thousand simultaneous channels with a duplex channel for TV transmissions. In addition, Cuba already has a ground receiving station with a converter capable of handling any of the three color television systems, and in 1981 set up a factory able to manufacture 300,000 radio and 100,000 television receivers.

12

Cuban Film and the Revolution

C uban cultural policy dealing with film and other art forms has been set down in a number of stages, beginning in the early days of the Revolution. Between 1959 and 1963, the basis was set with the establishment of numerous agencies, including the Instituto Cubano del Arte e Industria Cinematográficos (the Cuban Institute of the Cinematographic Art and Industry), and with Fidel Castro's 1961 intervention at the cultural seminar on "Words to the Intellectuals." The 1971 National Congress of Education and Culture and the First Congress of the Cuban Communist Party in 1975 further defined cultural policy, as explained in chapter 11.

When the Socialist Constitution of Cuba was adopted in 1957, it included a chapter dedicated to education and culture. A number of items dealt with the role of the media, requesting them to "popularize Marxist-Leninist ideology, the Party lines, the main aims of socialism, activities of the Young Communist League, and other mass organizations"; to emphasize more foreign affairs news; to be used in well-planned, organized approaches throughout the school system; and to criticize all areas of social development (also see chapter 11).

Three congresses of the Union of Writers and Artists of Cuba (UNEAC) further refined cultural and media policy. Especially important were the second congress in 1977, where the minister of culture, Armando Hart, outlined the developmental perspective of the Cuban cultural industry, and the third congress in 1982. In the 1982 congress, Hart reiterated the constitutional provision that "artistic creativity is free as long as its content is not contrary to the Revolution" and stated that the essence of Cuban cultural policy is to promote "a broad popular movement around culture in such a way as to facilitate precision and high aesthetic standards and the broadest creative freedom for the masses and the writers and artists springing from them" (Hart 1982, 5). The minister also added

> As government officials, our duty is not to set down standards which artistic forms should follow. Our duty among others, is to find political procedures and means for communication to exist between society as a whole and the artistic movement within it. The problem is to decide on the practical means by which society, and not just a government official, may exert influences over the artistic movement through the social conscience of the artists. In this regard, our mission as leaders consists of facilitating communication between the artistic movement and the rest of society, so that a relationship of mutual trust is established (Hart 1982, 5).

To understand the objectives of cultural institutions such as film, one must keep in mind the fidelities of the Communist party of Cuba: Marxism-Leninism, the interests of the working class, the struggle against capitalism and "all forms of man's exploitation of man," proletarian internationalism, and close ties with the masses. Perhaps this constitutional statute best sums up the party role:

> The *Communist Party of Cuba* emphasizes consciousness-raising and ideological preparation of the masses so they are educated in the values of communist morality; it helps to create the new man — who, stripped of bourgeois and petit bourgeois morality and ideology (based on individualism and egotism), governs his conduct by the most noble principles of collectivism, self-sacrifice, love of work, hatred of exploitation and parasitism, and the fraternal spirit of cooperation and solidarity among all the members of society and among the socialist countries and workers and peoples throughout the world (Communist Party, Cuba 1981, 3).

PRE-REVOLUTION AND EARLY REVOLUTION FILM

Although Cuba has a relatively long history of films — the first was produced and shown in 1897 — until the 1960s, the existence of a film industry was precarious. Before 1959, the industry was underdeveloped, depending on coproductions, mainly with Mexico, and characterized by "blatant commercialism, low technical quality, and limited artistic interest" (Hernández 1976, 1). A rough estimate placed the number of feature-length films made in Cuba between 1897 and 1958 at fewer than 150, excluding U.S. films using Cuba as a location. The earliest filmma-

kers employed historical and folkloric themes, and their films had to
compete with the imports. Other problems included the absence of large
capital investments, available technical resources, and a sufficient audience. Because most of the 595 theaters (149 in Havana) were under the
control of international distributing chains, they were required to show
the films of those chains before offering domestic movies. Along the
same lines, only through coproduction did Cuban films get international
markets, and these were limited because Mexico cornered the one market
Cuba could best appeal to—that of Latin America (Black 1976, 328).

Almost immediately after Castro took power, the Cuban Institute of
the Cinematographic Art and Industry (ICAIC) was created in March
1959, the result of the first governmental decree dealing with ideological
and cultural matters. ICAIC still regulates all aspects of film production
from filming to poster design. The core of ICAIC filmmakers came
from a group of leftist amateurs, who in pre-Revolution times coalesced
around the Sociedad Cultural "Nuestro Tiempo." Some of these people
(Santiago Alvarez, Julio García Espinosa, Tomas Gutiérrez Aléa, and

12.1   U.S. film companies, such as Warner, were replaced at the outset of the Cuban Revolution.

Manuel Octavio Gómez), who constitute ICAIC's base today, had organized cine clubs and experimental filmmaking activities.[1] They learned film through "practical ways" and were influenced by Italian neorealism. According to Santiago Alvarez, once ICAIC was created, the foreign influences became multiple as top documentarists from elsewhere were brought to Cuba to teach (Interview, Alvarez 1982). Named director of ICAIC was Alfredo Guevara, a schoolmate of Fidel Castro, who showed filmmakers how to educate and re-educate audiences about the nature of film. One of ICAIC's first goals was to identify talented filmmakers, some of whom were sent to Czechoslovakia for training. In other instances, internationally known directors were invited to Cuba to teach and direct films. To further develop the skills of local directors, coproductions were done with Czechoslovakia and other socialist countries. Because North American equipment was difficult to obtain, especially after the U.S. blockade of Cuba, filmmakers switched to equipment from Czechoslovakia, Poland, the Soviet Union, and England. In 1960, ICAIC published the first issue of *Cine cubano,* a film periodical still in existence.

By 1961, ICAIC ventured into successful projects such as Cuban Cinemateque and *cine movile* (mobile cinema), and at the same time the organization began to use stricter controls, including censorship. Cuban Cinemateque, formed in 1960, continues to provide daily programs to three Havana and one Santiago de Cuba theaters, to give films and assistance to the three national universities, to present weekly programs in all provincial capitals and three other major population centers, and to produce two weekly television shows. All of its programs are to "decolonize, cultivate and develop the public taste" and to "demystify film in general and in particular the ideology and language imposed by Hollywood" (Hernández 1976, 4). *Cine movile* was started in 1961 to bring movies to the remotest regions. Before 1959, the 1.6 million weekly viewers of films did not include rural people, as the theaters were in the capitals and large towns. The Division of Cinematographic Education made available trucks, boats, and later in 1969, mules to carry equipment to inaccessible areas, thus creating *cine mule.* By 1970, one hundred *cine movile* and about a dozen *cine mule* units existed (Black 1976, 330). Other innovations in those early Revolution years included ICAIC's development in 1960 of a weekly news program of national and international events, "Noticiero latinoamericano," directed then, as now, by Santiago Alvarez; the setting up in 1963 of an audiovisual department at the University of Havana, where educational films are made; and the re-establishment of the feature film industry.

By the late 1960s, Cuban films had received worldwide acclaim; in fact, they had received twenty-two international awards by March 1969. Much attention was given to documentaries and short subjects, as is the case today. From 1959 until 1973, only 50 full-length features were produced, while 210 documentaries, 85 educational short films, 94 animated cartoons, 94 film sketches for a popular scientific motion-picture encyclopedia, and more than 500 editions of the newsreel were done (Black 1976, 331). Reasons for this priority are that documentaries are less expensive in capital, material, and personnel and are more flexible and practical for mass education and mobilization. Hernández (1976, 5) listed six types of documentary subjects used by ICAIC: (1) internal politics and mobilization, especially the sociocultural achievements of the Revolution; (2) international relations or liberation struggles in the Third World; (3) Cuban customs and folklore; (4) history, especially since 1968; (5) education, especially technical and scientific; and (6) news events. Of 850 documentaries before 1970, 60 percent were newsreels. By the early 1970s, feature-length documentaries on individual revolutionary projects were produced.

Summarizing the first thirteen years of ICAIC, Hernández (1976, 6) said that film output had increased, a new generation of filmmakers had appeared, and both production and distribution had radically changed, as all commercial film theaters and companies were centralized under ICAIC. New audiences had also developed, and social and cultural significance had become the determining factors for film projects. Finally, films were being used to educate people about the Revolution.

FEATURE FILM POPULARIZATION

During ICAIC's formative years, feature films were limited in quantity and quality. Between 1959 and 1962, very few Cuban directors, except for García Espinosa and Gutiérrez Aléa, had the ability to do longer features. The few features that existed eulogized the heroes of the Revolution, and some resulted because of production help from foreign filmmakers. In the next five years, from 1963 to 1967, coproductions and the early work of the first ICAIC-trained directors filled theater screens, but not without considerable political controversy when post-1959 themes were presented. As censorship and also self-censorship by directors became the norm, the topics turned to pre-1959 societal ills, leaving contemporary issues to documentarists.

In 1968, the tendency changed with the international award-winning films, *Memorias del subdesarollo (Memories of Underdevelopment),* by

Gutiérrez Aléa, and *Lucia,* by Humberto Sola. In these and other films, the themes were more concerned with revolutionary reality, either dealing with revolutionary changes or historical topics linked to the present through the imagery of the "struggle" (Hernández 1976, 6). García Espinosa's filming of *Las aventuras de Juan Quinquin* in 1967 was responsible for some philosophical choices made by filmmakers to this day — the preference for mass versus popular culture and for process versus analysis. In fact, García Espinosa incorporated some of this thinking in his important 1969 essay, "For an Imperfect Cinema," where he said Cuba needed not "poorly made films which reveled in their own lack of polish, but a kind of filmmaking whose modernity, relevance and worth was a function of those elements which constitute the essence of artistic expression" (quoted in Burton 1982b, 344; Burton 1982a). The new emphasis on revolutionary militance provoked some directors, such as Eduardo Manet, Fausto Canel, and Roberto Fandión, to move to Europe.

Feature film production ceased during 1969–1970, because of a lack of raw film, the absolute priority given to documentaries, and the difficulty of producing high-caliber films that could simultaneously respond to political goals. However, in the early 1970s, ICAIC produced an average of five features yearly, compared to three per year before 1970. Besides this quantitative increase, there was a marked change in quality, and the films demonstrated more maturity and competence. Hernández (1976, 7) wrote that film had developed "new and important ways of confronting the difficult problems of creating revolutionary art."

As indicated earlier, ICAIC's leadership followed recommendations of the 1971 National Congress of Education and Culture, which stated that emphases should be placed on development of revolutionary values through historical analysis, the use of Third World solidarity themes, and a new look at contemporary revolutionary conflicts. Analyzing the twenty-three features made between 1970 and 1975, Hernández (1976, 8) reported that six dealt with Cuban solidarity with the Third World and anti-imperialist struggle; eight with selected historical aspects of Cuban life consistent with official political ideology; four with contemporary topics, either revolutionary accomplishments or problems still faced (such as the unresolved problems of ethnic and sexual equality); and five with Cuban cultural and artistic life. Among the directors of these films were Alvarez, with four; Hector Veitia, three; Manuel Octavio Gómez, Pastor Vega, Antonion Fernández Reboiro, and José Massip, two each; and eight others, one each. In Cuban films, the social theme is all important, and the actor is not allowed to predominate over the theme. As

Adolfo Llauradó, who would be considered a star in another culture, explained, "the actors and actresses serve the people and are not to be exalted" (Interview, Llauradó 1982).

By the late 1970s, film was recognized as an important factor in Cuban development. Marking its twentieth anniversary in 1979, ICAIC established the first of its projected annual film festivals in Havana on "New Latin American Cinema" (Aufderheide 1979). In that year, ICAIC produced five theatrical features, one full-length animated feature, two long documentaries, thirty-five short documentaries, thirteen animated shorts, and fifty-two newsreels. At least one thousand theaters, five hundred of which were mobile, operated in Cuba in 1979. The industry's overall production between 1959 and 1978 included 100 long feature films, 650 medium features, 950 weekly newsreels, and 150 cartoons. During that time, ICAIC films won more than two hundred awards in international festivals. Despite this volume of locally produced films, Cuban theaters must still depend upon many foreign movies. Aufderheide (1979, 22) estimated that only 4 to 6 percent of Cuban screen-time annually is devoted to Cuban film; the rest are chosen by ICAIC from Western and Eastern Europe, the Soviet Union, Latin America, and the United States. For example, in 1977 Cuba bought 120 titles. Not more than U.S. $1,500 was paid for any film (Besas 1978), partly because ICAIC is limited by a shortage of currency to import. Because of the U.S. economic embargo, ICAIC either uses already acquired American movies of the 1940s and 1950s or post-1959 movies obtained through prints made in Europe or Latin America.

In 1981, more than thirty-five million moviegoers attended ICAIC-controlled theaters to view the movies produced or imported by ICAIC. Cuban production that year included forty-five documentaries, fifty-two newsreels, ten animated films, and seven or eight features. In 1982, Alvarez said that ICAIC hoped to make ten features yearly, but quality and the needs of the people were priorities over quantity. He added that the number of films has been stable for a decade, also blaming Cuba's inability to increase production on a lack of resources resulting from the U.S. economic blockade (Interview, Alvarez 1982). ICAIC accomplishes its many tasks through four companies: Distribuidora Nacional, Empresa ICAIC (production), Empresa Servicio Técnicos de Exhibición, and Distribuidora Internacional. The organization continues to expand its technical capability; in the late 1970s, a black-and-white-processing laboratory was set up to allow for increasing production to six or seven features yearly. Previously, black and white film had to be sent to Spain for processing, as is still the case for color. Other agencies, such as the

Ministry of Education, the military, and television stations, have their own film studios.

Aufderheide (1984, 28) reported that Cuban cinema, on the occasion of its silver anniversary in 1984, released a number of fiction features that included "experiments from veteran directors and debut works from new talents." Among experiments was the first fiction feature made by documentarist Santiago Alvarez, *Los refugiados de la cueva de la Muerte* (Refugees from the Death Cave), which describes the aftermath of the 1953 guerrilla attack on the Moncada barracks. Describing the new productions as a third phase — the first being the controversial documentaries of the early 1960s; the second, fiction features of the late 1960s and early 1970s — Aufderheide (1984, 29) said, "This new burst of production, in which documentary is playing with fiction while fiction toys with daily life, grows out of the two earlier phases." More and more, Cuban film is changing from the "stark drama" of earlier days to treatments of the "more intimate contradictions of daily life" — to filming the real.

12.2 Santiago Alvarez, Cuba's most famous news and documentary filmmaker.

CONTEMPORARY MOTIVATIONS AND PHILOSOPHIES

Motivations that seem to be important in all aspects of Cuban growth affect the hardware and software development of mass media such as film. Adolfo Llauradó, who has appeared in more than twenty films, playing lead roles in *Portrait of Teresa* and *Lucia,* said that one such motivation is fraternal competition resulting in emulation. Filmmakers, he said, "strive to copy the best elements. If we have three months to make a film and we do it in two, other film crews will emulate that. It's conscientization or consciousness raising" (Interview, Llauradó 1982). Alvarez gave examples of the speed with which films are made. Some documentaries are finished in three or four days, with one day of shooting. Alvarez said, "We might go up to a week or two to do a documentary. I'm making two documentaries at the same time right now" (Interview, Alvarez 1982). Perhaps there is another reason for meeting fast schedules. Aufderheide (1984, 32) said that the filmmaking union, Syndicato del Impresa ICAIC, which is organized vertically to include everyone from truck drivers to directors, shares in scheduling decisions. Thus, "once a project is established, the director is responsible for bringing the film in on time and on budget; the whole cast and crew will win or lose accordingly because their salaries are tied to the estimated schedule" (Aufderheide 1984, 32).

Enrique González-Manet, Cuba's chief spokesman on communications issues, explained that Cuba seeks to set an example for other developing countries by establishing a clearly defined national communications policy, creating its own communications hardware and software, and practicing proletarian internationalism. By the latter, he said that Cuba is helping other countries develop their institutions, including the media, to help in the fight against colonization and to give an "example of what solidarity means." He added, "a country like us that needs help, gives help. If we develop our communications systems, we prove to the developing world that it can be done" (Interview, González-Manet 1982).

Talking about film specifically, García Espinosa said that one motivation is to generate "artistic products which have an impact on the population to counter the enormous quantity of alienating products which bombard that population from elsewhere"; he added, "This is an impossible task unless we can develop new concepts and norms of artistic productivity" (quoted in Burton 1982b, 344). Documentary filmmaker Alvarez probably best exemplifies the use of film to counter other countries' messages. He said that the source of his documentaries is the newspaper and that he is like a journalist, giving "subjective, not objective, information"; "I have the vocation of a journalist," Alvarez said, adding, "the artist should communicate with the audience as a journalist, not as an elite separated from the masses. I like to go to movies and participate with the public when they watch my films" (Interview, Alvarez 1982). Describing a recent anti–United States film he directed, Alvarez said that he employed stereotypes such as the Ku Klux Klan to give a very emotional impact. "I gave all the feeling I had to the film. I was filmmaker, participant, and protagonist," he said (Interview, Alvarez 1982).

As to the theory and purposes of documentary filmmaking, Alvarez said that there are "no guidelines to tell us how or when, or in what way, to make documentaries. We have spent days discussing this, determining the number of classes of documentaries, etc., but we never reached an agreement" (Interview, Alvarez 1982). There are some who would argue that Alvarez himself has developed an independent style, described by Aufderheide (1984, 31) as using the scantiest possible narration, powerful and shocking montages, snippets from magazines and newspapers, bold title cards, and provocative animation.

In ICAIC, theme choosing for films is free and open, and Alvarez has said that his own inspiration for themes is in the streets and outside the country.

> Reagan inspires me a lot so I am doing a film on Reagan. I saw him on television, in the papers; he is full of funny and foolish things so he inspires me to do a satire film on him. We do a lot of internationalist films. We have gone to Asia and Africa to make films. I have been to Vietnam twelve times. I interviewed Ho Chi Minh. And also Allende. You see this and you feel anguish. I'd like to go to Argentina now. Britain inspires me. [The Falklands War was in progress at the time.] I'm very subjective, a political animal. It comes out of my pores. I guess I am an internationalist chauvinist (Interview, Alvarez 1982).

Once scripts are done by the country's limited number of scriptwriters and by the directors themselves, they are checked by ICAIC staff, whose approval will be obtained depending on the point of view expressed. Alvarez said, "When doing a film, I make consultancies with people working in film. We can make our own film which is then seen by the ICAIC director and discussed. The director has advisors who have a lot of technical experience; they help others. They do not censor, but advise in the spirit of helping" (Interview, Alvarez 1982).

The movies initially are shown in a selected six or seven theaters simultaneously and then more generally throughout the island. The moviegoer is given a good deal for the price of one peso — documentaries, newsreels, and a feature film. There is no hierarchy among these types; Alvarez said that each genre has its own value.

Despite the high development of Cuban cinema, shortcomings still occur. All film personnel receive on-the-job training, which is supplemented by ICAIC-sponsored courses of three or four months staffed by foreign technicians. In 1984, there was talk of developing a film school to replace this apprenticeship system, in which filmmakers first work in the newsreel division, then move to short documentaries, and finally, perhaps, to features. Although Cuban television uses videotape, ICAIC does not yet have experience in this technology. Cuba does not manufacture film equipment and therefore must depend upon imports. Because of the long U.S. embargo, there is a chronic shortage of film and other supplies. Despite, or perhaps because of, these deficiencies, Alvarez believes it is a privilege to make films in a developing country such as Cuba. He asks, "After nearly one hundred years of cinematography, how many Latin American countries have film industries? Argentina, Mexico, Brazil, Nicaragua, and Cuba. We had to make a revolution to have a film industry" (Interview, Alvarez 1982).

At the end of the 1980s, the Cuban cinema industry is still tightly structured under ICAIC. It is designed to promote the Communist party and the government's campaigns both domestically and internationally. While fulfilling this mission, Cuban film has developed into an aesthetically important medium, welcomed and honored in many parts of the world.

13

Mass Media of the Dominican Republic

HISTORY OF THE MEDIA

Between the time of the first newspaper in 1821 and the year 1973, at least 1,367 newspapers and periodicals were published in the Dominican Republic (Martínez Paulino 1973). The number is worth calling attention to because of the late and, even then, hesitant origins of printing in the colony.

Isaiah Thomas claimed that the "printing press was early introduced into the Spanish part of this island, probably about the beginning of the seventeenth century," but added that "It was seldom used except for printing the lists and returns, and other papers for the different branches of the administration" (Thomas 1874).

What has come down to contemporary times, however, as the first printing in Santo Domingo is an 1801 imprint, *Estatutos de la regia, y pontificia, Universidad de Santo Tomás de Aquino* (Swan 1970, 11). La Universidad de Santo Tomás de Aquino also figured in the printing of the first two newspapers, as both of their editors were associated with that university.

The first newspaper was *El telégrafo constitucional de Santo Domingo,* issued 5 April 1821 by Dr. Antonio María Pineda, a forty-year-old man of letters. The paper was a semiofficial weekly dealing with information about the colony and international notices. Most of the first number was made up of decrees and orders, "Decretos y Ordenes de S. M. Comunicados al gobierno de esta provincia." Other headlines in this four-page issue were "Circular del Ministero de Gracia y Justicia," "Entrada de Embarraciones," and "Salida." The decrees and orders continued in the second issue of 12 April, which was eight pages and carried the imprint, "Santo Domigo, imprenta de Gobierno José María González. Año de 1821." Other issues seemed to be devoted to official business.[1]

In the third issue of *El telégrafo* of 19 April, one of the two letters to the editor called attention to a new periodical, *El duende.* Founded by Dr. José Nuñez de Caceres, who is credited with being the first *dominicano* to promote the liberty of the country, *El duende* was an independent weekly that relied heavily upon foreign reports from London, Paris, Naples, or Madrid. Some of those stories dealt with Santo Domingo from a foreign perspective. Letters, verses, and political and economic essays also were frequent.

By 1835, a third periodical, *El dominicano español,* was started by José María Serra. Still others of the 1840s were *La chicharro, El grillo dominicano, El grillo dominicano y familia, El eco dominicano,* and *El dominicano en el desierto,* which was described as a "very curious publication" (Martínez Paulino 1973, 24). Some of these were handwritten papers of a "revolutionary character."

By the 1850s, the oppositionist newspapers were established. Characteristic of them was *El eco del pueblo,* started on 27 July 1856 as the voice of politics, literature, and industry. A sympathizer of Buenaventura Báez, *El eco*'s objective was to oppose in a "systematic manner all the actions" of the government (Martínez Paulino 1973, 31). Put at the disposal of the pens of Antonio Bobea and Manuel María Gautier, *El eco* was edited by A. Gutierrez, and later by Gautier.

The troubled period from 1844 to 1873, when even the possible absorption of the island by the United States was considered, saw the development of many publications, including *El dominicano, Gaceta del gobierno* (later converted to *Gaceta oficial), El eco de Ozama, El corréo del Cibao, El dominicano* (a second version), *El española libre, El progreso, El porvenir, La república, El tiempo, El sol, El oasis,* and *El cibaeño* (Otero 1953, 481).

Otero (1953, 481) credited the year 1873 as instrumental in initiating material and intellectual progress in the country. He attributed part of the reason for the transformation to educator Don Eugenio María de Hostos, founder of cultural associations such as El Amigo de los Niños and Los Amigos del País. Accompanying this cultural advancement were periodicals such as *El orden, El eco de Yaque, El dominicano, El nacional, El liberal, La paz, La opinión, El centinela, El observador, El telegrama, El teléfono, El día, El album,* among many others.

When the country went through political and military upheavals—including the U.S. occupation beginning in 1916—between 1902 and 1916, the principal periodicals were *El dominicano, El nacional, Pluma*

EL TELÉGRAFO CONSTITUCIONAL

DE SANTO DOMINGO

del Jueves 5 de Abril de 1821.

13.1 Inaugural issue of *El telégrafo constitucional de Santo Domingo,* 5 April 1821, the first newspaper of the Dominican Republic.

y espada, El hogar (a literary review), *La bandera libre, La compañía,* and *El lápiz* (Otero 1953, 482).

The long reign of the dictator, Generalissimo Rafael Leonidas Trujillo Molina (1930–1961), spurred both improvements in communication facilities and reach and a diminishment of press freedom. Trujillo recognized the important role the media played in politics. During his era, the number of radio stations and receivers multiplied, newspaper circulations increased, and two television stations started, the first in 1952. Wiarda (1969, 16) wrote, "Though during Trujillo's dictatorship, the expanding communications media were employed to further the cult of the Generalissimo, the framework for a modern communications system was established."

Trujillo assumed power at a fortuitous time. The press was in a decimated state, having opposed, at great financial costs, the previous Vásquez administration. With the exception of *Listin diario,* other newspapers were near collapse in 1930. One Dominican editor wrote

> "The Chief" [Trujillo] found out that by paying lip service to the causes championed by the journalists it was relatively easy to win over to his side some honest but short-sighted editors.[2] Where double-talk was not enough, more subtle means were employed. Government jobs, juicy official printing contracts — up to that point monopolized by *Listin Diario* — outright subsidies and bribes, mixed with an occasional threat, usually did the trick and assured the allegiance of the more "practical and realistic" publishers (Ornes 1958, 189).

Those who did not support Trujillo were jailed, exiled, or murdered. Initially, *Listin diario* was itself a nonsupporter. However, after its printing contracts were withdrawn, its quarters assaulted by the dreaded "La 42," and its publisher imprisoned, *Listin diario* announced in 1932, two years in advance, its support for Trujillo's re-election.

By 1940, Trujillo decided he needed his own paper, and *La nación* was inaugurated on 19 February. The lackluster acceptance of the paper at first was changed by the generalissimo. Government advertisements were directed to *La nación,* businessmen were told to patronize it over other media, and government employees were required to subscribe. The result was disastrous to the few remaining papers. Between 1940 and 1942, *La tribuna, Diario de comercio,* and *Listin diario* folded, leaving *La opinión* and *La nación.*

Trujillo, reacting to U.S. criticism of his actions, mounted a moderate opposition campaign, asking *La opinión* to be critical. All went well with this farce until the paper carried a piece that criticized Trujillo;

13.2 *Listin diario* survived chaotic times, including those of the Trujillo dictatorship.

shortly after, the remaining two dailies were merged. After 1947, Trujillo relinquished ownership of *La nación* first to the dominant political party and then to a senator. By 1957, he was owner again.

In 1947, Trujillo put up the money for still another daily, *El caribe,* a paper described as writing news stories based on a "mixture of half truths, innuendoes and outright lies (until then Dominican newspapers had been plain, unsophisticated liars)" (Ornes 1958, 194). Seven years later, it was sold to German Ornes, who, after about a year, left to live in the United States, which he called an exile (Ornes 1958, 198–99).

The homage paid to Trujillo by the Dominican press bordered on putting him on a level with deity. In one 1957 *El caribe* article, the generalissimo was called "the Great, Savior of America, Orientator of the World and First Anti-Communist of the American Continent." Foreign publications and journalists were paid comfortable sums to write favorable accounts about Trujillo, which were then reprinted in local newspapers. Ornes (1958, 205) said that in a typical daily in Santo Domingo, Trujillo's name would be mentioned as often as a hundred times, preceded by his titles and several adjectives.

Besides control by ownership and news releases, Trujillo also ruled with a spate of laws. Law No. 1387 of 26 March 1947 is an example.

> [A] person of Dominican nationality who with the purpose of defaming the Republic or its institutions spreads false and malicious news among foreigners residing or passing through the Dominican Republic, or who transmits such news abroad by any means of communication, will be condemned to from two to three years in prison. If this offense is repeated, the offender is liable to the maximum penalty of the law, which is five years in prison. Foreigners found guilty of violations of this act may be summarily deported from the country by decree of the Executive (cited in Ornes 1958, 206).

A 1956 law required registration of agents and correspondents of foreign publications and thus sharply curtailed foreign reportage of the country.

Even the letters-to-the-editor columns were under the dictator's control. Contrived and written by members of the National Palace, the letters usually were attacks upon Trujillo's enemies. Thus, to be mentioned in "Foro Público" in *El caribe* meant government displeasure with one's actions (Ornes 1958, 207–8).

Broadcasting was also tied to the Trujillo power structure, since stations and networks were owned by Trujillo family members. A statement by Wiarda (1969, 44) aptly sums up the Trujillo control of the media.

El Periódico de la Familia Dominicana

20 CENTAVOS

El Caribe

Y conoceréis la verdad, y la verdad os hará libres. San Juan VIII, 32.

20 CENTAVOS

AÑO XXXVI — SANTO DOMINGO, REPUBLICA DOMINICANA, SABADO, 28 DE MAYO DE 1983 — Nº 11190

Cuba Ensaya Asaltos Anfibios Sofisticados

Por George C. Wilson
De The Washington Post

WASHINGTON — Cuba está practicando por vez primera desembarcos anfibios sofisticados que representan una amenaza para las naciones aledañas del Caribe, revelaron el jueves funcionarios norteamericanos.

Pontífice Elogia Labor de Obispos De Santo Domingo

Por Juan Carlos Gumucio
De The Associated Press

CIUDAD DEL VATICANO, 27 de mayo.— El Papa Juan Pablo II denominada la República Dominicana como "la avanzada del Nuevo Mundo en la fe" recuerdo hoy la labor pastoral de los obispos de ese país y un exhortó a seguir trabajando "por el ejército del cuerpo de la iglesia".

Fotos Prueban Apoyo Ruso a Nicaragua

Por The Associated Press

WASHINGTON, 27 de mayo.— La Casa Blanca expuso anoche fotografías aéreas para comprobar sus afirmaciones hechas hoy acerca del apoyo soviético a Nicaragua.

Cumbre Económica Buscará Fórmula Resolver Problemas

Por Alexander Higgins

WASHINGTON, 27 de mayo.—

Opina Reclama Estímulo Buena Elección Jueces

Por Tulio Sarragoza

CAEI Afirma Invasiones Harán Descender sus Zafras

Exhorta a Recordar A Héroes de Gesta

Por Luis Tejeda

Afirma Deporta A Indocumentado

Por Miguel A. Matos

Analiza Evolución de Banca

Por Tomás A. Fuentes

13.3 *El caribe* began in 1947 with Trujillo financing and much praise of the dictator.

Newspapers, radio, television, and all other means of communication had to be fully in accord with the official line emanating from the National Palace. No criticism of Trujillo was permitted. Reporters were told when and how to write a story; they could not independently check the facts supplied. Writers vied to praise Trujillo in an original manner, prompting a critic of the regime to remark that the only difficulty for Dominican newspapermen was to coin a new adjective. In the controlled press, the dictator used the letters-to-the-editor column to denounce "anonymously" those who had displeased Trujillo. The propaganda transmitted over radio and television was similar to that in the newspapers.

After Trujillo was assassinated on 30 May 1961, press controls were relaxed generally. The competitive press had a rebirth with the appearance of *Unión cívica, La libertad, Rápido, La verdad,* and *M-14-J (Movimiento 14 de Junio).* On 31 December 1961, *El caribe* was restored to German Ornes, and on 1 August 1963, a revised *Listin diario* appeared after nineteen years. The government expropriated *La nación* from its former Trujillo owners on 26 February 1962 (Hilton 1963, xxi), and three years later, the paper was dissolved. By the late 1960s, other newspapers had been started, including *Prensa libre,* a short-lived, reactionary daily destroyed by mobs in 1965; *La información* of Santiago; *Ahora,* a news magazine; and *El nacional,* a liberal daily offshoot of *Ahora.*

In addition to expanding the number of newspapers, the new government made other efforts to overcome the repressive Trujillo legacy, such as dissolving the isolation of all groups and individuals through communications, the formation of a journalists' group and a training institute, and the development of more educational and public affairs programs for broadcasting.

Broadcasting changed in the post-Trujillo years. The confused ownership structures — networks such as La Voz Dominicana, Radio Caribe, Radio Rahintel, La Voz del Trópico, and others that had the imprint of Trujillo on them — were clarified and given some order. (Trujillo had been known for intertwining his personal properties with those owned by the state). The number of radio stations increased, doubling from the last days of the dictator until the mid-1960s to seventy-six AM and nine FM stations, while the number of radio receivers quadrupled and the number of television sets increased tenfold (Wiarda 1969, 127).

The 1965 Revolution and subsequent occupation of the Dominican Republic by the U.S. military destabilized the press scene once more. As already indicated, *La nación* and *Prensa libre* died that year; *Listin diario* and *El caribe* were forced to shut down for six months because they were located in the area held by the rebels and also because they experienced labor difficulty; and *La hoja* was temporarily banned. In October of that year, *La información* was about the only newspaper publishing regularly. The government radio station, used as a tool by those who controlled it, changed hands a few times during the strife (see Waggoner 1967). Violence was prevalent; besides the wrecking of *Prensa libre*'s plant, three journalists were killed (McReynolds 1965).

In September 1965, the country's provisional president issued a decree temporarily suspending broadcasts emanating from Santo Domingo and its environs (except those from the government station) and tightened control over the state network's news in an effort to calm "the excitement of the masses" (Hofmann 1965).

When Joaquín Balaguer occupied the presidency for three terms from 1966 to 1978, a credibility and trust gap prevailed with the media, but as Pierce (1982a) maintained, an "all-out declaration of war" between the president and the press was avoided because Balaguer brought justice to the country and never persecuted print media in a sustained manner.

Although generally free under Balaguer, the media, especially radio, occasionally were subjected to interference or pressure. Single radio programs were banned and entire stations closed for content unfavorable to the authorities. Newspapers, especially *Listin diario,* faced harassing libel suits emanating from government circles. On a few other occasions, journalists were jailed, and in 1972 and 1975, three editors and columnists were murdered.

While Antonio Guzman was defeating Balaguer in the 1978 election, progovernment military forces tried to steal the election, shutting down television and radio. Some newspapers reacted by sustaining editorial campaigns against such actions.

The presidencies of Guzman and his successor, Salvador Jorge Blanco, expanded freedom of expression, despite a few troubling times. In 1980, when the Dominican Republic suffered severe economic problems, the authorities, fearing a popular uprising, censored broadcasting and films. In 1983, a bill passed by the Chamber of Deputies called for the establishment of a reporters' association with mandatory membership. Critics saw this as an attempt at de facto licensing of reporters (Morales 1984, 18).

CONTEMPORARY MEDIA

The Dominican Republic is among the select few media-rich Caribbean countries, possessing nine dailies, thirty nondaily papers, about 200 radio frequencies, 150 film exhibition locations, and six television systems. Most newspapers are fat with advertising; the major dailies contain forty to sixty pages, and tabloids, twenty to thirty-two. *Listin diario* and *El caribe* are considered the most important of the dailies and the most serious in their news approach. Radio is very visible in the country. One source showed that while in 1973 the Dominican Republic had one station for every 35,817 people, in 1987, the figure was one per 15,000 inhabitants (Rosario Adames 1987, 21). The Institute for Studies of Population and Development recently reported that for each one hundred dwellings in Santo Domingo, there were 143 radio and television receivers.

Most media are privately owned. The dailies are, and of the 198 radio stations, 180 belong to the private business sector, nine to religious groups, and two to the state (Rosario Adames 1987, 22).

Unlike those of most of the Caribbean, Dominican Republic entrepreneurs do not hesitate to invest in the media. One writer gave the reasons as the political prominence available to publishers and broadcast managers, the possibility of fast profits on small investments, and the growth of advertising revenues, especially those from government sources. He believed most publishers looked upon their newspapers as financial, not political, investments (Pierce 1982a, 297).

Group and cross-media ownership abound in the Dominican Republic. Five or six groups dominate daily journalism. The Pellerano family owns *Listin diario* and *Ultima hora,* as well as a radio station; Pepin Corripio has *Hoy, El nacional, Ahora* magazine, Teleantillas and Telesistem television channels, and HIJB radio station; and German Ornes and his family own *El caribe* and have links with a television and a radio station.

Some sources claimed that such concentration of ownership has impeded freedom of expression for the masses (Rosario Adames 1987, 22). One reporter said, "Oligarchies control the media here—four or five families. There is no outlet for views of the masses because the families that run the government also own the media" (Interview, Simo 1983).

Of course, the oligarchies disagreed. Rogelio Pellerano, publisher of *Listin diario,* assured the Inter American Press Association in 1988 that his country's press was free and open. If a threat to press freedom existed, he said, it resulted from the high costs of imported supplies, not from governmental or sectarian groups (*Inter American Press Association News* 1988).

The masses are served, however, by the use of formal or alternative media. In few places in the Caribbean have there been more experiments in the use of communication for education and development than in the Dominican Republic.

Radio Assisted Community Basic Education (RADECO), supported by the U.S. Agency for International Development, provides interactive radio instruction to children in rural areas deprived of primary schools. A part of the government's Secretariat of Education, Fine Arts, and Religion, RADECO maintains sixty-four centers in fifty-four communities in the southwest provinces. Members of the communities elect helpers, who, after brief training, teach children reading and writing through the fourth-grade level. The program was launched in 1983 (Berges Rib 1988; Hanssen, Kozlow, and Olsen 1983, 1, 11; Helwig and Friend 1985).

Another example is Radio Enriquillo, also in the southwest. Started in 1977 by the Roman Catholic Church, the station attempts to give a voice to otherwise voiceless sugar workers, with homegrown music, poetry, drama, news, discussions, worship, and shows for children and teenagers. Advertising is limited to only forty minutes of the eighteen-hour broadcast day. Cassettes are taken to villages by Enriquillo staff to solicit views on peasant problems; volunteer correspondents keep the station informed of news happenings (Lowe 1983; López Virgil 1983).

Mujer-Tec, an action and advocacy group for women, has worked to promote community action through the media. Its objectives center on developing women's technical and leadership roles in the media so that women, "through their work, can introduce positive changes that will benefit the status of all women" (Andújar 1982). The organization has been involved in training women in nontraditional communications jobs, in producing programs beneficial to women in areas of health, education, and employment, and in soliciting views of women concerning their problems. The hope of Mujer-Tec is to place women in media managerial and technical positions, 98 percent of which now are held by men.

Dominican journalism has long suffered from a lack of professionalism. Part of the problem stems from the media owners' refusal to share their huge profits with employees, who must work second or third jobs in other media or public relations. Additionally, most journalists have not had formal training; one estimate claimed the figure as high as 95 percent. According to one source, the situation is chaotic: "Explosive developments in journalism over recent years have resulted in the profession being entered by people lacking the essential qualification. Owners abuse this situation and hire non-qualified journalists at lower salaries, including students from the higher grades of journalist schools. This leads to a deterioration in the living standards of trained journalists of whom many are unemployed" (*IOJ Newsletter* 1987, 2).

The controversial establishment of the Colegio Dominicano de Periodistas (CDP) in 1983 was meant to control entrance into the profession, as only membership in the Colegio, obligatory by Law 148, qualifies one to practice journalism. The controversy has revolved around issues of professional protection of working journalists and freedom of expression. The Inter American Press Association, among others supporting publishers' interests, claimed that licensing of journalists (which it believes colegialization implies) takes away certain freedoms. The Colegio has about eleven hundred members (*IOJ Newsletter* 1982, 2). In 1988, the Supreme Court ruled Law 148 illegal, and the Colegio was banned.

In April 1984, when President Blanco took harsh measures against the broadcast media following street rioting, the Colegio challenged the government, the military, and the police to acknowledge the right of journalists to work freely. Blanco, worried that coverage would increase the rioting, closed television and radio stations and jailed and otherwise harassed journalists (Stix 1984, 3).

Unlike during the Trujillo days, such government interference as Blanco's is the exception. Censorship is not the norm, and officials often are available to reporters. The press law, dating to 1962, prohibits "all preventive measure, all intervention and all administrative control over expression of ideas or communication of facts." Exceptions are provided for offenses against "the honor of persons, social order or public peace."

To ensure minimal responsibility among newspaper owners, the law requires them to be adult Dominican citizens without a criminal record or foreign funding. Newspapers are required to correct errors without charge and cannot incite crime or disobedience of duty by military or police personnel. A vaguely stated section of the law forbids "offenses" to the president, false news that "perturbs the public peace," and "outrage against good customs." Also forbidden is publication of information about paternity suits, abortion cases, divorces, internal court discussions, or suicides of minors (cited in Pierce 1982a, 298–99).

In conclusion, the Dominican Republic mass media stand somewhat alone in the Caribbean, practicing a lively and, for the most part, a free type of journalism, which at the same time is financially profitable for the owners. Increasingly, in recent years, some groups have used the formal media for developmental and educational tasks.

14

Mass Media of the French Caribbean: Historical and Contemporary Views

Printing and periodicals apparently were not priorities of the early French authorities in the Caribbean colonies of Martinique, Guadeloupe, and French Guiana. According to Cave (1974–1975, 13–14), some sources believe that the first "brevet d'imprimeur" in the French Caribbean was issued to a Mr. Deveaux in 1729; he had probably introduced printing to Martinique two years earlier. However, in all three territories, the oldest evidence of printing that this author could find does not predate the 1760s.[1] Imprints of Pierre Richard's work in Martinique exist for the 1760s, but there is uncertainty about what was printed by Guadeloupe's first printer, Jean Bénard between 1765, when he arrived in Basse-Terre, and 1783, when a *Calendrier* appeared. In French Guiana, the oldest printed works seem to have been books, the first of which was a Report of Meetings of the National Assembly, published in 1777, followed by *Traité . . . sur les terres noyées de la Guiane,* a 350-page work from L'Imprimerie du Roi in 1788. The same imprint was on an *Almanach de Cayenne pour . . . 1789* (Cave 1974–1975, 8).

When considering what seems like a slow start for the development of a French Caribbean press, one must remember that printing arrived relatively late throughout the Caribbean. Except in the case of Spain, which used printing to propagate Roman Catholicism, the very nature of colonialism—with its heavy dependence on the metropolitan country and strong controls over local cultural institutions for political reasons—dictated against the creation of indigenous presses. Claiming that the French Antilles were always far behind in culture, even far behind other Caribbean states, one author stated that "cultural pabulum arrives by boat-mail from France" (Guérin 1961, 79).

The importance attached to the metropolitan country was reflected in the contents of colonial newspapers everywhere. In many instances, the first colonial newspapers were published to reprint news of the metropolitan country contained in European gazettes that had arrived by the latest ship. Thus, the colonial press usually was not designed for local people but rather for the colonialists, as Frantz Fanon said (1965), "to keep them in touch with civilization, *their* civilization."

The oldest surviving imprint of the French Antilles that this author has found certainly supports this view. *Gazette de la Martinique,* number 26 of which was published 25 June 1767 and is preserved in the Library Company of Philadelphia, devoted nearly all of its four pages (and most of its two-page supplement) to European news. The eight-by-twelve-inch *Gazette* carried datelines on its front page from "Dantzig 28 March," "Berlin 25 March," "Geneva 25 March" and "Thorn 26 March." Except for a letter headed "Magnifiques Seigneurs," which took up both columns of page two and one column of the next page, the rest of the issue had datelines from "London 31 March," "Rennes 28 March," and "London 6 April." The supplement included a declaration of the king of Spain, Martinique arrivals and departures, and prices in the colony and Paris. The paper thus carried virtually no local news (except for arrivals, departures, and prices) and no advertisements.

EARLY PRINTING IN MARTINIQUE

The *Gazette* was the work of Pierre Richard, one of the first printers in the French Antilles, who as "imprimeur du Roi" worked out of St. Pierre. Between 1767 and 1788, imprints in Martinique carried his name alone, but by 1791–1792, in a newspaper entitled *Affiches littéraires et politiques de la Martinique,* the signature was "Pierre Richard et La Cadre." Other early printers in Martinique were J. Francois Bazille in 1791 and J. B. Thounens, active in St. Pierre as Thounens and Vauchet in 1791, printers of *L'ami de la liberte et l'ennemi de la licence.* Shortly after, the firm printed under his name alone. Thounens called himself the first "printer to the people" and, after 1793, "Printer to the Committee of Safety, and to the Patriotic Society" (Thomas 1874). Thounens also printed the weekly *Gazette nationale et politique,* which existed from at least January 1788 to 16 April 1793. Under Pierre T. Thounens or J. B. Thounensfils, the enterprise continued until the 1840s. Cave (1974–1975, 13–14) said that J. B. Thounens must have moved to St. Lucia and Saint-Dominique to print there.

Another periodical in Martinique in the post–French Revolution era was *Le trinité,* published by "XYZ," probably in 1790.

Most newspapers of the nineteenth century were published in St. Pierre and contained general and local news, some of which was made up of official notices. As an example of the nature of the press in Martinique in a given year, *Hubbard's,* in 1882, listed five newspapers, of which three were triweeklies, one semiweekly, and one weekly. Four appeared in St. Pierre and one in Fort-de-France. The average circulation was between four hundred and seven hundred (*Hubbard's* 1882). Although many newspapers of both Martinique and Guadeloupe had short life spans (especially in the twentieth century when they often lasted as long as a political party or movement), there were exceptions. For example, *Le moniteur de la Martinique,* a semiweekly published in Fort-de-France, lasted at least from 1858 to 1923; *Le propagateur,* a weekly in St. Pierre, from at least 1854 to 1894; and *Les Antilles,* from at least 1850 to about 1902. *Les Antilles,* subtitled *Journal de la Martinique,* was a weekly published in St. Pierre. An issue this author saw for 6 January 1898 contained four pages, one and one-half of which were advertisements. The paper borrowed its news items from the newspapers of the United States, France, Guadeloupe, St. Thomas, and other foreign countries.

DEVELOPMENT OF PRESS IN GUADELOUPE

Shortly before Richard published in Martinique, Jean Bénard received a "brevet d'imprimeur" from Louis XV on 28 June 1764 (Blanche 1938, 167). He arrived in Basse-Terre, Guadeloupe, on 23 March 1765 (Gropp 1941).

With this permit, Bénard alone had the right to print administrative, judicial, and other works approved by the "intendant" (the treasurer) and to sell all imported works from the Royalty. During this time, nothing escaped the censorship of the intendant. For example, even ideas seen as compatible with the social state might be seen as incompatible with the policy of the colonies. Blanche presumed that the intendant had rights equivalent to France's director of library, in that when books were submitted to the intendant (and they all were), he told the censor about them. Blanche also believed that the intendant delegated his censorship powers to others. Of course, some things escaped censorship, including indecent, obscene, and subversive books, because the censors did not read them. Blanche (1938, 167) said that the number of books imported into Guadeloupe probably increased progressively after Bénard's printing house opened.

It is not known what use Bénard made of his printing permit, and it is possible he published a gazette and books, despite a restrictive ordinance of 30 April 1771. His printing permit passed to his son, Jean, on 28 February 1778. In 1783, a *Calendrier de la Guadeloupe pour 1783* appeared carrying this information: "Guadeloupe, chez Bénard, imprimeur-libraire du Roi, avec brevet de S. M. 1783" (Blanche 1938, 168). The son's widow became the proprietor of the press in 1788, for she is listed as printer of the proceedings of L'assemblée coloniale de la Guadeloupe in 1788. The same year, the first issue of *Gazette de la Guadeloupe* appeared under her name. The weekly, published in Basse-Terre, was usually four to six pages. She also published the second known newspaper, *Affiches, announces et avis divers de d'ile Guadeloupe,* a four-page weekly first published 3 September 1789, which lasted to at least 5 August 1790 (no. 48). Her two publications were very objective; they contained advice, news, and announcements but no political articles or comments (Blanche 1938, 169).

Concerning the policy of the royal printer and press during the French Revolution, Blanche said that virtually nothing is known. He said that possibly Widow Bénard's *Affiches* was published then, since issues of 1789–1790 survive (Blanche 1938, 170). Guadeloupe itself went through a turbulent period with an uprising of slaves from 1792 to 1794 plus a British invasion. Slavery was abolished in March 1794, when Guadeloupe, which had been proslavery, took up sides with the British.

One early Guadeloupe newspaper (possibly the third or fourth) that researchers such as Blanche and Cave failed to mention is *Journal républicain de la Guadeloupe*. Number 13, 24 April, "l'an 2 de la république français" (1794), preserved in the Library Company of Philadelphia, contains four pages numbered 65 to 68. Published in Basse-Terre, the eight-by-twelve-inch newspaper came off the press of Bénard and d'A. L. Villette. That Bénard's name was listed as the printer conflicts with Blanche's statement that Bénard had sold his permit to M. Cabre in 1792. Cabre has been identified with the printing in Pointe-à-Pitre of two early nineteenth-century newspapers, *Les affiches de la Guadeloupe ou la feuille universelle* (1803) and *Les affiches hebdomadaires de la Guadeloupe* (1806). He sold his establishment to a Mr. Ginet, who apparently published until 1809 *Gazette de la Guadeloupe,* an official paper (Blanche 1938, 172). After 1792, all printing was taken over by the government.

In 1804, Guadeloupe printing shops were reserved for the préfecture coloniale and the capitainerie générale. That same year, the capitaine général of Guadeloupe created a *Journal officiel de la Guadeloupe et dépendances* to publish official acts; it was replaced in 1805 by *Bulletin officiel de la Guadeloupe,* which lasted until 1809 (Blanche 1938, 171). A government printing office was established in January 1815 by the governor of Guadeloupe to print laws and ordinances in its *Gazette officielle,* a newspaper that survived throughout the nineteenth century under other names, such as *Journal officiel* and *Journal officiel de la Guadeloupe* (Blanche 1938, 172).

Besides the obvious control of printing exercised in the French Antilles through the issuance of printing permits, much legislation that further restricted publishing was enacted in the nineteenth century. The result in all three French territories in the Caribbean was that press freedom was tenuous, depending upon what was in effect in France. In 1816, the governor-general of Guadeloupe implemented an ordinance on printing and the press that remained in force for twenty years. This ordinance restored the previous censorship and authorization, provided for the appointment of two censors (one each for Basse-Terre and Pointe-à-Pitre), and instituted a license fee, payable in advance quarterly, for the professions of printer, bookseller, and editor. An ordinance of 9 February 1827 abolished the license fee but, according to Blanche (1938, 175), placed much authority in the hands of the governor, who became the "grand master" of printing and the press; no one could publish anything unless he permitted it.

In spite of the censorship, authorization, and license fee, a politically orthodox newspaper was started in Pointe-à-Pitre on 8 January 1817 by M. Jean-Baptiste Minee. The *Journal politique et commercial de la Pointe-à-Pitre* took various names, such as *Journal commercial, economique et maritime de la Pointe-à-Pitre* in 1824, *Journal commercial* in 1828, *Journal commercial de la Pointe-à-Pitre* in 1833, *La Guadeloupe, journal commercial . . .* in 1856, *Le commercial de la Guadeloupe* in 1860, and finally, *Le commercial,* before its disappearance in 1871. In 1833, M. Armand Haget, former Martinique printer, obtained authorization to open a print shop in Pointe-à-Pitre and started *Le courrier de la Guadeloupe,* which changed its name to *Avenir* (in 1841) and *L'avenir* (in 1845) before ceasing publication in 1878.

Through a 2 May 1848 decree, the provisional government proclaimed freedom of the press in the French colonies. The preamble of the decree recognized the need of colonial societies to have freedom of expression. This law abolished censorship of newspapers and other writings, allowed all newspapers to print without previous authorization, and stated that no periodical could be suspended or revoked administratively. However, the decree did have restrictive clauses. Another law of 7 August 1850 listed criminal offenses of the press punishable by three months to two years in prison and five hundred to four thousand francs in fines. Among such offenses were provoking to re-establish slavery, insulting in any way representatives of the metropolitan government, and inciting the public to resistance against the metropolitan authority (Blanche 1938, 177).

A law of 20 February 1852 abrogated the decrees of 1848 and 1850, saying they were not authoritarian enough, and vigorously returned the royal ordinance of 9 February 1827; it again gave the governor the right to commission printers, to authorize publication of newspapers, and to revoke newspapers in cases of abuse. Censorship was abolished in 1863, but the imperial decree of 5 July of that year established another strong rule that affected the press: authorization had to be obtained for publication of newspapers with political and socioeconomic content; moreover, administrative authorities had a right to warn the press, to suspend newspapers during certain times, to suspend papers with or without warning by proportion of general surety, and to hand press offenses over to correctional tribunals. Other changes occurred concerning press freedom with the laws of 14 February 1880 and 29 July 1881.

In 1892, the black people of Guadeloupe were promoting an honorable place in the society and a role in the government for themselves through a party and newspapers such as *Le peuple, Cri du peuple, La cravache petit bulletin officiel du Détachement socialiste Guadeloupéen,* and *Le bulletin du soir du Détachement Guadeloupéen du parti ouvrier francais.* These activities were directed mainly by M. Hégésippe Lígitimus (Blanche 1938, 182–84).

THE PRESS IN TWENTIETH-CENTURY MARTINIQUE

Through three academic theses supervised by Professor Xavier Yacono at Université de Toulouse, one is able to trace the development of the press in Martinique from the early twentieth century until the 1970s (see Louison 1971; DeLor 1970; Valdor 1973; all available on microfiche).[2] What is evident from these works is that the press definitely developed as a political tool during this century.

From the beginning of the twentieth century until 1940, Martinique was flooded with periodicals, about 110, partly because the many political organizations that existed needed their own outlets.

Louison (1971, 6) reported that between 1920 and 1939, nineteen printing firms operated in Fort-de-France, three of which published most of the newspapers (Imprimeríe Deslandes, fourteen; Imprimeríe Illemay and Imprimeríe Cooperative, seven each). Among the newspapers with political biases, eight were labeled by Louison as republican and radical. These ranged from the long-lived *La France coloniale,* an organ of the Democratie martiniquaise and Democratie coloniale, which was published as a biweekly between June 1900 and 20 February 1925, to *Le radical,* an organ of the Parti radical et radical socialiste, which published as a weekly from 11 March to 31 July 1937. Four others (*La democratie coloniale, L'aurore, La resistance,* and *L'action socialiste*) were socialist. The longest-lived of these was *L'aurore,* published as a biweekly organ of the Défense républicaine between 5 February 1919 and 15 June 1935. *La resistance,* a biweekly of the Fédération de la Martinique parti socialiste, was published from 23 January 1925 to 25 May 1937. Louison also listed seven "newspapers of the left" and three of the right. Among leftist newspapers, *Justice* was the organ of five different organizations before finally becoming the Parti communiste français paper in 1936. Rightist newspapers included *La riposte,* which lasted about seven months in 1925; *L'etincelle,* a weekly of Groupement national d'evolution sociale in 1936–1937, and *Le journal des contribuables,* a bimonthly of La Ligue des contribuables de la Martinique between 1938 and 1941. Eight other political papers of various persuasions were listed, including *Le flambeau,* a weekly promoting Marcus Garvey's Pan-Africanism, and *La libre pensee,* an anticlerical paper.

The ten commercial newspapers promoting economics and corporations were primarily published in the 1930s, and most of them had very brief lives. In addition, six literary, satirical, or sports periodicals appeared in the 1930s but survived usually just a year or less.

Besides the more specialized periodicals mentioned above, Martinique also had at least ten major dailies and weeklies for general circulation between 1920 and 1939. Among these were *La depeche,* a short-lived daily (April to October 1926) of politics, literature, and economics; *Le cablo,* a two-page daily between 1935 and 15 December 1936; *L'information,* a daily in 1935; *Le martiniquais,* a four-page daily that lasted for a few months in 1937; *Le radio quotidien,* which published Havas News Service copy for three months in 1937; *La presse,* which was established in 1937 and continued after World War II as *La petite patrie; La clairon,* established as a daily in 1939; *Le courrier des Antilles,* a weekly started in 1921; *La paix,* started on 1 February 1913 and lasting until the 1970s; and *La paix dominicale,* a religious weekly that appeared for two months in 1920.

All newspapers of Martinique during the first four decades of this century had a limited number of pages (usually two to four) and sparse circulations. In fact, as late as 1947, newspapers usually had circulations of between twenty-five hundred and fifty-five hundred.

During World War II, from 1939 to 1945, newspapers had to be authorized and very few were allowed to publish in Martinique. Louison (1971) reported that only two newspapers were created in the early 1940s, both patterned after Vichy regime models in France.

In the 1945 to 1958 period, according to DeLor (1970), about twenty-five to thirty periodicals were continued or established in Martinique. Again, many were of a political nature, such as *Le progressiste,* a weekly after 1958 which promoted Parti progressiste martiniquais; *La voix socialiste,* a weekly publication of the Fédération socialiste (SFIO) de la Martinique; *La voix Républicaine,* a weekly of the Républicains et des socialistes de la Martinique (established in 1951); *Rénovation,* established as a monthly in 1940 as the "organ l'expansion martiniquaise dans le monde"; *L'appel,* a weekly devoted to the "defense des interêts généraux de la Martinique dans le cadre de l'Union Française" (established in 1955); *Les nouvelles,* a weekly started in 1953; and *Le rappel,* a weekly journal of the M. R. P.: Fédération de la Martinique which was started in 1946.

For the years 1958 to 1970, Valdor (1973) listed papers continued from previous eras, such as *Justice,* a Communist party weekly of eight thousand circulation in 1970; *Le progressiste; Le populaire de la Martinique; Les nouvelles; La paix; La petite patrie;* as well as newcomers such as *Présence socialiste,* a bimonthly of the Fédération de la Martinique du parti socialiste unifíe; *Le combat,* newspaper of the Défense de la Martinique, Départment française, started in 1967 as a weekly; and *France-Antilles,* a daily established in 1964.

RECENT INFRINGEMENTS ON THE FRENCH ANTILLEAN PRESS

Throughout its more recent history in the French Antilles, the press at times believed it was being victimized by the authorities. This occurred in 1963, when groups such as the Front de Défense des Libertés Publiques, made up of local organizations, attacked what they believed were abuses by the prefect of Martinique, who they alleged created a repressive regime by banning meetings, seizing newspapers and pamphlets, and transforming French radio in the Antilles into a propaganda tool (Mitchell 1968, 244). Later in 1963, pressures against French Antillean newspapers continued with seizures of *L'etincelle,* the official organ of the Guadeloupe Communist party, and *Progrès social,* also of Guadeloupe.

The latter newspaper ran into difficulties with the authorities again in 1965 when its editor, Rémy Bébel, was arrested for attacking the Guadeloupe administration's handling of municipal elections "more effectively than wisely" (Mitchell 1968, 249). Bébel was transferred to Paris, where he was imprisoned for a week.

CONTEMPORARY MEDIA

Martinique and Guadeloupe are served by media that are parts of large Parisian media concerns, by an unusually large number of radio stations, and by a plethora of special interest weeklies.

The one daily on the two islands is *France-Antilles,* published in Fort-de-France with editions for both islands. It is part of the Robert Hersant media group, which controls at least twelve of France's most important dailies, including *Le figaro* and *France soir,* about ninety radio stations, and other interests. One in five of France's newspaper readers purchase an Hersant paper daily. Until 1978, a Guadeloupe edition of *France-Antilles* was provided only on Monday, Tuesday, Thursday, and Saturday.

By Caribbean standards, *France-Antilles* is large, averaging sixteen to twenty pages, and expensive (3.80 Fr, or U.S. $.60, on weekdays, and 4.60 Fr, or U.S. $.82, on Saturday). The paper takes the reactionary position of its French owner, who is known for his right-wing politics. Canadian researcher, Alvina Ruprecht, described the paper as a mixture of a French regional newspaper and the sensational, usually nonpolitical *France soir* (Interview, Ruprecht 1988).

Guadeloupe director and editor-in-chief, Alfred Ollivrin, said that Hersant does not interfere in the *France-Antilles'* day-to-day operations. Hersant has put his son, Philippe, in charge of the French West Indies operation, and according to Ollivrin, Philippe visits the newspapers three or four times a year and telephones at other times to keep in touch. Ollivrin explained: "We have the responsibility to make choices. But, we are chosen by Hersant [to be in management] because we have the same views as Hersant. It is obligatory to have the same view" (Interview, Ollivrin 1988).[3]

Hersant's media group in the Caribbean is structured under a parent company, Société Publi-Print (*France-Antilles*), a national advertising agency located in Martinique. Publi-Print operates the daily paper on both islands, as well as Radio Bis on Guadeloupe and Radio RV7 on Martinique. Also under Publi-Print are the free advertisement weeklies owned by Hersant, *971* on Guadeloupe and *972* on Martinique.[4]

14.1 Guadeloupe edition of *France-Antilles,* major
daily of the French Antilles owned by media magnate
Robert Hersant.

A television station was also in Publi-Print's plans in 1987–1988, but Ollivrin believed that another private interest would be given the islands' third television channel. "The government licensing board has ambiguous, too complex laws on concentration of ownership, and it thinks Hersant already has too many media properties," Ollivrin explained. Publi-Print was tied in with a group of local business people who had been pirating television from the United States; their joint proposal disintegrated when Hersant could not agree with the terms (Interview, Ollivrin 1988).

France-Antilles sees itself not as a press of opinion but, according to Ollivrin, as one of information. He added, "We're French 'liberals'— liberals in the sense of a free market" (Interview, Ollivrin 1988). In fact a scan of the paper's pages demonstrates a lack of opinion and an emphasis on sensationalism and commercial sales.[5] Advertisements, most in full color, load nearly every page; additionally, a page is given to classified advertisements. The other nineteen pages of *France-Antilles* include five devoted to Guadeloupe news, mostly of social and business gatherings; seven to sports, with many photographs of participants; one to French affairs; one to France and world news; one to women's issues; and one to features, including foreign comic strips, a horoscope, and a crossword puzzle. An advice-to-the-lovelorn column is written by a Guadeloupean, and some political cartoons are provided by a Martinique artist.

French Caribbean and other regional events are covered by a mixture of island and metropolitan France reporters. The Guadeloupe *France-Antilles* employs ten to fifteen journalists, with a ratio of two Guadeloupeans to every French person. The Martinique edition has twenty reporters. Other journalists claim that *France-Antilles* and the government radio and television stations usually assign metropolitan France reporters to important island or regional stories.

Discussing the problems of newspapers in the French Antilles, Ollivrin said that there was much competition among the many media for advertising revenue and admitted that *France-Antilles* fared very well. He said that the distance between France and the islands and the distribution of the papers were other difficulties. The Guadeloupe office of *France-Antilles* rents a special plane to deliver copy to Martinique every day, and "sometimes we are late," he said. The price of newspapers (even weeklies cost U.S. $.53 to U.S. $1.80) is exorbitant, twice as expensive as in France in relationship to buying power. Ollivrin said that newspapers suffer because the public does not have much money nor a reading tradition—"They'd prefer to see television or listen to radio" (Interview, Ollivrin 1988).

Other Paris-based media in the Caribbean are Société nationale de radio-télévision française d' outre mer (RFO), state-financed radio and television, and Radio caraïbes internationale, financed by private and public metropolitan interests. RFO has been described as one regional subunit of metropolitan culture "defined in terms of the dominant national culture which is European French" (Ruprecht 1988, 8). For example, its forty-five minutes of daily news emphasizes events directly related to metropolitan France institutions. Before 1982, state broadcasting monopolized as private broadcasting had not been permitted.

Radio and television broadcasts of RFO, according to one radio official, give the impression that because Guadeloupe and Martinique are French, they are better culturally and financially than the rest of the Caribbean. She added that these programs project a patronizing attitude and provide the message through slanted coverage that if the islands were to become independent of France, they would suffer the plight of the rest of the region (Interview, Mekel 1988). Thus, a problem-plagued island such as Haiti is given much coverage, especially on television, with visuals showing poverty and chaotic situations. "They don't use pictures of Barbados, which is a stable, independent country," the same radio official said (Interview, Mekel 1988).

RFO broadcasts solely in French. The station director rationalized that Creole, the language of most of the people, is not appropriate for national radio because it is a "regional dialect and technically inadequate for weather or traffic reports" (Ruprecht 1988, 5). Neither RFO nor RCI is known for controversial programming.

In fact, to make local television more controversial, relevant, and realistic, the conseil régional in 1986 commissioned Télévision Caraïbes to produce and air fourteen news-magazine shows based on, and originating from, the Guadeloupean population. Journalists organized a team of nonjournalist interviewers from various towns to conduct on-the-spot spontaneous interviews on current topics. These programs commenced airing in early 1987 but were abruptly stopped.

Otherwise, virtually no local programming exists on RFO television. The latest figure on Guadeloupe is four hours monthly, plus a twenty-minute news bulletin on RFO-1 five days a week (Ruprecht 1988, 6). Most of the other shows on RFO-1 and RFO-2 emanate from France, with 20 percent of all shows (such as "Santa Barbara," "Dallas," or "Hotel") coming from the United States. Some short video clips of local singing groups are inserted to fill in around programs. The commercials use Antillean actors and actresses.

RC1 broadcasts thirty minutes of news daily, but like RFO radio, it

steers away from conflict-oriented coverage. Instead, the station emphasizes human interest stories and metropolitan France–related events.
Since January 1988, France-Inter, a state-owned station, has been coming into the French Caribbean directly from France via satellite on the
AM band.

Besides RFO and RC1, the other popular radio stations on Guadeloupe are Radio Bis, Radio Galaxy, and Radyo Tanbou. Radio Bis and
its Martinique counterpart, Radio RV7, concentrate on music and talk
shows, ignoring news almost entirely. A local bulletin is given at 7:30
A.M., as well as hourly, two-minute news flashes via satellite from Sud-
Radio in France. Radio Bis aims at a young radio audience, usually
upper class and metropolitan-oriented. French and U.S. music predominate, but every hour at least two "very high quality" Guadeloupe records
are played. The choice of records is decided by the director of programming, who is from France, as are half of the disc jockeys (Interview,
Ollivrin 1988).

The station that stands out as different in the French Caribbean is
Radyo Tanbou, financed by Le Mouvement patriotique, an umbrella
group formed by local organizations that support the independence
party, Union pour la libération de la Guadeloupe (UPLG). Operating out
of an apartment in Point-á-Pitre, the station uses the barest equipment
and a largely volunteer staff to provide "intellectually demanding and
politically stimulating programming" (Ruprecht 1988, 11). The studio is
furnished with a dining room table, assorted kitchen chairs, and a
bench; the staff is made up of six journalists, one news director, and ten
technicians, only three of whom are paid.

Yet, even with such a modest operation, Radyo Tanbou has become
the third most popular station behind RFO and RC1. According to a
recent poll conducted by a Paris agency, RFO and RC1 captured a total
of 43 percent of the Guadeloupe audience while Tanbou had 15.8 percent
(Ruprecht 1988, 9). Its popularity can be attributed to a number of
characteristics: use of Creole, local and traditional music, many interviews and much information, and local and regional news sources. Unlike the more than seventy other stations of Guadeloupe and Martinique,
Radyo Tanbou does not resort to escapist content, such as games or
phone-in quizzes. All sectors of society are sought for their views, and
the audience is encouraged to phone in examples of injustices, thus acting as free-lance correspondents (Ruprecht 1988, 11).

At least ninety minutes of news make up the daily schedule of
Tanbou, blocked in twenty-minute to one-hour packages at 6:30 A.M.,
12:30 P.M., and 6:00 P.M. Most of the stories deal with local or neighboring islands' events. In addition, detailed information programs of forty-

five minutes to two hours are broadcast daily on different topics. On Mondays, there are specials on sports and on history; Wednesday programs focus on economics and on schools and education; on Saturdays, health and international concerns are addressed; and Sundays feature culture stories. Other in-depth broadcasts are provided regularly on social welfare and the environment, and the issue of independence is addressed for forty-five minutes weekly by the UPLG. All of these shows use volunteer guests — specialists from governmental, educational, union, and professional organizations — and most of them encourage audience participation via telephone (Interview, Mekel 1988). The most popular Tanbou program is "What Do You Think About It?" on Sunday mornings. A journalist presents the main events of the week, after which the audience is allowed to react by phone.

Among the problems Tanbou faces are lack of money needed to update the antiquated equipment and to pay the many volunteers and lack of time to solicit advertising. The station uses very few commercials because the volunteer staff members are working full-time jobs elsewhere during the day when advertisers can be approached. Surprisingly, the station has had minimal problems with the government. In 1983, the authorities threatened to close Tanbou, claiming the station stored arms in its studio. While police searched the premises, a crowd demonstrated outside, and the authorities left. Shortly after, the UPLG called for a demonstration in support of Tanbou and against the government action, and ten thousand people appeared (Interview, Mekel 1988).

Ruprecht (1988, 18–19) explained why the government has kept its hands off Tanbou despite its often adversary nature.

> Radyo Tanbou shows it is well aware of the limits of state tolerance because it instigates a self-imposed censorship. . . . While this collective "we" does ask embarrassing questions, while it does broadcast events which other stations do not air because of their controversial or "delicate" political nature, while it does offer resistance by questioning power relations, protesting openly, and proclaiming the need for change, Radyo Tanbou does not advocate violence. In fact, it does not propose any concrete acts of any kind.

Guadeloupe and Martinique are very unusual among Caribbean countries for their large numbers of radio stations. Each has at least three dozen stations, most of which are authorized and some of which are private operations. Guadeloupe actually has forty-three private stations and one semi-private station, as well as a state-sponsored national network. Various political parties, religious groups, and important people have started their own stations. Even small villages often have a station with a limited range and broadcast schedule.

For example, on Guadeloupe, Radio Massabielle is a Roman Catholic station, which proclaims that cultural tradition should be a product of Western values; Radio Souffle De Vie and Radio Vie Meilleure are Protestant outlets. Radio Gaïac is Guadeloupe's Communist party station, Radio Inité is "Independantiste," and Radio Galaxy is private and business-minded with a rightist perspective.

Television expansion is also accelerated in the French Antilles. As indicated earlier, the Commission nationale de la communication et des libertés (CNCL) in mid-1988 considered the possibility of a third channel. Among the proposals were those of Canal 10, backed by Edouard Boulogne and a group of Guadeloupe businessmen with support from French right-wing parties; Canal 4, supported by Jacques Faed; Guadeloupoe-Télévision, under Michel Hamousin, a Guadeloupean producer working in Paris; and Télévision Caraïbes, already described (Interview, Ollivrin 1988; Ruprecht 1988). Canal 10 had already begun telecasts in 1988, even before a CNCL decision, and irregularly and illegally provided fare from the United States and Mexico via satellite.

Just as there are many broadcasting stations, so are there dozens of weekly newspapers and monthly magazines in the islands. In Guadeloupe, at least thirteen widely read newspapers and magazines exist. The majority of them serve political purposes, and most are relatively expensive.

On bookshop and convenience store shelves in Guadeloupe are newspapers such as *Match,* an eight-page Socialist party organ founded in 1943; *Le progrès social,* a four-page weekly serving the "defense of Guadeloupe" interests against those of colonialism; *Combat ouvrier,* a Trotskyite weekly; *Lendèpandans,* a six-page weekly of the UPLG; *L'etincelle,* an eight-page, forty-four-year-old organ of the Communist party; and *Criterium,* a photo-packed, ten-page sports weekly.

Among the magazines are *Antilla, Sept, Antilla kréyol, Koubari, Expression,* and *Guadeloupe 2000 Magazine.* The relatively free press in Guadeloupe and Martinique allows a range of periodicals from far-right Catholic to far-left Trotskyist. Circulation of weeklies ranges from three thousand to seven thousand.

Writing in 1979, Zandronis (p. 11) identified some of the above publications, as well as others such as *Jakata,* a twelve-page monthly promoting Guadeloupe's independence; *Lekol,* a thirty-two page, political monthly; *Madras,* an eight-page periodical of L'union des femmes guadeloupéenes; *Le jeune garde; Guadeloupe roman;* and *Corail.*

Martinique also is served plentifully by such periodicals. In 1979, this author found at least twenty to twenty-five specialized periodicals in the bookshops he visited in Fort-de-France. For example, among political newspapers were *Martinique avenir,* a six-page weekly of the Rassemblement pour la république; *Révolution socialiste Antilles,* an eight-page weekly "pour la construction du Parti Communiste Révolutionnaire"; *Rénovation,* a two-page bimonthly of the "L'Expansion antillaise dans le monde"; *Justice,* a twelve-page weekly of the Communist party; *L'Indépendant de la Martinique,* a two-page monthly of the "Défense des intérêts économiques de la Martinique"; *Le progressiste,* a sixteen-page paper of the Martinique Progressive party; and *La parole au peuple,* a twelve-page newspaper promoting the independence movement of Martinique. Most of these periodicals listed not only editors but also "political directors." Regional general-interest magazines, such as *Le naif qui va plus loin, Le naif,* and *Carib-Hebdo,* all published in Fort-de-France, were available, as were cultural periodicals, such as *Toi . . . Antilles,* an interesting mixture of emphasis on hair beauty, ceramics, art, jazz, macramé, etc., published monthly in Fort-de-France. *Choubouloute* was a sixty-six-page weekly in English and French oriented to the tourist, with television-radio schedules, lists of restaurants and museums, and many advertisements. At least two women's magazines were published: *Grain d'or,* a twenty-eight-page weekly, and *Femmes martiniquaises,* an eight-page monthly. Some of these periodicals still survive in Martinique, notably *Le progressiste, Révolution socialiste Antilles,* and *Justice.*

In the South American portion of the French Caribbean, French Guiana, mass media are very underdeveloped. A small daily, *Le radio presse* (circulation of fifteen hundred), was published in Cayenne in the 1970s. However, by 1988, the major newspaper, *France-Antilles Guyane,* appeared only twice weekly. Owned by Robert Hersant, the paper was not closely affiliated with its sister daily in Guadeloupe and Martinique (Interview, Ollivrin 1988).

Interestingly, French Guiana has been used as a launching site for high-powered radio and telecommunications projects. In 1979, the European-made Ariane rocket was fired from Kourou, freeing Europe from U.S. space technology and providing another alternative for Third World satellite launchings. A high-powered radio relay station was instituted in 1982, equipped with six 500-kw transmitters, and broadcasts Portuguese programs to Brazil, Spanish shows to other parts of Latin America, and English productions to North America.

CONCLUSION

The press of the French Antilles has been very closely related to that of France. The regulations under which the French Antilles press has operated have been those of the metropolitan country, as have been the contents of all the mass media. The latter point is not surprising, for the importance attached to the metropolitan country is reflected in contents of colonial newspapers everywhere.

For most of its lifetime, the French Antillean press has been partisan to one or another political party. Again, this is similar to the other colonial experiences, including those of the Dutch and former British Caribbean. What is different is that although the major Commonwealth Caribbean nations and the Netherlands Antilles colonies have political newspapers, in most cases they are secondary to the main dailies, most privately owned, that serve more general informational roles. In the French Antilles, there is only one major daily owned by a France-based group; most of the rest of the press is political party–oriented and –owned.

Only infrequently does one hear of contemporary incidences of freedom-of-press violations in the French Caribbean. At first glance, this could be interpreted as a hands-off policy on the part of the government. Others, however, would suggest that where government control is nearly complete, the usual flare-ups in press-government relationships do not exist. In the case of the French Antilles, the very political nature of contemporary newspapers would indicate a modicum of freedom, for some of the political sheets do take critical stands against the government. It may be that these political sheets, because of their small circulations, are not taken very seriously by officials and therefore do not represent threats.

In all of the Caribbean, not many countries have the wealth of the media operations in Guadeloupe and Martinique. Except for Cuba and the Dominican Republic, no country has as many radio stations as do the French Antilles, and very few have as many television channels.

15

Haitian Mass Media

Nineteenth-century and twentieth-century journalism in Haiti has seldom been free, an irony when one considers that Haiti was the second independent country in the Western Hemisphere and the first black republic in the world.

The hundreds of newspapers in the 1800s lived precarious and short lives, partly because of persecutions by various heads of state; in the present century, the media have faced the iron hands of the U.S. Marine Corps and one Haitian president after another. The culmination of this oppression was nearly thirty years of methodical Duvalier control.

If there was a time when the press flourished, it probably was in the latter eighteenth century, in the waning years of French colonization and in the beginning era of independence.

HISTORY OF THE PRESS

Printing was introduced to the French colony about 1725. Cabon (Brigham 1940, 5) wrote that a librarian, Joseph Payen, published a book on his press at Léogane in that year. Not much else is known about early Haitian printing except that between the time of the Treaty of Paris and the outbreak of the French Revolution, the colony had about fifty journals. This was in comparison with French provinces, which had only four or five journals each. Logan (1968, 86) said that the newspapers were subjected to official censorship, but the Inquisition had no jurisdiction over the French colony.

The first newspaper was the weekly *Gazette de Saint-Dominique,* issued in 1764 by the printer, Antoine Marie. Renamed *Affiches améri-*

caines after 1776, the paper survived until 1796, claiming as many as fifteen hundred subscribers.[1] Logan (1968, 86) wrote that besides the usual news and announcements of travelers, local events, entertainments, and sales of slaves and other property, *Affiches* also used articles about Indian ruins, topography, and hydrography.

A monthly *Journal de Saint-Dominique* was started in 1765; its sixty-four pages were equally divided between belles letters and items on agriculture, commerce, diseases, climate, science, and natural history. The *Journal* was short-lived because of lack of subscribers, as were *Iris américaine,* a poetry periodical of the 1760s, and *Gazette de médecine* of 1778–1779. Survival was difficult because of the limited number of readers, the high cost of paper, and the necessity of importing presses from France.

Other periodicals after the French Revolution were *Courrier de St. Dominique* in 1790, *Le Républicain* in 1793, and *L'ami de l'egalite* in 1792 (Brigham 1940). Articles in some of these papers were so fiery that a member of the Colonial Assembly asked that "the liberty of the press be abolished for having caused the ruin of Saint Dominque." He explained that the "colony was flourishing; but since it has been allowed to write on all kinds of subjects, tranquility and wealth have disappeared" (Desquiron 1988, 13). One paper that promoted French propaganda was *Bulletin oficiel de Saint Dominique,* published in July 1798 by P. Roux. Otero (1953, 381) wrongly called this the first periodical of Haiti.

After the slave revolt that made Haiti an independent country in 1804, the *Gazette politique et commerciale d' Hayti* was published as the country's official newspaper.

The printing press was an important instrument on the island. Rotberg (1971, 36) reported that the town of Cap Français, which in 1789 had twenty thousand inhabitants, possessed a printing company as well as several newspapers. When Henri Christophe became Henri I, King of Haiti, and moved his palace to Sans Souci, a well-equipped Imprimeríe Royale d' Hayti was established. Christophe, though illiterate, had literacy aspirations for his kingdom, which he hoped to realize through the press. Established in 1817, Imprimeríe Royale carried on the work started by the royal government between 1811 and 1816, when its printer, P. Roux, brought out about twenty titles. Most of these works were decrees, broadsides, and treatises.

The director of the royal press at Sans Souci was a Monsieur Buon, and the first publication of the press was the 1817 *Almanach royale d'Hayti.* The almanac was first published at the Cap Haitien Press in 1813. Also in 1817, the royal press printed a political essay by Pompée-Valentin, the Baron de Vastey, in which he refuted another writer's claim that the only way Haiti could prosper was as a part of France (Esterquest 1940, 178). The third title from this press was a play by the Count of Rosiers in 1818, and the final three works, in 1819, were the 1820 *Almanach Royale,* Baron de Vastey's essay on causes for Haiti's revolution and civil wars, and another essay by the Count of Rosiers (Esterquest 1940, 179).

Throughout the nineteenth century, many newspapers appeared,[2] as did many publication decrees, and repressive actions were frequent. For example, the famous journalist Pierre Frédérique was exiled three times and died as a pauper in New York; Joseph Courtois lived in exile for years, and as early as 1820, the Haitian president had a journalist named Darfour executed in public (Desquiron 1988, 13). On 28 October 1885, "Loi sur la Presse" was passed, guaranteeing freedom of the press but with responsibility. To assure the latter, the law required registration of publications with the Secretairerie d' Etat de L'Interieur, providing the name of the periodical, the place of publication, and the publisher (Shearman and Rayner 1926, 128–30).

Between 1804 and 1949, at least 885 newspapers were published in Haiti. Oldest among the surviving newspapers is *Le nouvelliste,* founded in 1896 by Cheraquil and Henry Chauvet, and *Le matin,* started in 1906. The Chauvet family still owns *Le nouvelliste.*

Suppression of newspapers was very frequent during the U.S. occupation of Haiti from 1915 to 1934. In fact, the declaration of martial law by the United States forces in September 1915 was used mainly against the press (Balch 1972, 122). The U.S. administrators and marines were tough, allowing presidents Philippe Sudre Dartiguenave, Louis Borno, and Sténio Vincent to act only as puppet rulers. Censorship was heavy-handed, and at any given time several editors languished in jail. Throughout the 1920s the telegraph was censored by the U.S. military, which also controlled Associated Press and United Press dispatches through Marine Corps representatives. In 1927, at least seven editors were jailed at the same time; on 26 July they addressed a letter to *The Nation* in the United States complaining about infringements on press freedom (*The Nation* 1927a).

The U.S. Marines' most effective weapons against Haitian journalists were "preventive imprisonment" and the press laws. Among the latter was the stipulation that the government's legal representative in the courts could issue a summons against press personnel anytime he saw fit. Thus, the writer of an offending article, along with the manager and editor of his publication, would be arrested and imprisoned. Once in jail, the journalists were likely to remain there without examination by a magistrate or judgment of a court. Jailed journalists were denied paper and writing materials, and if their newspapers wrote stories considered offensive to the marines while they were in prison, they were hauled before the court for a new sentence.

The Nation (1927b, 166) reported that in 1924, the U.S. authorities even jailed the press operator of *Poste;* a year later, they "went still further, and locked up all the compositors of the *Courrier haitien,* while, under the direction of an American officer, gendarmes brought coffee sacks and piled into them all the type in the composing room, which they took in a truck to the record office of the civil tribunal."

After the United States departed, the press continued to be victimized by Haitian leaders. President Vincent in the 1930s reintroduced censorship, jailed editors without trial, and suspended their publication. His successors, Elie Lescot, Dumarsais Estimé, and Paul Magloire, followed this pattern in the 1940s and 1950s. During Magloire's administration, the police broke up and carried away the press and type of the daily *Haiti démocratique* and arrested its editor and deputy (Rothberg 1971, 184).

Despite these setbacks, dailies survived in Port-au-Prince, with nine to twenty-five appearing on the streets by the 1940s. The number depended upon the political situation, according to A. J. Liebling, who wrote, "Whenever an election impends, newspapers blossom like an hibiscus, practically everywhere you turn" (Liebling 1948, 65). The nine regulars in 1948 were *Le nouvelliste, La nation, Haiti-Journal, Le matin, Le soir, Le République, Le reveil, La phalange,* and *L'action.*

Liebling (1948, 65) was struck by the poetic quality of writing in dailies, attributing it to the number of poets who doubled as reporters or editorial writers "to balance their budgets." He said that Port-au-Prince journalism seemed to be a "ball of rhetoric skillfully bounced from one ball of intelligence to another." In 1948, foreign news received little attention in these dailies, which stressed local political and aesthetic topics, according to Liebling. Rodman (1961, 158–59) agreed that Haitian newspapers were "primarily vehicles of literature and polemics rather than news." Except for *Le nouvelliste,* Haitian dailies were not known for their independence, he said, adding, "All the other dailies rumble with indignation and view with alarm but are far from independent."

HISTORY OF BROADCASTING

Broadcasting began in Haiti on 22 October 1926, when the 1-kw Radio HHK aired programs dealing with agricultural innovations and education. Nine years later, HH2S and HH3W, owned by wealthy local businessmen, became the first commercial stations. Others came onto the scene after the 1950s: Radio 4-VEH in Cap Haitien in 1950; the government's Radio Commerce in 1956; the Protestant Radio Lumière and Jesuit Radio Manrese, both in 1959; Radio Nouveau Monde, 1969; Radio Métropole, 1970; and Radio Haiti-Inter, 1971 (Tarter 1985, 47).

By 1980, sixteen stations were broadcasting from Port-au-Prince and nineteen from other cities. Almost all were independently funded through the sale of commercial time. Radio licensing and monitoring are still handled by the Conseil national de télécommunications (CONATEL), founded by presidential decree of 27 September 1967.

Radio Lumière, which is Haiti's only radio network with five stations, was started by David Harti of Worldteam. The original station was very basic technically, using welded irrigation pipe as a tower and a homemade antenna. After 1979, the network was decentralized to meet local village needs (Thatcher and Tarter 1983, 34). A 1976 poll showed that Lumière was the most listened-to station among the lower classes of Port-au-Prince.

The popularity of radio has soared over the years because of its inexpensive nature, because of attacks on government in the 1980s, and because of the use of Creole. By the end of the 1970s, at least one station (Haiti-Inter) broadcast four hours of entertainment and one hour of news daily in Creole (Pierce 1982b, 435). The station was on the air nineteen hours daily.

TéléHaiti, operating via cable with channels in English and French, was started in 1959. Owned primarily by Americans who derived their profits from more than 19,000 cable hookups, TéléHaiti controlled the television market until 1979. In December of that year, the first over-the-air station, Télévision nationale, was started. The station has had financial help from the Vatican.

THE DUVALIERS AND THE MASS MEDIA

Dr. François ("Papa Doc") Duvalier's ascendancy to the presidency in 1957 ushered in the most oppressive period in the history of Haitian journalism. During his fourteen years in power, Duvalier imposed censorship, closed newspapers, jailed and exiled journalists, barred foreign correspondents, subsidized papers favorable to him, and forced publication of stories and editorials that glorified his rule.

Writing about the press when Duvalier took over, Logan (1968, 165) reported that there were seven dailies (*Le nouvelliste, Le matin,* and *La phalange* were the largest and oldest) with a total circulation of about fifty thousand. Others contended that this was an inflated figure and that the top daily circulation did not exceed four thousand (Rotberg 1971, 203). The papers were in a vulnerable position; limited in circulation, they had to rely on subsidies from the church or state with consequent influences on their policies.

Duvalier was brutal in his attacks on the media. By the late 1950s, *cagoulards* (hooded Duvalierists who attacked at night) carried out his dirty work, which was termed "machine gun censorship" by *Editor and Publisher* in its 27 September 1958 edition. Haitian soldiers checked all cables and phone calls in and out of the country, and Duvalierists wreaked havoc on the media even slightly disagreeable to the authorities. In the spring of 1958, the offices of *Miroir* and *L'indépendance* were wrecked, and Georges Petit, editor of *L'indépendance,* was jailed for the seventeenth time in his life. When an aide to Duvalier bombed the tri-weekly *Le patriote,* injuring two printers, the police arrested the publisher, Antoine G. Petit, son of the already-jailed Georges (Diederich and Burt 1969, 112).

In 1960, the Catholic newspaper, *La phalange,* was ordered not to publish any information about the political situation except that released in official bulletins. Simultaneously, Duvalier's Ministry of Information stepped up its propaganda efforts for the "glorification of the self-proclaimed 'Spiritual Leader of the Nation'" (Logan 1968, 165), increasing the number of radio shows on the government's "Voice of the Republic" and the number of press releases exclaiming Duvalier's virtues.

About the same time, censorship policies were strengthened, *La phalange* was closed, and critical items in foreign periodicals circulating in Haiti were scissored (Hilton, 1963, xx–xxi). In 1963–1964, after the *Haiti Sun* was closed and its editor expelled, Duvalier sought to change his international image through Miami-based public relations agencies (Diederich and Burt 1969, 320). Most of those efforts failed as human rights groups continually denounced the regime.

By the beginning of the 1970s, the credibility of the Haitian media was dismally low. Newspapers, not permitted to publish without Duvalier's personal approval, were financially dependent upon him for subsidies and newsprint allocations. The result was the printing of sycophantic editorials, some supplied by the government, and "long reports of cultural events, gossip, home economics, verbatim texts of presidential speeches, and news of sports" (Rotberg 1971, 352). The front pages of the eight dailies and five weeklies featured pronouncements of Duvalier and other officials or long accounts of foreigners' reactions to a Haitian diplomatic or other accomplishment. Crime and other unfavorable news were ignored, as was anything remotely connected to politics (Rotberg 1971, 352).

TéléHaiti and about twenty-five independently owned radio stations avoided any information that could be construed as hostile to the regime. Instead, television featured U.S. movies and presidential messages, and radio featured Western popular music.

When Duvalier died in April 1971, his mantle of president-for-life passed to his son, Jean-Claude, also known as "Baby Doc." For the first eight or nine years of his nearly fifteen-year reign, "Baby Doc" gave the illusion that press-government relations had improved. He instituted the first presidential press conferences, used the annual press day as an occasion to proclaim meaningless press-freedom messages, and permitted the independent press to be replenished through thirteen new periodicals in Port-au-Prince (Fowler 1981). However, when criticism of the regime's policies became too severe in the eyes of the authorities, clampdowns were inevitable.

Early in "Baby Doc's" presidency, newspapers criticized the government in coded language. As Treaster said (1986a), "They worked in a kind of vague, coded language, heavy on double entendre, innuendo and implication. The most popular writing form was the meandering essay, and that is the style that predominates in the newspapers today. Fact and opinion tend to run together, and there is often more advocacy than objectivity."

More direct attacks against the government occurred after a 1975 famine when *Le petit samedi soir* editorialized that the government had no interest in ending the disaster. The paper was briefly closed for that remark and was closed again a few months later when it said that all Haitians were "only free on bail." By the end of 1975, when it printed a petition, accusing the Tonton Macoutes (the Duvaliers' goon squad) of brutality, *Le petit samedi soir* became the most widely read daily, equalling *Le nouveau monde*'s eight thousand circulation (Ahmed 1979, 51). The Tonton Macoutes reacted by hounding reporters in 1976; in June, a reporter for *Le petite samedi soir* was killed after investigating the plight of strikers.

The publishers of *Le petit samedi soir* was Dieudonne Fardin, suspected by the press to be a dupe of the United States and used as a safety valve for criticism of Duvalier (Ahmed 1979, 51). Fardin mixed sycophancy with criticism and was careful not to attack Duvalier power directly or to call attention to the embezzled millions of the president (Chamberlain 1986, 35).

A rival liberal weekly, *Hebdo jeune presse,* founded in 1975 by Bob

Neree, complemented Fardin's attacks with stories about abuses by the Tonton Macoutes and press-freedom restrictions. Although Neree was warned, he did not let up until his father was hospitalized for injuries sustained because of his writings. In December 1978, Neree closed *Jeune presse.*

By 1977, after twenty years of Duvalierism, the following five newspapers had been closed by the authorities: *La phalange, L'indépendance,* the *Haiti Sun, Le patriote,* and *Haiti miroir.* Dailies that remained were the three government organs (*Le nouveau monde,* the *Haiti-Journal,* and *Le jour*) and *Le nouvelliste, Le matin,* and *Panorama.*

"Baby Doc" strengthened his media apparatus in 1978–1979, creating an information office (Conajec) to promote the new ideology of "Jean-Claudism" and establishing the governmental television channel and a powerful radio station. In 1980, as his father had done earlier, he used U.S. public relations firms to stem criticism and build a favorable image.

Morales (1983, 18–19), like others, believed that Duvalier allowed some dissent during this period to gain favor with the Jimmy Carter administration, which tied economic aid to clean human rights slates. In 1979, however, the noose began to tighten for journalists. *Le petit samedi soir* was told to refrain from further protests against the rigged elections of February, to which publisher Fardin theatrically reacted by burning all nine thousand copies of one issue "in the name of feeble Haitian democracy."

A 1979 press law set a penalty of up to three years' imprisonment for criticisms of Duvalier or his family. Comments about lower-ranking officials landed journalists one-year jail terms. Additionally, printing companies had to submit all work for governmental approval three days prior to publication, and journalists applying for a license to work had to provide much information about their families. Using the rationale that parents complained about "ghastly sexual scenes," the government required film and theater directors to obtain authorization from three ministries—National Education, Youth and Sport, and Social Affairs.

After much outside criticism, Duvalier formed a commission to rewrite the press legislation. Surviving in the new draft, which was proclaimed in March 1980, were the journalist licensing requirement and the three-year penalty for criticisms of the president and his wife. As Pierce (1982b, 432) explained, press laws were of minimal importance; a simple, but much more effective control mechanism had long been in place.

> It operates through the Ministry of the Interior, the office in charge of police work—and therefore the most important ministry in Haiti.

No elaborate list of prohibited subjects is given out, but when a journalist displeases some dignitary he hears about it. This notice comes in two forms – by telephone and by summons to the ministry. The first is considered sufficient for minor offenses and for pliant persons. In the second, government agents are sent to pick up the offender and take him to the ministry. He is told his journalism is considered harmful to the nation. If he repeats his offense, it is suggested, he may face either official or "popular" action. The latter, on the surface, implies retaliation by irate citizens supporting the government. In reality it means hoodlums on official subsidies.

Duvalier's government abandoned any pretense at liberalization in November 1980. Using the Anti-Communist Law of 1969, the authorities conducted the most severe crackdown on mass media in nearly a decade, interrogating, detaining, and expelling nearly every independent journalist and closing radio stations and newspapers. Among the scores of political opponents arrested were eighteen top critical editors and reporters, who were given one-way tickets to the United States. Closed at least temporarily were Radio Haiti-Inter, Radio Métropole, Radio Cacique, and Radio Progrès and the following newspapers, *Le conviction, Le petit samedi soir, Régard, Coquerico,* and *Inter-Jeune* (Americas Watch 1984, 4).

The next five years were dotted with instances of suppression. In February 1984, Duvalier staged parliamentary elections and announced the end to arbitrary arrest and torture. He said that newspapers were free to write what they wanted. Three politician-journalists who took him at his word suffered the consequences. Christian Democratic party leader Sylvio Claude, also editor of *Conviction,* had to go into hiding when the police seized five thousand copies of his magazine and his press. Also closed were *Fraternité,* an organ of the Social Christian party edited by Gregoire Eugène, and *L'information,* published by Pierre-Robert Auguste, who was beaten by police. Arrested with Eugène and Auguste was Fardin of *Le petit samedi soir.*

Radios Lumière and Soleil, which reported these arrests, were warned by the authorities, and Soleil went off the air for a few days after being threatened by masked thugs. Also during the summer of 1984, the director of state television was dismissed for talking too much with foreign journalists, and Claude's home was raided by police, who beat his daughter and seized the next day's galleys of *Conviction.*

Perhaps because the church was a bit immune from government, the religious stations, Soleil and Lumière, continued their critical broadcasts. In 1985, however, the director of Soleil was expelled, and later that year, the station, along with Radio Lumière and Radio Ave Maria, closed. Strong pressure, including some from Washington sources, forced Duvalier to reopen Radio Soleil after eighteen days on 23 December (Chamberlain 1986).

On 31 January 1986, Duvalier reneged on a promise to Washington that he would resign. Instead, he declared a state of siege, silencing all media except state radio and television and *Le nouveau monde.* A week later, he and his family fled Haiti.

Journalism had sunk to a dreary state during the last years of Duvalier. Main "independents," such as *Le matin* and *Le nouvelliste,* most radio stations, and the independent television channel had been conditioned to obey, preferring to "hide behind the immunity and sober despatches of the local correspondent of the French news agency" (Chamberlain 1986). They carried very little news, concentrating instead on government releases, notices of social events, essays on the arts, and reviews of noncontroversial books. They steered away from anything slightly controversial, faithfully called Duvalier "president-for-life," and did not question this or other taboo topics, such as the first lady, government officials, or the system that kept them in power (Americas Watch 1984, 10; Treaster 1986a).

CONTEMPORARY MASS MEDIA

Mass media in the immediate months after Duvalier's fall acted similarly to their counterparts in post–Japanese occupation Asia or the post-Marcos Philippines. They reported on almost everything, ran unverified information, and used what Treaster (1986a) termed "sentimental reflex," letting the audience know whether they approved or disapproved. The emotion-charged atmosphere led to much confusion about what constituted objectivity.

Some of the exile newspapers returned from the United States and seemed to be favored. The government daily was renamed *Haiti libérée,* and the oppositionist *Le petit samedi soir* lost most of its militancy, instead reflecting the conservatism of the now-wealthy businessman, Dieudonne Fardin, its publisher. Dozens of political weeklies filled out the print media scene (Chamberlain 1986, 37).

Five months into this relaxed state, the interim government of Henri Namphy issued by decree a new press law, thought by some to be as tough as the Duvalier law. This legislation included several requirements: (1) professional journalists had to register with the Ministry of Information, (2) to work as a journalist one had to possess a high school education, university diploma, or the equivalent, (3) it was an offense to publish or broadcast anything that would "bring harm to good morals and to public order," (4) sources of broadcast information must be mentioned in the news report, (5) and right of reply must be offered concerning any article or broadcast considered defamatory to any person or entity (Treaster 1986b, A–2).

Among Haitian journalists, the minimal educational requirement was most worrisome, since more than one half of them did not have a high school education. The government said that this requirement would upgrade journalism, but the journalists' associations saw it as threatening, with too much decision-making in the hands of the authorities.

The Inter American Press Association (IAPA) generally took issue with the loosely worded nature of the law as well as with individual clauses. Singled out as dangerous by IAPA, in addition to the five restrictions above, were those making it an offense to publish "acts of accusation and proceedings of biased commentaries, before a decision of justice, to influence witnesses, jurors and judges"; to obtain by fraudulent means, the journalist's identity card; to make death threats by voice of press; to publish any document that may harm the morals of youth and children, and to utter "injurious and outrageous" words over the airwaves, thus constituting "public injury." Nevertheless, the law remained in 1988.

Tenseness prevailed from 1986 to 1988, as the country tried to restore the democratic process. Strikes, demonstrations, and a violent, aborted election kept the public and the mass media uneasy. During the bloody strikes of June and July 1987, radio and television journalists from at least Métropole, Cacique, Haiti, and Arc-en-Ciel were fired upon because of stories they reported. Also, shots were fired at seven radio stations, and cameras, film, and tapes were confiscated.

It was to be even worse as elections approached in November. In the three months leading to the scheduled election, every major radio station had been hit by gunfire; in November, Radio Lumière was knocked off the air when gunmen broke into the broadcast tower and set it afire. On election day, 29 November, thugs opened fire on Radio Soleil's office and transmitter, injuring one staff member and incurring damages to equipment that closed the station for a week. Four other stations shut down because of similar attacks. A Dominican Republic camera operator was among the more than fifty people killed in what were to be the first democratic elections in three decades. When the election finally occurred in January 1988, Leslie Manigat, a political science professor, emerged as head of state; he was removed five months later in a military coup led by Namphy.

Manigat began his term with a media blitz previously unknown in

Haiti. He used what was called *kozé Anba Tonél* (talking to the people in an outdoor tropical setting), a monthly press conference, and speeches to the nation. One source felt he failed to communicate, soaring "high above the average interrogator, especially in French, but flying high made him vulnerable to outdistancing his audience" (Diederich 1988, 10).

Within a month after his election, Manigat was accused of trying to suppress the media. His army chief and information minister separately warned the press not to publish unverified news appearing in the foreign press. Newspapers, radio stations, and television channels used self-censorship, as they were caught in a double bind. If they published information offensive to the army, they risked repercussions; if they remained silent, they might lose their audiences to the rumor system, *le télédiol* (Diederich 1988, 11).

More than two hundred journalists work in Haiti. Most are inadequately trained; Haiti has no real journalism school. Almost all are poorly paid. The journalists are divided into two groups—those who belong to the Association des journalistes haitiens and those who are members of the Federation haitienne de la presse professionelle.

Besides dailies such as *Le matin* and *Le progressiste haitien,* a state paper started in 1988, U.S.-based papers circulate in Haiti. Among these are *Haiti observateur* and *Haiti-Progrès,* both of New York, and *Haiti en marche, Haiti demain,* and *Haiti Tribune,* all of Miami. In the summer of 1988, *Haiti-Progrès* complained that its 25–31 May edition was seized by airport security (*Haiti-Progrès* 1988, 6, 22–24).

The media still suffered governmental repression in 1989. In April, four radio stations—Radio Haiti, Radio Antilles, Radio Métropole, and Radio Liberté—sustained considerable damage after they were fired upon by Presidential Guard troops. The Haitian president, General Prosper Avril, denied issuing orders to disrupt the stations. He offered to help repair them.

Radio is still the most pervasive, and perhaps the most persuasive, mass medium in Haiti. Of the radio stations, Radios Lumière and Soleil have the largest share of listeners, according to a recent poll. This may be attributable to their oppositionist natures and also to their grass-roots and participatory characteristics.

Radio Soleil, ten years old in 1988, remained the greatest voice of opposition, although it did not originate that way. Founded at the urging of Haiti's Catholic bishops' conference, the station was first seen as a religious and educational tool. However, very quickly Radio Soleil became a political force, acting as the voice of the masses. The station broadcasts in Creole, promotes developmental projects, and serves as

HAITI PROGRES

Haïti 4 gdes
Diaspora: 3.75

11 Rue Capois, Port-au-Prince, Haïti Tél.: 2-6513
1398 Flatbush Avenue, Brooklyn N.Y. 11210 (718) 434-8100

Le journal qui offre une alternative

Vol 6 No 10 8 au 14 Juin 1988

HAITI PROGRES

REGALA IMPLIQUÉ
DANS LE TRAFIC
DE DROGUE!

GRAVES TENSIONS ENTRE «DÉPUTÉS» ET GOUVERNEMENT

Les duvaliéristes s'opposent catégoriquement à toute séparation effective entre police et armée!

A l'époque de Jean-Claude Duvalier, la fonction des députés était nette et claire, elle se résumait en cette expression significative *«députés-/-approuve»*. Les députés servaient uniquement de chambre de résonance et de paravent officiel à l'action gouvernementale. Les temps auraient-ils changé? Aujourd'hui, les parlementaires semblent au contraire manifester un systématique refus aux propositions qui leur sont soumises et auxquelles ils s'opposent avec une énergie entraînant même certains fâcheux «écarts de langage».

LE DÉPUTÉ LUC FÉLIX: «DES INJURES GRAVES ET PUBLIQUES»

Il m'a été ainsi le mardi 31 mai, jour où la Chambre des Députés analysait le projet de loi du ministère de la Justice et de la Police, dirigé par le premier ministre Martial Célestin. La discussion était si chaude qu'à un certain moment, Luc Félix, député de Jérémie, perdit toute mesure, se permettant certaines «incartades» qui—notait sentencieusement le journal gouvernemental—*peuvent éclabousser le prestige du Parlement*. Il faut en effet reconnaître que

Suite à la page 10

Au centre, le «premier ministre» Martial Célestin que l'on voit ici sommolant aux côtés de Leslie Manigat. Parlant de lui à la Chambre Législative, le député duvaliériste Luc Félix s'est écrié: «Force l'effet de l'âge? Car il commence à vieillir, il a déjà un pied dans la tombe... A-t-il pris la raison? Il se perd... il est perdu... Le nœud de la question: le secteur macoute refuse la séparation de l'armée et de la police

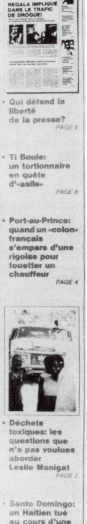

New York: une Haïtienne brûlée vive dans le métro

Un attentat horrible a eu lieu ce vendredi 3 juin à Brooklyn. Mona Pierre, une Haïtienne de 39 ans, travaillait dans sa guérite de métro à la station de Halsey Street/Wyckoff Avenue à Brooklyn quand un individu s'est approché d'elle pour lui demander qu'elle lui remette l'argent de sa caisse. Employée seule depuis le 6 juillet dernier par la Transit Authority, et toujours à l'essai, Mme Pierre a refusé. Furieux, l'assaillant a introduit un liquide inflammable à travers le guichet et y a mis le feu avant de l'enfuir. Luttant contre les flammes qui auraient envahi la guérite et s'attaquaient à ses vêtements, l'employée a réussi à sortir et à atteindre les escaliers de sortie de la station, mais à était trop

tard, 80% de son corps étaient brûlés. «Les seules parties de son corps qui n'étaient pas brûlées étaient ses mains et la partie de ses ongles», a dit le détective de la police du métro, Harry Harris. Quant à Richard McNamee, un passager qui venait de quitter la station et qui a été alerté par la fumée de l'explosion, il a vu notre compatriote en flammes: «J'ai vu une chemise en train de fondre le feu de son corps...»

Mme Pierre a été transportée au New York Hospital-Cornell Medical Center mais elle s'est expirée le lendemain, samedi, à 6h39 du matin.

Le fait que la Transit Authority ait annonce une récompense de 10.000 dollars

Suite à la page 19

Mona Pierre, une Haïtienne de 39 ans, employée de métro dans le quartier de Brooklyn, New York. Agresseur, elle a été victime d'un assaillant qui, faute de pouvoir emporter la caisse, n'a pas hésité à incendier la guérite où elle faisait son travail

---

15.1 *Haiti Progrès* serves Haitians and exiles in the United States.

the mail and telephone for the dispossessed. For example, Radio Soleil daily carries forty-five minutes of messages in which "a man tells his parents in far-off Jacmel when he will be home; one man tells another that a mutual friend has died; a woman wants her family to send money; another man says he hasn't heard from his brother and is worried."

The older Radio Lumière epitomizes the "small is beautiful" and the "pedagogy of the oppressed" concepts espoused by Schumacher and Freire. Content has been localized and made simple, staff has been indigenized and given upward mobility, and equipment has been made appropriate, including the use of solar power. As early as 1978, Radio Lumière dealt in two-way radio, dispatching men on motorcycles to remote villages where they taped people's views (Thatcher and Tarter 1983, 34). Radio Nationale also featured developmental fare over the years. Another oppositionist station is Haiti-Inter, which had been closed from 1980 to 1986.

That media must walk a tightrope lest they invite the displeasure of government, unruly mobs, or advertisers is exemplified by the situation of Radio Métropole. A station that sounds like Paris FM radio, Métropole tries to be objective and careful. Caroit (1987) reported that the station often quotes Agence France Presse, in French, about Haitian events that happen right outside Métropole's windows. Despite such moderation, three of the station's ten reporters have been attacked by soldiers, and some big merchants have withdrawn advertisements because of the way the station handled stories. Perhaps this example best typifies the precarious nature of Haitian journalism.

16

History of the Mass Media in the Netherlands Antilles: Beginnings to the 1969 Revolution

It is ironic that the first newspaper in the Netherlands Antilles was published on St. Eustatius, which today is devoid of newspapers and ranks as one of the least populated and least prosperous of the six islands of Aruba, Bonaire, Curaçao, Saba, St. Maarten, and St. Eustatius (Hartog 1948; 1984).

The *St. Eustatius Gazette* was published between 1790 and 1793. Printed by Edward Luther Low, who advertised that he did all "manner of printing . . . with case [care?] and dispatch," the *Gazette* was part Dutch and part English. In a notice calling on the subscribers to pay their bills, Low assured them that "their neglict [*sic*] will lay him under many inconveniences" (Hartog 1944, 79). Hartog said that the *Gazette* may have existed even before the above dates, since St. Eustatius was in a golden age before the British conquered the island 3 February 1781. He speculated, "As in the meantime the North Americans had gone to trade elsewhere, the former prosperity never came back. Given the fact, however, that even after about ten years there was still a weekly (the *Gazette*) available makes us think that maybe, it has also existed during a more prosperous era" (Hartog 1944, 122).

By 1905, only three issues (those of 23 June 1790, 28 December 1792, and 25 January 1793) of the *Gazette* remained, owned by Father Jan Paulus Delguer. Father Delguer quoted from these issues in a 1905 newspaper article. One notice asked for the return of a "Run Away": "A negro woman Dinah, belonging to Mr. Charles Chadwick of St. Martinus, about 5 feet high, rather square over the shoulders, a remarkable hairy face breast, a reward of eight Joes will be paid down on her delivery to Captain Chadwick at St. Martinus." The following advertise-

16.1 The *St. Eustatius Gazette,* 31 August 1792, the
first newspaper of the Netherlands Antilles.

ment offered by Rhelim Coole gives an indication of what one man
thought about his wife: "Run away last night my wife, Bridget Coole;
she is a tight neat body, and has lost one leg. She was seen riding behind
the priest of the parish through Termoy; and we never was [sic] married.
I will pay no debt that she does contract, she lisps with one tooth, and is
always talking about Fairies, and is of no use but to the owner." [n.b.!]

The second recorded newspaper in the Netherlands Antilles was *De
Curaçaosche courant,* a weekly first published 11 December 1812 as the
Curaçao Gazette and Commercial Advertiser. The newspaper became
the *Courant* in 1816 and has been the weekly official organ of the gov-
ernment on Curaçao since then. The first publisher of the *Courant* was
William Lee, who had been in the printing business in Caracas and came
to the islands in March 1812 after an earthquake, which killed 12,000
Venezuelans, destroyed his shop. Salvaging as much of his printing
equipment as possible, Lee set up his print shop in nearby Curaçao.
Upon his death in 1823, Lee's wife took over the newspaper. Along with

the Stockdale sisters in Bermuda and Mrs. Bénard in Guadeloupe, she had to have been one of the first female printer-editors in the Caribbean. Hartog (1968, 227) wrote of Lee's *Courant:*

> When the need of a newspaper was beginning to be felt and Lee attempted to supply it, one of those supporting him was Governor Hodgson, who appointed him Printer to the King's Most Excellent Majesty. Lee, in return, for certain privileges, also printed official announcements. Until the opening years of the 20th century the *Curaçaosche Courant* continued to perform its dual function of newspaper and semi-official gazette. However, when other papers took over the dissemination of news, Curaçao's oldest newsletter restricted the scope of its activities to official publications.

Apparently, the *Curaçaosche courant* did not reach neighboring Aruba, fifteen miles away. Hartog (1961, 196) thought it was "odd among the stream of news issuing from the governor's pen, we hardly find any mention of the *Curaçaosche courant,* though this paper was the newspaper for Aruba; the press organ deemed worthy of faithful mention each month, the news bulletin repeatedly referred to as 'circulating,' that paper is *De Volksvriend* (the *People's Friend*)." But, as Hartog (1961, 196) explained, this paper was not published in the islands.

> It has taken us quite some doing to solve the question as to what kind of paper this *People's Friend* might have been. After a good deal of research we could be certain that no paper of that name ever left the Curaçao presses. In the Netherlands, however, this almanac-like nineteenth century name was smugly borne by some ten more or less pretentious papers. . . . The famous paper proved to be . . . the monthly magazine of an organization with a very long-winded name: The Dutch Society for the Promotion of Abolishment of Strong Drink! It was circulated here at the order of the minister of the colonies, after having seen the light in 1846. The *People's Friend* drew out its existence till the century's close. This was the source whence the Arubans derived their news.

Information was transmitted between Aruba and Curaçao primarily through monthly reports from the Aruban lieutenant-governor to the governor on Curaçao. Such reports pertained to births, deaths, marriages, and the weather.

The lack of an abundance of newspapers during the eighteenth and nineteenth centuries can be attributed to at least three phenomena: insufficient educational and cultural training, small and isolated populations, and a mixture of languages. On Aruba, no form of education existed as late as 1816, and only thirty-one pupils were enrolled in a Mr. van Eekhout's 1824 school. The situation was not much better on Curaçao, according to Hartog (1961, 155); he reported that "the Company, holding the view that education was a matter concerning the clerical authorities rather than themselves, did not bother greatly about it. Sometimes old service men, whatever their qualifications, settled here as teachers. Usually keeping a one-room school here, they sometimes entered the service of the wealthier families as tutors."

When Governor Kikkert arrived in Curaçao in 1816, he reported the state of education as wretched, it being "customary for persons without means of subsistence to found schools in order to earn a living, even though they themselves might have hardly any education at all" (Hartog 1961, 156). It was only during the second half of the nineteenth century that schools attracted children in appreciable numbers.

Because of the small, isolated populations, communications took place despite the lack of newspapers. The oldest population figure recorded for Curaçao is for 1635, when there were 462 inhabitants, including 50 Indians. By 1789, the population rose to 19,544, but by 1833, it dropped to 15,027, mainly because of the departure of a number of Jewish families. In 1816, Aruba had only 1,732 inhabitants, while Bonaire had 1,135 (Hartog 1968, 222).

Portuguese, Dutch, English, Spanish, Papiamento, and Gene[1] are the languages that Antilleans have coped with over the years. Today, most residents of Aruba and Curaçao speak three or four languages—usually Dutch, Papiamento, English, and Spanish. Spoken by the Jewish population during the eighteenth century, Portuguese became the dominant language of the islands. From Portuguese, a "corrupt variant" called gibberish, or "papiamento" (from the Portuguese *papear,* meaning to jabber or mutter; or from the Spanish *papear,* to speak incoherently) arose among the less-educated class.

Despite the existence of earlier newspapers, 1812 should mark the beginning of journalism in the Netherlands Antilles, for in that year the main island of Curaçao received its first printing press. Before that time, mass-communicated items were duplicated either in manuscript or sent to New York to be printed. As a result, Curaçao was one of the last major Caribbean islands to have a press.

The presses must not have been put to full use, for between 1812 and 1884 only twenty-one periodicals were published in Curaçao, eighteen of which appeared between 1870 and 1884. In fact, Hartog does not list any newspaper on Curaçao besides the *Courant* until 1864, when

Shema Israel was published as an organ for the Jewish community. But there were a few printing presses in the islands, according to Hartog (1968, 301–2), who said,

> . . . and thus the first printing office of the [Catholic] Vicariate came into being at Barber in 1843, to be followed in 1848 by a second at Santa Rosa. The latter was founded when the parish priest on returning from leave, not only brought a printing press with him, but also a printer . . . to operate it. . . . While no product of the Vicariate's printing office at Barber has come down to us, we still possess several booklets printed at Santa Rosa, both Dutch and Papiamento specimens. The mission priests displayed great publishing zeal. Between 1850 and 1901 they brought out no fewer than 72 titles.

In 1865, *El evangélico liberal* was published, followed in 1870 by *Onpartijdige. Civilisadó,* a paper of the people as its motto proclaimed, was the first newspaper to use Papiamento in 1871. A weekly, the *Impulse,* was the other creation of 1871. Periodicals of 1872 were *L'Echo de Curaçao,* in French and Spanish, and the weekly *De onajhankelijke.* The Spanish weekly, *El imparcial,* was one of the longest-lived of the early Curaçao newspapers, surviving from 1874 to 1916. Other early Curaçao journals were, in 1875, *El corréo de las Antillas, Progreso,* and *De vrijmoedige,* a weekly that lasted until 1920; in 1879, *Boletín de la libreria de Agustin Bethencourt e hijos;* and in 1883, *El ensayo, El liberal,* and *Revisor.*

Amigoe di Curaçao, the oldest contemporary newspaper, was founded 21 December 1883 as a weekly. From the beginning, it was a voice for the Roman Catholics, founded by the first Dominican apostolic vicar of Curaçao, Father Henricus J. A. van Ewijk. Originally, *Amigoe* was bilingual (Dutch and Papiamento), but after 1900, the only Papiamento that remained was in its nameplate. The language was dropped because in that year *La cruz,* also a Catholic weekly, published in Papiamento. *Amigoe* went to twice weekly publication in 1935 and to daily publication in 1941.

In Aruba, the first periodicals came six decades after Lee's *Courant. Express Office,* of which little is known, was published in 1874, followed by the weeklies *El semanario* (1890), *De Arubaansche courant* (1894), and *El farro* (1899). *Semanario,* trilingual in Spanish, Dutch, and Papiamento, published "news and particulars" during its five-year lifetime. Its publisher-editor, William "Cornelis" Gruenings, was extremely critical of the Roman Catholic Church. *De Arubaansche courant* and *El farro* were also trilingual; the former was published and edited by Jan

Jacob Beaujon, and *El farro* was edited by a merchant, Leonardo Macabéo Henríquez. Despite these efforts, it was not until 1931 that printing took place in the "modern sense," according to Hartog (1961, 301).

Prior to the establishment of the first wireless station in Curaçao in 1908, the islands communicated with the outside world by being on certain steamship lines. There were no steamship lines calling at Curaçao before 1850, but in that year the Curaçaosche Pakketvaart Maatschappij (Curaçao Packet Company) connected the islands to the St. Thomas route, thus coupling Curaçao with the British steamer service calling at St. Thomas. Of course, mail was the medium of communication, but oftentimes foreign newspapers were delivered to Curaçao hotels. Hotels charged local residents a fee to read these periodicals; strangers were not charged.

A conflict that almost ended in war with Venezuela is given credit for setting up the first wireless connection for Curaçao. Hartog (1968, 269) wrote, "When therefore in 1908, Dutch warships were sent to patrol the area off the Venezuelan coast, a complete set of wireless equipment arrived here. It was powered by a petrol generator and petrol was very hard to come by in the Curaçao of those days."

The wireless saw limited use until it was put at the disposal of the public in 1921. Before then, it was not used to communicate with the outside world directly but only to reach ships and the islands of the insular territory. Aruba had wireless capability in 1911, but the Arubans used theirs only to communicate with Curaçao. Only one man on Aruba knew how to operate the wireless; when he was sick, there were no wireless transmissions.

Aruba's isolated position is illustrated by Hartog's analysis (1961, 249) of the journal of Lt. Gov. Hendrik J. Beaujon, who was in command of Aruba from 1911 to 1921.

> The word "war" does not even occur there; not a single allusion is made to the upheaval of European conditions. A person not knowing about it from other sources would not be able to gather from this painstakingly kept diary that there had ever been a war at all.

> The wireless had already been introduced in those days. But it did not report the outbreak of war. Was the battery spent? Or was there not enough wind to set the little mill going? . . . not until some days after the war [World War I] had started was intelligence about the fact received by means of the *Boletin Comercial,* a paper published in Curaçao. Sailings from Curaçao to our island taking place only at irregular intervals, this newssource was received here in the form of neatly tied up piles of back numbers.

Such isolation did not lend itself to newspaper development. Hartog (Interview 1968) explained that "there could not be any newspapers in Aruba until deep into the 19th century because Aruba was a closed society until the 19th century. No Negroes settled here till 1800 and there was just one white man here before then." Between 1874 and 1945, Aruba had forty-two publications, only one more frequent than weekly; most of them were bilingual or trilingual. Dutch seemed to be used most, either solely or in combination with other languages.

On the other hand, during the period 1812 to 1945, Curaçao had 211 publications, fourteen of which were dailies. The first dailies in Curaçao, and thus in the Netherlands Antilles, were *Express Office* in 1885 and *Oficina maritima* in 1886. Fifty-five publications were launched in the two-decade period from 1880 to 1899, compared to only sixteen for the eras before 1880.

Because of the scarcity of publications, any newsletter or regularly printed promotional organ was classed as a periodical. These included publications of hotels, movie theaters, radio stations, racing clubs, the British Consulate, sports organizations, civic clubs, churches, anticlerical organizations, and political groups.

TWENTIETH-CENTURY COMMUNICATIONS

The development of oil refineries on Curaçao and Aruba in the early decades of the twentieth century brought the islands partially out of isolation, but one has only to look over a list of firsts to realize that formal communications structures had a late start in the Netherlands Antilles.

For example, the first daily on Aruba was not issued until 1938. *The Aruba Post,* as the paper was called, was edited by Simson Vieyra, who "used bad English to promulgate news items from all over the world. Being a telegraph operator by profession, he simply jotted down bits of broadcasts by American news agencies, and printed them without more ado. As a cultural manifestation, the importance of this paper was zero" (Hartog 1968, 404). By 1946, the *Post* had floundered when a bookseller acquired it and formed the *Arubaanse courant,* which became a successful daily by 1952. Later it was merged with *La prensa* of Curaçao.

There are other indications of the late start of formal communication. Only five thousand wireless sets were in use on Aruba in 1952, and only eight thousand on Curaçao. The Antillean book trade was stagnant until 1948, when a bookseller's shop opened in Oranjestad. The first Aruban movie theater was opened in 1919, and the island's first drive-in theater in 1968.

As with its print media, Curaçao had earlier development of electronic media than did Aruba. The first films were shown in 1897. Called "cinematographic views," they employed a train oil lamp as the source of light. After 1908, the "cinema proper" was established in Curaçao, using imported pictures from Caracas and an electric generator for a power source.

Private individuals in Curaçao had experimented with radio broadcasts at the beginning of the 1930s, and in 1933 Curaçaose Radio Vereniging (Curaçao Broadcasting Association) entered the field. From Curaçaose Radio Vereniging, an executive body called Curom was initiated in 1937. At first, Curom avoided the use of advertising. The broadcasting chain of Horacio E. Hoyer was established in March 1954 when

16.2 Old studios of Radio Hoyer, a broadcasting group established in 1954 by Horacio Hoyer.

Radio Hoyer I went on the air. Radio Hoyer II followed in March 1957, and Hoyer III in Bonaire in 1960.

In 1955, Carl Heilegger organized Radio Caribe, the third commercial station on Curaçao (Curom was government subsidized). Aruba has had radio broadcasting only since the 1950s. Voice di Aruba was the first commercial station, followed in 1958 by Radio Victoria and Radio Kelkboom and in 1962 by Radio Antilliana. Television arrived in Curaçao in 1960 and in Aruba in 1963.

THE 1969 REVOLUTION

Antilleans believe that Aruba and Curaçao changed drastically after revolts devastated Willemstad, Curaçao's capital, in 1969. In turn, the mass media also made significant changes (see chapter 17 for discussion of those changes), and the approach of the 1970s was a watershed period.

In 1969, Curaçao had three daily newspapers, three radio stations, one television channel, and a magazine. Aruba had one daily (the other paper, which called itself an Aruban daily, *Amigoe di Aruba,* was actually a Curaçao product), four radio stations, one television channel, and a few assorted governmental and industrial publications. Bonaire had one radio station, and the three Windward islands of Saba, St. Eustatius, and St. Maarten did not fare that well.

Curaçao dailies were *Amigoe di Curaçao, Beurs-en nieuwsberichten,* and *La prensa.* The former two were in Dutch, while *La prensa* employed Papiamento; all had nearly the same circulation of eight thousand to nine thousand and the same number of pages daily, eight to sixteen.

La prensa was founded in 1928 as a Spanish daily by Jorge Bartoloméo Suárez, whereas *Beurs-en nieuwsberichten* was created as a Dutch-language neutral newspaper in 1935. A *Beurs* editor said that the title, meaning "news from the stock exchange," is "ridiculously misleading." He added, "We have very little stock market news; people think I'm a financial expert when I know very little about the market. It's just a name the paper has" (Interview, van Goens 1968). The most influential Curaçao weekly in 1969 was *La cruz,* a Papiamento organ of the Roman Catholic Church. Official publications were the weekly *Curaçaosche courant* (1812); *Voorlichting* (1956), an irregular Government Information Service (GIS) periodical distributed to forty-four thousand people; and *Corsow,* another irregularly issued GIS publication. The latter two used Papiamento and Dutch. Two party newspapers came into existence

16.3 Popular Aruba and Curaçao newspapers at the
time of the 1969 revolution.

after the first political parties were initiated in the 1940s — *Democraat* (1945), a monthly in Papiamento, Dutch, and English published by the Democratische Partij, and *Nacional* (1967), a weekly in Papiamento published by the Partido Nacional di Pueblo.

Another category of Curaçao publications was the union or labor periodical, including *La unión* (1922), a weekly in Dutch and Papiamento; *Petrolero* (1963), a monthly in Papiamento published by the Petroleum Workers Federation; *Voz di C. F. W.* (1967), a monthly in Papiamento of the Curaçaosche Federatie van Werknemers; and *De ambtenaar* (1937), a Dutch-language monthly. Circulations of the labor newspapers were from twenty-five hundred to three thousand.

Still other Curaçao publications were *Opinion* (1964), an irregularly issued Papiamento magazine; *Vito* (1965), a monthly in Dutch and Papiamento; *El venezolano* (1966), a Spanish monthly; *Antilliaans juristenblad* (1953), a Dutch quarterly; *Radio teatro television* (1965), a Dutch and Papiamento weekly; and *Cooperador* (1964), published in Papiamento. The circulations of these periodicals ranged from two thousand to three thousand.

Aruban-based periodicals in 1969 were headed by the G. J. Schouten newspapers — *Chuchubi* (Chirping Bird), a Papiamento weekly founded in 1947, and the *News,* an English daily established in 1962 — and by the Catholic-owned *Amigoe di Aruba,* a Dutch daily. *Amigoe di Aruba* and *Arubaanse courant* actually were incorporated into Curaçao newspapers. *Amigoe di Aruba* was a verbatim copy of Curaçao's *La prensa; La prensa–Arubaanse courant* was distributed on both islands. The fifth Aruban newspaper was the *Local,* an English weekly tabloid founded in 1948. All five publications had circulations from fifteen hundred to thirty-five hundred, and all published from eight to sixteen pages. In-house publications on Aruba were *Aruba Esso News* (1940), a biweekly English-Papiamento organ of Lago Oil, and *Barcadera News* (1964), an English monthly issued by Aruba Chemical Industries.

Still other Aruban periodicals were *Justicia* (1955), a Dutch quarterly of two hundred circulation; *Noticiero di I.O.W.U.A.* (1964), a Papiamento-English monthly; and *Reportero grafico,* a Papiamento bimonthly.

Bonaire had one publication, *Eco di Bonaire,* a monthly organ of the Partido Democratico Bonairiano. Published in Papiamento, *Eco* had a circulation of twenty-five hundred. The *Windward Islands Opinion,* created in 1959 as an English weekly, published on St. Maarten with a circulation of one thousand.

Over the years, a few other publications appeared in Bonaire and the Windward Islands. *De kampioen,* a Papiamento monthly, was issued as an organ of the Soccer League of Bonaire in 1934. It consisted of one mimeographed sheet. St. Maarten has had at least five other publications. In 1911, there was *St. Maarten, Day by Day,* an English weekly that lasted until 1920. Its editor, Josiah Waymouth, battled officialdom regularly, expounding on the many interisland political and economic problems. In 1922, the *Dutch Windward Island Times,* an English fortnightly, was printed on St. Kitts, British West Indies, and transported to St. Maarten. *New Life,* "published at such dates and as often as circumstances under God permit," also was edited by Waymouth. The English-language periodical had an extremely religious background and heralded itself as a messenger of God. In the first issue, Waymouth discussed his unsuccessful fight against the government through his *Day by Day. Bovenwindsche stemmen (Windward Voices)* was a biweekly in English, despite its nameplate. Like all other periodicals published on St. Maarten, *Stemmen* also was issued by the Methodists. At first, the paper dealt mainly with religion, politics, and news. *Stemmen* died in 1942. *De slag om slag (Tit for Tat)* was published on St. Maarten in 1934 as an English weekly very critical of the political and economic actions of the government. Editor Anthony R. Waters-Gravenhorst Brouwer was jailed frequently for his opinions. The periodical ceased to exist by 1939 (Hartog 1944, 24, 79–81).

MEDIA PROBLEMS

Smallness has been the root of most media problems in the Netherlands Antilles—small populations, small land areas, and small advertising markets.

The largest and most populous island, as well as the center of government and culture, is Curaçao, thirty-eight miles long and from two to seven and one-half miles wide. Aruba is nineteen miles long and two to six miles wide.

So small are the islands, as are many of the other Caribbean territories, that newspapers in Curaçao had a gentleman's agreement with the courts and police not to use any lawbreakers' names. To give offenders (whether murderers or petty thieves) anonymity in such an interpersonal society, only initials were used in police stories (Interview, Hermelijn 1968).

Because the societal characteristic of "personalness" is so dominant in the Netherlands Antilles, newspapers often have been careful of criticism lest it be taken personally. One editor did not like to criticize the government because he might not be able to depend on officials as sources in the future (Interview, van Goens 1968). In the late 1960s, the three dailies of Curaçao informed movie theatre owners that they were using too much sex in their newspaper advertisements. The four owners reacted by drastically reducing their newspaper advertising budgets (Interviews, Maas 1968 and van Dongen 1968).

With the second highest per capita income in the Caribbean and an illiteracy rate of only one or two percent, the Netherlands Antilles still had a relatively low newspaper readership rate in the 1960s. Editors explained that Antilleans, especially those in the suburbs, did not care too much about what was happening in the world. They were interested in local news, particularly police reports from radio broadcasts, many of which were in Papiamento (Interviews, Maas, van Dongen, and Maduro, all 1968).

Although Netherlands Antilleans could read Dutch (as well as English, Spanish, and Papiamento) and nearly all papers were in Dutch, the people did not like that language, according to two editors (Interviews, Maas 1968 and Panneflek 1968). Economic reasons accounted for the print media's preference for Dutch. News via telex was relayed from the Netherlands, and in most cases the newspapers could not afford to have it translated into Papiamento. Papiamento's structure allows it to be translated more easily for radio than for the print media.

Newsstand and street sales of newspapers were almost nonexistent before the 1970s; it was too easy to home-deliver the newspapers with only 70 square miles (as in Aruba) or 180 square miles (Curaçao) to cover. The dailies, *Amigoe di Curaçao, Beurs-en nieuwsberichten,* and *La prensa,* had circulations in Aruba; only *Amigoe* had a separate Aruban news-gathering and circulation office and an Aruban edition. At the time, Aruban copy for *Amigoe* was placed on a night flight to Curaçao; the following day, the printed *Amigoe di Aruba* copies were likewise flown to Aruba at 4:45 P.M. Problems developed with canceled flights or hapless airline personnel who put the copy or printed editions on wrong flights. *Amigoe* at times ended up in Santo Domingo and Caracas (Interview, Maas 1968).

The mini nature of the Antilles was accused of hindering press freedom. One government official said that the smallness of an island government intimidated some editors; they felt that the government was breathing down their necks (Interview, Suares 1968).

Press freedom is guaranteed in the Antillean Charter, but editors in 1968 were quick to point out instances of press suppression, usually of a subtle form. The ownership of influential newspapers was also bothersome. Of three dailies published in Willemstad and circulated in Aruba, two (*La prensa* and *Beurs*) were owned by the Democratische Partij (a political party), which had been in power since 1954. The third daily, *Amigoe,* was owned by the Roman Catholic bishop of Willemstad, as were the two influential weeklies, *La cruz* and *La unión.* Editors admitted with a defeated shrug of the shoulders that they ran everything that the government or church stipulated (Interview, Panneflek 1968). "Anything the Democrat party wants in our paper, we can't say no. Same with *Amigoe* and the church," van Goens said. He added, "The press is not free; you can't fight church and government. We're used to the lack of press freedom, so what can you do about it? If you fight for freedom of the press, you will not get any more news" (Interview, van Goens 1968). Hermelijn believed, though, that there was press freedom in Curaçao; in fact, he said, sometimes the "press is embarrassingly free. The fact that press critics can voice their opinions means we have freedom of press" (Interview, Hermelijn 1968).

The only influential Aruban newspapers not controlled by a Curaçao party or the church were the *News* and *Chuchubi,* both operated by G. J. Schouten, who took great delight in using his papers as antigovernment journals. Learning to cope with repercussions, Schouten sold *Chuchubi* for one-half guilder (U.S. $.25), making the 8½-by-11-inch magazine-format newspaper "one of the most expensive in the world" (Interview, Schouten 1968). "For six months, *Chuchubi* was adless because of government pressure; occasionally, merchants ran advertisements, saying, 'We're with you in your fight, *Chuchubi,* but they wouldn't sign the ads,'" Schouten said. Eventually, he told advertisers either to sign their advertisements or to "go to hell."

Besides attacking the government, *Chuchubi* also took frequent shots at the Roman Catholic Church. On an island where more than 90 percent of the inhabitants were Catholic, *Chuchubi* regularly featured a page devoted to sex, informing "girls that the pill is for birth control and not colds" (Interview, Schouten 1968).

On Curaçao, Guillermo Rosario, editor of the magazine *Opinion,* had similar problems with the government. Rosario edited a weekly, *Un po ko* (A Little One), in which he regularly criticized the government. Rosario said that the newspaper was stenciled because no printer "had the guts to print it," afraid of losing the many governmental printing contracts (Interview, Rosario 1968). Unable to obtain advertisements, *Un po ko* relied solely on circulation. Rosario contended that one could write anything but should be ready to face the consequences, usually in the form of "foolish charges" brought by the government. He was arrested at least three times by the authorities.

Amigoe editors in Curaçao and Aruba insisted that complete freedom of the press existed in the islands. They pointed out that though the government tried to suppress information sometimes, the final decision of publishing rested with the editors (Interviews, Maas 1968 and van Dongen 1968). The editor of *Amigoe di Curaçao* recalled only one instance where the government interfered with the press; an *Amigoe* reporter was not received in the government offices for a short period (Interview, Maas 1968).

In the 1960s, Antillean newspapers used daily front-page editorials. Editorials in *Beurs* were distinguishable from other copy because they were set in reverse, white on black, and called the "Black Column" (Interview, van Goens 1968). Every week, the dailies ran a page each devoted to teenagers and women. Editors explained that there was not much "society" in the islands, and women's pages were devoted more to features, recipes, and fashions rather than to weddings and engagements (Interviews, Maas 1968 and van Goens 1968). Another feature of the dailies was the serialized novel, received from the Netherlands via telex.

As they are now, reportorial staffs were very small; *Amigoe* had five employees working its Curaçao newsroom while *Beurs* had three. The dailies depended upon stringers throughout the islands and the many governmental and church handouts. For international news, they clipped Netherlands newspapers through contractual agreements with them. *Amigoe* and *Beurs* also subscribed to a Dutch news agency. News services of the United States were not used because they were too expensive and required translation. Photographs of international events were flown from the Netherlands, taking one or two days to reach the islands.

Because of the limited market, the advertising ratio of the Netherlands Antilles newspapers was relatively low. Most newspapers had two pages of advertisements on days when they ran eight pages, and five when they carried twelve. The most profitable advertisements were those called *schakels* (links) in *Beurs* and *zoekertjes* (small seekers) in *Amigoe* (Interview, van Goens 1968). Similar to classified advertisements, they were usually one column-inch deep and sold for six guilders (U.S. $3) per insertion. In 1969, thought was being given to dropping Saturday editions because of a lack of advertising and the five-day work week. Antillean newspapers did not publish on Sunday; editors followed the Dutch thinking of not needing those editions (Interviews, Maas 1968 and van Goens 1968). Morning papers did not exist in the islands because the people started work early and did not have time to read.

According to some editors, people were attracted to journalism because of its social status (Interviews, van Dongen 1968 and Maas 1968). A number of former newspeople had gone on to become government or business officials. On-the-job training predominated because of the lack of journalism courses. Of the colleges, only Radulphus and Peter Stuyvesant had school newspapers, and no journalism training programs were offered. *Amigoe,* and for some time, *Beurs,* brought editors from the Netherlands to operate their newsrooms. Usually on four-year contracts, they were free to return to the Netherlands after that time. Gradually, importation of editors disappeared because it was costly to bring them to the Antilles, accustom them to the cultures, and then lose them.

Competing actively with the newspapers in the late 1960s were Telearuba and Telecuraçao, owned by the government and leased to the Bartell Media Corporation of the United States. Newscasts on Aruban television were two five-minute presentations, one in Papiamento, the other in English. Telearuba used Associated Press dispatches and local correspondents. Telecuraçao had two fifteen-minute newscasts daily, one each in Papiamento and Dutch. Besides local correspondents, the station used Columbia Broadcasting System and Associated Press news.

High per capita incomes (because of the Esso and Shell refineries on the islands) and a Latin philosophy of "enjoy today, pay tomorrow" accounted for the islands' extensive television set ownership. On Curaçao, eighteen thousand of the twenty-five thousand homes had receivers in 1968; 70 percent of the ten thousand Aruban homes also had sets (Interviews, Maduro, Christensen, Pitsch, Hoyer, and Hernandez, all 1968).

17

Mass Communications
of the Netherlands Antilles in the 1980s

Perhaps the Netherlands Antilles represent, in a microcosm, the changes that Third World mass communications underwent in the 1970s (see Lent 1971a, 1971b). During that decade, the quantity and quality of the mass media changed profoundly. The number of dailies on the capital island of Curaçao doubled, and two radio stations were added in Aruba. More importantly, mass media usage of the indigenous language, Papiamento, became much more pronounced in this multilanguage area. According to some media managers, this resulted from the growing consciousness and awareness of a national identity after the 1969 revolution that shook Curaçao. Dependence upon the Netherlands by the mass media diminished enough that island newspapers no longer were edited by Dutch journalists on secondment (leave). Broadcast programming included much more Caribbean music, and newspapers used more local content, including in at least one case locally drawn comic strips. By 1980, there was talk of a regional news service to avoid the heavy reliance still placed on the Dutch agency, ANP. Professionalization of journalism was promoted during the decade by the formation of press clubs, publishers' associations, and the Stichting Grafische Communicatie (SGC—Foundation Graphic Communication), by the writing of a code of honor, and by a keener awareness of the beneficial roles of mass media on the parts of government and the society at large. Education in mass communications began in earnest with workshops sponsored by SGC and, in some cases, overseas training.

MEDIA IN THE 1980s

Curaçao now has six dailies, compared with three in 1968, the year portrayed in chapter 16. In addition to *Amigoe* (the oldest, dating to 1884), *Beurs-en-nieuwsberichten,* and *La prensa, Nobo* was established in 1973 as the first daily to be sold widely in the streets, followed by *Extra* and *Awor.* The three newcomers, as well as *La prensa,* are in Papiamento. The dailies' total circulations (including distribution to other islands of the Netherlands Antilles) range from the largest, *Amigoe* and *Nobo,* each with thirteen thousand, to *Awor* and *Extra,* with seven thousand to eight thousand. The most widely read, according to a

17.1 Curaçao tabloid dailies that sprouted in the 1970s, *Awor, Extra Aruba,* and *Nobo.*

1980 survey, are the flashy *Nobo* and *Extra.* Four are afternoon papers, while *Awor* and *Extra* became the first successful dailies to publish in the morning. There are no Sunday newspapers in the Netherlands Antilles.

The magazine industry is not nearly as developed. Although Oltheten (1977, 57) showed twenty-seven titles with a total circulation of 49,700 for the entire Netherlands Antilles, one Curaçao magazine editor thought the magazine revolution was yet to develop. Leslie Roosberg, editor of *Tempu* (a "social, cultural bi-weekly with a circulation of 1,500"), said that no "real magazines" exist in the region, adding that the islands always have depended upon other countries for magazines (Interview, 1980). He had thought that the industry would be better developed by the mid-1980s. Besides *Tempu,* two other magazines appeared in Curaçao in the late 1970s — *Waya,* a weekly devoted to popular arts, and *Wega,* a biweekly sports magazine. Roosberg said that the magazine business of the Netherlands Antilles was plagued by "too little equipment, money, and staff," the result of which was high mortality. For example, *Kambio,* an Aruban cultural magazine, died in 1979, as did *Siman,* a cultural magazine in Bonaire (Interview, Roosberg 1980).

The oldest — since 1937 — and one of the most powerful radio stations of the Netherlands Antilles is Curaçao's Curom (AM). The other Curaçao stations are Hoyer I (AM and FM), Hoyer II, Radio Caribe (AM and FM), and Korsow (FM). The Hoyer stations and Radio Caribe were started in the 1950s, while Korsow was established in 1976. Interestingly, a few stations take the surnames of their owners; Hoyer stations were founded by H. E. Hoyer, Radio Kelkboom is owned by J. Kelkboom, and Radio Caruso Booi is owned by Hubert Booy.

Telecuraçao, operated by Antilliaanse Televisie Maatschappij N.V., has been Curaçao's only television system since it was opened in 1957. It is on the air from 4:30 P.M. until midnight daily and from noon to midnight on Sunday. A 1980 survey showed that in both Curaçao and Bonaire, television was the most popular medium. In Aruba, radio had that distinction. The least popular in all the islands was newspaper (Interview, Heiligers and Salsbach 1980).

The advertising industry also has shown recent growth along indigenous lines. Roosberg said that advertising grew rapidly after 1972, with local advertising offices taking root. Of eight agencies in Curaçao, six are locally owned, and two have some foreign capital. The largest is R. J. Dovale Advertising. Unlike many Third World regions, Antillean advertising is not dominated by U.S. interests. Roosberg added, "Many advertisements, contrary to before, are produced here. Many more radio and TV commercials are done in Curaçao. Previously, all advertisements came from the United States or Venezuela. Now, there is no J. W.

17.2 *Tempu,* one of the pioneer magazines of the Netherlands Antilles.

Thompson–type big company owning any sector of business" (Interview, Roosberg 1980).

Thus, for a population of 159,500, Curaçao has a total of twelve mass media—six dailies, five commercial radio stations (plus two noncommercial FM stations), and one television channel.

In Aruba, one daily, one weekly, seven radio stations, and a television system serve sixty-three thousand people. The *News,* a daily in English for twenty-five hundred subscribers, is published by the irascible, self-proclaimed watchdog of government, G. J. Schouten. The weekly, also in English, is the *Local.* Twice daily, a bulletin (*DN Bulletin*) is distributed to each hotel with news of interest to tourists. In the 1970s, the Aruban government started a daily in English and Papiamento, but it did not survive. Additionally, all Curaçao dailies have independent editors stationed in Aruba, and they telex stories to Willemstad.

Of Aruba's seven radio stations, five are AM and two are FM (Voz di Aruba and Radio Carina). Four were started in the 1950s, the oldest being Radio Kelkboom and Voz di Aruba, both started in 1954. Radio Carina, which claims the highest listenership (Interview, Gómez-Lampkin and Dieffenthaler 1980), went on the air in 1978, and Radio Caruso Booi did so in 1979. Television came to Aruba in 1963 with Tele-Aruba; the station, now under the control of Antilliaanse Televisie Maatschappij N.V., converted to full color in 1979.

Newspapers are published in the other Netherlands Antilles islands, but on an irregular and less permanent basis. At various times since 1975, Bonaire had the *Bulletin* (a monthly in Dutch and Papiamento) and the *Bonaire Weekly* (English, 400 circulation). St. Maarten's newspapers were the *St. Maarten Star* (English, weekly, 1,000 circulation), the *New Age* (English, weekly, 700 circulation), the *Clarion* (English), the *Morning Mirror* (English), and the *Windward Islands News Day* (English, weekly, 700 circulation) (Snow 1977, 14; Oltheten 1977, 54; SGC 1979?). Others were the *Saba Herald* (English, weekly, 350 circulation) and the *Statia Gazette* (English, weekly), published on Saba and St. Eustatius respectively. The circulations of these newspapers must be put in perspective with the island populations: Bonaire, 8,800; St. Maarten, 11,800; St. Eustatius, 1,400; and Saba, 1,000.

Broadcasting in these islands are Hoyer III, an AM station begun in Bonaire in 1961; PJD 2, an AM station dating to 1961 in St. Maarten; and Voice of Saba, an AM station started in Saba in 1971. West Indies Television, a 100-watt channel in St. Maarten, began operations in 1972.

OWNERSHIP AND CONTROL

Unlike some parts of the Caribbean (especially the U.S. and Commonwealth sectors), the Netherlands Antilles has not had outside ownership of the mass media for a number of years. In fact, broadcasting regulations prohibit foreign ownership. Editors of *Amigoe* said that in 1979 a Netherlands newspaper had designs on starting a daily in the islands, but the idea did not see fruition (Interview, Heiligers and Salsbach 1980). Also unusual for a Third World region is the minimal government ownership of the mass media; only the television stations are government owned in Aruba and Curaçao, and they are managed by an independent company. Cross-channel and group ownership also are not prevalent in the Netherlands Antilles. *Beurs* and *La prensa* have a common ownership, and *Amigoe* and *Nobo* have a cooperative printing arrangement, but the latter cannot be construed a group. The parent company of *Amigoe* and *Nobo* owns Rotoprint, a modern offset plant that prints both papers. *Nobo*'s editor explained that when his paper started in 1973, it arranged a printing contract with *Amigoe*. He added, "When *Amigoe* moved, they didn't have money to set up a new shop. We had the money and became partners with *Amigoe* in the printery. The deal was for one of the partners to operate the printery and so we at *Nobo* did. However, *Nobo* and *Amigoe* have separate staffs and stockholders; it is just a business marriage" (Interview, Daantje 1980).

However, one similarity between the media of the Netherlands Antilles and those of other Caribbean islands is their affiliation with political parties and other special interest groups. Again, the situation in the Netherlands Antilles is not as aggravated as in neighboring states. *Amigoe* is owned by the Roman Catholic Church, but its editors claim they receive no interference from the bishop. In their words, "We hardly hear from him. He continues to own it because of historical precedence" (Interview, Heiligers and Salsbach 1980). Of course, the possibility of interference is always present, and at least two journalists recalled a former bishop who used the paper to back a political party with which he was sympathetic (Interviews, Daantje 1980 and Roosberg 1980).

Although radio stations are not owned by political parties and, in most cases, are not connected with political movements (Interview, Cuales 1980), the same cannot be said as categorically for the press. Two dailies, *Beurs* and *La prensa,* do not hide their connections with the Democratische Partij (DP), which would be difficult to do anyway since the chief editor of *La prensa* is also a member of Parliament and served as secretary of DP during his editorship. Knowing the political stance of the shareholders of these dailies (the Winkel and Jonckheer families), the editors use editorials and letters to promote the DP (Interview, Roosberg 1980). The situation at *Nobo* is more difficult to analyze. Although a former prime minister, R. J. Isa, is a major stockholder in the paper, there is not agreement on his political aspirations. When *Nobo* subtly attacked the central government in 1980, one source thought that Isa might be making a comeback (Interview, Roosberg 1980). Of course, *Nobo*'s editor, Carlos Daantje, denied this possibility, stating that Isa had no interest in returning to politics; Daantje provided background on *Nobo*'s stockholders.

> When *Nobo* started, *Amigoe* was heavily involved politically, and *Beurs* and *La prensa* were on the opposite political side. As a third group, we just wanted to do our duty. I said 50 percent of *Nobo*'s stock should be held by Arubans, 50 percent by Curaçao residents. It is still the same. In Aruba, four stockholders have equal parts of the 50 percent, while in Curaçao, there were three — R. J. Isa, Arthur Jesurun, and myself. After two years, Jesurun pulled out and I bought his stock, so that today, I have 66 percent, and Isa, 33 percent, of the Curaçao half (Interview, Daantje 1980).

Nearly all editors agreed that the mass media were concerned with promoting political parties and/or with making money. *Amigoe* editors said, "It is handy to defend a party. All papers [except *Amigoe*] choose a party to back" (Interview, Heiligers and Salsbach 1980). Roosberg lamented that the motivations of media owners were mainly political or commercial and claimed that this is a handicap. He would like to see more media take the direction of Radio Curom, which, he said, is not tied to any commercial or political group and has become the first station to do radio journalism independently and objectively (Interview, Roosberg 1980). Daantje said that while it is true that the media are politically or commercially oriented, it is equally valid that one must make money to provide public service (Interview, Daantje 1980).

The television services have changed for the better. For years, Tele-curaçao and Tele-Aruba had boards of directors chosen on a political basis. Today, the five- to seven-member boards are chosen according to professional capabilities.

ECONOMICS

Competitiveness and smallness of the market do not allow broadcasters and editors to let their guards down on financial matters. Aruba and Curaçao are glutted with mass media, which, until very recently, practiced cutthroat competition. The prediction is that some media will die, especially *Awor,* and possibly Radio Antilliana and Radio Caruso Booi, both in Aruba. But the same prediction was made to this author in 1968, and as noted above, the opposite happened. In fact, while gloomy statements were being made in 1980, a number of individuals were attempting to obtain radio licenses.

Daantje fears that the Dutch-language dailies may be in danger because of the emphasis on the "national" language. Already, these papers are losing circulation, but up to this point, they are surviving on their advertising revenue. The islands' businesses still use Dutch. Speaking about the seven commercial radio signals of Aruba and the twelve different media of Curaçao, Cuales said, "There is not enough revenue for all this. Those already in a financial bind would run in circles—not enough money, therefore not enough programming, therefore not enough advertising. This will happen especially with some newspapers" (Interview, Cuales 1980).

No doubt some newspapers and radio stations are making money. Roger Snow, director of SGC, said that for the first time in 1979 the big five dailies (all except *Awor*) were in the black. *Nobo,* for example, made a profit by "running a tight ship and taking care of cost control" (Interview, Daantje 1980) and, it might be added, by sensationalizing the news. Outsiders are surprised that in a small place such as Curaçao, a newspaper can show a profit, especially because all materials must be imported at extra costs and because distribution problems are created by the attempt to be regional (Interview, Daantje 1980).

Some economic difficulties are caused by the publishers who engage in what Snow called "a stupid type of competition" that kills rather than builds. When Snow came to Curaçao in 1972, he advised the formation of a publishers' association aimed at combining many of the newspapers' common interests (Interview, Snow 1980). The publishers' association, which became a reality in 1977, has not been a panacea for all problems. *Amigoe* editors thought that if the six Curaçao dailies had a better organization, more cooperative ventures could be undertaken to stave off financial blight. They said that with such a cooperative, newsprint and equipment could be bought more inexpensively in bulk, and horrendous distribution costs could be sliced. The four afternoon dailies belong to a joint distribution company, Districo; the morning *Awor* and *Extra* do not. Because the dailies want to portray an Antillean-serving image, they distribute via air freight to all islands, which makes for costly circulation. The newspapers, through their press clubs, are appealing to the government for lower air freight, telex, and telephone rates. One editor predicted that if the government did not lower these rates, the costs would be passed on to the subscribers, a damaging proposition. He showed that in Aruba only twelve thousand families are potential subscribers, and because of increased newspaper prices, most have already become two-newspaper families (one each in Dutch and Papiamento). Previously, he said, a family would subscribe to all five (Interview, van der Schoot 1980).

MEDIA/CULTURAL DOMINATION AND INDEPENDENCE

Without the usual fanfare associated with a state's emergence from under the cultural domination of a metropolitan country, the Netherlands Antilles made great strides in the 1970s towards creating a national identity. As indicated earlier, the impetus was probably the promotion of Papiamento. As Cuales pointed out, "From the banker to the doctor to the shoeshine boy—if they know Papiamento, they speak it. Maybe the 1969 riots played an incidental role in popularizing Papiamento as there was more attention given to local culture. Until 1973, of the three dailies, two were in Dutch, one in Papiamento. Today, there are four Papiamento and two Dutch dailies. Also, all island parliaments now use Papiamento" (Interview, Cuales 1980). The switchover is also evident in radio. Formerly stations used very little Papiamento, but by 1980, Caribe, Curom, and Hoyer I were all totally in the native language. Korsow was split between Dutch and Papiamento. Only Hoyer II is completely Dutch.

Cuales emphasized that Papiamento in the Netherlands Antilles has a different position than patois in other parts of the Caribbean. "Patois is a marketplace language only, while Papiamento is the language of everything here. The wide use of Papiamento is natural," he added. The limited use of the language—on only three islands of the world—makes for costly problems. First, nearly everything received by the media must be translated; second, exchanges of radio and television programs or newspaper stories are not possible (Interview, Cuales 1980).

Daantje recognized the wider use of Papiamento as important culturally; however, he does not believe the 1969 riots were that important in the changeover.

> The increase in the use of Papiamento is not the result of the 1969 riots. The government let the riots explode because it did not believe that something like that could happen here. After the riots, quite a few people saw an opportunity to come forward to push a local cultural identity. When I started in journalism twenty years ago, it

was hard to get people to read Papiamento. They read Dutch poorly
and wrote it well; they wrote Papiamento poorly and read it well. In
the early 1970s, the people just got interested in Papiamento (Interview, Daantje 1980).

The minister of culture of the Netherlands Antilles, Jacques Veeris,
said in 1980 that he was in the process of reviewing the cultural relationships his government had with Holland and Venezuela because he believed they have not benefited Antillean cultural development. Veeris
said that "When television was started sixteen years ago, we had a Hol-
land-appointed person who chose the programs for our station. Then a
Dutch foundation sponsored 300,000 guilders yearly for television shows
on the order of 'The Week in Holland.' Thus, Holland decided what we
saw on TV" (Interview, Veeris 1980). Veeris changed that relationship. In
1980, meetings were held among representatives of the Ministry of Culture, Telecuraçao, the Dutch-sponsoring foundation, a Dutch television
company, and others to restructure programming. The result is that
Antilleans have about 90 to 100 percent of the decision-making power.
They prefer that the Dutch foundation money be sent to Aruba and
Curaçao for the production of local shows. Since Veeris believed that the
cultural impact of Venezuela is too strong in the islands, he also talked
with the Venezuelan Cultural Center to bring about changes (Interview,
Veeris 1980).

Not following the policy of some Third World countries (including a
few in the Caribbean), the Netherlands Antilles does not regulate the
importation of music. The result is that Aruba's Radio Carina is made
up mostly of U.S. music, and Curaçao's Radio Curom fills its music
schedule with 70 percent foreign music. Despite these figures, Cuales
was not alarmed.

> The difference between ten years ago and now is that there are ten
> times more local bands. There has been quite a surge in local music
> that has come with the greater consciousness of local values. It was
> here all along and 1969 brought it to the forefront. The imported
> music on radio is not in conflict with the local culture, partly be-
> cause of the cosmopolitan atmosphere of Curaçao. It is not unusual
> to meet Americans daily, so we do not get upset hearing U.S. music.
> Plus, we are at the crossroads of North and South America. It is not
> unusual to hear U.S. pop, local bands, calypso from Jamaica, a
> Dutch song, or Spanish ballad. We understand all of it (Interview,
> Cuales 1980).

Not much progress has been made in changing the dependence of island media upon the Dutch news agency, ANP, for news and features, although the agency has been accused of using too much European news not relevant to the islands (Interview, van der Schoot 1980). The *Amigoe* editors said that "indeed, there is imperialism."

> In Holland, people blame the U.S. of [*sic*] dominating news flow, but they forget Holland has been doing the same to Netherlands Antilles and Suriname. We are interested in regional news but we can't afford to pay correspondents on other islands, the result being we have to depend upon ANP. During the recent coup in Suriname, all news had to go via ANP to Holland and then via ANP back to the Netherlands Antilles. *Amigoe* did send its own correspondents to Suriname (Interview, Heiligers and Salsbach 1980).

Occasionally, there has been talk of setting up a news agency in the Netherlands Antilles that would have the scope of the Caribbean News Agency (CANA). In fact, the director of CANA visited Curaçao in 1979, but with the aim of contracting *Amigoe* and other papers to CANA. No action had been taken by 1980. Talks have also proceeded with the Netherlands Antilles government and with a Netherlands university, both interested in establishing a regional news agency.

Even without the aid of regional news and feature services, some newspapers have made their contents more localized. *La prensa,* for example, runs Friday comic strips drawn by its own artist. *Amigoe* hoped to do the same but was having difficulty obtaining the services of an artist. The other dailies either use Spanish- or English-language comics. Additionally, most datelines in the Netherlands Antilles newspapers are now from the region, and papers such as *Amigoe* have written their own analysis of international events.

PROFESSIONALISM

Among the most striking differences between the Antillean media of the late 1960s and the early 1980s were the organizational efforts for making the public aware of media roles and for upgrading newspapers and broadcasting. In the early 1970s, individual press clubs were formed in Aruba, Bonaire, Curaçao, and the Windward Islands. Besides performing social roles, the clubs have been instrumental in sponsoring a yearly Antillean Press Congress, writing a Code of Honour, and having 1 September declared Press Day. They have also lobbied for less expensive telex and telephone rates, radio connections, and duty-free printing supplies and tapes. The press clubs have been very active in raising the political and media awareness of the public. Before elections, they organized political meetings to which each party sends a representative. They have also sponsored lectures on drug abuse, and during their annual congresses they have delved into problems associated with oil exploitation, energy, police activities, and unification of the islands. The presidents of the island press clubs make up a regional governing board called Persraad.

Newspaper owners are organized into the Nederlands Antilles Verenigde Dagsbladpers on Curaçao and the Gremio Professional di Periodistenan Arubano on Aruba. The latter has changed the character of governmental press conferences. Previously the Aruban government called press conferences with two hours' notice to the media. After several boycotts of the conferences by GPPA members, the authorities extended the notice to twenty-four hours (Interview, van der Schoot 1980).

The organization that has changed the profession most significantly is the Stichting Grafische Communicatie (Foundation Graphic Communication), directed by Roger Snow. Dedicated to the promotion of graphic communication in the islands, SGC has promoted children's books in Papiamento, workshops for journalists, printing facilities in the smaller islands, articles of cultural and educational value in the daily press, establishment of weeklies and monthlies, an awareness of the role of communication for development, and a media textbook for high schools. Discussing the beginnings of SGC, Snow said,

> When I set up the publishers' association, I noticed gaps — there were no monthlies, no children's books, very little use of Papiamento, no real standards, poor newspaper formats. To change all this, I realized I needed a center, but a center needs money. The government could do it, but the government could abuse such a project, or the people might not accept it if government sponsored. So in 1977, I set up SGC as a "paper" organization and then sought funding from a large foundation in Holland. I also set up projects through the sponsorship of other nongovernmental foundations. The board of SGC is made up of top people in the islands, so when we take on a project, we have the trust of the public (Interview, Snow 1980).

One of the first projects SGC sponsored was a symposium on the role of the media in the development of the Netherlands Antilles, an awareness-raising effort. Believing there was very little educational and cultural fare in the dailies, SGC received funding from an agency in the Netherlands to subsidize each newspaper (including those in the Windwards) — 1,000

guilders monthly if they devoted four pages during that time to education and culture. *Amigoe* started providing this service through a special
section called *Napa.*

In an effort to make high school children more interested and critical of daily journalism, SGC published *De krant op School,* a booklet to
be used in the classroom (similar to newspaper-in-the-classroom projects
in the United States). Each school is offered thirty free copies of the
booklet; additional copies cost fifty cents each. Also, each school is
asked to "subscribe" to five copies of all newspapers daily for two
months; SGC pays for these subscriptions. The foundation planned a
similar booklet on radio and television. Snow said that the children's
books project developed because of the "diversity of language training
here. Children grow up in Papiamento; then when they are six, they
learn everything in Dutch. This is disastrous. They cannot continue reading Papiamento because there is nothing for children in that language"
(Interview, Snow 1980). In 1979, with the help of an association of
Antillean women, SGC organized a short story contest for six- to nine-
year-olds. A monetary award and publication of stories were promised
the winners. Forty stories were selected from the three hundred to four
hundred entries. Initially, four illustrated books of these stories were
published and sold inexpensively throughout the islands.

SGC also conducted a project similar to the one the Trinidad *Express* did for smaller islands' papers of the Commonwealth Caribbean
for at least one Dutch Windward island. Because Saba had no infrastructure for communication (only an old stencil machine), SGC obtained Netherlands funds to set up an offset press in the island. A Sabaan
was trained to operate the printery, which publishes the *Saba Herald,*
under the auspices of SGC. Snow also hoped to establish a neutral radio
station in St. Maarten to serve the Windwards.

Apparently, SGC was an originator of the controversial media
council proposed for the Netherlands Antilles, and it also worked on a
training scheme for Third World journalists. Concerning the latter,
Dutch media and other organizations offered 1.3 million guilders yearly
for the training of Third World journalists through two courses of fifteen weeks each. When the SGC and Minister of Culture Veeris heard
there was a desire to offer the training in a developing state, they offered
Curaçao as the site. Another SGC proposal was the development of an
institute of mass communication at the University of Netherlands
Antilles to do research and to take charge of SGC training courses and
the above-mentioned 1.3 million guilders program.

Local training in newspaper and radio techniques was started by
SGC in September 1979. Four short courses were offered in 1980–1981,

and other workshops were organized for the Windward Islands and for training in photography and small-newspaper management. The need for training had been a problem for years. A few individuals had received training in the Netherlands or Barbados, but for the most part, newspeople had no schooling at all, except for what was obtained on the job. Daantje said his "biggest problem is to get competent people in the administrative and editorial staffs. If you pay well enough, you get competent people. But if you want trained people, you have to train them yourself. And you need competent people on your staff to do the training" (Interview, Daantje 1980). Cuales agreed that the biggest problem in radio is getting adequately trained radio journalists. At Radio Curom, much on-the-job training takes place, although three of the station's five newspeople are graduates of a Dutch journalism school. Cuales said that because other stations seem only interested in sales, and not news, they do not have training schemes. Thus, a station such as Radio Korsow was known to use high school children as free-lancers. On Bonaire, there are only three professional journalists serving all the media; again, there is a heavy reliance upon free-lancers — such as teachers and other educated citizens — to send in news. Because of the training problem, radio and newspapers have suffered some embarrassing, unprofessional moments, when blackmail, vulgarity, and other unethical practices occurred (Interview, Gómez-Lampkin 1980).

The editors of *Amigoe* touched on another aspect of the problem of personnel availability saying, "Our biggest problem is that a small group of people is trying to do what other newspapers do with more people. If we have to deal with a story about oil, or finance, or some other topic, we have to talk to someone quickly or read a book on the topic. We have to be a jack-of-all-trades and don't have time for specialization. Often, our journalists are accused of not knowing enough about subjects they cover. This is true; they don't have the time" (Interview, Heiligers and Salsbach 1980).

Finally, the islands do not have an infrastructure to support research in mass communications. By 1980, only one individual had formal work in academic mass communications research. The University of Netherlands Antilles, set up in the late 1970s, is only now getting around to dealing with the social sciences.

GOVERNMENT-MEDIA RELATIONSHIPS

The most talked-about government action regarding the press in 1980 was a proposal for a media council. The idea called for an eleven-member council that would advise the Netherlands Antilles government on mass media affairs. The membership was to consist of three persons chosen by the Antillean Television Corporation, the Antillean Broadcasting Association, and a daily press association; three persons chosen from the press; four to represent island territories; and one to represent the government of the Netherlands Antilles. Only the latter was to be chosen by the government.

Although the decree concerning the council was vague on the types of advice that would be sought by the government, media personnel had their own ideas. Daantje said that he could not conceive of the government's using the council for its own benefit. Instead, he thought "the council will help the media. For example, radio stations complain they have to pay import duties on tapes; now they can complain to the council" (Interview, Daantje 1980). Another editor thought the council would be a place for citizens to complain about irresponsible advertising (Interview, van der Schoot 1980), while G. J. Schouten saw the council strictly as a control mechanism (Interview, Schouten 1980). Probably closer to what is meant by a council were the views of the Minister of Culture, Jacques Veeris, who said:

> The council is a positive action to have the press in a body that counsels government on communication. In fact, the newspapers asked for the council. Radio Curom and *Amigoe* have broad views on the council, while *Beurs, La prensa,* and the Aruba section of *Extra* worry and make a big scene out of anything that looks to them like a restriction on press freedom. Simply put, the council allows media to suggest to government. At the moment, the communication structure of the Netherlands Antilles is very poor. Media are commercially operated to give information to the public in the cheapest way possible. So, the government should give the media a hand to be broader, more positive, less dependent upon commercials, and to play a bigger role in the country. That's how I approach the media council—the media can have input in government media policy (Interview, Veeris 1980).

At the time, the authorities sought the advice of the media concerning the proposal and planned to reword parts of the document to appease them.

Generally, the relationship between the government and the mass media is much more cooperative and congenial than in the late 1960s. The central government instituted a "meet the press" monthly and worked not only to remove from the books discriminatory laws related to broadcasting but also to revamp the government information services,

RVD. Access to the central government is rather open. For example, the meet-the-press sessions are televised. Additionally, there is a regular television interview show in which ministers answer unscreened questions of representative newspeople. Parliamentary sessions of the central government have been transmitted by radio since the advent of the 1980s, and members of parliament are invited to participate in a triweekly radio show in order to question ministers on various governmental topics.

Veeris said that the government information services had not been working the way he had hoped, so a special press liaison officer was appointed in the Council of Ministers. Concerning government information services, he said, "RVD is a problem. We inherited a weak management, an office that is handled too politically. Each succeeding government brought in its people — none professionally trained. I have sought help from the Holland RVD in restructuring our own" (Interview, Veeris 1980).

Because of an incident involving an international press-monitoring body, the antiquated broadcasting laws of the Netherlands Antilles were overhauled. The Inter American Press Association, upon seeing the broadcast laws and assuming they were being used regularly, declared that there was freedom for the press but not for broadcasting in the Dutch islands. Article 7 of the Radio Law, which stipulated that programs had to be taped and tapes and scripts forwarded to the ministry before broadcast, was abolished in the early 1980s. Although this regulation had not been applied by 1980, nevertheless, its potential danger was present. Similar regulations have also been scrutinized by government (Interview, Cuales 1980).

The government has helped the media in other ways, most notably by waiving the payment of duty on the importation of newsprint and by advertising in the newspapers. The latter has been misused by the government of Aruba, according to Schouten, who contended that his newspaper (the *News*) and *Beurs* and *La prensa* have been denied government advertising because of their oppositionist stance (Interview, Schouten 1980). One editor reacted that Schouten's newspaper is designed for tourists who would have no need for the government advertisements (Interview, Daantje 1980).

Editors and broadcasters claimed that they investigate government without repercussions. Cuales said that when Radio Curom carries critical editorials of the central and insular governments, the authorities request rebuttal time but do not "tell the station who do you think you are" (Interview, Cuales 1980). *Amigoe* has carried exposés of illegalities in government without harassment from officials.

The government-media relationship is more tense in Aruba, but it is certainly not at the explosive level. The island government there has been accused of abusing broadcasting by asking for undue airtime, by censoring broadcasting, by withholding official invitations to certain newspapers, by forcing critical announcers off the air, by denying advertisements to newspapers, by temporarily operating their own propaganda daily, and by having designs on owning a radio station (Interviews, Cuales, Schouten, and Gómez-Lampkin, all 1980).

CONCLUSION

Mass communications in the Netherlands Antilles was drastically changed from the 1960s to the 1980s, and for the most part, positively. Four dailies and most radio stations now use the indigenous language, and the contents of the media have been localized. The first fully professional journalists returned from the Netherlands to join island staffs, and local training schemes have been drawn up. Radio has made moves toward performing journalistic functions. The media have organized into working press clubs and associations, and a better dialogue has occurred between the government and the media. SGC and others have popularized the concept of using communications for developmental purposes, and despite the growth in numbers of media, most have moved a bit beyond the survival level.

However, much remains to be done at the close of the 1980s. Virtually no educational media exist in the islands, broadcasting is called a "mental pollutant" because of its intense commercialism, and little intercommunication exists between the Netherlands Antilles and the rest of the Caribbean. The media, still dependent upon a Dutch news agency, must make strides towards setting up a regional agency, and more concern for the "small" media (folk, mimeograph, cassettes, etc.) is necessary if development messages are to receive larger audiences. Advertising also needs closer scrutiny, even though it is mainly locally owned.

18

Suriname Mass Media: A Brief Overview

HISTORICAL DEVELOPMENT

Suriname had its first newspaper in 1774, *De wekelijksche woensdagsche Surinaamsche courant,* started by Beeldsnijder Matroos. In about ten years, the authorities subjected the press to restrictive censorship. By 1787, *Surinaamsche spectator uitgegeven* was censored by the governor, and nine years later, *Nieuwsvertelder of zamenspraak tusschen louw en krelis* faced a similar fate (Kalff 1923–1924).

A rather large number of printing presses and newspapers developed in the colony, and during the British sovereignty of 1804 to 1816 at least ten printing shops operated. Paramaribo newspapers at the time published only official notices, advertisements, and foreign news, the latter picked up from newspapers of Barbados, Demerary, the United States, or occasionally, Europe (Samson 1950, 80).

Measures taken against Suriname newspapers remained arbitrary until about 1864, when Governor van Lansberge referred to a royal decree upon suspending a newspaper for three months. The decree gave him full powers to take action, but he first had to consult with the Colonial Council (Samson 1952, 227).

Both the Netherlands and Suriname governing bodies had occasions in the latter nineteenth century to complain about the local press. However, not many sanctions were meted out. In the twentieth century, the story was different; lawsuits were brought against editors for libeling governors, and in 1932 draft ordinances were sent to the legislative body with modifications to the penal code. The ordinances were meant to guarantee the safety of the colony, public order, and public authority. Under these ordinances, the governor was given full power to name

Ao. 1859.

Donderdag

No. 147.

8 December.

SURINAAMSCHE COURANT EN GOUVERNEMENTS ADVERTENTIE BLAD.

Gouvernements-Secretarie.

Paramaribo, den 7 December 1859.
Bij Gouvernements Resolutie van gister No. 6, is aan Jacoba Linch, zich noemende Jacoba Rebecca de Haas, vergund, om met weglating van haren familienaam Linch, dien van de Haas te voeren, en om bij haren voornaam Jacoba, dien van Rebecca te voegen en zich alzoo te blijven noemen:

Jacoba Rebecca de Haas.
De Gouvernements Secretaris,
E. A. van EMDEN.

Gouvernements-Secretarie.

Paramaribo, den 7 December 1859.
(16155) Alzoo bij het Bestuur het verzoek is gedaan om den slaaf *Johannes*, geboren in 1801, moedersnaam onbekend, van den naam van plantage *Killenstein*, gelegen in de divisie *Beneden Cottica*, te doen afschrijven.

Zoo worden degenen die vermeenen mogten redenen van bezwaar daartegen te hebben in de gelegenheid gesteld om binnen den tijd van veertien dagen, na de dagteekening dezer, van hun vermeend regt of pretentie aanteekening ter Gouvernements Secretarie te doen.

De Gouvernements Secretaris,
E. A. van EMDEN.

Gouvernements-Secretarie.

Paramaribo, den 7 December 1859.
(16155) Alzoo bij het Bestuur het verzoek is gedaan om den slaaf *Constant*, geboren in 1838, moedersnaam *Bobé*, van den naam van plantage *'t Vertrouwen*, gelegen in de divisie *Beneden Cottica*, te doen afschrijven.

Zoo worden degenen die vermeenen mogten redenen van bezwaar daartegen te hebben in de gelegenheid gesteld, om binnen den tijd van veertien dagen, na de dagteekening dezer, van hun vermeend regt of pretentie aanteekening ter Gouvernements Secretarie te doen.

De Gouvernements Secretaris;
E. A. van EMDEN.

Gouvernements-Secretarie.

Aanzoek voor Vrijgeving.

1859
2 Dec. Van de slavin *Amba* of *Jaba*, geboren in 1810, dochter van *Maria*, (overleden), toebehoorende aan F. M. Schietlood.
  » Van het slavenkind *Qurina Maria*, geboren in 1859, dochter van Cla-

rista, toebehoorende aan Martha Levij.
De Gouvernements-Secretarie,
E. A. van EMDEN.

Derde Afkondiging.

Benoodigd voor 's Gouvernements dienst.

Diverse KLEEDINGSTUKKEN enz., voor de Landslaven, waarvan de monsters ter Administratie van Financiën bezorgd worden.

De bus der inschrijvings-billetten ter Gouvernements Secretarie, alwaar eene specifieke lijst der benoodigde goederen is aangeplakt, zal geligt worden op Donderdag den Asten dezer maand, des voormiddags ten 10 ure.

Paramaribo, den 5 December 1859.
De Administrateur van Financien,
A. de MAN.

(15888) De Exploicteur bij het Geregtshof in de kolonie *Suriname*, zal op Vrijdag den 9 December 1859, des voormiddags ten half negen ure, publiekelijk bij executie verkoopen:

De slaven *William, Hendrik, Eduard, Rudolf, Carel, Cornelia, Leentje, Sophie, Heintje, Marius, Richard* en *Amelia*, aankomende wed. J. del Monte geboren Ezechiëla.

De slaven *Marjus, Thomas, Kwasiba, Phillida, Georgina, Constant, Sinda, Anna, Rudolf* en *Adolf*, aankomende B. Arrias geboren de la Parra.

De slaven *Kees* of *Christiaan, Albertus, Willem, Jan, Contessa* en *Caro*, aankomende de wed. M. Naar.

Den slaaf *Johannes*, aankomende boedel J. Valois.

De slaven *George, Constant, Jetta* en *Anthonij*, aankomende boedel F. van Sachten.

De slaven *Alexander* en *Bebo*, aankomende E. en C. M. J. Freubel.

De slaven *April* en *Hendrik*, aankomende E. Emanuels Jz.

Het Huis en Erf La. O No. 4b., aankomende S. J. Samson.

Eene billardtafel, drie Hanglampen en vijf Speeltafels, aankomende J. J. Salomons.

Paramaribo, den 7 December 1859.
SIMON ABENDANON Sz.

(15889) De Exploicteur bij het Geregtshof in de kolonie *Suriname*, zal op Vrijdag den 9 December 1859, des morgens om half ne-

gen ure, publiekelijk bij executie verkoopen:

De slaven *Antoinette, Jacoba, Wilhelmina, Christina, Henrij, Maria, Johannes* en *Albertus*, aankomende wed. J. A. Knipschaar geboren Stoelman.

Paramaribo, den 7 December 1859.
SIMON ABENDANON Sz.

(15890) De Exploicteur bij het Geregtshof den 9 December 1859, des voormiddags ten half negen ure, publiekelijk bij executie verkoopen:

De slaven *Adriaan, Johanna, Cathanina, Augusta, Johanna Elisabeth*, en *Frans*, aankomende A. Goedschalk weduwe J. J. Burkheim.

Paramaribo, den 7 December 1859.
SIMON ABENDANON Sz.

(15649) De Exploicteur bij het Geregtshof in de kolonie *Suriname*, zal op VRIJDAG den 30-ten December 1859, des morgens ten half negen ure, publiekelijk bij executie verkoopen:

De Plantaadje **Bent'shope** c. a. gelegen aan de *Warappa kreek*, aankomende John Bent, nu boedel.

De verlatene Plantaadje **Breedevoort** c. a. gelegen aan de rivier *beneden Commewijne*, aankomende de minderjarigen M. A. — W. — H. E. — J. C. — en A. Jackson.

Paramaribo, den 7 December 1859.
SIMON ABENDANON Sz.

MARINE.

De Kapitein Luitenant ter Zee, Kommandant Z. M. Zeemagt in de kolonie *Suriname*, zal aanbesteden de navolgende leverancien ten dienste der alhier gestationneerde Zeemagt, als:

De levering van VERSCH BROOD, gedurende den jare 1860, de levering van VERSCH RUND VLEESCH tot ultimo Junij 1860 en de levering tot laatst gemeld tijdvak van de onderstaande ARTIKELEN als:

P. **1200** Ned. **RIJST**.
» **1000** » **KOFFIJ**.
» **600** » **SUIKER**.
» **1500** » witte **ZEEP**.

De voorwaarden der aanneming zullen ter inzage liggen op het bureau van den Heere Kol. Magazijnmeester, alwaar de inschrijvings billetten, benevens de monsters voor zoo ver betreft de laatst gemelde artikelen, zullen worden aangenomen van af den 20n. tot den 24n. December 1859, op welken laatsten datum dezelve, des morgens ten 10 ure, geopend en de leverancien, aan de publications liable to suspension after he had consulted with the advisory council. After a certain time period, he could actually suspend the periodicals if he thought this was advisable. Although the legislative body objected, saying such an ordinance would be an infringement of press freedom, the governor had his way when the regulation came into being on the strength of a royal decree. In 1938, and again in 1950, newspapers were targeted as liable to suspension.

Periodicals other than newspapers began in Suriname with almanacs, probably the first of which was *Surinaamsche almanach* of 1788, followed by *De lantaarn* of 1792 to 1801, *Surinaamsche staatkundige almanach* of 1793, as well as others (Benjamins and Snelleman 1914–1917, 679). By 1933, Oudschans Dentz (1933) listed 153 newspapers and other periodicals that appeared in Suriname.

Radio had its origins in 1935 with the setting up of Algemene Vereniging Radio Omroep Suriname (AVROS), followed by Radio Paramaribo in 1957, Radio Apinto in 1958, Radio Dihat Ki Awaz in 1962, and Stichting Radio-Omroep Suriname (SRS) in 1965. Although planning had taken place for a few years, the first television station was Surinaamse Televisie Stichting in 1964. The station, according to a 1975 survey, broadcast 70 percent in Dutch and 30 percent in English. The same survey showed the breakdown of programs: entertainment, 45 percent; news, 25 percent; education and culture, 17 percent; children's shows, 10 percent; and religious shows 3 percent (Bruijning and Voorhoeve 1977, 522–23, 604).

Apparently, the first films were shown in Paramaribo as early as 1899 by C. G. Heilbron. The largest number of films in any given year came from the United States; between 1953 and 1955 there were 1,076. In that same period, there were 163 films from India, 97 from Italy, and 31 from England; others were from France, the Netherlands, and Mexico (van Gorkom 1957, 77, 80). Indian films are popular because 37 percent of the population are Hindus.

CONTEMPORARY SITUATION

Two major daily newspapers were published in Suriname throughout the 1980s—*De ware tijd,* under government control, and *De west,* privately owned by E. A. Findlay. *De ware tijd*'s circulation of twenty thousand was about twice that of its competitor. The only television channel was Suriname Television, also government controlled. After a military coup of 1980, the only radio stations that broadcast regularly were governmental, although by middecade stations such as Apinto,

Rapas, and Stem Van de Revolution were allowed to resume.

Telecommunications in Suriname are governed by a national corporation, TELESUR, which shares a third of the investments made in the communications earth station at Cayenne, French Guiana. Three of every hundred Surinamese had telephones in the early 1980s; the number was expected to increase to thirteen per hundred (*CETTEM Newsletter* 1982, 4).

The media scene has been somewhat unstable since Suriname threw off Dutch colonial reins in 1975. In February 1980, the eight hundred-man army took over, installing Lt. Col. Desi Bouterse as the head of government. Morales and Ballard (1985, 63) reported that after the 1980 coup, "There has never been a time when the former Dutch colony's press has been without restrictions."

During the takeover of government itself, *De west* was occupied by soldiers, and some of its equipment was destroyed. By April, the daily, *Free Voice,* clashed head-on with the authorities for reporting on public beatings of petty criminals. Editor Wilfred Lionarons was detained for two days. During the next two years, he was summoned by military leaders seven times for warnings, his paper was confiscated on one occasion, and he was placed on a death list (Lionarons 1985). In July 1981, the National Military Council announced that censorship was to be implemented for all media to "protect the revolutionary process."

A Suriname journalist, Edward N. Drop (1982), rationalized the government's actions, stating that Suriname had become the victim of counterrevolutionary forces hostile to the progressive Bouterse government. In fact, he said that such forces were very much involved in propaganda destabilization. In March 1982, during an attempted coup, these forces succeeded in closing all radio stations except the state station, which they used to start a "slanderous campaign of lies," according to Drop; the government forces quickly recaptured a radio station (Drop 1982).

Also in 1982, the Progressive Media Workers Association of Suriname was formed with resolutions on the establishment of the group, the national situation, a new information order, and the quality of information. A code of ethics was adopted. Bouterse gave his country's support for the New World Information and Communications Order (NWICO) at its inaugural meeting. He referred to international press campaigns against his government, similar to those carried out against Chile's Allende and Jamaica's Manley. Additionally, he denounced the way the Netherlands, through its news agency, censored news of happenings in Suriname.

Other 1982 happenings changed the role of the media. In October, the authorities banned the media from reporting critical remarks directed at Bouterse. On 8 December, the military tightened its grip on the opposition, "eliminating civilian participation in the government and putting an end to even the very little discretion in editorial judgment" surviving (Morales and Ballard 1985, 63). During a fracas, four journalists and eleven opposition leaders were killed, and media offices were burned and bombed. As a result, *De wek* and stations Apinto and Rapas were closed.

Within a year, the clampdown was all but complete; most of the news of Suriname was provided by the government-financed Suriname News Agency. Justifying the death of the once-outspoken Suriname press, the editor-in-chief of the news agency, Edward Naarendorp, told the *New York Times* that the press had to be an agent of social change, overcoming backwardness. He added that the new press was an improvement, serving the interests of "workers, peasants and women," rather than just elites and the middle class. Some Suriname citizens disagreed, according to the *Times,* believing that events unfavorable to Bouterse were not reported. Also, the rules tended to change as the government sought different allies, Naarendorp said (LeMoyne 1983).

The former editor of *Free Voice,* Wilfred Lionarons, interviewed in exile in the Netherlands, said that censorship had eased somewhat by 1984. Some newspapers reappeared on the condition that they abstain from all criticism. Lionarons viewed this with alarm.

> I guess that is even worse than the censorship we experienced in the first years of military rule. At that time they had a censor on every newspaper, so at least you could talk to the man and discuss what would be allowed and what not. Now all journalists are in doubt all of the time. The result can be seen in Surinam's [sic] press today, which is extremely careful and undaring. None of them wants to be banned for confronting the military. They know that would lead to physical violence against journalists — several of them had already experienced this before December 1982. So what we have now are newspapers writing on "safe" subjects. A lot of foreign news, from the wires of UPI and AP. The remaining pages are filled with pictures, puzzles and fictional stories. For instance, I recently found the complete *Three Musketeers* in one of the papers (Lionarons 1985, 16).

Discussing the same cautious characteristic of the Suriname press, Morales and Ballard (1985, 64) described the new rules.

> The new system was set up by a series of agreements signed between representatives of the government and the owners of the media in

which both parties consented to state controls being limited in exchange for politically cautious editorial policies. It was stipulated that the press must "make every effort to serve the nation's interest" and refrain from publications and programs that could in any way damage national interest, security and law and order. Editors are to check with the Prime Minister's office when in doubt over the wisdom of reporting on a particular issue.

In May 1985, official censorship was dropped, permitting "conservative criticism." Bans on several radio stations and *De wek* were removed. However, incidents still occurred. In February 1986, Linus Rensch, editor of the weekly *Brandpunt,* fled to French Guiana after receiving word that he and his family were to be arrested. *Brandpunt* had been outspoken in its criticism of the government. In late 1987, the International Press Institute protested to Bourterse when the government refused visas to thirty Dutch journalists who wished to cover the September referendum.

It is unlikely, however, that many incidents concerning internal press freedom will erupt. As Lionarons indicated, self-censorship can be a deadly silencer.

19

Mass Media in Puerto Rico

The Puerto Rican mass media in the 1980s dashed off in the direction of their mainland U.S. counterparts as if independence and local autonomy were alien concepts. They tied themselves to large Puerto Rican or mainland groups, adopted U.S. big-business journalism practices, and, in the case of television, rationalized that islanders craved stateside English-language programming.

By 1988, the skids had been applied to this U.S.–based development, as a main daily folded, at least four television channels stood the chance of selling out, and Puerto Ricans reaffirmed their preference for locally produced television fare. Nevertheless, Puerto Rico remained one of the few media-rich Caribbean territories, with four dailies, forty weeklies, eleven television channels with twenty-one translator stations, thirty or more cable outlets, and more than 110 radio stations (see various articles by Carty; Cintron 1983; Fores-Caraballo 1988).

HISTORICAL DEVELOPMENT

Much like a few other Caribbean countries, Puerto Rico had its first press rather late, in 1806. Between 1806 and 1808, the first newspaper, *La gaceta de Puerto Rico,* appeared; the exact date has not been confirmed, and three different historians designate 1806, 1807, or 1808 as the inauguration.[1] All sources agree that the second periodical was *Diario económica de Puerto Rico,* published in 1814 by the island's first *intendente* (treasurer), Alejandro Ramírez. *El cigarrón* also debuted in 1814, after which there was not a new periodical until 1820, when *El investigador* appeared. In 1821, *Diario liberal y de variedades* became the first daily. According to Pedreira (1970), press development was slow, with two new periodicals in 1822 and not another until 1839. In 1845 and 1846, there was one each; in 1842, two; 1850 and 1852, one each; 1855, two; 1856, one; 1857, three; and 1859, one.

Between the time of the first newspaper in 1806–1808 and the year 1840, then, eight periodicals appeared, and the next twenty years saw the establishment of thirteen more. From then on, according to Pedreira (1970), the growth was rapid and prodigious, with 126 appearing between 1861 and 1880, 498 between 1881 and 1900, and 574 between 1901 and 1920. The individual years with exceptionally high numbers of periodicals were 1898 with forty-three, 1899 with fifty-five, and 1900 with forty-eight.

Among the periodicals during the latter part of the nineteenth century were the first English-language newspapers, such as the *New Sun,* the *Puerto Rico Mail,* and the *San Juan News* of 1898, and the first to use the telegraph to obtain information, *El telegrama* of the late 1880s.

The establishment of the doctrinarian press after 1870 had much to do with the proliferation of periodicals. Growing numbers of intellectuals began to support the development of political parties, correspondingly leading to an expansion in the quantity and quality of newspapers and journals to promote their causes (Negron-Portillo 1980, 41).

Among the liberal newspapers of the time was *La democracia,* the main voice of the *hacendado* social class and its political party, El Partido Liberal Reformista (later Partido Autonomista). Started in 1890 by Luis Muñoz Rivera, *La democracia* published three times weekly until 1893, when it became a daily. Intellectuals, such as Mariano Abril, Eugenio Astol, and Luis Cabrero, wrote for the paper, always fully confident of Puerto Rico's attainment of self-government. Later, when voting reformist Luis Muñoz Marin returned to Puerto Rico in 1929, he became editor of *La democracia* before launching his own campaign paper, *El batey* (Davey 1979). The paper always had one of the highest circulations, although it was seldom financially secure. Its final issue was in 1945.

Reading the Puerto Rican press of the 1940s, Liebling (1948, 60) said, was like reading U.S. papers in Spanish. Of the four San Juan dailies, three were tabloid (*El imparcial, La democracia,* and *El universal*) while *El mundo* was standard size. Liebling reported that all the dailies used much U.S. "syndicated fodder" and were sensationalistic. The rowdiest was *El imparcial,* which used staged photographs much like the *New York Evening Graphic* of the late 1920s and 1930s.

Radio grew out of the efforts of members of the Club de Aficionados de Radio—Jesús T. Piñero, Ramón Mellado, and Joaquín Agusti.

Agusti helped develop the first commercial station, WKAQ, which grew out of Compañía Telefónica and was responsible in 1922 for setting up the first radio transmitter.

By 1951, at least twenty-four radio stations served owners of the 128,000 receivers on the island. Most survived on shoestring budgets, as few industries could afford radio time. Most advertisers were mainland U.S. companies. As a result, stations often worked with minimal staffs, prompting Kingson and Cowgill (1951, 167) to write, "Talent is there. It is simply overworked, untrained, underpaid, and limited in the forms in which it can express itself." Stations hoped professionalism would improve after Puerto Rico's first radio training program was set up in 1951.

The contents of Puerto Rican radio in the 1940s and 1950s were more explicit than those of the mainland stations. The very popular *novelas*, which made up a sizable portion of all programming (there were at least forty per week in 1951), dealt with syphilis or adultery (Kingson and Cowgill 1951, 160).

Television started in Puerto Rico in 1954 with WKAQ-Telemundo, owned by Angel Ramos. It was followed by WAPA (Channel 4), WKBM (11), WRIK (7), WIPR (6), and WTSJ (18), the last in 1964.

Although advertising obviously had existed in Puerto Rico previously, the first agency handling accounts was the West Indies Advertising Company, initiated in 1933 by Felix Muñiz. Agency growth was slow until after World War II. In 1958, the Advertising Agency Association of Puerto Rico was started; when it was incorporated in 1963, there were nine members. Twenty-nine agencies belonged in 1972, when Puerto Rico had at least fifty agencies, ten of which were branches of mainland U.S. companies. Advertising research began with the Business Research Institute in 1953 and Clapp and Mayne Incorporated in 1969. The Puerto Rican government in 1970 issued a proclamation prohibiting deceptive advertising and practices; earlier, in 1958, it had set up regulations governing roadside signs and billboard advertising (Piedra 1972).

Public relations on a formal scale is a very recent phenomenon. Piedra (1972, 58) reported that in the early 1970s, some advertising agencies had public relations departments, varying from one person handling $50,000 to $80,000 billings to ten-person, $150,000-billings operations. Also, a few small independent public relations agencies did up to $50,000 in billings.

CONTEMPORARY MASS MEDIA

Newspapers
With the death of *El mundo* in 1987, Puerto Rico continues to be served by four dailies and an alternative weekly, *Claridad. El imparcial,* started in 1918 by a local writer, José Perez Lozada, had ceased much earlier in December 1973. Never steady financially, *El imparcial* first closed in 1932 because of the Depression, reopened a year later under Damaso Ayuso, and in 1970, ended up in the hands of a group headed by Miguel Angel García-Mendez, chair of the Estadista-Republican party (see Kershen 1953a).

El mundo was the oldest continuous daily when it announced its closing in July 1987. Started in 1919 by Romualdo Real, the paper eventually was owned by Angel Ramos and was part of his group, which by 1966 included WKAQ-Telemundo (the number one television channel since its 1954 start), WKAQ radio-El Mundo (with network affiliates of WORA in Mayaguez, WPRP in Ponce, and WABA in Aguadilla), and Film and Dubbing Productions. When Ramos died, the group was placed under the Angel Ramos Foundation, chaired by his widow, Argentina S. Hills. The foundation was affiliated with the Knight-Ridder newspaper group on the mainland through the widow's marriage to a top official of that group, Lee Hills (see Anderson 1977).

Strikes in at least 1965–1966 and 1972 had serious consequences for *El mundo,* which saw its circulation plummet from 180,000 in the mid-1970s to less than 100,000 by the time it converted to a tabloid in 1985. At the time of the daily's peak in the 1970s, the parent foundation owned Telemundo Inc., Creative Film Producers, Cine Revista Internacional Inc., El Mundo Inc., and El Mundo Broadcasting Inc. The television interests, WKAQ-Telemundo, were sold to John Blair and Company in 1983.

The English-language daily, the *San Juan Star,* has been owned by U.S. groups from its beginning. Cowles Communications Inc., at the time owner of *Look* and major dailies, especially in Des Moines and Minneapolis, opened the *Star* in 1959. The venture was risky, as English-language dailies were not known for their popularity, despite the fact that 700,000 people on the island spoke the language. Angel Ramos had tried on two occasions to publish an English-language daily. From 1940 to 1945, he published the small *World Journal;* in 1956, he revived it for a short nine months. The *Star* followed the pattern of not being able to gain a sizable part of the market; its first two years witnessed a loss of $600,000. In 1970, the paper's circulation was barely up to 40,000 when it was sold to Scripps-Howard, another mainland group, for $9.75 million. Capital Cities Broadcasting also considered purchasing the *Star* (Ettlinger 1970, 12).

El nuevo día, which circulated to Ponce and its environs since 1911, became more of a national paper when it moved to San Juan in 1970. Before it had been known as *El día.* The Ferré family, involved in politics and big business, own *El nuevo día* and radio stations. The daily is based on the ideas of Luis A. Ferré, founder of the New Progressive party and governor of the island in 1968. He was part owner of WRIK-TV when it went on the air in 1958. Another Ferré, Maurice, was mayor of Miami, Florida, for four terms. The Ferrés own many large corporations, which in 1977 had a total capital of $215 million. Among these are Puerto Rico Cement Company, Florida Lime, St. Regis Paper and Bag Corporation, as well as others in sugar, iron, development, investment, glass, pulp, and clay. Antonio Luis Ferré, president of *El nuevo día,* is a director or official in twelve other corporations, and members of the family in another ten (Anderson 1977, 35). By 1986, *El nuevo día* moved into the top circulation spot with 140,000.

The other dailies are *El vocero* and *El reportero,* also tabloids. *El vocero* was started 29 April 1974, apparently to replace *El imparcial.* Incorporated by Gaspar Roca and a group of local investors, *El vocero* for years has seemed to be the most independent paper, with no ties to other media in Puerto Rico or to the mainland United States. The paper uses a simple, lively style.

Besides the dailies, *Claridad,* a proindependence Socialist party weekly, has been around since the late 1950s. *Claridad* circulated as a daily for some time; in 1976, its 22,500 circulation placed it last among the five dailies. Puerto Ricans depend upon *Claridad* to report upon social and economic problems (Carty 1987, 34) in a climate where these can be glossed over because of the big-business nature of the media.

Puerto Rico has a very small book trade compared to its use of newspapers and magazines. In 1977, book sales brought in $16.5 million. Eighty-eight percent of all books sold were imported, and the island industry exported only 6 percent. In 1979, the importation-of-books market was $20.5 million, and those from the United States made up $13 million. Of books produced in Puerto Rico, 50 to 75 percent are from government agencies.

Broadcasting and Film

The big media story in the 1980s revolved around television and cable. Recognizing that Puerto Rico was a lucrative television market and carried potential as a Spanish-language producer, U.S. mainland investors bought channels profusely in 1986, investing over $150 million. Simultaneously, cable television expanded; at least, 100,000 homes had hooked up to one of about thirty systems by 1986. The largest is Cable TV of Greater San Juan, launched in 1973 and declared bankrupt in 1977, when its present owner, Harris Cable Corporation of Los Angeles, took over. The prediction was that Puerto Rico would have one hundred cable stations and 300,000 to 500,000 cable homes by 1988 (Dinhofer 1983; also see chapter 22).

Before the pivotal year of 1986, WKAQ-Telemundo (Channel 2) and WAPA-Televicentro (Channel 4) controlled 90 percent of the island's television market. They had undergone recent ownership changes, much as other stations would experience later. In 1983, WKAQ-Telemundo was bought by John Blair and Company for $55 million, and after over two decades of local management, it was run by a mainland U.S. broadcaster. The following year, WAPA-Televicentro was purchased by SFN Communications, with Hallmark Cards as one of the main stockholders. Earlier owners of WAPA were, successively, the Winston-Salem Company, Columbia Pictures, and Western Broadcasting (Astroff 1987, 14). The $154 million paid for WAPA also included television stations in Columbus and Augusta, Georgia and Stockton-Sacramento, and three radio stations in Montana. The management of WAPA also owned 50 percent of Pegasus Broadcasting of Chicago. SFN originally was a textbook publisher.

When U.S. companies realized that $161.6 million in advertising revenue was generated for a population of three million in 1985, they scrambled to get into the market. Within the next year, Lorimar-Telepictures set up KLII (Channel 11), with 20 percent ownership by Radio Caracas[2]; Malrite Corporation of Cleveland bought 70 percent of WLUZ-Telelúz (Channel 7)[3]; Oklahoma broadcast owner James C. Leake owned WPRV-TV (Channel 13); and Lane Gawick held WSJU-TV (Channel 18). The last two programmed 90 to 100 percent in English, based on the rationale that Puerto Ricans would grow to prefer non-Spanish programming. Two other new stations entered the market in 1985: WRWR (Channel 30), established by PLD Investments and Bay Broadcasting and programmed with English-language U.S. shows dubbed into Spanish; and WMTD (Channel 40), a university-owned station featuring Public Broadcasting System shows, all in Spanish. The latter, the first university-owned television station in the Caribbean, was started by the Ana G. Mendez Foundation.

While these changes were occurring, two schools of thought prevailed. One, represented by WKAQ, WAPA, and KLII, believed that Puerto Ricans wanted their own programs, reflecting island values and the Spanish language. The other view, that of U.S. mainland broadcasters such as Leake, held that Puerto Ricans, especially young people, were tired of old television formats, such as the serials, and wished to be plugged into the U.S. Anglo culture.

By 1988, it was obvious that the channels retaining Puerto Rican programs were much more successful. At the top was WKAQ-Telemundo, with 50 percent of the $100 million television market. The reasons given for its continued success were its good programming, the upheavals of management at other channels, and the uncertain future of smaller stations.[4] WAPA slipped to about 19 percent of the market, and in a flurry of activity in 1988, tried to recapture its audience by doing three Puerto Rican sitcoms and other local productions for a total of eight or nine hours daily. Also in second place with 19 percent was the Lorimar-Telepictures' Tele-Once. Malrite's station, changed to WSTE (Super Siete), made a major thrust, moving from 4 to 13 percent of the audience in two years.

Channels whose managers had thought Puerto Ricans were eager to watch Anglo products in English fared so poorly that they either switched to local television or tried to sell out. WPRV, which originally intended to telecast only in English, switched to 40 percent Spanish; it and others, such as Tele-Once, WSJU, WRWR, and possibly WAPA, were mentioned as up for sale in 1988. Hallmark was considered a likely buyer of Tele-Once, which had a price tag of $50 million.

Radio is very popular in Puerto Rico; 90 percent of the homes have receivers. Almost all stations have Spanish-speaking disk jockeys, and some air U.S. rock music. The other program formats are *salsa,* easy listening, public radio, religious, and all news.

Puerto Rico is among the handful of Caribbean nations involved in filmmaking. One or two low-budget features are produced yearly by production houses such as Zaga Films or Sono Films. In 1988, Zaga had two films in the theaters, *La gran fiesta* and *Tango Bar.* Sono Films also operated Sono Inversiones, a producer of film commercials that appear on seventy screens, and Sono Sucesos, a documentary service. Other companies in branches of filmmaking are Logros, the first company to make movies for television in 1979, and Crescendo Audio Productions, which in 1984 used its subsidiary, Double Talk, to dub films. Crescendo and its branch are financed by a Texas-based company, BFC.

The Puerto Rico Film and Television Arts Institute (FOMENTO), created by law in 1974 but not operative for another five years, promotes indigenous film production, attracts offshore filmmakers for locations, and provides incentives to local producers. The major film exhibitor is Wometco, with twenty-two locations. The company also distributes thirty-five to forty films yearly and is the owner of forty-two theaters in Miami, about one hundred throughout Florida, and others in Alaska and the Dominican Republic. United Artists owns fourteen Puerto Rican theaters, Victor Carady's Regency Caribbean owns fifteen, and the Cobb Circuit (headquartered in Atlanta) owns nine.

In the early 1980s, the island had 165 theaters, but many have closed since then because of the recession and the growth of cable and videocassette recorder usage. For example, by 1982, fifteen home video clubs had cut into theater attendance with their $12 million in sales. Sales of at least 150,000 to 200,000 movie theater tickets were lost to video in 1981–1982 (see chapter 22).

At the end of the 1980s, filmmaking received a boost from a U.S. tax law set up to spark development in Puerto Rico. Section 936 of the 1986 Tax Reform Act grants a 100 percent tax credit generated in a Puerto Rican subsidiary. As a result, U.S. investors have been willing to invest in local films. Additionally, the Puerto Rican Cinema Institute worked to coordinate government services for local film production (Lenti 1988). Also, in 1988 Puerto Rico's first Festival Cine San Juan was inaugurated.

FREEDOM OF EXPRESSION

Freedom of the press is doubly guaranteed by the constitutions of the United States and Puerto Rico. The latter was written when the island became a free associated state in 1952.

Despite these constitutional guarantees, a number of threats and obstacles do hinder Puerto Ricans' rights to free expression. The first relates to ownership of newspapers and broadcasting stations. The cross-media, cross-industry ownership tied to mainland corporations and to island economic and political elites has ensured that the status quo is maintained. We have already seen examples of dailies and television stations that are parts of island and transnational groups. Additionally, media managements are made up of many North American executives, and most advertising agencies are branches of multinational corporations or their local affiliates.

The effects of such ownership trends on sensitive topics such as independence and social change are devastating. Astroff (1987, 21) reported on an analysis of television news in Puerto Rico that showed proindependence and social change news either was not covered, was broadcast days late, was slanted and partially reported, or was given negative associations. She said that this was not a new phenomenon; as early as 1931, the Radio Corporation of Puerto Rico (a subsidiary of ITT) refused to broadcast speeches of the leader of the independence movement. She added that, tied as they are to the elite segment of society, broadcasting stations have "a long history of ignoring or delegitimizing political alternatives to Commonwealth or statehood" (Astroff 1987, 20).

Agencies such as the Federal Bureau of Investigation have been vigilant in pressuring the mass media to downplay, ignore, or negate the independence movement. The FBI has been accused of planting "friendly" editorials in newspapers (especially *El mundo*) that associated proindependence with communism, Castro, or violence; of spreading malicious misinformation about independence leaders; and of threatening the loss of broadcasting licenses (Astroff 1987, 21). In 1987, the FBI searched the home of a journalist and the offices of *Pensamiento crítico* on the pretense of looking for evidence to arrest proindependence militants. Copies of the periodical, subscription lists, and equipment were seized.

Other pressures abound. In 1983, a police reporter for *El reportero* was beaten and threatened with death for articles she wrote on police corruption, and a *Star* reporter also was harassed for his investigative reporting. At the same time, economic pressure through manipulation of advertising faced *El mundo* and *El reportero,* because they carried opinion articles contrary to the line of the government. One of the most subtle pressures involved a local ratings company, Mediafax. Senate hearings revealed that Mediafax gave high audience ratings only to radio and television stations that helped pay for the polls. Tommy Muñiz, owner of Channel 7, sued Mediafax in the early 1980s, when his viewing audience fell by 50 percent, according to the poll. Finally, a bill that would have required licensing of journalists failed to pass the Puerto Rican Senate in March 1981. Failure to obtain the license would have been met with fines or imprisonment (Cintron 1983).

20

Newspapers in the Virgin Islands:
A Historical Overview

Although meriting but a footnote in the literature of the region, newspaper publishing in the U.S. Virgin Islands (St. Thomas, St. Croix, and St. John) has a history dating to 1770—predating that of any country in Africa and of most in Asia. In fact, the Virgin Islands boast the oldest surviving Caribbean newspaper, the *St. Croix Avis,* which has been printed under that name since 1844 and which traces its development from the first newspaper of the Virgin Islands, then called the Danish West Indies, in 1770.

Nearly the first 150 years of that history, while the Danes ruled the islands, were conservative, and the role of the press was restricted by regulation and licensing. Still, the newspapers published during that time are rich reservoirs of governmental and societal doings, commercial transactions, and anecdotes. Leafing through the well-preserved, early issues, one finds a letter written by a St. Croix–born youngster, Alexander Hamilton, who later became secretary of the treasury of the United States; an advertisement inserted by a trader, Benedict Arnold, later to become better known as the most infamous U.S. traitor; and other advertisements for everything from "houses of diversion" to "four Negroe Women, with Three Children."

After 1915, when the case for press freedom was successfully presented before the Danish king (and two years later, when the islands became U.S. property), a more liberal stand is evident in the newspapers. Less elitist than before, newspapers began carrying slogans indicating that they wished to be the voices of the oppressed, laboring classes.

EARLY PUBLISHING

Moravian missionaries are credited with writing the first books in the Danish West Indies. In 1770, J. C. Kingos wrote a children's book, *Kreool ABC buch,* and J. M. Magens wrote a grammar of Creole; both were published by Daniel Thibou in Christiansted, St. Croix (Varlack and Harrigan 1977). That same year, the *Royal Danish American Gazette* of St. Croix appeared on Saturday, 7 July. Publisher George Thibou wrote in that first issue,

> The Publisher of this Paper returns his most grateful thanks to those Persons who have already favored him with their subscriptions; as he will take every step to merit their future favours; he still hopes for further encouragement, and desires those who incline to encourage the Press to send in their names to the Printing-office in Queen-street. Subscriptions for the Gazette are taken in at the above Office, at Mr. Williams and Mr. Malloy's taverns, at Mr. Hunter's store, and by those who are entrusted with subscription papers.

Page one was divided into three columns, one of which was devoted to advertisements—for a tavern, coppersmith, chariot for sale, etc. The other columns of the first number were datelined "London, April 27" and gave news obtained by letter from various cities of Europe. The *Gazette* published primarily in English on Wednesday and Saturday, days when the planters came to town. It was physically attractive, with clean printing and layout and woodcuts, which were used to decorate advertisements. Some advertisements were translated into Danish.

From the beginning, the *Gazette* was a popular advertising medium. The second issue devoted two and one-half columns of the front page to advertisements, and the third issue, the entire page. Typical ads were those renting or selling slaves, seeking information on runaways and "strays," and settling bills. Not so typical was a 1 August 1770 advertisement for the opening of "a House of Diversion for young Gentlemen, Bachelors, Widowers or any other who may be inclined to favour . . . house with their company," offering handsomest "drest" [women?], ages 14 to 18, "not to exceed it," in "black, yellow or brown." Those interested were to inquire of "Yellow Margy." In the fifteenth issue (25 August 1770), the following notice appeared: "Stopped from a Negroe some Days ago, A pretty large Silver Tube, for the smoking of Segars, whoever can prove the property, may have it again, by paying for this advertisement. Enquire at the Printing office." Among other items advertised was the *St. Christopher Almanack* for 1771, "calculated to serve all the other Charibbee Islands," and sold at the *Gazette* printery.

Whether the *Almanack* was printed at the *Gazette* or abroad was not indicated. Benedict Arnold's advertisement appeared in the 11 December 1773 *Gazette:* "Just imported from Quebec, in the Brig Harriat and to be sold by the subscriber at Mr. Burry's Tavern, very reasonable for cash or crop pay A CARGO OF EXCELLENT DRAUGHT AND SADDLE HORSES, single and in pairs. Also, English Pease, Brown Bread, Pickled and Smoaked Salmon. Benedict Arnold."

The nonadvertising content seemed to be composites of letters and other information concerning affairs in Europe, which is not surprising since most colonial newspapers of the world were designed primarily to serve the elite residents with news of the metropolitan countries. Some of the headlines give a clue to the "news" provided: "Thoughts on Various Subjects"; "By Command of His Majesty. Particulars to be observed in giving up the lists of Slaves in Each Quarter"; or "A Robbery." Occasional letters to "Mr. Printer," and to others, if they included news or good style, were used. Probably the most famous letter in the *Gazette* was that of Alexander Hamilton to his father describing the devastation of a hurricane that hit the Danish West Indies in 1772. The *Gazette* also covered the American Revolution, "loyally publishing George Washington's war dispatches, letters and other Revolutionary War reports on its front pages as fast as rebel boats could ship them in" (Lewisohn 1970, 178).

The *Royal Danish American Gazette* changed its name to the *St. Croix Gazette* in 1801, back to its original name in 1802, and then to *Dansk vestindisk regerings avis* in the same year, the name it carried until 1844, when it changed to *St. Croix Avis.*

Other newspapers published in the first half of the nineteenth century included the *St. Croix Gazette,* number 61 of which is dated 1 August 1808; the *St. Thomas Gazette,* the first newspaper on that island, started in 1809 as a biweekly by Jonas Englund; the *St. Thomas Monday's Advertiser,* which existed, according to evidence, in 1810; the *Royal St. Croix Gazette* of 1815; and the *St. Thomas Tidende* (*Sanct Thomae tidende*), a biweekly (and later daily) published from at least 1815 to 1917 (see Dookhan 1974, 142; Hague 1980, 12-A, 96-A).

Early on, the Danish government established strict press regulations. Under a Danish law of 1779, the government set up censorship and provided that only subsidized newspapers be given a royal grant. Until 1916–1917, newspapers were paid for printing legal notices and proceedings of the Colonial Council. However, as Lewis (1972, 283–84) pointed out, some courageous editors took issue with the autocratic Danish authorities.

[All papers] bore their titles as government property and their editors were required to pass an examination before the police authorities before being licensed. The papers tended to be, then, bulletin boards for official notices, a characteristic still discernible in papers of the present day such as the *St. Croix Avis.* At the same time, that kind of government press law did not prevent the emergence, in the Danish period, of independent editors like Leroy Nolte, John Benners, William Murta, and John Lightbourn, whose liberal tradition was carried on after the transfer by editors like Conrad Corneiro, Abram Smith, and Alton Adams, as well as by the creators, like Jackson and Francis, of a more radical type of newspaper.

ST. CROIX AVIS: 1844 TO THE PRESENT

The long-lived *St. Croix Avis,* which has carried that name since 1844, was not, as Lewis indicated, one of those that challenged the officials. Subsidized by the government, the *Avis* existed to serve the plantocracy, publishing official notices in a conservative tradition. The paper went through a series of owners and editors after the time Richard Hatchett published and edited it between 1844 and 1851. When Hatchett died in 1851, his widow, Harriet, became the owner, and from 1852 to 1871, two other relatives owned and edited the paper—Hans Hatchett from 1852 to 1866; Peter B. Hatchett from 1866 to 1868, and Hans again from 1868 to 1876. Lauritz Holm took over the paper in 1872 and two years later passed it to Christian Dahl, who was editor until 1877. For six months in 1877, Julius Knuthsen edited the *Avis.* He was followed by John T. Quin from 1877 to 1878, Faludan Muller from 1878 to 1879 and Albert Hanschell from 1879 to 1884. In May 1884, Quin, who by then was inspector of schools, purchased the *Avis* and ran it until his death. Quin, an author and scholar of distinction, made the paper more educational and provided more coverage of foreign news. When he died, the paper's foreman, Gustave Johansen, was requested by the government secretary to put his name beside Quin's in the masthead, because "no newspaper can be published by a dead man." Thus, Johansen was recognized as the new editor, and the government subsidy passed to him. He tried to carry on the *Avis* conservative tradition, but in the early decades of the twentieth century, the paper's policy came under severe attack as contrary to the welfare of workers.

Johansen published the *Avis* until 30 June 1940, when Canute A. Brodhurst, Miss Montclaire Creque, and Ariel Melchior, Sr., purchased it. Brodhurst was editor and publisher from 1942 until his death in 1980.

The *Avis* made some moves toward liberal stands in the first years under Brodhurst, questioning government policy in a few editorials, saying it would not "tolerate any molestation with its news sources, especially its reporters, by any one," and favoring better housing and higher wages for the masses. However, since at least the early 1970s, the paper has reverted to being an official bulletin board (*St. Croix Axis* 1969; *Editor and Publisher* 1969; Carty 1975). An anonymous source in 1977 claimed that the paper was controlled by government advertising and that, because its editor was in the good graces of the ruling party, he received government favors (Letter to author).

GAINING OF PRESS FREEDOM

Besides the *St. Croix Avis,* at least nine other newspapers published between 1850 and 1915, when the request for press freedom was granted. Among these were the *St. Thomas Tidende,* the *St. Thomas Times,* the *St. Thomas Herald,* the *St. Croix Bulletin, Lightbourn's Mail Notes,* the *Bulletin with which is incorporated the St. Thomas Commercial and Shipping Gazette,* the *Danish West Indian, Y.M.A. Voice,* and *West End News.*

Among the editors who deviated from the government line were John Lightbourn, publisher of *Lightbourn's Mail Notes* and self-proclaimed (in the newspaper's logotype) "printer and manufacturer of Rubber Stamps"; William Murta of the *St. Thomas Herald;* and Leroy Nolte, publisher and editor of several newspapers, including the *Bulletin* and the semiweekly official newssheet, *St. Thomas Tidende* (Zabriskie 1918, 153). Nolte also printed the *Danish West Indian,* edited by Pastor Herman Lawaetz on St. Croix. Lawaetz was a Dane who organized community theater and the New Century Movement to encourage blacks to become more interested in insular improvements. An attack of malaria forced him to return to Denmark in 1903 (Lewisohn 1970, xvi).

One newspaper singled out by Jarvis (1938, 79) as being militant in the 1870s was the *St. Thomas Tidende.* Jarvis said that the administration in the 1870s was intolerant of criticism and used the law to muzzle the press, thus drawing the fire of the "militant editor" of the *Tidende.* In the mid-1870s, under another administrator, Governor Garde, the press, and especially the *Tidende,* was "censorious" and roused the wrath of the government, according to Jarvis. *Tidende's* license was revoked, after which its editor started the *St. Thomas Times.* Shortly after, *Tidende* was resumed under new management, and it and the *Times* "went into combat, leaving the government alone" (Jarvis 1938, 79).

By the 1880s, Danish West Indian newspapers used the telegraph to obtain news; most of them carried columns labeled "Telegrams" or "Cablegrams." In 1918, when the West Indian and Panama Telegraph Company set up headquarters in St. Thomas, it received a U.S. $4,000 annual stipend to issue a daily news bulletin in both St. Thomas and St. Croix. The bulletin, in turn, was copied by the two dailies in St. Thomas and the three in St. Croix.

While the telegraph revolutionized news dissemination, a young teacher and clerical worker from St. Croix made radical changes in the functions of the press. David Hamilton Jackson, born in 1884, had become by the age of thirty a top labor leader in the islands. In 1915, the people raised funds to send him to Denmark to represent their cause before King Christian X. His main pleas were for the raising of the wage scale and the granting of a free press in the English language. Lewisohn (1970, 358) said, "The implication that the workers could not be held in check forever and might well strike helped Jackson win consent for the free press." He is credited with getting the 1779 press law rescinded on 11 February 1916 (by Governor Helweg-Larsen), thus eliminating censorship and press subsidies. But upon his return to the Danish West Indies, he was labeled a troublemaker and a radical by the press, which was still controlled by the planters and the government. He immediately started his own newspaper, the *Herald,* in Christiansted on 29 October 1915, and it has since been called the first free newspaper in the islands. Made possible through contributions of Crucians at home and in New York City, the *Herald,* a daily with a motto of "Liberty — Equality — Fraternity," became the voice of the oppressed and laboring classes (Hill 1971, 61–62; see "Liberty Day Nov. 1" n.d., 4). By January 1917, the *Herald* had obtained its own equipment with the purchase at auction of the *Avis* press (*St. Croix Avis* 1969, 59). Westergaard (1917, 257) said that Jackson started a paper called the *Labor Union* in November 1915, but no other evidence of that paper exists. In 1917, the three Danish islands were sold to the United States, and the controlling U.S. Navy regime was hostile to an independent press. Immediately the navy became the target of the *Herald* and its successors.

In 1921, the *Emancipator* joined the *Herald* in crusading for the masses. Using the motto, "Be Not Afraid — Dare," *Emancipator* editor Rothschild Francis dared to the extent that the most significant libel case in the islands' history involved him as a defendant. The local court ruled against Francis, whereupon he appealed to the Third Court of Appeals in Philadelphia. The judge reversed the decision, saying that the "courts of the Virgin Islands are not instrumentalities for the regulation of the public press" (Hill 1971, 84–85, 213). Some people believed that the judiciary had been used to "correct the evil influence of an 'ignorant' and 'corrupt' local press."

The high moral tone of the *Emancipator* was reflected in this page-one story for 6 August 1921.

> Not guilty. Last Monday a boy . . . Ivan Foster (age 13), native of Tortola, was brought to the Police Station by John Gibbs. The charge against Foster was wanton and wilful removal of two ducks from the premises of Gibbs. The boy pleaded that his mother neglected him, he wore a large marine jacket and his pants (if they should be so called) where [*sic*] badly torn. Our editor asked the boy to spell CATTLE, which he was unable to do; it did not surprise us any, since he was born in an environment which fosters ignorance and upholds superstition. It's too bad—this boy is not guilty—he never had a chance and is simply a product of a damnable environment. Why not deport this lad and save us the expenses of feeding him? Our boys have better opportunities and they should be grateful to their benefactors.

The 1930s and 1940s saw the birth of a political party movement and attendant politically inspired newspapers, such as *Mortar and Pestle, Cocomacaque,* and *Progressive Guide;* the *Progressive Guide* was the organ of the first political party in the Virgin Islands, and the party bore the same name. Among those who organized the Progressive Guide and its newspaper were Carlos Downing, later editor of the British Virgin Islands' only weekly, and Earle B. Ottley, later a prominent senator and originator of the *Home Journal* (1951 to 1973). With his brother, Randolph, Ottley founded the *Photo News* (1945 to 1951), the first picture newspaper in the islands (Hill 1971, 156). Earle Ottley also was listed as editor-publisher of a Frederikstad paper, *News Current* (Lewisohn 1970, xix). Lewis (1972, 284) said that newspapers have been used too often for political platforms, citing the *Photo News* and *Home Journal,* the latter of which, through the 1960s, was "regarded by many as the defender of official policy and of the Ottley-Paiewonsky political machine that controlled that policy until the changeover of 1969."

Virgin Islands legislators made 1968 a bad year for press freedom. First, through an economic squeeze, Senate President Earle Ottley's *Home Journal* stood to benefit, while the *Daily News* and others suffered. When legislation was passed to limit advertising of public documents to one newspaper each on St. Thomas and St. Croix, it was a foregone conclusion that the St. Thomas contract would go to Ottley and his *Home Journal.* Second, that same year, Governor Ralph Paiewonsky had to veto bills introduced by legislators to license annually all publications in the islands. Third, Sam Ballard, editor of the *West End News,* a biweekly of Frederikstad, was severely castigated by the senators and told to leave the islands, under threat to his life and property *(Editor and Publisher* 1968, 12, 22; Inter American Press Association 1970, 21).

Worst of the political sheets, according to Lewis (1972, 284), was the *Virgin Islands Times,* conceived in 1963 by Governor Paiewonsky and his friend, Leo Harvey, of alumina big-business interests. This political weapon, Lewis said, had successive editors who were controlled by a United States senator, who was himself carried on the payroll as a reporter at U.S. $500 a month. When the *Times* lost credibility in the community, its editor was dismissed by the paper's Washington lobbyist and sent off the island.

DAILY NEWS: 1930 TO 1978

The *Daily News* of St. Thomas, the only other surviving daily in the Virgin Islands, was established during the Depression year of 1930. As a result, Ariel Melchior, Sr., and J. Antonio Jarvis, who started the *Daily News,* faced difficulties obtaining start-up capital. After the banks turned down loan requests, Melchior approached a friend for a loan of U.S. $300 to publish a souvenir booklet; he hoped to use the profits to finance the *Daily News.* With a circulation of one hundred at first, the newspaper struggled, selling full-page advertisements for forty cents (Melchior 1981, A-8). Jarvis, a man of many professions (teacher, artist, author, principal, and librarian), edited the paper for the first decade, after which it became the sole property of Melchior. In 1940, the *Daily News* acquired the equipment of the defunct *Emancipator* and started the first magazine in the Virgin Islands, the *Record,* as a weekly (Cuthbertson 1981).

When the *Daily News* was started, two other newspapers were also published in St. Thomas — one representing shipping and commercial interests, and the other, the labor unions. The *Daily News* was meant to be for general circulation. After forty-eight years, the Melchior family sold the paper to the U.S. group, Gannett Company Inc., on 15 February, 1978.

CONCLUSION

In the rich history of newspaper publishing in the Virgin Islands, one sees wide variations in the number and duration of papers from one island to another. St. Croix, first with a newspaper in 1770, has been the place of publication for at least twelve newspapers. St. Thomas, which had its first newspaper in 1809, has, at the minimum, supported eighteen newspapers. On the other hand, only two newspapers were published in St. John, the first of which was the *Drum* in 1972.

The quality of the newspapers in different periods is much more difficult to assess. For although many newspapers, after Jackson's trip to Copenhagen, have been praised as agitators for social change and watchdogs of government, those newspapers that published before his intercession cannot be denied their important roles as advertisers, communicators (although to the elites), and carriers of otherwise-lost historical information. On the other hand, a number of newspapers published since 1915 have acted on their own volition as government and political stooges, while a few nineteenth-century newspapers, at great risk, took adversary stands in regard to the authorities.

21

Mass Media in the Virgin Islands:
A Contemporary View

The U.S. Virgin Islands (St. Croix, St. Thomas, and St. John) and the British Virgin Islands (Tortola, Virgin Gorda, and other very small islands) must have one of the highest densities of mass media per population and area of any territories in the world.[1] St. Thomas, with only thirty-two square miles, has two television systems, one cable service, five radio stations, and a daily newspaper; St. Croix, with eighty-four square miles has a television service, four radio stations, and a daily; Tortola has an inactive television station, a radio station, and a weekly newspaper. Because of their proximity to one another, the islands are served by their neighbors' media as well as by those of Puerto Rico.

The survival of these media is hard to understand when one considers the difficult market in which they operate—a tourist-oriented business community in which the black population is not represented. Additionally, the cultural history of the islands—especially that of St. Croix, which has been colonized by seven countries—would not seem conducive to sustained growth of institutions such as the mass media. Yet, as indicated in chapter 20, St. Croix has had a newspaper since 1770, and its *St. Croix Avis,* which has appeared under that name since 1844 but traces its roots to 1770, ranks among the oldest surviving newspapers in the Caribbean. St. Thomas had its first newspaper in 1809. The first newspapers in St. John and Tortola appeared in 1972 and in 1959, respectively. In fact, the British Virgin Islands have had only two newspapers: the first, which was the *Tortola Times,* and the *Island Sun* (see Penn and Penn 1968). Broadcasting had a late development; radio and television arrived in the U.S. Virgin Islands in 1950 and 1961, respectively, and in Tortola in 1965 and the 1970s, respectively.

The diversity of this cultural background is evident today. Most mass media are owned by "outsiders." The regulations under which they operate are those of metropolitan countries applied to microstates. Moreover, a large amount of the content originates primarily in the mainland United States and may not be relevant or helpful to the islands. For example, a 1981 survey of editors and broadcasters showed that 62.5 percent thought that the programming of the media was not adequate and that there were not enough local shows (Vaughn 1981, 7).

Using case studies, this article will assess contemporary mass media in the Virgin Islands. The approach is by medium and by island.

NEWSPAPERS

Serving the islands today are the *Daily News* of St. Thomas, the *St. Croix Avis,* the *BVI Beacon,* and the *Island Sun* of Tortola. (The *Avis* is not profiled here because its editor refused to meet with me.) Also popular is the *San Juan Star,* an English-language daily in Puerto Rico. Owned by the Scripps-Howard group, the *Star* sells three thousand to five thousand copies in the U.S. Virgin Islands (Interview, Collins, 1981).

St. Thomas Daily News

The main newspaper of the Virgin Islands is the *Daily News,* published in Charlotte Amalie. A part of the Gannett group since 1978, the *Daily News* previously was in the hands of the Melchior family. For most of its life, the *Daily News* has faced hard times. Throughout the 1950s, the circulation was usually one thousand or less. Worse yet, circulation revenue exceeded that of advertising by 25 percent. Melchior made ends meet by running a gift shop for tourists at the *Daily News* (Kershen 1953b; Cuthbertson 1981).

Melchior was forced to sell to Gannett because of high operational costs and spiraling inflation; as he explained it, "the Ma and Pa trend in journalism as I knew it ceased to exist" (Cuthbertson 1981, 30). His son, Ariel Melchior, Jr., said that Gannett was chosen because of that company's philosophy of improving newspapers while keeping them independent. He added, "After a man puts fifty damn years of his life into his paper, he wants it retained the way it was—not as a political or vested-interest paper. I don't feel the community lost anything with this

21.1 Virgin Islands newspapers: the *St. Croix Avis* and the *St. Croix Mirror,* the *BVI Beacon* and the *Island Sun* of the British Virgin Islands, and the *Daily News* of St. Thomas.

sale" (Interview, Melchior 1981). Although there has been some disagreement with this statement, the consensus is that the *Daily News* has improved in content and appearance; the circulation has increased by two thousand to a total of ten thousand. For three weeks in March and April 1981, the newspaper shook the foundations of St. Thomas politics with a series on corruption, done jointly with Gannett News Service staff members (Thomas 1981).

Melchior said that Gannett does not get involved with the editorial side of the *Daily News* and expects the local staff to be responsible for increasing advertising and circulation. Benefits derived from Gannett ownership, according to Melchior, include receiving the Gannett News Service; linking with Gannett national advertising representatives, although the paper is too small to use this service much; being able to organize more efficiently with much more resources at hand; and receiving increased employee benefits (Interview, Melchior 1981).

Since the Gannett takeover, the *Daily News* has purchased a monthly regional magazine, *Virgin Islander,* formerly owned by Harry Blair and in 1981 published by his widow, Maureen O'Hara Blair, of U.S. movie fame. Melchior did not believe the *Daily News* planned to acquire other islands' media but would not "hazard a guess whether Gannett plans to buy other media in the Virgin Islands" (Interview, Melchior 1981).

Like most newspapers in small territories, the *Daily News* has faced problems concerning access to information. As Melchior said, "The government has never wanted to talk to us and cabinet members are told to be silent. But, the problems are not that blatant. People just clam up when it involves controversial matter" (Interview Melchior 1981). A 1981 survey of media personnel showed that 43.7 percent were worried about government-media relationships (Vaughn 1981). Other problems included inadequate facilities, isolation from the mainland where supplies and other materials must be obtained, and a dependency upon Puerto Rican advertising and the middlemen who handle shipping of supplies. Concerning facilities, the newspaper has been housed for years in a two-hundred-year-old former mission school owned by a Moravian Church. In fact, Ariel Melchior, Sr. attended classes there as a boy.

Tortola Island Sun

In 1981, the only newspaper in the British Virgin Islands, the *Island Sun,* was published by Carlos Downing, earlier an organizer of the first political party in the U.S. Virgin Islands, where he was an important orator. Downing said that he edited the newspaper "to keep him busy". Social security benefits he received from the U.S. government enabled him to keep the *Island Sun* alive (Interview, Downing 1981). The weekly, with a circulation of seventeen hundred to two thousand and "up during the tourist season," has been edited in a one-room building in Roadtown.

The *Island Sun* has depended upon bartering and free services. CANA-Reuters cablegram news is provided free by Cable and Wireless, and other news is received from the British Information Service and the local government. The paper is circulated free of charge to other islands and the U.S. Virgin Islands by interisland boats. Downing explained that "if the boat services need advertising, we give it to them free" (Interview, Downing 1981).

He said that relationships between the *Island Sun* and the government normally were friendly. The government provided him press releases and did not attempt to censor; in fact, the government provided a special postal rate to the newspaper. Even though Downing had been a U.S Virgin Islands senator and councilman and founder of the *Progressive Guide,* he said that he did not use the *Island Sun* as a political organ. Also, because of the smallness of the islands, the paper did not carry crime news from the magistrate's courts; according to Downing, "If we put that crime news in, it would look like we have a lot of crime here, which is not good for tourism. Also, if we put it all in, everyone would be in the paper in the course of a year or two."

BROADCASTING

William Greer, a consulting engineer for Puerto Rican and Central American radio stations, started the first radio stations in St. Thomas, St. Croix, and Tortola. Greer founded the first station in the region, WSTA, in St. Thomas on 1 August 1950. The following year, he developed WIVI (now WSTX) in St. Croix, and in 1965, ZBVI, Tortola's only station.

Two Americans, who went to the islands in semiretirement, started the second radio station in St. Thomas and the first television service in the Virgin Islands. Robert Moss and Robert Noble came to St. Thomas in the early 1960s to establish a radio station, but because of an FCC freeze on new radio stations, they started WBNB television instead. Both had been important figures in U.S. television. Moss had produced shows such as the "Perry Como Show," and Noble, vice president of ABC sales, was a nephew of Edward J. Noble, owner and a cofounder of the ABC network. When the FCC freeze was lifted, Moss and Noble established WBNB radio in 1962. The partnership was dissolved in 1968, with Noble retaining the radio station and Moss keeping WBNB television. In 1969, the radio station's call letters were changed to WVWI (Mickelwright 1980). Most of the ten Virgin Islands radio stations are owned by outsiders; in fact, WVWI in St. Thomas has prided itself on being one of the very few locally owned stations.

In the 1970s, the British Virgin Islands had its own television service, ZBTV, Channel 5. Dave Antoniak, with Columbia Pictures, started the station but ran into numerous problems. Through U.S. Department of State intervention, he was allowed to beam Channel 5 to the U.S.

Virgin Islands, which stirred up animosities with his St. Croix rival, Channel 8. In retaliation, the owner of the St. Croix station, with permission from the FCC, put up a translator on the St. Croix tower of Channel 12 (the Public Broadcasting System outlet on St. Thomas), thus blocking out ZBTV's signal. This proved disastrous, as ZBTV had been seen via cable until Cable News Network, operated by Ted Turner, took over the cable system in 1981. Antoniak appealed to the British government, asking that the FCC be requested to have the translator removed. However, the FCC ruled in favor of Channel 8. ZBTV had other difficulties, such as "faulty equipment and shaky administration," both of which forced it off the air numerous times and thus affected its credibility. When last revived in 1979 (Interview, Brewley 1981), ZBTV used mostly U.S. programs because of its affiliation with Columbia (Colli 1979, 25).

Besides WBNB and ZBTV, other television systems are WSVI, Channel 8, the ABC affiliate on St. Croix; WTJX, Channel 12, the PBS station on St. Thomas; and the Cable News Network. Since 1978, WTJX has operated a news-satellite ground terminal, which remedied the previous procedure of having all programs flown or mailed to St. Thomas (*Variety* 1978). Cable television came to St. Thomas in the mid-1960s. However, because of island jealousies, the government of the Virgin Islands, headquartered in St. Thomas, maintained until the early 1980s that St. Croix did not need cable. Once that policy was changed, another stumbling block remained; the utility company on St. Croix denied the use of its poles to St. Croix Cable. There was also controversy between two companies over ownership of the poles. St. Croix Cable then proceeded to wire the island home by home, using underground cable, stringing wire from house to house, and putting up its own poles (*News Front* 1981).

WVWI—St. Thomas

As mentioned before, WVWI, as WBNB, started in 1962 by Moss and Noble, and Noble is still president of the Thousand Islands Corporation, licensee of the station. WVWI has remained one of the few Virgin Islands radio stations entirely locally owned; Lawrence (Ric) Ricardo, vice president, said, "All the money earned here stays here" (Interview, Ricardo 1981).

The station's serious commitment to the St. Thomas community has been reflected in its programming, half of which has originated locally. Ricardo said that the station has broadcast hours of governmental hearings and other meetings (a costly operation), because the "community is good to us and we want to put something back." Whereas most Virgin Islands stations are predominantly music, WVWI prides itself on its news, information, and sports. The CBS affiliate pioneered in the early 1980s by offering a ninety-minute "Newswatch" show between the 6:30 A.M. and 8:00 A.M. "drivetime," when competitors said that it was foolhardy to offer news. The magazine show, with a mix of CBS and local news, sports, commentary, features, and weather, has proved to be very popular because the Virgin Islander "takes his news seriously" and is "better informed than his mainland counterpart" (Interview, Ricardo 1981).

Programming has remained in standard English, because "even the local population is turned off by dialectal [calypso] language." Sometimes, dialect is used in music shows and commercials, but standard English is much more prevalent; it is the language most islanders speak, except when they are in a "laid-back situation" (Interview, Ricardo 1981).

As with other Virgin Islands stations, WVWI does not exchange programs throughout the Caribbean, partly because most are meant for local audiences. If something of significance happens in the Eastern Caribbean, WVWI sends its own personnel and equipment to report.

The station's stable staff is attributed to a hiring policy that favors either native born Virgin Islanders or outsiders who have been residents in the islands for years. Ricardo said that most other Virgin Islands stations hire "gypsies who drift from place to place looking for a year's vacation in the sun" (Interview, Ricardo 1981). What training is done occurs on the job, unlike most other stations, which bring "freelancers off the street and provide no training." The islands do not have professional organizations that could initiate training schemes; the several efforts to establish a press association were to no avail. In 1981, however, a Virgin Islands' version of the 4-As was created for the five advertising agencies of St. Thomas and other media personnel.

Government-media relationships have been good, according to Ricardo, as journalists have access to officials and documents, can broadcast sessions of the legislature, and can "call up the governor anytime." The government has not placed heavy taxes or duties on imported equipment, tapes, or program material.

Most of the difficulties WVWI has faced are those associated with the infrastructure of the islands — power outages, expensive utilities, and poor telephone and postal services. As an example, electricity costs for WVWI more than doubled between May 1980 and May 1981, rising from U.S. $1,553 to U.S. $3,400.

WSTX—St. Croix

St. Croix's oldest radio station, WSTX (formerly called WIVI), has been under two ownerships since its establishment in 1951. The owner since 1968—the Virgin Islands Broadcasting Corporation, owned by William Carpenter of North Carolina and Tony de la Cruz of Puerto Rico—has no other business interests. Vice president Robert Miller said that ownership of most Virgin Islands broadcasting by outsiders has not sparked any real controversy.

WSTX, which in the early 1980s reduced its daily hours of broadcast from twenty-four to eighteen because of expenses, for years thought of itself as the only legitimate news broadcaster of St. Croix, despite a one-man news staff. The station dialed Washington seven times daily for network news. Miller said that using network news was difficult because of expenses, geographical distances, and the smallness of the St. Croix market. "Much of our network news is not even sponsored," he added (Interview, Miller 1981). The smallness of St. Croix has created other problems, according to Miller: "Gathering local news is very difficult as, culturally, people do not go out on a limb to provide information. Basically, local news is geared to press conferences and functions. Also, people will call and ask that their names be taken off the police report for fear of being victimized. Sometimes we don't broadcast their names because of the peculiar situation of everyone knowing everyone else" (Interview, Miller 1981).

In St. Croix, as in all the Virgin Islands, radio is primarily entertainment. WSTX uses a black-oriented music format with Caribbean, soul, and disco music. The station provides community-oriented programming in the form of two weekly talk shows hosted by a local physician; it also broadcasts bulletin board notices hourly for one or two minutes and thrice daily for five minutes each. During the prime listening period of 6 to 8 A.M., when television is not on the air, WSTX airs emergency messages, acting almost as a telephone for Virgin Islanders who have links in other territories. WSTX, as with most stations, has not used much dialectal programming for the same reason given by its counterpart in St. Thomas—the people understand English well enough.

In St. Croix, the media have been free to cover legislative hearings and have been spared local regulations governing broadcasters. Miller said that there had been talk of the U.S. Virgin Islands government setting up a regulations committee, but he thought the idea was nonsensical because the "government cannot run its own affairs" and certainly would not be able to do a better job than the FCC. The stations abide by the same equal-time rulings that stations follow on the mainland, with the difference that in St. Croix some politicians never stop campaigning and thus buy time weekly. Also, there exists no firm rule on the amount of time provided the government, as in the former British colonies. Miller said that, unfortunately, the media have been "reduced to using a lot of the government release material because of their lack of news-gathering staffs and because there is not much else" (Interview, Miller 1981).

Staff training and debilitating production costs also hinder WSTX. On-the-job training prevails and the applicants are usually of less than trainable quality, Miller said. He added:

> We are swamped with applicants who are nearly illiterate—many from the continental United States. We get some local high schoolers on the air, but graduates here do not have a good enough education to enter the business. They think we at WSTX should teach them to read and write. If we don't put them on the air, the community complains that we don't have enough local people. We go the middle ground by putting them on after coaching them. Then we catch flack from the educated members of the community for such poor quality.

Miller said that the economic bind stations have found themselves in is similar to "Russian roulette." "We have to sell a bunch of spots to pay our U.S. $30,000-a-year electricity bill or to buy water at U.S. $100 for 3,000 gallons," he said (Interview, Miller 1981).

ZBVI—Tortola

Virgin Islands Broadcasting Ltd., the licensee for ZBVI, is also owned from outside the area by Bermuda Broadcasting Company Ltd., Communication Investors Ltd. of California, and Pacific Broadcasting Company; the last two are the property of Scott Killgore. The 10,000-watt station reaches all of the U.S. and British Virgin Islands, Puerto Rico, and parts of the Eastern Caribbean.

ZBVI programming is mainly local, 70 percent of the shows being music from the United States and the Caribbean. Exceptions are the few government-run talk shows used once or twice a week; in fact, the government is entitled to an hour of broadcasts per day. An affiliate of the BBC News and Mutual Sports Network, ZBVI has three fifteen-minute newscasts daily and provides five minutes of news on the hour. Ten-minute BBC newscasts are used three times daily, and there is also a fifteen-minute BBC commentary. The station is used as a telephone by islanders who are allowed to give messages free of charge. Obituary notices, aired early in the day and at 4:10 P.M., cost U.S. $4.50 each. The station, which broadcasts sixteen hours on Monday through Thursday and eighteen hours on Friday and Saturday, limits its airtime to 6 A.M. to 9 P.M. on Sunday. General manager E. Walwyn Brewley explained that on Sundays, residents watch TV or attend movies, so the station is closed early to allow the engineer to work on the transmitter (Interview, Brewley 1988).

The station has had an unusual relationship with the local government. According to Brewley, the authorities have not been interested—and have not wanted involvements—in ZBVI for fear of having to subsidize it. Under an agreement of 26 September 1964, the station pays U.S. $1,000 yearly to the British Virgin Islands government for a license, which can be revoked if, in the opinion of the authorities, the station is not operated in the best interests of the public. Brewley was not worried about this happening because if the government were to revoke the license, it would have to purchase the station, which it does not want to do. Thus, stipulations in the license specifying the number of minutes per hour of commercials (ten) and the percentage of BBC programs that must be carried are not met by ZBVI.

On the other hand, the station has done virtually nothing to provoke the government with its content. Brewley said, "We have no editorials, no exposés of government. The government, which is very touchy, provides us with news releases, gives us a day or two advance notice about press conferences, at which we submit questions beforehand. We can tape press conferences, and we can tape legislative sessions live if they are important. But, usually we have to take notes at these meetings" (Interview, Brewley 1981).

Equal time during political campaigns is not an issue in the British Virgin Islands. There is no limit on the amount of time a candidate can purchase except that of the candidate's own financial resources. So far, the islands have not progressed to the stage where parties or individuals complain about unequal time allotments.

Economic problems have plagued ZBVI, including the high expenses (such as a monthly electricity bill of U.S. $2,500 to $3,000) and the very small market. Three-fourths of all commercials come from the U.S. Virgin Islands, Puerto Rican, or international advertising agencies.

Brewley's biggest problem has been obtaining a local, trained staff. He has resorted to using expatriates from other Caribbean islands, a tenuous situation because they are issued work permits that can be pulled by the government. However, Brewley said that the government would not revoke a permit of an employee without first calling him (Interview, Brewley 1981). Training is done on-the-job by the program director, who received his training in the same manner. Brewley himself became general manager with no broadcast experience at all. In fact, he was an accountant, hired by the owners to help make the station economically viable.

WBNB-TV— St. Thomas

WBNB-TV is owned by a mainland U.S. cross-channel group, Worrell Newspapers. Worrell, which owns two other TV channels and thirty-eight radio stations, takes an active role in WBNB and wants it to be a major station of the Caribbean. Between the time Robert Moss owned it in the late 1960s and 1980, when Worrell bought it, other owners were Federated Media of Elkhart, Indiana, and Island Tele-radio Service, an enterprise comprised of blacks from the Virgin Islands and the continental United States.

General Manager Joe Potter said that the changes in ownership resulted from a difficult market in which 80 to 85 percent of the local blacks were not represented in the business community, which is geared to the tourists. He explained that businesses see no need to use television advertising; they are operated by "whites," whose investment interests are different from those of the community. Potter said that they are not concerned with the community's likes because they do not get much business from local people (Interview, Potter 1981).

WBNB is the only Virgin Islands television with a local news show, which is very expensive to sustain. The newscast, which featured Associated Press wire news and CBS clips that were three or four days late, was doubled to one hour in the early 1980s when WBNB obtained a satellite hookup. The station, like other Virgin Islands television stations is faced with community pressure for longer hours of transmission— presently they are from 1:30 P.M. to 1:30 A.M. —and for more local and current content. At the time, Potter said that mainland U.S. programs did not suit the needs of the Virgin Islander: "We have to use CBS shows often not relevant here. We have to bend to ratings carried out on the mainland. For example, "White Shadow" was popular here but not on the mainland, and CBS dropped it. On the other hand, "M.A.S.H." is not big here but is renewed because of high United States ratings" (Interview, Potter 1981). WBNB was criticized in 1981 because its CBS shows were not current; it took seven days for them to be dubbed and shipped to St. Thomas.

Some commercials and parts of some programs used the local dialect, but Potter hesitated to use more. He said that the "people think we're making fun of them by using dialect"; moreover, with the "mix of immigrants here, it is difficult to know what the local language is" (Interview, Potter 1981).

Programs usually are not exchanged with other Caribbean island stations because, according to Potter,

> It is not easy to do business with our fellow Caribbean islands. In the independent British islands, the class system is very prevalent and it is hard to get a clear-cut decision from anyone. It is hard to travel through the islands because of bureaucratic procedures in customs and immigration. In some islands, one must obtain a government license to sell advertisements. Also, the Caribbean islands television stations are not doing much locally that is adventuresome, and most are government operated and therefore do not attack the government (Interview, Potter 1981).

WBNB claimed it had easy access to the Virgin Islands government, although the chief executive was hard to approach and did not hold press conferences.

Although for years WBNB barely survived economically, during its first year under Worrell the company had U.S. $800,000 in billings. Worrell further improved the station by putting in U.S. $240,000 in capital improvements in 1980–1981 and by arranging for a satellite hookup and increased power to reach four hundred miles in any direction. Hoping to be a Caribbean-wide station, WBNB has made a major thrust toward Puerto Rico, and at least 46 percent of the station's advertising sales have been off-island.

CONCLUSIONS

Virgin Islands mass media can be characterized by (1) a historical tradition dating to 1770; (2) a high density of media per population and geographical area; (3) a high percentage of outside ownership and affiliation, including Gannett, Bermuda Broadcasting Company, Pacific Broadcasting Company, Worrell Newspapers, ABC, CBS, BBC, Mutual Sports, PBS, and CNN; and (4) a relationship with government that does not include censorship, licensing, or other types of overt harassment common elsewhere in the region.

Many problems have kept the Virgin Islands mass media from reaching their full potential. Newspapers suffer from inadequate facilities, dependency upon Puerto Rican and mainland U.S. advertising, large geographical distances from sources of supplies and equipment, and problems associated with smallness — hesitancy to carry sensitive information and an incapability to sustain an advertising market.

Broadcasters listed even more difficulties, including operating within the framework of island jealousies and animosities and an infrastructure that has high utility rates with less than adequate service. Others include lack of local programming; poor news gathering and reporting, with a heavy reliance on press conferences and releases; no arrangement for the exchange of programs between islands, or for the professionalization of the field; inadequate on-the-job training, oftentimes of freelancers; and the same dependency on Puerto Rican and mainland U.S. advertising that newspapers experience. The islands also provide an unusual market where most of the local population is not represented in the business community and where media personnel must work under colonial-inspired regulations in an area that is becoming nationalistic.

II

Topical Perspectives

22

Communication Technology in the Caribbean: Deepening Dependency Decade

For centuries, the Caribbean has been the clay from which metropolitan countries molded their treaty arrangements, their economic policies, and their overall expansion plans. Some islands, such as St. Croix and St. Lucia, alternated flying different flags and sometimes became the victims of European treaty agreements. Most islands provided the slave labor and raw materials to keep European powers flourishing. The result was that Caribbean people had difficulties determining their cultural roots, a sense of who they were, and their worth.

When the mass media entered the region, they certainly did not represent cultural institutions with which West Indians could identify. Instead, they were a means, as noted by Frantz Fanon (1965, 71), for the European explorers to keep in touch with *their* civilization. Similarly, telecommunications systems, once they were set up in the latter nineteenth century, were more oriented to linking the islands to the outside world than to one another.

The dependency in technology and the resultant cultural domination not only persist but have been greatly magnified, to the extent that one writer pointed out that even indigenous cultural forms are not acceptable to the region unless given the "okay by North American critics and or public. A Bob Marley or Sparrow, an Otis Wright or a Joseph Niles languishes in relative obscurity while the music of an Elton John or a Harry Belafonte, an Andre Crouche or Staple Singers dominate our airwaves year after year" (Marshall 1985, 8).

The foreign domination of telecommunications and the mass media has reached the crisis point throughout the region, with most efforts to avert the problems being "too halting, too unsure and too minor in scope to seriously challenge the 'tentacles' which CNN, cable TV, video, radio, film, coca-cola, designer jeans and musical fads have wrapped around our cultures" (Marshall 1985, 8).

TELECOMMUNICATIONS

Foreign countries and multinational and transnational corporations took a keener interest in Caribbean telecommunications in the 1980s. If the United States government did not spark this interest, then it helped to keep it alive. For example, just as it published advertising and marketing manuals on how to capture various country markets in the 1920s, the Department of Commerce in 1986 published a "Telecommunications Equipment Markets in the Caribbean/Central American Area" report providing profiles of thirty-two countries and territories, presumably designed to help large corporations learn hardware needs (Wetzel 1986).

A number of reasons have been given for the augmented interest in Caribbean telecommunications. The chief reason proposed is that the islands became economically and strategically important to the United States. With Ronald Reagan's election and the coincidental sweeping into power of right-wing governments in the region came the created need to wipe out (and keep the area free of) Marxist ideologies. The local governments went along with this U.S. policy, partly because a number were of the same ideological tint as Reagan but also because they faced economic recession. As a result, the Caribbean Basin Initiative was spurred on by the Reagan government, established, and then used in a blackmail fashion — open up island economies to private foreign investment or be denied U.S. assistance. As Brown (1987, 21) wrote, "Deregulation, free enterprise and open markets" were encouraged, and in that context, "Communication technologies are conceived as commodities for consumption or as products for manufacturing and assembling."

In line with this policy, offshore information assembly and processing industries have sprung up throughout the Caribbean. Barbados attracted a U.S. microelectronics firm, and Jamaica in 1984 brought in its first offshore information processing with Telemar Jamaica Inc. At the latter, workers store printed copy on computer disks for U.S. clients. Other businesses were attracted to the region for the same reasons they flocked to Southeast Asia earlier, most notably the low wages. Thus, when the Caribbean was not being used as the playground for U.S. tourists, it was performing as the sweatshop for that nation's industrial leaders.

Another reason some Caribbean nations became important to foreign corporations was the legal tax haven the islands provided. For example, film producers (mainly from the United States) and other business people use the Netherlands Antilles to legally avoid or defer U.S. taxes on foreign revenues. Other foreign-based producers use the Netherlands Antilles to get their U.S.–derived income out of the United States without paying taxes.

The need to entice foreign business and new industrialization, as well as to continue to attract tourism, was translated into a need for better communications facilities, also brought in from outside. Thus, in the mid-1980s the Montego Bay offshore data-processing firm planned a satellite teleport, including the purchase of a data transmission satellite, and the U.S. Virgin Islands completely modernized their telecommunications system to lure tourists and offshore business.

Of course, as a modern telecommunications infrastructure was provided for the Caribbean, a correspondingly heavy reliance on foreign-produced supplies materialized. It has always been obvious that the increased push for new information technologies has been to provide markets for foreign companies, as expressed by a Barbadian broadcaster who lamented, "When we go to the operations committee meetings [of INTELSAT], the people there are mostly interested in selling us equipment, not so much in helping us with our problems" (quoted in Hoover 1986).

Why have not local governments reacted more vociferously against these types of technological and cultural domination? Some explanations given by a recent consulting group were that the governments (1) expect new technologies to maintain social order for them, (2) are reluctant to remove a satisfying and status-conferral activity for the influential classes, (3) give a low priority to communications planning vis-á-vis other development priorities, (4) have neither the time nor the skills to deal with the problem, (5) react to direct political pressures not to deal negatively with outside cultural influences, and (6) are hoodwinked by the U.S. government-sponsored Caribbean Basin Initiative, which stresses communications infrastructure development and discourages local planning (Caribbean Council of Churches 1986, 5).

Still other reasons for a lack of telecommunications policy were listed by Hamelink (1985) as (1) a fragmentation of the communications sector that incapacitates it in competing for scarce resources, (2) the high degree of personalism in decision-making regarding communications, (3) the lack of a research and development tradition in the communications sector, (4) the "political discontinuities" that mitigate against coherent communications policy development, (5) the national interests that take precedence over regional interests and (6) the fact that private-sector interests often supersede those of the public interest in bargaining for scarce resources.

In some countries, decisive policy formulation was hindered by the fragmentation of domestic agencies controlling telecommunications. For example, in Trinidad and Tobago, the minister of public utilities and national transportation oversees telecommunications and assigns radio frequencies, while the Public Utilities Commission regulates rates; the government-owned Trinidad and Tobago Telephone Company Ltd. controls domestic phone services and Trinidad and Tobago External Telecommunications Company Ltd. (51 percent government owned and 49 percent owned by Cable and Wireless) controls all overseas services. In Puerto Rico, regulation of telecommunications is split between the Federal Communications Commission, the Puerto Rico Communications Authority, and the Bureau of Public Utilities of Puerto Rico for local licensing. In French Guiana, Guadeloupe, and Martinique, the local government Agence de Telecommunications handles local operations, but planning, purchasing, and policy (including frequency allocation) are done centrally by DTRE in Paris. Compañía Dominicana de Teléfonos (CODETEL), a wholly owned subsidiary of GTE, operates the main national telephone and data communications network, limited mobile service, all international telephony, and datacom in the Dominican Republic. TELERAN, a minor regional company, has limited service in agreement with CODETEL, and All America Cables and Radio Inc. (ITT) and RCA Global Communications offer international telex over channels leased from CODETEL.

In many other countries, telecommunications services are under the ministry of information. Exceptions are Bermuda, where they are handled by the Department of Telecommunications under the Ministry of Industry and Technology; the British Virgin Islands, where they are under the Postmaster's Office in the Ministry of Communications and Works; the Turks and Caicos Islands, where services are handled by the General Post Office; Haiti, where everything is handled by the government monopoly, Telecommunications d' Haiti (Teleco); the Netherlands Antilles, where the government-owned Landsradio Telecommunicatie Dienst Nederlandse Antillean is in charge; and Jamaica, where control is centered in the Telecommunications Branch of the Ministry of Public Utilities and Transport.

Perhaps Brown (1987, 22) best summed up the reasons behind the development of Caribbean telecommunications and the lack of clear policies.

> The new communication technologies have all but succeeded in incorporating the English-speaking Caribbean into the North Ameri-

can cultural orbit. That incorporation has been assisted by the ideological orientation of regional governments as well as by the scope and power of the technologies themselves. Lacking institutional co-ordination and information management capabilities, the conditions do not now exist in the Caribbean for the formulation or implementation of coherent, rational and regional communication policies.

Multinational Corporations and Transnational Organizations

Among the multinational corporations in the Caribbean, Cable and Wireless is the most influential, probably because it has had such a long lead time. At one time it controlled nearly all telecommunications in the region. In fact, some islands' telecommunications systems are still wholly operated by Cable and Wireless, including those of the British Virgin Islands, the Cayman Islands, Dominica, Montserrat, St. Lucia, St. Vincent, Turks and Caicos, and Anguilla. A wholly owned and operated subsidiary of its London parent, Cable and Wireless handles all traffic in the area, with sixteen subscribers in as many islands.

RCA Global Communications Inc. maintains offices in the Dominican Republic, Puerto Rico, and the Netherlands Antilles and direct circuit correspondents in fifteen other Caribbean countries. Western Union Telegraph Company offers standard IRC services, exports television broadcast services to some islands over its Westar satellite, and has direct circuit correspondents in seven countries.

As might be expected, a former subsidiary of the ubiquitous United Fruits (later United Brands) had control over some telecommunications. TRT Telecommunications Corporation, which began as a subsidiary of United Brands, was recently purchased by UNC Resources, at which time the company sold some of its direct operations to local governments. TRT Telecommunications still has direct circuit correspondents on thirteen islands.

Other huge U.S. telecommunications corporations flood the Caribbean. ITT Communications Services Inc. has subsidiaries in the Dominican Republic, Puerto Rico, and the U.S. Virgin Islands, an office in Puerto Rico, and direct circuit correspondents in thirteen countries. MCI International Inc., which purchased Western Union International from Xerox in 1982, has standard IRC services but is negotiating for direct telephone services to Bermuda and Jamaica. With offices in Haiti, the Netherlands Antilles, Puerto Rico, and Central America, MCI has direct circuit correspondents in ten islands. AT & T Communications offers voice traffic only in ten areas, plus direct circuit correspondents in twenty-eight countries.

Smaller operations are Continental Telephone Service Corporation (CONTEL), with subsidiaries in Barbados and the Bahamas, and GTE Corporation, with a sole subsidiary in the Dominican Republic.

At least eight transnational organizations deal with Caribbean telecommunications. Some function solely as forums for the discussion of problems. Among these are the 809 Conference, a biannual meeting of operations from twenty-three Caribbean countries in the 809 dialing area; the conference was organized by AT & T and the Caribbean Telecommunications Council in 1985 to foster telecommunications development and consists of sixty organizations, including operators, manufacturers, educational institutions, and law firms. The Caribbean Association of National Telecommunications Organizations (CANTO) has been more action oriented. Made up of eight English-speaking nations (Antigua, the Bahamas, Barbados, Belize, Guyana, Grenada, Jamaica, and Trinidad and Tobago), CANTO meets yearly to discuss regional cooperation; the CARIISAT regional telecommunications satellite is an outcome of the group.

Others involved in telecommunications include the Caribbean Broadcast Union (CBU), since 1970 a forum of broadcasters from seventeen Commonwealth Caribbean and Netherlands Antilles states. Among its main activities, CBU has sponsored training and exchange programs and arranged for common circuits for the broadcast of overseas events. The Caribbean News Agency (CANA), formed in 1976, provides a written service as well as a daily radio service for individual broadcasters in fifteen Commonwealth Caribbean and Netherlands Antilles countries.

Also, a regional representative in the Caribbean for the International Telecommunications Union handles coordination and technical assistance matters, simultaneously acting on behalf of the United Nations Economic Commission on Latin America and the Caribbean in its telecommunications projects.

Telecommunications Equipment Suppliers

Telecommunications equipment for the region is imported mainly from the United States, Canada, Japan, and the United Kingdom, and to a lesser degree from France, Germany, Sweden, Holland, and Italy. Before the U.S. invasion, Grenada imported from East Germany, and because of a U.S.–imposed embargo, Cuba has bought equipment from Argentina, the USSR, and Czechoslovakia, as well as from Japan, Canada, France, and Great Britain. Cuba is different in that it designs and manufactures its own telecommunications equipment, including its own computer (Interview, Gonzaáles-Manet 1982). Over the years,

Cuban technicians have installed and operated telecommunications systems in smaller countries of the world.

A country that did not import much equipment for a long period was Guyana. Multinational companies have not been in much evidence there, probably because the country is economically bankrupt and cannot pay for equipment. In more recent times, NEC sold an earth station to Guyana, and Brazil, which is willing to accept Guyanese dollars, sold cable.

Other countries have not hesitated to upgrade their telecommunications infrastructures using large inputs of supplies from multinational corporations. For example, Jamaica brings in equipment from eight corporations, mainly from the United States and Canada, including Motorola, Harris, RCA, NEC, and Northern Telecom. The Canadians have made the biggest push for the market; their Northern Telecom is the most prominent supplier, especially of Jamaica Telephone, where it is also involved in training. The Canadians are also supplying and directing most of Trinidad and Tobago's telecommunications modernization program, with Northern Telecom and BCI dominating. In fact, Northern has one of its two Caribbean offices in Trinidad; the other is in Puerto Rico. Other suppliers are GTE, American Laser System, and Continental Page. Northern Telecom is the chief supplier of equipment for the Bahamas.

In most cases, supply lines follow old colonial links. Cable and Wireless and other British firms have dominated in parts of the Commonwealth Caribbean, and in the French Caribbean all equipment is French and supplied by Thompson and other French corporations. In Haiti, France's CCCE is financing 70 percent of the U.S. $11.2 million project for thirty thousand new telecommunications lines at 5 percent over fifteen years, and the other 30 percent as an outright grant. Before 1984, Ericsson had been the main supplier. Interestingly, given France's virtual monopoly of television equipment in its former territories and other French-speaking countries, the United States has been granted the contract to upgrade Television National.

In the Netherlands Antilles and Suriname, Philips is important; in the latter country, it is the most evident, followed by GTE. Surinamese engineers now are sent to Holland and Japan for equipment maintenance training. Japanese, Italian, and United States companies also supply Suriname's needs. Other suppliers of the Netherlands Antilles are Siemens, Motorola, and General Electric.

CODETEL's association with GTE gives that corporation most of the Dominican Republic market, with smaller shares going to Western Electric, Farinon, and Philips Cables. A country that has a very wide

range of foreign suppliers is Antigua. Besides Cable and Wireless, others
include GEC, also of Great Britain; Wandel Goltermann of West Germany; and GTE, Racal-Milgo, Racal-Vadic, Databit, Coherent,
Farinon, Extel, Teletype, and Wang, all of the United States.

National Economies and Telecommunications

The accelerated modernization of the infrastructure of the Caribbean in the past decade has had debilitating effects upon national economies. By the mid-1980s, some islands actually slowed down development
and expansion. For example, Bermuda and Belize were on downswings
until more foreign capital could be attracted, and the British Virgin
Islands, like some others, had lowered its telecommunications budget
for 1985–1986. But most countries seemed to forge ahead, getting involved in ever more expensive technologies without considering the dependency relationships that were nurtured.

Despite the financial squeezes faced by numerous Caribbean countries, they continue to borrow to upgrade telecommunications. Thus,
tiny Anguilla, which in 1971 did not have electricity (except two or three
private generators), now has underground cable systems sponsored by
Cable and Wireless, as well as push-button telephones with call-forwarding features. The Dominican Republic, facing a shortage of foreign exchange and the parity of its peso to the U.S. dollar, still completely
automated its telecommunications network, incorporating digitalization
and fiber optics. It was able to do this because Fujitsu proposed a telecommunications plan to the government with financing already in mind.
The Swedish government also had financed some consulting work for
Dominican Republic telecommunications.

Other examples are readily available. Guyana, which has foreign
currency shortages, announced a U.S. $50 million telecommunications
expansion program in 1985. Annual government subsidies, no doubt
financed from abroad, will be required to expand. Jamaica and Trinidad
and Tobago have faced recurring financial constraints concerning telecommunications, yet their expansion surges ahead.

The self-supporting Jamaica Telephone Company (JTC), for example, finds it difficult to fund programs because of the paucity of foreign
exchange, yet it is moving into fiber optics in transmissions in Kingston,
computerization of domestic and international networks, modernization
of the rural system, digital microwave transmission in the South, and an
improved local telex service. To finance its U.S. $104.5 million development plan for 1982 to 1986, JTC borrowed from the Caribbean Development Bank, Canada's Export Development Corporation, and others. In

1983, the company alone had loan indebtedness of U.S. $44.5 million. As another example of the scope of financing needed, JAMINTEL (Jamaica's satellite program) requires U.S. $95 million to expand during the 1981–1997 period.

Trinidad and Tobago's telephone company, Telco, also has had an ambitious development program despite persistent financing problems. Telco has moved into fiber optics and solar-powered microwave, and in 1983 it initiated a U.S. $12 million Rural Development Program, which extended telecommunications to 75 percent of the villages. In 1985, Telco began serious consideration of cellular use in cooperation with the U.S. Trade and Development Program of the U.S. Department of State. Estimated to cost U.S. $9.85 million from 1987 to 1991, this program has been funded by AT & T, Motorola, and Northern Telecom. Telco's capital-spending budgets were U.S. $100 million for each year between 1983 and 1985, and a larger figure was expected for 1986. In 1981, the telephone company's loss was T.T. $72.2 million, and with outstanding loan debts of T.T. $174.9 million, Telco requested a major consumer rate increase. Loans have been provided by the World Bank, Japan's Exim, and Canada's Development Corporation.

Puerto Rico has borrowed extensively to meet the huge expenses required to upgrade its communications systems. The Puerto Rico Communications Authority recently borrowed U.S. $30 million from REA, and the Puerto Rico Telephone Company apparently must be receiving outside funding to meet its U.S. $120 million annual construction budget. From 1986 to 1990, expenditures for switching equipment will amount to U.S. $594 million.

BROADCASTING

From their origins, Caribbean broadcasting services depended upon outsiders for their equipment, ownership, and programming.

Examples of dependency through equipment have already been cited. But what happens when the technology supplier or controller does not get its way? A case in point is the British Virgin Islands, where the cable company, BVI Cable TV Ltd., requested a U.S. $6 monthly increase of its customers in February 1987. When negotiations with the government broke down in March, the cable company withdrew from the air four twenty-four-hour satellite stations it transmitted. After two weeks, when the government capitulated to a $4 increase, the service was restored with the implied condition that when BVI Cable adds another station (WOR-New York), the remaining $2 can be assessed.

Although shares of the Caribbean media have increasingly become localized (usually through government or large local entrepreneurs), some foreign ownership continues. Trinidad and Tobago Television is partly owned by CBS, and a few systems (on Barbados, for example) are owned by London-based Rediffusion.

But the island where outside investments in mass media have been the most marked is Puerto Rico. For example, by the mid-1980s, U.S. companies scrambled to get a larger role in Puerto Rico's television market. Of the main stations, WAPA-Televicentro was successively owned by a number of U.S. companies, including Columbia Pictures, Western Broadcasting Company, SFN Communications, and recently, Pegasus, also owner of U.S. mainland stations. Telemundo moved from ownership by the widow of media magnate Angel Ramos (she later married the chairman of the Knight-Ridder Group of newspapers) to Harris and now to Reliance Capital, both of the United States. Other new channels included WLUZ, owned by the Malrite Communication Group of Cleveland; KLII, owned by Lorimar Telepictures; WPRV, owned by Oklahoman James Leake; WSJU, owned by Lane Gawick (Astroff 1983, 6; also, *Variety* 12 March 1986 and 25 March 1987). Reasons for the intensified interest in owning television in Puerto Rico include the availability of good production facilities, the possibility of developing a superstation to serve the U.S. Hispanic population, and a relatively good television market when compared to other parts of Latin America.

One scholar, in labeling Puerto Rican television as dependent, said it was similar to other industries on the island, with "close ties to U.S. industry, a dependent elite, and a large expatriate element . . . thus understandable that the establishment and development of television in Puerto Rico has to be understood in light of two fundamental factors: first, the great expansion of industrial commercial capital . . . and second, the colonial dependence of Puerto Rico on the United States" (Astroff 1983, 5).

In the area of programming, the situation has worsened in the Caribbean. With more sophisticated technological capabilities allowing for less expensive and quicker transmission, the region is inundated with foreign programming, mostly from the United States. The August 1986 *South Magazine* claimed that foreign television content ranged from 50 to 98 percent in various Commonwealth Caribbean countries: "The percentages of foreign programming, mainly from the U.S., tell their own story. In the Bahamas, there is now 100% foreign domination of television. In Antigua and Barbuda . . . , 60% U.S. programming, with the other 40% mainly made up of government information programmes. In Trinidad and Tobago 76%."

Even countries that previously worked diligently to produce more local television now opt for the U.S. shows. Jamaica, which during Manley's administration had the highest percentage of locally produced programs in the Commonwealth Caribbean (25 percent), used 88.3 percent foreign shows by 1985. In fact, if news and Jamaica Information Service shows had been dropped, local programming would have ceased to exist (Wilson 1985). In one year alone, 1985–1986, there was a 75 percent drop-off in local programming (Hoover 1986, 34) because of competition from satellite and home video, both usually pirated. JBC-TV has had a long-running dispute with the United States Motion Picture Export Association over rebroadcast of copyrighted material.

The United States impact on television programming has remained as pervasive on other islands. On Dominica, which has one cable and two television networks, most programs originate in the United States and are picked up by satellite. On Barbados, although there is a yearly survey of the most popular television shows, the actual rates are set by the program's ratings in the United States, not in Barbados. Nine of the ten most popular television shows are from the United States; the other is the local nightly news.

When a local program is produced, it is often a copy of a U.S. show. Some producers contend that this must be the case to win audience approval. But one veteran Caribbean broadcaster does not buy the argument that Caribbean drama must be in the context of "Dallas" because "Caribbean people are accustomed to 'Dallas' and will not accept local materials" unless done in the "Dallas" mold. He said that Caribbean television can accommodate the abundance of drama indigenous to places such as Jamaica and Trinidad and Tobago as well as the "Dallas" variety (Cholmondeley 1984, 14).

An island that has proved Cholmondeley correct is Cuba. Seventy percent of Cuban television programming is nationally produced for a total of eleven thousand hours yearly. Of the remaining 30 percent, three-fourths comes from socialist countries and the rest from the West, including U.S. cartoons and other programs received free via satellite (see chapter 11). In fact, Cuba produces enough programming to seek overseas markets (*Variety* 25 March 1987, 104).

In the rest of the Caribbean, radio is also predominantly United States–oriented, with most stations acting as jukeboxes for popular music. Of the average eighteen hours daily on Commonwealth Caribbean stations, 55 percent is music (mostly Western pop); 29 percent is made up of interviews, talk, phone-ins, and educational broadcasts; and fifteen percent is news. One-third of all news is from the British Broadcasting Corporation, Voice of America, and Canada Broadcasting Corporation.

As examples, the two stations of Bermuda Broadcasting Company take most of their programs from U.S. sources, and in Guyana, the predominant music of radio is either North American popular music or gospel music. The latter has pervaded most of the region as U.S. Christian groups, supported by their large budgets and realizing the big-business possibilities of the electronic church, have set up gospel stations on many islands (Anguilla, Antigua, Dominica, St. Kitts, and Jamaica among them) or have bought radio time to provide instant music for instant religion. More than most other Caribbean people, Jamaicans have been upset with North American evangelism as a cultural force. One government official there, who deals with folklore, reported that evangelistic forays into the hinterlands have destroyed folk forms (Hoover 1986, 47).

One broadcaster said that the only thing local and innovative in Commonwealth Caribbean radio during the past decade has been the talk show. He believed that the low quality of local radio programming resulted not from financial constraints, as some broadcasters contend, but instead from a shortage of trained personnel (Cholmondeley 1984, 15). His point about talk radio is well taken. On Jamaica, radio call-in programs are especially popular. Of ten such shows, four are open-mike and the rest are call-ins to a doctor, a psychiatrist, a pediatrician, a consumer affairs advocate, a lawyer, and a nighttime social advisor and spiritual healer. A survey of 268 adults in Kingston showed that they preferred the open-mike shows (Surlin 1986, 461).

A liberalization of broadcasting laws in France has had some effect upon stations in French Guiana, Martinique, and Guadeloupe. Some private stations have been licensed, including a few owned by French Caribbean political interests. However, all three territories are served by branches of French companies, such as Radio France Outremer or Tele-diffusion de France, and by relays of Radio France.

Generally, as with telecommunications, Caribbean broadcasting lacks meaningful regional or country policies. One system, that of Bermuda television, has been described as, "muddied by a series of government decisions and non-decisions regarding satellite and cable pay TV, policy toward satellite technology and videotaping of (U.S.) copyrighted programs, programming quality, and the structure of local regulation" (Wetzel 1986).

To help remedy the situation in the region, a resolution calling for an area-wide broadcasting policy was proposed at a seminar on communications and development held in St. Lucia in 1985. Sponsored by the CARICOM and the Caribbean Institute of Mass Communications, the seminar reported that "no progress has been made by governments to counteract the massive penetration of our societies by foreign culture and political thought through the new communication technologies such as broadcast satellites."

Accordingly, delegates called for license stipulations that require a significant and increasing percentage of local programming; limiting of the percentage of imports from any one country out of the region; government facilitation of local programming; recognition by the commercial sector and advertisers of their social responsibility to sponsor Caribbean shows; regional cooperation of producers to create programs with a Caribbean outlook; and research emphases on the effects of foreign programming on society and youth.

Satellite Broadcasting

Dependence upon U.S. television programming has been greatly enhanced by satellite transmission. Six Commonwealth Caribbean countries have satellite ground stations linked to INTELSAT. Suriname owns one-third of an INTELSAT Standard A station in French Guiana and operates a Standard B station at Paramaribo for traffic to the United States and South America. Cuba's EMTELCUBA has two satellite earth stations, one is INTELSAT, supplied by NEC in 1979, and the other is INTERSPUTNIK, set up in 1973.

In addition, the Caribbean is within the overspill of U.S. domestic satellites, enabling regional television systems to easily pick up the signals. At the beginning of 1986, Jamaica, with a population of 2.3 million, had seven thousand dishes in the hands of the economic, political, and technocratic elites who pirate U.S. television.

Other countries have allowed private entrepreneurs to set up relay stations to retransmit material directly from satellite through cable or on VHF channels. In St. Kitts and Antigua, private enterprise has been permitted to set up such cable systems to directly compete with national systems. In Belize, Dominica, St. Lucia, Guyana, Turks and Caicos, Montserrat, and St. Vincent, where state broadcasting of television does not exist, cable hookups via satellite dominate. Such systems do not carry local programs, and as indicated in chapter 5, the foreign shows even contain foreign advertisements.

The U.S. government and media conglomerates do not concern themselves with possible cultural and economic impacts upon these territories by such an abundance of U.S. programming. Instead, they voice some objection to the losses incurred because of piracy, arguing that the islands should pay for the overspill of U.S. satellites. Even that concern is not taken up very persistently or loudly, which makes one wonder if the policymakers on the matter might be willing to lose some profits now for the long-range advantages of addicting the Caribbean people to U.S. television.

Concerning payment of copyright fees for the imported television, some Caribbean policymakers have counter-argued that U.S. movies and television have been adequately paid for in the past and that none of that money ever found its way back to the region. One writer even suggested that a development fund to encourage Caribbean programming be established with copyright fees (Rudder 1985, 133).

The U.S. Federal Communications Commission joined the controversy on 7 June 1983 when it released a "Notice of Inquiry" to start a comprehensive process to develop policies and guidelines for the construction and use of satellite and cable transmission to the Caribbean during the 1985 to 1995 decade. The agency, claiming that the Caribbean is the only area in the world where satellites dominate telecommunications, reported that 66 percent of United States-Caribbean traffic is routed over satellites and that twenty-one cable systems provide services to the region (see discussion of Belize satellites in chapter 6). In fact, satellite radio has entered the region also. In 1985, GEM-FM in Milwaukee, with a transmitter in Montserrat, began broadcasting U.S. pop music twenty-four hours daily via satellite. The news and the sports mingled in also originate in the United States (Brown 1987, 21).

Cable Television

Cable television permeates the area. Almost all of it is brought in from the United States via satellite, a large portion of it is pirated, and all of it is owned by private (mainly United States) operators. At least the following have cable television: Antigua, Belize (one, plus seven independent satellite carriers), Bermuda (a pay cable network), the British Virgin Islands, Dominica, Haiti, Jamaica, Montserrat, Puerto Rico, St. Kitts, St. Lucia (two, one owned by Cable and Wireless), and St. Vincent. During the mid-1980s, cable systems were in the talking stages for the Dominican Republic, Trinidad and Tobago, and Turks and Caicos (a satellite rebroadcast operation).

Puerto Rico has experienced one of the most profound growths of cable. Initially, in 1976, Puerto Ricans received HBO, some local films, and Virgin Island stations via cable. Then, by 1980, satellite hookups enabled them to see programs from WTBS Atlanta, WOR New York, WGN Chicago, and the Spanish International Network. Three years later, they had a choice of twenty-one cable channels; for a package of twelve, they paid only U.S. $11 monthly. The most recent figures for

1986 showed at least thirty cable channels (with twenty-four in English) and more than 90,000 subscribers (see *Variety* 30 March 1983, 37, for background), and predictions for 1988 called for 300,000 to 500,000 subscribers. The largest company is Cable TV of Greater San Juan, owned by Harris Cable of Los Angeles, with annual billings of over U.S. $12 million by 1983.

Jamaica began construction of a cable television system in 1983, with proposed subsystems in Kingston, Montego Bay, and Ocho Rios. Government-built and government-operated, CTS hoped to use programs from satellite services of the United States. At its birth, an economist predicted that the system would use very little local programming and that consumers would not be buying Jamaican but would instead be "increasing their consumption of imported goods and services"; he added that the foreign currency drain caused by buying foreign programs would be $1.5 million annually, or .8 to 1.4 percent of Jamaican income (Snyder 1983).

Some national broadcast systems use satellite transmissions of U.S. cable and network programs. For example, in Barbados, a retransmission of CNN's "Daybreak" morning news program has been carried four hours on weekdays, with a series of local scenes substituted during U.S. commercial breaks. Jamaica Broadcasting Corporation Television also fills large amounts of time with satellite-received and other canned programming (Cozier 1986).

The situation is almost unchecked in the smaller islands. For example, in the Windwards, cable systems such as those of Helen Television in St. Lucia, SUG TV in St. Vincent, or Marpin TV in Dominica, all have erected receiving dishes through which they take satellite transmissions of U.S. networks. In the Leeward islands of St. Kitts–Nevis, Antigua, and Montserrat, the situation is equally serious (see chapter 5).

Videocassettes

Videocassette recorders, combined with satellite-to-home reception, also play havoc with national television programming, international copyright regulations, and film attendance. With virtually no government control over outside influences on the mass media generally, an elusive technology such as home video has free reign, especially in countries without national television systems (such as Guyana and Belize), or in countries that lack variety in over-the-air or cable television fare.

For example, U.S.–originated programming is available twenty-four hours daily in St. Lucia, where an informal infrastructure of videocassette playback units has been privately installed. Thus, U.S. films and television shows are widely viewed, legally and illegally, via satellite downlinks and videotape rental parlors (Caribbean Council of Churches 1986, 2, 4). In Barbados and Trinidad and Tobago, home video is popular enough to keep a number of rental firms in business (thirty-three in Barbados), dispensing the whole gamut of materials from U.S. television shows (including their commercials) to pornographic films. The market is so saturated with these imports that local producers are discouraged before they begin (Hoover 1986, 33).

Only recently have some Caribbean voices spoken out against the influx of imported videocassettes. One Caribbean Broadcasting Union official quoted government authorities as saying that video is useful in keeping people off the streets, that it could be used as a pacifier of the dispossessed, perhaps otherwise angry, masses; listing the "high and growing" penetration of VCRs as one of six major problems for Caribbean broadcasting, he asked if he and other broadcasters were on "death-row or will be in the back waters for so long that it would seem as if we had received a life sentence" (Rudder 1986, 125). A Guyanese writer blamed videocassettes for bringing into the homes in his nation "irrelevant and questionable North American life-styles"; the practice has an impact, he said, "on clothes and hairstyles of the young," and "it has highlighted gangsterism; encouraged consumerism, through TV/video advertisements; and even contributed to the rate of immigration to North America" (Forsythe 1983, 53). As mentioned in chapter 6, Belizeans also complain often about the U.S.–inspired consumerism encouraged by home video.

Home video, cable systems, and an economic recession have been blamed for a significant drop in cinema attendance in Puerto Rico. In 1983, film billings decreased by 8 to 10 percent, and between 1981 and 1983 they had decreased by 20 to 25 percent (*Variety* 30 March 1983, 37); as a result, cinema houses closed in some areas. Compounding the problem was a September 1983 law that cracked down on the portrayal of sex in theaters and thus drove that audience to home video (*Variety* 21 March 1984).

Interestingly, video proliferated quickly in Puerto Rico, despite a 19.8 percent import duty on hardware and the fact that almost all prerecorded cassettes are in English without Spanish subtitles. By 1984, about 150,000 to 200,000 videocassette recorders and 250 video clubs existed on the island. San Juan alone had over thirty legal sales and rental outlets. Of course, much of the videocassette trade is illegal; piracy is very prominent, with some films appearing on the market before their official release in city theaters.

The very few surveys of home video in the Caribbean reveal a number of reasons for its popularity. At the top, of course, are the relative inexpensiveness and convenience of viewing video in the home, but added to that—at least in Puerto Rico and Guyana—is the safety factor. A Guyanese wrote that home video was preferred to cinema attendance because there was less likelihood of one's automobile being stolen at home. He also provided the most curious reason for video's popularity: "And there is the notion, respected by Guyanese housewives, that video is there to keep women at home while, even in isolated cases *and* places, the roving husband enjoys *his* video shows in the second home of his so-called *essential* 'deputy' wife" (Forsythe 1983, 53).

Just as the television receiver was perceived as a status symbol earlier, the VCR represents that position in the 1980s. (I recall visiting Caribbean homes in the early 1970s and seeing television sets adorned with pictures of each family member standing next to the prized possession.) Owning a video camera as well as a VCR is even more of a status symbol because of the capability to record and play back family and community events, such as weddings and parties. In at least Jamaica and Guyana, reports showed that the VCR is considered an alternative form of babysitting.

In countries where national television programming is considered weak, partly because of dull governmental shows, home video has become another source of adult entertainment. The obverse does not always apply. For example, Puerto Rico has about ten television channels, plus the many cable possibilities, yet more than 14.6 percent of the television homes and 3.8 percent of the total homes have VCRs. The Dominican Republic, on the other hand, which also has a number of television channels (at least five or six), has a low VCR penetration of only 2.5 percent of the television homes and 0.2 percent of the total homes. One researcher said that the variety of programming on the channels offsets the need for home video in the Dominican Republic, as does the poor state of the economy (Straubhaar 1986, 14). In a small survey Straubhaar conducted, he found that even among those who could afford a VCR, very few did so; that video rentals were not widely available; and that the private video clubs emphasized U.S. and Mexican films.

Economics was cited as a reason in 1984 for the low penetration of VCRs in St. Kitts–Nevis. The head of broadcasting said that the VCR, just coming into the island then, was not very prominent because cassettes availability was not very high. He predicted that video would become important as the people craved more violent or sexually explicit content than that offered by the government television service, or if that service did not otherwise serve the public need (Interview, Caines 1984).

Home video, unlike more formal media systems, is sometimes introduced to an area without much notice. For example, in Jamaica, video emerged at the time of the 1980 national elections, and political parties campaigned with a series of short, vivid, and amateur videos shown in televised commercials. When some people realized they too could make a television program, or at least record a family event, they asked friends traveling to Miami to bring back a VCR. A few video clubs sprang up — first in Kingston, then in Montego Bay and other towns — to serve as viewing theaters and tape-lending libraries. The few elite people who owned VCRs became members by purchasing a cassette at the exorbitant price of U.S. $77 to $93, for which they were permitted to borrow up to three cassettes for U.S. $27. Prerecorded cassettes cost U.S. $102 for a one-and-one-half-hour tape to U.S. $115 for two-and-one-half to three-hour films. These prices, along with that of the VCR (U.S. $1,595), make home video an expensive proposition in Jamaica. Yet Jamaicans not only buy the VCRs but they also purchase the one-inch cameras to go with them. Of course, costs are reduced because much copying goes on (some tapes are fifth or sixth generation) and foreign travelers bring back tapes to share with friends. Some of these are recorded off the air in Miami, London, or New York (Thomas 1983). By 1985–1986, Jamaica had a video penetration of 7.8 percent of the television homes and 0.1 percent of the total homes. (See chapter 6 for discussion of video in Belize.)

Incongruous as it may seem, the two Caribbean territories where home video has experienced the fastest growth — Puerto Rico and Guyana — are also the most economically strapped. Despite a 25 percent unemployment figure, Puerto Rico has witnessed a boom in the home video business. Between 1980 and 1982, twelve video clubs were started, and they had U.S. $12 million in sales in 1982 alone. That year, the oldest club had fifteen-hundred members and an inventory of five thousand cassettes. The video clubs sold a host of products at high prices — a prerecorded motion picture cassette for U.S. $75; a blank cassette for U.S. $16; a VCR for U.S. $800 to $1,200; a giant seventy-two-inch television system for U.S. $4,000 — as well as other products, including video games. Videocassettes rented for U.S. $2 to $4 daily, and the rate continued to drop in the mid-1980s. Most customers are upper-middle-class professionals (*Variety* 19 May 1982, 54).

In Puerto Rico, sex has been a popular theme of videocassettes, accounting for 20 to 30 percent of the rentals. Other popular cassettes have been *S.O.B., Paternity, For Your Eyes Only, Rocky, Mommie Dearest,* and classics such as *Dr. Zhivago, The Sound of Music, The Godfather,* and John Wayne films. One writer reported that if a customer checked out four videocassettes for a weekend, one would be sexual for a couple to enjoy, one would be a Disney cartoon for the children, and two would be English-language movies for the entire family (*Variety* 19 May, 1982, 54).

Guyana, which has experienced extreme economic problems, had a fourteen-fold increase in home video between 1980 and 1983. Despite price tags of U.S. $2,000 or more on a VCR, the Guyanese imported an average of thirty per week in 1983; some were gifts from relatives in the United States. By 1983, there were an estimated 16,000 VCRs in 3.4 percent of the television homes of Guyana. Some households had two or three models to facilitate home copying.

By 1983, there were nine video clubs, each with an average paid-up life membership of 160, as well as an estimated 500,000 cassettes in circulation, including many pirated versions. Seventy percent of the cassettes originated in the United States, while 15 percent came from Canada, 12 percent from the West Indies, 2 percent from Western Europe, and 1 percent from Venezuela and Brazil. A prerecorded cassette cost U.S. $60.

A 1983 survey showed that viewing preferences in Guyana consisted of (1) morning viewing by housewives in suburban and middle-income urban areas, (2) evening and night viewing by professionals, public servants, and manual workers, (3) all-day Saturday and Sunday viewing by young people and children, and (4) weekend viewing (except Saturday morning) by working adults. The favorite fare were romantic dramas, comedies, sports events, serials, musicals, horror films, Westerns, courtroom dramas, and old movies. Indian films were liked by the large East Indian population, and pornography, uncensored by the Film Censorship Board, was seen by some adults and teenagers. Viewers gave their reasons for watching home video—entertainment, an escape from reality, and a form of home education. They believed that besides those benefits already mentioned, home video also united the people in this multiethnic community through video parties and kept children off the streets (Forsythe 1983, 53).

ALTERNATIVES

Although in most Caribbean countries virtually nothing has been accomplished in setting policy for telecommunications and broadcasting, there have been a few exceptions. As indicated in chapter 11, Cuba maintains a well-structured system that promotes social change to benefit the masses—not foreign or domestic entrepreneurs. It is alone in the region in implementing a national communication policy and in working toward creating its own technology. For a brief time under Maurice Bishop, Grenada attempted mass mobilization to bring about social change through various government organs, including radio. The Grenada experiment did not succeed because of the short rule of Bishop, as well as because of structural, technological, and other restraints (see chapter 9).

For the most part, viable alternatives to imported telecommunications technology have not been found in the Caribbean. But some individuals and small groups have worked seriously to offset North American cultural forms by re-emphasizing and attempting to preserve the local popular media from the onslaught of television; by using media for developmental purposes; and by producing—admittedly in very rare cases—larger amounts of Caribbean-oriented programming.

The Caribbean possesses traditional creole and African communication forms that have received more attention recently after they were threatened with extinction or superimposition from outside. Among these, perhaps calypso and reggae music are the best known. There have been concerns that both cultural forms may be losing their authenticity as they are recorded and modified for larger overseas audiences. Cuthbert (1985), while pointing out that reggae is popular mainly among Jamaican lower-class youth, said that with its internationalization, it also has been muted. Another scholar showed that the use of radio and recording equipment to enlarge the audience for calypso beyond the islands has meant that the music has lost its topicality and timeliness and has become a type of "homogenized calypso." (Hoover 1986, 28). Lewis (1981, 20), analyzing the work of the calypsonian called "The Mighty Shadow," said that calypso has been "metamorphosed from earthy spontaneous outpourings to a sophisticated and profound socio-political and cultural medium of expression." Perhaps the "homogenized calypso" is preferred by local authorities, who often have been the butt of the lyrics.

No doubt, the political clout of this music has been great. For example, in the 1950s, when the calypsonians threw their support behind Trinidad's People's National Movement, the opposition was crushed. Later, in 1977, when Eric Gairy's press restrictions did not allow political dissent in Grenada, calypsonians formed a breakaway tent (organization), "We Tent," to protest through their music (McLean 1986, 89). In Barbados, folk and protest calypsos have been banned from radio because of their controversial material. One calypsonian, "The Mighty Gabby," whose work was banned for questioning Barbados's military buildup and the invasion of Grenada, let it be known that he considered calypso a political weapon. In his song "Calypso," he claimed calypso as

22.1 Loudspeaker trucks have been useful alternative forms of communication in the Caribbean. (*Photo by John A. Lent*)

his music, to be used to protest conditions under which his children must grow—a weapon that would liberate him. Like other calypsonians, "The Mighty Gabby" has also protested the U.S. media and cultural invasion of the territory. In his 1985 "Culture," he sang about the futility of setting up a cultural plan for the Caribbean when North American television shows penetrated the region. Another calypsonian protested that there was so much Americana on television that it seemed as if the "Yankees are still here in Trinidad."

Some islands have progressed further than others in preserving indigenous cultural forms. Jamaica seems strongly committed; it has a national campaign, "Memory Bank," which tries to preserve the experiences and wisdom of elderly people, and encourages street theater groups. To preserve the authenticity of the steel band, a group in 1980 persuaded Trinidad and Tobago Television to film the steel band concert outdoors, not in confining studios. St. Lucia's Folk Research Center and Adult Literacy Program uses traditional media—especially popular theater—to promote "conscientization"; the center also is active in documenting and preserving folk forms. In St. Vincent, the New Artists Movement attempts to do the same, while in Dominica the People's Action Theatre, using traditional communication forms, gets entire villages to participate in skits of real-life situations, especially those concerning development problems. Since 1974, the Banyan Experiment in Trinidad has been successful in producing low-cost television programming that preserves folklore and looks at social reality (Taylor 1976; Taylor 1982; *World Broadcast News* 1981).

Other countries have mobilized communication forms for developmental purposes, although broadcasters believe that most officials, except for those of Cuba, are lackadaisical about developmental communications. When communicators get together anywhere in the world to discuss communication for development, they spend inordinate amounts of time promoting high technology–oriented media. They believe that with telecommunications, computerization, and advanced broadcasting systems, people's attitudes, beliefs, and behaviors can be changed for individual and societal welfare. Similar thinking has been expressed at the few conferences on communication and development in the Caribbean, ever since one of the first in Guyana in 1974.

Besides the above-stated uses of traditional communication forms for development, there have been some isolated instances of using cost-efficient, community-inspired media for social awareness and change. In Cuba and the Dominican Republic, broadcasting has been used to teach literacy and numeracy skills, in both cases employing cost-effective methods (Hanssen, Kozlow, and Olsen 1983). One experiment in the

Dominican Republic has used radio effectively as an interactive medium. At Radio Enriquillo, a problem is discussed on the air early in the week, after which cassettes are distributed to the villagers for their feedback. The recorded messages are then played over the air later in the week. This station also uses a village correspondent network to provide information useful to the people, such as news of a bridge washout or the breakdown of an irrigation pump (Lowe 1983, 14). In Haiti, Radio Lumiére covered all of that country with developmental programs using a community approach to broadcasting (Thatcher and Tarter 1983).

Not much can be reported about Caribbean broadcasters' lowering the number of imported programs. For a time in the early 1980s, the two major television stations of Puerto Rico opted to decrease imports in favor of more local soap operas, musicals, and situation comedies, with the goal of finding Spanish-language markets elsewhere for these productions (*Variety* 30 March 1983, 65).

These micro-experiments, however, are grossly insufficient to change the pattern of outside domination of telecommunications and broadcasting that has persisted for generations. A coordinated effort of Caribbean governments screaming, "Enough!" and backing up the shout with drastic actions like the nationalization of telecommunications and/ or the creation of regional policies might curb the onslaught of outside influences, but this would be temporary. The economies of the region, in all probability, cannot maintain the elaborate services already in place.

The buildup of information technology generally has a momentum of its own. It is seductive and addictive, and it traps developing countries the way drugs trap addicts. Enamored with information technology, these nations sample some of its paraphernalia—a telephone system here, a microwave service there, or a broadcasting station elsewhere. In the process, they become a bit dependent. In turn, the multinational, transnational, and national corporations and governments push more powerful and much more expensive gadgetry, and the dependency deepens. By the latter part of the 1980s, it seems that the Caribbean has already advanced to the second stage of dependency.

23

National Development and Mass Media with Emphasis on the Commonwealth Caribbean

T his chapter deals with two things, the first an incontrovertible fact and the second a troubling question. Together they provide the focus for much of the argument concerning mass media in the Third World.

The fact is that there is a discomforting gap between what governments *state* as their goals and strategies in developing a national culture and consciousness and in presenting useful developmental information to the public and what they *do*.

There is a great deal of verbiage in the world today about Third World nations finding their own developmental paths and, in the process, de-emphasizing some of the outside influences. Criticisms have been voiced against the "Big Four" international news agencies domination of what has been called a one-way flow to the Third World; against the foreign values, attitudes, and life-styles conveyed via television programs, music, and advertising from the West, the North, or the North Atlantic; and against the "old development paradigm," which emphasizes big media with its sophisticated and expensive technology and vertical, one-way flows of information.

The call has been for the establishment of more national and regional news agencies or news pools; more locally developed broadcast programming, advertising formats, and messages suited to the national culture; and more adoption of what was bound to be called the "new development paradigm" — horizontal communication between Third World countries and areas within those countries; participation of the people in designing media messages and packages; and more reliance on the use of feedback, folk or traditional media, and appropriate or intermediate stages of media technology.

The old and the new paradigms are the two extremes. Apparently, to get from one to the other is not a "leapfrog" maneuver, as has sometimes been thought. Too many difficulties intervene. Probably the most prevalent problem relates to economics: If a nation is not going to use foreign media products and technology, if it will no longer tolerate foreign ownership and patronage of its mass media, how will it afford to operate its media systems? One alternative—the one most obvious in much of the Caribbean—is for the national government to assume this responsibility. This has been especially evident in parts of the Commonwealth Caribbean, Cuba, and the Francophone Antilles. For example, when Radio Demerara was sold to the government of Guyana in 1979, only one medium, the struggling *Mirror,* could be said to be privately owned. After Jamaica's Manley government purchased the *Daily News* and Radio Jamaica Rediffusion (RJR) in 1978, the two main Gleaner Company dailies remained the only privately held media. Government ownership of the mass media fit into Guyana's plans concerning national development. Government official Kit Nascimento said that all media channels must be used to support the development process and that the government cannot leave to chance matters such as media ownership and content. Guyana's former prime minister justified publicly that the government had a right to own media. In Jamaica, Manley had been more cautious, saying that freedom of the press is subject to the question of social responsibility and that the national interest should be the overriding concern of the media.

Despite common beliefs to the contrary, government ownership of the media does not mean economic stability in all cases. A former broadcasting official in Guyana, Ron Sanders, pointed out some adverse effects of national development upon economic aspects of broadcasting. Sanders wrote that when in the mid-1970s companies were nationalized and merged, thus creating monopolies, the need for advertising was eliminated. The two radio stations in Guyana felt this squeeze and began operating in the red. The lack of advertising support affected all other parts of the broadcasting operation—programming, training, and organization. It even affected a developmental goal of regionalizing broadcasting for easy access of the people and the promotion of national aims; this project had to be abandoned for lack of money. Government thinking became awkward and conflicting when one of the stations, owned by the foreign Rediffusion, sought to sell out, and the government had to ask Rediffusion to stay on because it could not afford to purchase the station at that time. This would *have* to be an embarrassing situation for a government that in 1977 had said "out with all foreign media" (Sanders 1978b, 12).

The Jamaican government's purchase of the *Daily News* and RJR went more smoothly. The ailing *Daily News,* according to the government, was purchased to ensure its continuance. RJR was bought and converted into a "people's station," with 24 percent of the ownership by government, 25 percent by RJR workers, and 51 percent by the "people." The "people" were defined as twenty-three organizations (sixteen of which were trade unions), and no single group owned more than 10 percent of the whole.

Besides government and the "people" as alternative owners, another possibility is mixed ownership. Actually, the RJR ownership is mixed, and the Caribbean News Agency (CANA) is unique in the world among news services for its mixed ownership; the proportion of its shares held by privately owned media is slightly higher than the proportion of shares held by the government. Of course, as the government owns, and presumably controls, more mass media outlets, there are fears that the important dynamic of criticism may be lost.

Perhaps another economic alternative is one I suggested in 1972; because of the thinking at the time, the suggestion was largely ignored. My belief then (as now) was that media on a big scale should not be contemplated until the government or some other entities (preferably the latter) have the resources to keep the media local and independent. Perhaps Guyana was alone in the Caribbean in attempting to do this; it was one of the few countries to hold off acquiring television. It seems that other states have confusedly equated progress with acquiring the latest piece of equipment or paraphernalia of modernity, with little thought about who will benefit from it or what it is to be used for. Thus, a tiny state such as Antigua has had its own color television system for years, as have other microstates. A color television system (and a national airline) almost seems to be a gift a nation gives itself upon becoming independent. It is very difficult to convince governmental and media people to think in terms of intermediate stages of development and to use more of the small media that have been successfully implemented in some parts of the Third World. As a result, one does not see much use of audiocassette technology, blackboards, or wall newspapers in the Commonwealth Caribbean; however, a few experiments with alternative media used to bring about social change did take place in Haiti and the Dominican Republic.

Another area where there is a discrepancy between what Caribbean governments and media *say* they want and what they *do* is the content of development messages and the manner in which they are presented. The stated desire is to present development messages on topics of life-or-death consequences to as many people as possible in an understandable, interesting way without including foreign values and attitudes. That is the goal; it is seldom approached. Cuthbert (1976), for example, pointed out that although most advertisements in Jamaica now feature black faces, they still perpetuate the consumption-oriented tastes of the developed world. She pointed out conflicting messages: "At best the population receives conflicting messages from advertisements: The Workers Bank encourages savings and the airline and furniture store encourage spending; the Family Planning Board encourages responsible parenthood and the ad for Dragon Stout (which is said to have virility-inducing qualities) says that Dragon 'Puts it back.' "

In a four-month content analysis of the six main newspapers of Jamaica, Guyana, Trinidad, and Barbados, Archer showed that although these papers were giving information on food and nutrition, they were not doing so as effectively as possible. He concluded that though there were many recipes given, very little was said about the nutritional values of the meals. Many of the recipes were meant for special occasions, not for the daily living of the masses. He said that much of the literature on food and nutrition consists of recipes, shopping tips, and cooking hints, while relatively less of it concentrates on the importance of human nutrition, nutritional requirements of the body, nutritional values of food, etc. Archer said that most of the presentations in the media on food and nutrition are artless and dull (Archer 1976). This is a common complaint about most development messages. Sargent (1979) wrote that advertisers will spend thousands or millions of dollars preparing messages for the public, while government and other development agencies fire out messages without understanding their audiences or the impact of messages. They assume that the public is anxiously awaiting the next development message.

Thus, especially in the Commonwealth Caribbean, the governments and the media are somewhere in a transitional zone between where they say they want to be and where they are in regard to the issue of mass media and national development. If nothing else has been done in the past decade and a half, the problems have at least become known. Through seminars and conferences sponsored by UNESCO, Stichting Grafische Communicatie, Caribbean Food and Nutrition Institute, International Broadcast Institute, Friedrich-Ebert-Stiftung, Friedrich Naumann Stiftung, Caribbean Institute of Mass Communication, and some governments, topics such as perspective of media management, mass media and food and nutrition, and communication for development purposes, among others, have been discussed.

During this same time, foreign ownership of the Caribbean mass media all but vanished, except in the French and U.S. Caribbean. Outside owners were replaced in most instances by local governments or regional or local business conglomerates. Also, some attempts at using

more local and regional media content were made, especially by the
Caribbean Broadcast Union, which promoted exchange of programs; by
the Caribbean Publishers and Broadcasters Association, which helped
set up CANA and the Caribbean Press Council; and by various Cuban
institutions, which sponsored regional training, film festivals, and exchanges. Also important were the efforts by the Caribbean Institute of
Mass Communications and by Cuba's UPEC and ICAIC, which began
training Caribbean journalists.

Many efforts have already been made, but there are areas where
much work remains: allowing the people to participate more in setting
their own media agendas; using the traditional media for development
purposes; and defining more specifically what key development topics
need to be communicated, whether they be ecology, food and nutrition,
intermediate technology, energy, or family planning.

The troubling question that persists is whether the media can adopt
national development goals and still retain their integrity, independence,
and free enterprise spirit. In short, can freedom of the media exist side-
by-side with the promotion of government-inspired national development aims?

This issue probably takes up more time of the Commonwealth
Caribbean and other governments and media than any other. It stems
partly from the tradition endemic in the region of the press playing the
role of the opposition, and it is more pronounced in these states than in
many other areas in the Third World because of the small number of
media. For example, in the Commonwealth Caribbean, where most
newspapers are politically owned or affiliated, the tendency is to have
two (and sometimes three) papers in a country, one progovernment and
one antigovernment.

The debate is also tied up with ownership. Managers of privately
owned media fear that governments, in the guise of promoting national
development, will force the sale of or will confiscate all media. They also
believe that a lot of the government-inspired development messages are
designed not for the public good but instead for the good of the national
leadership—that they represent the leaders' efforts to perpetuate themselves in office. They worry that once a government controls all the mass
media, the critical function in a society can be lost. They believe that as
governments emphasize a national development role for the media, press
people will become frightened that they might incur the anger of the
authorities and, in the process, they may choose to self-censor.

On the other hand, government officials and managers of government-owned media contend that privately owned media are selfish, concerned with entrenched interests, and not open to alternative socio-eco-

nomic organizational forms. Such criticisms have been made of the *France-Antilles* of Guadeloupe and Martinique, of the huge corporation-owned dailies of Puerto Rico and Barbados, and of the *Gleaner,* among others. As a University of the West Indies lecturer, Gordon Draper (1977, 17) said,

> Private ownership is no less restrictive. . . . Moreover, given the commercial nature of this ownership form, the main criteria of performance become profit. The media must conform to ensure there are no advertising boycotts, which would threaten their revenue position, and hence their profitability. When the prime concern becomes profit therefore, good responsible journalism must take second place. The owners become less concerned about the media playing their optional role in the development process.

Government officials also charged privately owned mass media with irresponsible journalism, with distorting facts and lying about the government in an attempt to bring it down.

The battleground where all of this was most evident was Jamaica in the 1970s. One author wrote that whereas the *Daily Gleaner* stood for capitalist enterprise, alliance with the West, and a conservative sensibility, the Manley government of the 1970s represented socialist development, Third World alignment, and an insurgent spirit (Kopkind 1980). The government, believing the *Daily Gleaner* represented a small group of elite Jamaicans afraid of losing their privileges, accused the paper of distorting information about Manley and other officials. Others who joined the fray criticized the *Daily Gleaner* for its selfishness, its oppressive treatment of employees who would not take antigovernment stands, and its distortion.

On the other hand, *Gleaner* officials said that the democratic socialist government of Manley demanded cooperation or extinction. They believed that Manley would not be satisfied until the government owned all the mass media and used them for the "psychological reorientation of the society."

What is evident is that as governments and the media spar over these issues, a lot of good time that could be given to national development goals, whether inspired by the government, or by private agencies such as the independent media, or by both, is lost. To ensure that the media can be used for the nation's welfare, it is necessary to adopt the principle that freedom of the press should be freedom from government control as well as from economic control by groups promoting their own self-interests rather than those of the larger society.

24

Mass Communications Research:
Background and Problems

Until the 1980s, mass communications was not a research topic of interest to the few scholars who regularly concentrated on the Caribbean, a strange situation because the region teems with unique historical, sociological, and political phenomena of relevance to mass communications. Although the situation has changed slightly in recent years, mass communications research is still very immature. A number of reasons can be offered. Writing in 1972, I said that the relatively underdeveloped nature of mass communications research in one part of the region, the Commonwealth Caribbean, could be attributed to at least three factors.

> (1) European and American scholars have felt the islands too small and insignificant for serious exploration; (2) the diffuseness of this group of tiny islands dotting the sea has been responsible for deterring scholars; (3) journalism scholars have been ignorant of the potential of conducting research in the region. On the other hand, the islanders, having been under colonial tutelage for centuries, never thought they possessed institutions worthy of investigation; nor did they have the time to indulge in the luxury of research (Lent 1975).

These reasons, in addition to others, still stand today. Because of authoritarian governments, some of the nations are not enthusiastic about being studied and others are still dependents of European countries, where some of their communications policies have been made and where research materials about them exist.

Finally, mass communications research traditionally gestates in journalism schools, which until recently did not exist in the Caribbean.

In fact, journalism education began in 1942, when Cuba had a program. Today about eight schools or departments operate (see chapter 25). That almost all of these schools developed during the past generation is an encouraging sign, although until now very little research has emanated from them.

There are other indications that the Caribbean media are slowly being recognized as researchable topics. First, more West Indian students are going abroad to pursue graduate studies in communications; in the process, they are writing theses and dissertations on Caribbean media. For example, in the 1960s and 1970s, at least six theses or dissertations done in United States and Canadian universities dealt with Puerto Rican media; all written by Puerto Ricans. Nine papers were written about Commonwealth Caribbean media. Before the 1960s, though, there were very few theses written on Caribbean topics. In a survey of broadcasting theses from 1920 to 1973, Kittross (1978) found only seven, the oldest dating to 1951. Since the late 1970s, at least twice that number have dealt with mass communications in the Commonwealth Caribbean, Puerto Rico, Haiti, Cuba, and the Netherlands Antilles. Without any pretense at comprehensiveness, this chapter mentions at least fifteen in that time frame.

A second indication of the area's growing importance is the fact that national governments and other agencies — such as UNESCO, the International Communication Institute, and the International Organization of Journalists — have taken some interest in the region's media, sponsoring seminars and other types of events that have led to an increase in the book-length and periodical literature on Caribbean mass media. For example, Cedar Press has published small books on the law relating to Caribbean media (White 1977) and on women and the media (Cuthbert 1975); the *Caribbean Quarterly,* in unprecedented moves, devoted two special editions in 1976–1977 to research on Caribbean media. *Caribbean Studies, Granma Weekly Review, UPEC, Ciencia, Cine cubano, CEMEDIM, PAJ News,* and *Caribbean Contact* also have carried regular articles. Outside the region, periodicals that have discussed aspects of Caribbean mass communications include *Index on Censorship, Variety, IAPA News, IPI Report, Development Communication Report, COM-BROAD, IOJ Newsletter, Democratic Journalist, Media Development,* and *Studies in Latin American Popular Culture.*

The chapter surveys the research done on all aspects of mass communications in the Spanish-, French-, Dutch-, and English-speaking Caribbean, including the continental countries of Belize, French Guiana, Guyana, and Suriname. The research is described under two categories, historical-bibliographical and descriptive (infrastructure, audience, and content analysis). Representative or the more important studies are mentioned under each category. Also included is a section on problems and needs of mass communications research in the Caribbean.

TYPES OF STUDIES

Historical-Bibliographical

By far, more research has been done on historical and bibliographical aspects of Caribbean mass communications than on contemporary topics. A group of dedicated librarians, archivists, and antiquarians, many of whom worked during the first quarter of this century, was responsible for the majority of this work. These researchers usually worked at documenting the existence of periodicals and newspapers; however, occasionally they wrote narrative histories on various aspects of mass communications.

In the Spanish-speaking Caribbean, these listings of printed media appeared in journals such as *Revista de las Antillas* and *Boletín histórico de Puerto Rico,* both in San Juan, and *Boletín del Archivo Nacional* and *Boletín oficial de la Secretaría de Comunicaciones,* both in Havana. For example, *Revista,* in its June 1914 issue, carried an article on the first daily in San Juan, while *Boletín histórico de Puerto Rico,* in at least its 1915 and 1919 issues, had directories of Puerto Rican periodicals and an article on liberty of the press as its existed in Puerto Rico in 1870.

During the 1923 to 1936 period, *Boletín del Archivo Nacional* of Havana had a thorough, continuous article that included facsimiles of historical Cuban periodicals. The same journal, for the 1916 to 1929 period, carried the series by Joaquín Llaverías y Martínez (director of Cuba's National Archives) on Cuban press history. This series provided profiles of hundreds of Cuban periodicals. In at least its 1929 to 1930 issues, *Boletín oficial de la Secretaría de Comunicaciones* also included listings of Cuban newspapers and magazines. Still other listings were compiled by Fermín Peraza y Sarausa from 1933 to 1944 and for publication in *Anuario bibliográfico cubano* and by Carlos Manuel Trelles y Govín between 1911 and 1915 for publication in *Bibliografía cubana.* Some of the latter's work included historical descriptions of the press.

Medina's *La imprenta en la Habana 1707–1810* (1904) must be considered one of the earliest and most comprehensive book-length histories of Cuban printing, while works by Rodríquez-Demorizi (1944) and Pedreira (1941) were important in describing the histories of periodicals in Santo Domingo and Puerto Rico, respectively. The Pedreira book included a valuable appendix listing Puerto Rican periodicals by provinces. A 1919 monograph by an American, Jesse William Sanger, gave the first glimpses of advertising usage in Cuba; Camarena (1927), Amiana (1933), and Despradel and Mata Díaz (1937) discussed periodicals, press freedom, and printing in the Dominican Republic.

Similar early studies and listings of the presses of the French-, Dutch-, and English-speaking Caribbean remain among the best work done. No scholar has approached the excellent caliber of Cabon's history of Haitian journalism, completed in 1919 and reprinted with help from American Antiquarian Society staff member C. S. Brigham in the American Antiquarian Society *Proceedings* in 1939 and as a separate monograph in 1940 (Brigham 1940). This century-and-a-half history, written in French, first appeared in *Petite revue hebdomaire,* Port-au-Prince, 12 April through 14 November 1919. Haitian journalism also received substantial treatment in the second volume (pages 314–407) of Ulrick Duvivier's *Bibliographie generale et methodique d' Haiti* (1941). Esterquest (1940) reported about a little-known Haitian press of 1817. What Cabon did for Haitian journalism history, Lénis Blanche (1935) did for press history in Guadeloupe with a fifty-five-page monograph and with a section of his more general *Histoire de la Guadeloupe* (Blanche 1938).

Historical research on the Dutch territories in the Caribbean, including Suriname, appeared occasionally from the 1920s to the 1950s in *West-Indische gids,* a journal published in The Hague. Again, the main work was completed by a librarian-historian, Johan Hartog, who published his descriptive *Journalistiek leven in Curaçao* (1944). Hartog, head of the library in Oranjestad, also mentioned the press in more general histories he wrote about Aruba, Curaçao, and St. Eustatius and in articles in *West-Indische gids* and other periodicals. As recent as 1984, Hartog wrote about the *St. Eustatius Gazette.*

Early historical studies of the Commonwealth Caribbean were carried out by Frank Cundall, by writers for the American Antiquarian Society *Proceedings,* and by printing buff Douglas McMurtrie. Cundall, probably the foremost British West Indian press historian, was longtime director of the Institute of Jamaica, which holds one of the best collections of British West Indian newspapers. He wrote a number of monographs and articles, probably the most detailed being his *History of Printing in Jamaica from 1717 to 1834* (1935). This monograph, reprinted from the centenary edition of the *Jamaica Daily Gleaner* (13 September 1934), includes detailed biographical and bibliographical notes and photographs of newspapers. The October 1916 *Proceedings* devoted 122 pages to Cundall's "The Press and Printers of Jamaica Prior to 1820," a work that documents the Jamaican newspapers available in the Institute of Jamaica, the British Museum, the Royal Colonial Institute, the Record Office of London, the Library of Congress, the American Antiquarian Society, and twelve other libraries.

Other issues of the *Proceedings* during the first three decades of this century included historical descriptions of British West Indian newspapers. In the April 1926 *Proceedings,* Waldo Lincoln described newspapers available in the American Antiquarian Society Library in Worcester, Massachusetts (Lincoln 1926). C. S. Brigham later annotated and added extensively to that list, which should be republished by the society. Lincoln's work appears in other issues as well, describing a visit to the West Indies in search of old newspapers (1913) and listing Bermuda newspapers (1924). William McCulloch (1921) described other Commonwealth Caribbean newspapers in the 1929 *Proceedings;* James Rodway (1918) wrote an excellent study of British Guiana journalism in 1918; and Wilberforce Eames (1928), wrote on "The Antigua Press and Benjamin Mecom, 1748–1765."

McMurtrie traveled the world writing about the first printing in at least the United States, parts of Europe, Asia, and the Caribbean. His research usually appeared in library or book-publishing journals, and his reports were reprinted as short monographs by printing schools or by McMurtrie himself. In the Caribbean, he described the first printing and newspapers (and in some cases provided a checklist of published materials relating to journalism history) of the Dominican Republic (1942a), Dominica (1932), Barbados (1933), Bermuda (1928), Jamaica (1934a, 1934b, 1936, 1942b), Trinidad (1943c), Tobago (1943b), and Antigua (1943a).

Finally, among older works on the history of journalism with references to the Caribbean, is Isaiah Thomas's *The History of Printing in America,* first published in 1810 and reprinted later (Thomas 1874). The original manuscripts, with marginal notes by Thomas and additions by others, are stored in the American Antiquarian Society. Oswald's book (1968) also has references to the history of Caribbean printing.

Among contemporary historians of Caribbean printing, the most prolific is Roderick Cave, a British librarian who has written a series of articles that has appeared in various journals and has been reprinted, along with others' works, in two volumes entitled *Working Papers on West Indian Printing* (1974–75, 1976), published by the Department of Library Studies, University of the West Indies. Cave has researched printing in most Commonwealth Caribbean areas, including Tobago (1976), Turks and Caicos (1974–75), the West Indies (1978a), Belize (1974–75), Trinidad and Tobago (1974–75, 1976), Jamaica (1974–75, 1976, 1985), and the Cayman Islands (1976). The *Working Papers* are useful volumes because they reprint old documents on printing and deal with specialized topics, such as "West Indian Merchants' Stock: Books of Thomas Craddock" and the use of slave labor in West Indian printing houses. Bradford F. Swan (1956) compiled a checklist of printing in Antigua from 1748 to 1800 and tried to treat the printing history of the entire Caribbean region in a forty-eight-page monograph, entitled *The Spread of Printing. Western Hemisphere. The Caribbean Area* (1970), but the latter was superficial. To cover the early printing in Hispaniola, Jamaica, Barbados, Antigua, Bermuda, the Bahamas, Dominica, Grenada, Montserrat, St. Kitts, Martinique, Haiti, and the Netherlands Antilles, as Swan attempted to do, is not feasible. Both Cave and Swan emphasized the Commonwealth Caribbean in their histories, as I did in my book, *Third World Mass Media and Their Search for Modernity: The Case of Commonwealth Caribbean, 1717–1976* (1977b), the first comprehensive treatment of historical and contemporary perspectives of British West Indian mass communications. My book was an extension of my doctoral dissertation (1972). Other historical theses and dissertations on Commonwealth Caribbean mass communications history include Erwin Thomas's (1978) study of the beginnings of broadcasting in Barbados, British Guiana, Jamaica, and Trinidad; Gerald Smeyak's (1973) history of Guyanese broadcasting; and Martin Renalls's (1968) treatment of the development of Jamaican documentary films.

In the Spanish-speaking Caribbean, recent historical works have dealt with Cuban broadcasting (Martínez-Victores 1978), the Cuban press (Leon Enrique 1975), Cuban cinema (Agramonte 1966; Valdez Rodríguez 1963), printing in colonial Spanish America, including the Antilles (Thompson 1962), and the reaction of the Puerto Rican press to the United States from 1888 to 1898 (Chiles 1975). Others were Alegría's (1960) history of the Puerto Rican press, and Martínez (1978), Martínez Paulino (1973), and Matéo-Nin (1974) on Dominican Republic journalism, the former on clandestine publications. The French Antilles were well served with three theses done at France's Université de Toulouse. The authors covered Martinique's press in relation to politics, providing detailed listings of periodicals. Louison (1971) covered 1920 to 1939; DeLor (1970), 1945 to 1958; and Valdor (1973), 1958 to 1970. In 1980, I also wrote an article on the French Antillean press, based on archival evidence in Martinique and elsewhere. In fact, I found evidence of an earlier press than those previously known in the collection at Philadelphia's Library Company. U.S. Virgin Island press history was treated to a limited degree in Hill (1971), Lewisohn (1970), and Zabriskie (1918), and I wrote one of the first histories of these islands' presses based on research in the St. Thomas and St. Croix libraries (see chapter 20).

Melchior (1981), longtime St. Thomas editor, shared some of his memories as a journalist.

Theses and dissertations include Negron-Portillo's history of Puerto Rico's *La democracia* (1980), Torres-Ramos's history of instructional television (1974), Piedra's development of Puerto Rican advertising (1972), and Vélez Aquino's study of Puerto Rican press reaction to the shift from Spanish to U.S. sovereignty (1968). Recent historical studies of the media in the Netherlands Antilles include Radio Hoyer's anniversary book (Radio Hoyer 1959?) and my articles in the *Gazette* (Lent 1971a, 1981b).

Journalistic endeavors that have dealt with the history of the Caribbean media are the many anniversary numbers of newspapers, especially the centenary issue of the *Port of Spain Gazette* (21 September 1925); the 125th year issue of the *St. Croix Avis* (May 1969); the *Barbados Advocate-News* (1 October 1970); the *Jamaica Daily Gleaner* (9 September 1934; 31 December 1966); and the fiftieth anniversary edition of the *St. Thomas Daily News* (1 August 1980). Also useful have been the collections of extracts from various historical newspapers; these include *Caribbeana* (1741) for extracts of the *Barbados Gazette,* the *Journal of the Barbados Museum and Historical Society* (1958) for the *Liberal,* Davies (1984) for the *Bermuda Gazette,* Neita (1953) for various Jamaican newspapers, and Extraits (n.d.) for Martiniquan newspapers.

Among current bibliographies, the most complete is my work devoted to Caribbean mass communications, which contains 2,653 sources (1981a). An abbreviated version of this compilation appeared in the *Journal of Broadcasting* (Lent 1976a), and an updated version appeared as part of a world bibliography (Lent 1987). I have compiled another 3,500 sources for a forthcoming bibliographic volume. My bibliographies on mass communications in the Commonwealth Caribbean have appeared in *Third World Mass Media and Their Search for Modernity* (Lent 1977b), in a *Caribbean Studies* (1974) article, and as a Temple University monograph (Lent 1976b). Mota (1985) has pulled together an excellent bibliography on Cuban press history. More general bibliographies on the Caribbean, such as Comitas (1968, 1977) and Dodge (1987), and on Latin America (Okinshevich 1966) also include citations.

Descriptive Studies

This category includes infrastructure (state of the media) studies and audience and content analyses.

INFRASTRUCTURE STUDIES. The status of some Caribbean mass media has been reported for years in international agency (see UNESCO 1947–51, 1964, 1965, 1975; Nippon Hoso Kyokai 1977; Frost 1947 to date; FBIS 1975) and national government handbooks and yearbooks (such as *Jamaica Yearbook*).[1] However, most of these treatments were sketchy, usually providing a list of outdated statistics concerning mass media. More detailed surveys were contained in feasibility studies usually conducted by outside agencies. One of the best of these was Roppa and Clarke's study (1969) on regional cooperation in news and broadcasting exchanges in the Commonwealth Caribbean. This survey, commissioned by UNESCO, resulted from extensive interviewing in the islands. Other feasibility studies were done by the United States Information Agency to cover all media and by Barrett (1945) to cover British West Indies broadcasting. In their theses, Thomas (1972) discussed establishing an educational television home economics program in Puerto Rico, and Otero (1973) explored the feasibility of starting a Puerto Rican communications media center.

Inventories, surveys, and policy analyses of telecommunications in the region include works by Wetzel (1986), a Department of Commerce publication on equipment markets; by Hamelink (1985), a report on the entire region; and by González-Manet (1982), who has contributed a number of works on Cuban telematics. Development communication was surveyed by the Canadian Foundation for Caribbean Development and Cooperation (1984), and Cuthbert (1975) reported on women in communication for development.

The first contemporary, book-length survey of the mass media in the region is my own (Lent 1977b); I interviewed more than one hundred media managers, conducted historical studies, and analyzed the content of various media of the Commonwealth Caribbean. I also wrote shorter infrastructure articles on the Commonwealth Caribbean mass media that appeared in many journals.[2] Other more recent books treating aspects of mass communications on a regional basis include International Organization of Journalists (1982), the proceedings of a conference of journalists in Grenada; Soderlund and Surlin (1985), an edited collection of papers from a University of Windsor conference; and Brown and Sanatan (1987), profiles of media in the Commonwealth Caribbean countries.

Among still other surveys of Commonwealth Caribbean mass communications are Dorcas White's *The Press and the Law in the Caribbean* (1977), Maddison's case study (including Jamaica) of using broadcasting to combat illiteracy (1971), Hosein's controversial analysis of Guyanese press freedom (1975b),[3] Sanders' survey of broadcasting in Guyana

(1978a), and Central Rediffusion's treatment of commercial broadcasting in the British West Indies (1956). Still other more recent works on the Commonwealth Caribbean are Charles (1981) on satellite use and Cuthbert (1979) and Burke (1981) on the Caribbean News Agency. The media of individual countries of the English-speaking Caribbean have been analyzed by Lynn (1981), covering media for national development in Jamaica; by Shaw (1981), covering public relations and the multinational alumina corporations in Jamaica; by Walters (1979), covering Jamaican freedom of press; and by me (1985), covering governmental shifts and the Grenadian media.

The media of the Spanish-speaking Caribbean have also been studied. Surveys of Cuban mass media were conducted by American researchers John Nichols (1979, 1982a, 1982b, 1982c), Jim Carty (1978a), and Howard Frederick (1986) and by Soviet writers whose works have appeared in *OIRT Information, Democratic Journalist,* and other journals and books (see Okinshevich 1966; Informational Organization of Journalists 1976). Cuban cinema has been analyzed regularly by Burton (1977, 1978, 1979, 1982a, 1982b) and in essays that have appeared in *Cine cubano* and books, such as that of Meyerson (1973). López (1981) studied Cuban radio's development in a neocolonial society; Ratliff (1987) analyzed the media's promotion of Fidel Castro; Wertheim (1977) compared Cuban educational television with that of El Salvador; and Rodríguez Méndez (1976) looked at the press. Waggoner (1967) analyzed the news and mass media of the Dominican Republic, and Condero et al. (1976) studied Santo Domingo media directors. Recent Puerto Rican media research was reflected in the works of Vélez (1983), Manléon de Benítez (1978), and Sánchez Betances (1976), dealing with television; Paláu (1979), covering the press; and Nicolini (1987), presenting Puerto Rican leaders' views of media.

Werker (1974), in a University of Amsterdam monograph, studied functions of the mass media in Suriname, while Costa Gómez (1957), Oltheten (1977), Roosberg (1977), and I (1971a; 1981) carried out surveys of the media of the Netherlands Antilles. Oltheton and Roosberg did book-length works, Roosberg's resulting from his doctoral work in the Netherlands.

Concerning other countries, Brutus (1982) published a work on the Haitian press and Vaughan (1981) and I (1986) both wrote about the U.S. Virgin Islands' media.

AUDIENCE STUDIES.   Because audience studies are often considered vital to the commercial success of broadcast media, they have existed for years in nearly all Caribbean nations. Originally, these analyses were done by outside agencies such as the U.S. Information Agency (USIA) or by parent agencies of the Caribbean broadcast stations. USIA conducted audience studies on the Voice of America and Radio Havana audiences in Central America (1968) and on foreign radio listening in Cuba (1963, 1968). Rediffusion International Ltd. of London, which until recently owned a number of stations in the Caribbean, did studies of Radio Caraibe's audiences in Guadeloupe and Martinique in 1968 and market profiles of Guyana in 1970; it also studied the Bahamas in 1970 and Barbados in 1965.

Radio audience surveys in Jamaica can be traced to at least 1956, when Radio Jamaica and its parent, Rediffusion International Ltd., published a guide to mass information (Radio Jamaica and Rediffusion 1956). Other surveys, some of which included television, were done by Marketing Advisory Service Ltd. (1965) in the early 1960s, Radio Jamaica (1965, 1969), Market Research Ltd. (1973), and CRAM International Ltd. (1971). Market profiles of Trinidad were done by the Rediffusion outlet, Radio Trinidad, in 1967 and 1969. The only survey I have seen on the Dutch territories was done by International Christian Broadcasters (1966) with the audience of Aruba's station PJA-6.

In addition to the commercially oriented surveys, others exist that take on more academic characteristics. Among these are Farace's analysis (1968) of local news channel preferences among Puerto Ricans; Green's study (1951) of how Dominican Republic citizens use communications; Hosein's report (1975a) of the mass media preferences, awareness, and credibility of urban St. Lucians; and Singham's book (1968) on voter behavior and the use of mass media in Grenada. In one of the few development-related studies done in the Caribbean, Rodríguez (1967) compared media exposure to adoption of farm practices among Puerto Rican tobacco farmers. In other academic surveys, Tarter (1978) studied audience participation in broadcast programming in Haiti; Straubhaar (1986) interviewed Dominican Republic residents concerning their use of videocassettes; and Skinner (1984) discussed foreign televiewing in Trinidad and Tobago.

CONTENT ANALYSES. Not many studies that analyze the contents of Caribbean mass media can be found in the literature, and until recently, the few that did exist concentrated almost entirely upon the Commonwealth Caribbean. I (Lent 1977b) used impressionistic analyses to discuss the contents of Commonwealth Caribbean print and broadcast media in 1970, 1971, and 1976. Systematic analyses appeared in theses completed by Findley (1969), who compared longitudinally the symbols of nationalism, socialism, and scientism as found in the *Jamaica Daily Gleaner;* by Darville (1972), who studied editorial coverage of the 1967–1968 Bahamian elections by two Nassau dailies; by Campbell (1978), who conducted a longitudinal study of the *Sunday Guardian* of Trinidad and Tobago; by Snitkey (1974), who analyzed Cuban radio newscasts; and by Astroff (1983), who discussed dependency by looking at Puerto Rican television programs. Belizean television has been the subject of much study in recent years, as writers such as Barry (1984), Lapper (1984), Oliveira (1986a), and Roser et al. (1986) discussed the country's dependency on the United States for all of its programming. One other content analysis with some relevance is the Bovenkerks' study (1972) of how Surinamese and Antilleans are portrayed in the Dutch press.

PROBLEMS AND NEEDS

Mass communications research in the Caribbean is still being done on an ad hoc basis; typically, a few individuals carry out studies they favor. There have been virtually no cooperative, concerted, and longitudinal projects of relevance and use to larger population segments. The Caribbean should not be singled out for this criticism, since this kind of mass communications research is endemic to many parts of the world. It may be the result of the individuality of the journalism-trained people doing the work.

The Caribbean faces a number of problems — again, many of which are characteristic of other parts of the Third World — chief of which are a lack of direction, government strictures or sensitivities concerning some research, a lack of a tradition of mass communications research in the universities, and a shortage of trained researchers.

To conserve the limited resources available, there is a need for more cooperative, rather than competitive, ventures among researchers in individual nations and throughout the region. Perhaps researchers should join to explore communications issues across language-related regions, over longer periods of time, and with various research methodologies. For example, with the emphasis on developmental communications in some areas of the Caribbean, studies should compare the use of developmental information in different countries, analyzing media content and comparing it both with what the decision makers expect of the messages and with audience perceptions of the messages.

There are also needs for (1) a clearinghouse to handle information relating to mass communications, thus centralizing what are now scattered materials; (2) the systematic collection and preservation of back issues of newspapers, broadcast tapes, and other primary research materials, which are now being destroyed by the elements; (3) the creation of a region-wide mass communications journal to serve as a stimulus and outlet for research; (4) the establishment of mass communications research components — with curricula, faculties, and other resources — in at least one university in an English-, Dutch-, Spanish-, and French-speaking country; (5) the growth of journalism history and biography series — similar to that of Cave at the University of the West Indies — which would tap information from old media still existent and from media pioneers; (6) studies of the roles of traditional and interpersonal communications in these small and compact societies where such roles are very important; (7) studies of the effects of multinational corporations and the earlier colonialism upon the mass media of the Caribbean; (8) more content and audience analyses of all media in all regions; and (9) more mass communications research on geographical areas that have been slighted, such as French Guiana, Suriname, Martinique, or Guadeloupe.

Some progress has been made: several universities have become involved in communications research, folk media forms are being used and studied (see chapter 26), and media and cultural imperialism by multinational corporations has become a topic of concern.

25

Education and Training
in Mass Communications

Mass communications education and training took root in the Spanish-speaking Caribbean more quickly than it did in other territories. Cuba had its first school of journalism in 1942, only seven years after Argentina initiated the first Latin American program. The Dominican Republic followed with a school in 1953. In the 1970s, Puerto Rico, Guyana, and Jamaica started programs. In his surveys of Latin American journalism education, Nixon (1981, 14) found that of the twenty countries reported upon, Haiti was the only one that had never attempted journalism education; he said that is the case because most media workers there are not full-time journalists.

At the advent of the 1980s, Nixon listed the following programs in the Caribbean: Cuba—Escuela de Periodismo at both the University of Havana and the University of the Orient; Dominican Republic—Instituto Dominicano de Periodismo (with a two-year program) and Departamento de Comunicación Social, Universidad Autonoma; Guyana—Program in Communication Studies, University of Guyana; Jamaica—Caribbean Institute of Mass Communications, University of the West Indies; Puerto Rico—Escuela de Comunicación Pública, the University of Puerto Rico, and Programa de Comunicación Pública, the University of the Sacred Heart.

Puerto Rico's two schools were stimulated by grants from the island's Angel Ramos Foundation, named after the late owner of the San Juan daily, *El mundo*. The foundation believed that the schools should deal in all types of communication education, not just newspaper. Funds have been provided for scholarships, seminars, and a visiting professorship.

Netherlands Antilles journalists traditionally received their training and education through workshops or study at universities in the Netherlands. After 1979, the Stichting Grafische Communicatie (SGC — Foundation Graphic Media) offered a series of five journalism workshops, each built on the previous ones. Specialized workshops on photography, small newspapers management, printing, and broadcasting also were offered. SGC has been involved in many aspects of professionalism — running seminars, making students aware of the media, promoting children's books in Papiamento, offering printing facilities on smaller islands, and establishing a periodical press (Interview, Snow 1980).

Because Netherlands Antilles newspapers are understaffed, day-long workshops were considered inappropriate by SGC, and the organization resorted to week-long sessions carried out after working hours. The foundation also has worked with the young University of the Netherlands Antilles in organizing international workshops in journalism and communication policy (see *Antillen Review* 1981).

CUBA

Of all Caribbean nations, Cuba has the most sophisticated and varied mass communications training programs. Having successfully advanced media education and training within the country, Cuba has expended much energy in recent years on international education. The International Film and Television School and the José Martí International Institute of Journalism have been inaugurated for this purpose. The latter has hosted courses for Latin American journalists, varying from two to four months, in theoretical and practical aspects of the profession, specialization areas, and the new information order.

The International Film and Television School, set up in December 1986 to help developing countries, had the famous Argentine filmmaker Fernando Birri as director. Birri announced that the school would be antiacademic and would produce films. Producing a new type of professional capable of mastering the techniques of film and television was the school's goal, he said (Valenzuela 1986). The school, which will train three hundred students at any given time, is divided into three levels: basics, experimental workshop, and advanced seminars. A multinational faculty provides an assortment of training experiences, including guest lectures from well-known international artists.

The government of Cuba provides facilities for the school, and the initial equipment and funds came from the New Latin American Film

Foundation. The institution is independent of the Cuban government (Castañeda 1987).

As indicated earlier, journalism education began in Cuba in 1942. Today, the education and training of journalists occur primarily on three levels: through courses and seminars offered by the Unión de Periodistas de Cuba (Union of Cuban Journalists, UPEC), at programs in the two aforementioned university faculties, and on the job.

UPEC, created in July 1963, has been at the forefront of much of the education and training in Cuba since the 1958 revolution. Its aim is the political, ideological, cultural, and technical improvement of its twenty-seven hundred members. UPEC has sponsored courses and symposia; developed a network of at least ten thousand amateur volunteer journalists throughout Cuba (and offered journalism courses in the provinces for them) (Interview, Benitez 1982); regularly published two trade periodicals, *UPEC* and *Fototécnica,* as well as other training materials; initiated training programs for nationals of other countries; and developed a media research storage institute, Centro Estudios Medios Difusión Masivos (CEMEDIM) (Interview, Coro Antich 1982).

UPEC's charge in journalism education was spelled out at the second Congress of Cuban Journalists in November 1966, which said that the organizations should: systematize the general, as well as specialized, education of journalists, especially in fundamental aspects of economic production in Cuba; teach each journalist a second language by 1970; systematize the education of correspondents in the interior; promote the interchange of journalists in certain aspects of professional practice; allow journalists to attend courses at universities; set up correspondence courses for journalists; and provide better cultural and ideological facilities for them (*Democratic Journalist* 1967; International Organization of Journalists 1976, 167–74). In 1967, UPEC established a Seminary of Professional Education, offering training sessions for active journalists over a six-month period. It also developed language courses for journalists and published a bimonthly professional periodical, *Boletín del periodista.*

Beginning in 1974, UPEC offered courses for nationals from other countries; that year, sixteen young people from Equatorial Guinea were trained. These courses led to the creation of UPEC's International Centre for Journalist Training, which offers two types of instruction—a basic course for young journalists from developing countries and seminars for Latin American journalists on media functions and ideological penetration by "North American imperialism." So far, two developing-countries courses, each of six-months' duration, have been offered. These include written examinations and practical exercises to test each stu-

25.1   Professional and trade periodicals dealing with Cuban mass media: *Fototécnica, Cine cubano* and *UPEC*.

dent's effectiveness and are concluded with a one-week work experience in a provincial newspaper. The Latin American seminars are attended by journalists who have worked in the profession for a considerable time. Participants are chosen by colleges or syndicates of journalists in Latin American countries. Between 1976 and 1980, the number of participants was twenty-one to thirty per year, and participants represented thirteen to sixteen countries. Participants received lectures from some of the most distinguished Cuban journalists. UPEC has also sponsored Cuban journalists to lecture and offer courses in Ethiopia, Mozambique, Nicaragua, and Grenada (Treffkorn 1982, 15–18). The post-Revolution, formal journalism schools were started at the University of Havana and the University of the Orient in 1963 and 1969, respectively. Total enrollment in these two programs and their two branches is about five hundred yearly. The University of Havana, which enrolls about fifty new students per year in its five-year program, has graduated about three thousand journalism specialists. Many have been students from abroad, mainly from the Soviet Union, Eastern Europe, North Korea, Vietnam, and parts of Africa and Latin America. The schools educate both young people and professional journalists who are returning for degrees. The latter meet with faculty members once a month until the end of the semester, when they spend fifteen days on campus taking examinations (Interview, Trelles 1982).

Irena Trelles, head of the faculty at the University of Havana, discussed the origins of the university's journalism school: "Before the Revolution, journalism was studied here. But it was necessary to start a specialty after the Revolution because the old type of journalism did not accommodate the needs of the Revolution. In addition, a lot of journalists left Cuba during the Revolution. We started in a nonscientific style. In 1975, the plan was modified where research became more rigorous and systematic in order to see which disciplines and topics to discuss" (Interview, Trelles 1982).

The modified study plan emphasized "basic" subjects, such as literature, philosophy, political economy, and history, in the first year. On the second level, a mixture of basic and specific subjects was offered, including grammar, writing, and methods of bibliographic research. The final cycle of courses dealt with a specialty and included theory and practice of journalism, written press, radio, and television. All through the program, however, students put into practice the knowledge they learned in the classroom; they wrote research papers, including a final diploma exercise, and incorporated ideology into their work. In 1982, this plan was being "corrected."

Writing skills are honed in "practica," limited to twelve to fifteen students and mainly taught by professional media personnel who collaborate with the full-time faculty. There is no laboratory publication, although students do contribute to university journals. The research project, which usually takes a semester to complete, is based on methodology inherited from sociology — surveys and content analyses. Trelles said that the program has used content analysis in a "very limited way so far" to characterize the profile of Cuban publications (Interview, Trelles 1982). Discussing the proportion of ideology to technique-oriented work, she said,

> Students are formed as ideological cadres so we do not separate

ideology from technique. Ideology is always present. We believe all journalists are ideological workers, although not all of them are party members. We emphasize no absolute ideology, except that students should not distort truthfulness, exactness, analysis, and historical analysis. In Cuba, we have the possibility of reaching a higher objectivity as we do not have economic pressure that the capitalist system has (Interview, Trelles 1982).

Carty (1978b) reported earlier that at least sixty-three courses at the journalism school dealt with some aspect of Communist ideology. Political education along ideological lines, according to a party official, takes place in a number of contexts. He said there is a high-level national school of political education and that others are operated by all mass organizations (trade unions, Committees for the Defense of the Revolution, etc.) and at the state and provincial levels. The differences between these schools and the universities are that the latter are open to all, do not have objectives for cadre work, and study social sciences from a humanistic view (Interview, Margolles Villanueva 1982).

Candidates for the journalism program at the University of Havana are evaluated on the grades they have obtained. There is no limitation placed on the number of students entering journalism, nor is there an attempt to have a balance between rural and urban or male and female students.

The majority of faculty members were educated in Cuba, where they received their master's degrees in a specialty in arts and letters (such as linguistics, history, grammar, classics, literature, technical and scientific information, journalism, or art history). Trelles said that some have taken courses abroad, in the Soviet Union as well as in capitalist countries (Interview, Trelles 1982). The faculty is supplemented with professional media personnel, some of whom work full-time for the university.

Textbooks vary also. Besides using translations of Soviet and North American books, the school lately has added more works written by Cubans and published in Cuba. Trelles said that North American journalism has a "great influence" in the school's instruction: "We use structures that are those in the United States, for example, the inverted pyramid" (Interview, Trelles 1982). My analysis of media-related books in the UPEC bookstore in 1982 showed that, as would be expected, most depended on Soviet theory. Locally written, professional books have been encouraged by a royalty scheme that pays authors on a per page basis; the rate of royalty is increased for more technical books. On a book with an initial press run of ten thousand, a new author would receive 6 pesos per page (U.S. $4.92) and a well-established author on science, 16 to 20 pesos per page (U.S. $13.12 to $16.40). This scheme has been described as a good incentive that has spurred a number of people to write (Interview, Coro Antich 1982). Books and periodicals are relatively inexpensive in Havana; a paperback text costs considerably less than a dollar, and a trade journal such as *Cine cubano* about twenty cents.

After graduation, students are placed in positions according to where they reside and the needs of the media in that locale. The Central Planning Board of the party is responsible for the placement. Whether the assignment is made strictly by the board or by the student's choice depends upon the student's scholastic record (Interview, Trelles 1982). Graduates, like all other Cubans, must first complete two years of social service to the country.

Graduation from a journalism school is not a prerequisite for working in the field, although today only a very small minority have not received a higher education. Jacinto Grande, director of the youth daily, *Juventud rebelde,* discussed the way training has moved from the job site to the university since his paper was started in 1965:

> When we started, young people had an attitude about journalism, but they didn't know anything about it. Our first problem was to train journalists. Now, almost all journalists have graduated from the university. Initially, in the 1960s, journalists worked for us and studied at the university at the same time. Now, we have created a professional attitude and we can require that a beginning person be graduated from the university. Getting our journalists to a university level education is one of our main successes. Originally, we just looked for people who wanted to work in journalism. Now, we ask for graduates — not just journalists, but lawyers and historians also. We select personnel in cooperation with the school of journalism (Interview, Grande 1982).

An official at Radio Havana Cuba, the external broadcasting system, also said that he usually hires graduates from Havana's school of journalism; although, he added, there are certain persons among the station's two hundred staff members who do not need degrees — veteran journalists, recognized specialists, or foreigners in the language departments (Interview, Prado 1982).

Finally, a branch of mass communications that did most of its training on the job is documentary filmmaking. Cuba's most popular documentary maker, Santiago Alvarez, said that all of the personnel working at the Cuban Institute of Cinematographic Art and Industry (ICAIC) learned their skills while at that agency. ICAIC offered its staff occasional three- or four-month courses, often led by foreign technicians from both socialist and capitalist countries. Alvarez said, "Most of us learned film through practical ways. When ICAIC was born, all of us were marked by the neorealism of Italian films, but as the organization grew, the foreign influences became multiple. In its first few years, ICAIC brought in top documentary artists from abroad. They taught us, and now we are the school of documentary film in Cuba" (Interview, Alvarez 1982).

These experiences may be exceptional in Cuban mass communications. Although a few positions are still filled by nongraduates, the trend in the past decade or more has been to augment the level of education required of those aspiring to media careers.

COMMONWEALTH CARIBBEAN

Formal mass media education in the English-speaking Caribbean was nearly nonexistent until 1974 when a diploma program was instituted at the University of the West Indies at Mona, Jamaica. Traditionally, most of the media training in the region was given in short in-service workshops organized by the Caribbean Publishers and Broadcasters Association, the Press Association of Jamaica, the U.S. Information Service, or the University of the West Indies Extramural Department. Some training was accomplished abroad, usually under the sponsorship of the BBC or Thomson Foundation.

Other organizations, then and since, also offered short courses. The London-based Commonwealth Broadcasting Association gave on-site training in late 1975, and the Thomson Foundation of Cardiff helped train at conferences in Barbados and elsewhere.

But the genesis for the first permanent, formal training program was the Jamaican government's request for a UNESCO consultant to discuss a training scheme in 1968. Simultaneously, the University of the West Indies included in its 1970–1972 expansion proposals a training program in communications media. Because of immediate funding difficulties, the one-year diploma course in mass communications was not established until October 1974. For the first few years, the Jamaican government provided the bulk of the financial support for the program, later called the Caribbean Institute of Mass Communication (CARIMAC). By 1984, the Jamaican government funded CARIMAC, while the Bonn-based Friedrich-Ebert-Stiftung sponsored the communications training program there (Interview, Brown 1984).

Thirty students, seventeen of whom were Jamaicans, were enrolled in the institute by 1975–1976. To be admitted, they had to be graduates of an approved university in a relevant field or individuals with practical experience in mass media or other qualifications of special relevance to the course. Courses taken by the students during their year of study at the institute in the mid-1970s included "History, Politics and Culture of the Caribbean," "Principles of Sociology and Economics," "Communication Principles," "Professional Communication Skills," "Writing and Editing for Print Media," and "Broadcast Writing and Production."

After only two years of operations, in the fall of 1976 the program expanded from being solely a one-year diploma course to also offering a three-year degree curriculum leading to a bachelor of arts in communications. Under the new structure, first-year students took "Communication Principles," "Use of English," and two courses chosen from language, literature, liberal arts, or physical sciences. In their second year, mass communication majors enrolled in "Broadcast Writing and Production," "Newspaper Writing and Editing," "Visual Communication," "Development of Civilization," or "History of the Caribbean," and one course chosen from liberal arts or physical sciences.

Five courses were required in the final year, chosen from "Advanced Radio-Television-Film Production" or "Advanced Journalistic Techniques," "Communication Analysis and Planning" or "Advertising Methods and Strategies," "Communication and Society," "Caribbean Study," and one course in liberal arts or physical sciences. Additionally, students pursuing the mass communication option had to complete one two-month or two one-month periods of supervised internship with a media enterprise.

The first director of the institute, Dr. Peter Pringle, cited a number of the problems in developing a mass communications training program in the region. Initially, he said, the main problems dealt with a lack of equipment and insufficient awareness on the part of university officials of the unique requirements associated with equipping such a curriculum. "The administration's concept of equipment was one typewriter," he said; "originally, the building housing the institute was designed without providing for television instruction. We spent the first year convincing administrators of the importance of TV" (Interview, Pringle 1976).

Another problem encountered is common to many Third World nations embarking upon mass media training for the first time—the lack of lead time between the conceptualization of the program and its implementation. Foreign lecturers were hired to teach in the University of the West Indies program before it was actually ready, and they had very little chance to acquaint themselves with the region or the university.

Other difficulties Pringle emphasized dealt with the diversity of the students, their expectations, and the prejudices of the mass media for which they aspire to work. Pringle explained,

> Because we group together the islands of the Commonwealth Caribbean and we have students enrolled from nine different island nations, it is a challenge to come up with content relevant to all. How can you discuss press law or freedom of the press, for instance, when these concepts differ so widely from island to island? Also, students are drawn to the program from all levels and disciplines, so in any given class there will be those who have been station managers; at the same time, there are new recruits to the field (Interview, Pringle 1976).

Institute students complained about the language in use, pointing out, for example, that they use British style manuals, when, in fact, Caribbean English is different from standard English. They also avoided using the inverted pyramid as an expediency measure, explaining that Caribbean people have a great deal of time to devote to reading, which they enjoy.

Pringle said that because the Caribbean society suffers from a certain degree of snobbery, his program did not receive the enthusiastic support of media personnel. "Great importance is attached to degrees here, and mass media people are fascinated by those who go abroad for their education," he added. In other cases, "mass media look to us to turn out graduates who have an education, but not training in journalism. They don't want us to train journalists; they think they can do that better" (Interview, Pringle 1976).

The conservative nature of the region, according to Pringle, also hindered institute trainees from practicing new journalistic concepts: "The usual reaction of editors and broadcasters to our students is, 'Don't you come here with those fancy ideas.' Media people have imitated the formats and styles of their predecessors so that newspapers, for example, look like they did a generation or two ago. Our students, after leaving the institute, are frustrated that they cannot apply what they learned with us" (Interview, Pringle 1976).

Finally, the authoritarian relationship between Commonwealth Caribbean governments and the mass media presented problems for institute lecturers. For example, one of Pringle's fears was that "once we make an impact and governments see how communication can be used to manipulate, the politicians may wish to incorporate us as part of government information services." He added, "We're seeing that already by the number of students the governments are sending to our course. People who control the purse strings will want us to train people to carry out their activities" (Interview, Pringle 1976).

In 1976, lecturers said that it was virtually impossible to teach students about the critical function of mass media. One student, an information officer from Belize, explained that he could not criticize government policies; he would be fired. As Pringle said, "Governments don't have to suppress down here. All they have to do is remind media personnel that if they don't keep quiet, they will lose their jobs. Of course, there are not enough media in the islands to accommodate those who have lost their positions. This leaves a chilling effect on media people" (Interview, Pringle 1976).

More than a decade after Pringle's experiences, CARIMAC offered a one-year diploma and the bachelor of arts in mass communications. The diploma program required "History, Politics and Culture of the Caribbean," "Principles of Sociology and Economics," "Communication and Society," "Media and Language," and "Communication Techniques." Required courses for the bachelor's degree were, in the first year, "Use of English" and "Communication and Society"; in the second year, "Communication Techniques," "Communication Research Methods," and "History of the Caribbean"; and in the third year, "Communication Techniques," "Communication Analysis and Planning," and "Caribbean Studies" (a mini-thesis).

Broadcasting courses concentrated on production, although training of announcers and presenters also was offered. Students produced broadcasts that could be aired; print journalism students published a laboratory newspaper. Techniques courses were offered in modules (each of five weeks' duration, eight hours per week) on audiovisual production, film production, print journalism, radio production, and television production. Each module included anywhere from four to fourteen courses from which to choose.

About 120 students are enrolled in the CARIMAC courses, very few of which are theoretical. After nearly fifteen years in operation, the institute still has to cope with editors who hesitate to hire the graduates (Interview, Brown 1984). However, Brown (1986, 14) suggested that this situation is changing rapidly. "There is no major media house in the Caribbean now that advertises vacancies without requiring at minimum a diploma in mass communication," he said (Brown 1986, 14).

CARIMAC, having made achievements in teaching and training, plans to build up its research capability and to move into the telecommunications field. However, these plans may depend upon additions to the faculty, which now is made up of six instructors (Brown 1986, 15).

26

Popular Culture in the Caribbean:
A Literature Review

Snippets of Caribbean popular culture have recently made the international scene, as Africans, Europeans, and other Americans dance to the rhythm of reggae, cheer on world-famous West Indian cricket or baseball players, and party at overseas versions of Carnival. Occasionally, they may listen to commercialized calypso, read a novel, play, or short story of one of the many Caribbean literary geniuses, or take in a Cuban film at an art theater.

Corresponding to this internationalization has been the development of a field of study among scholars. However, the study of Caribbean popular culture, much like that of the field generally, has been very recent, uneven—with some artifacts receiving much attention while others go unnoticed—scattered, fragmented, and tentative.

Reasons for this state of affairs can be found in the diversity of backgrounds of those researching the field, in general academic snobbery, and in the definition of popular culture itself. Anthropologists, economists, journalists, ethnomusicologists, historians, and sociologists, among others, have contributed to the literature. These different approaches to the subject are, no doubt, beneficial, but with so many disciplines involved, popular culture specialists remain "academic boat people," drifting about without a home.

Popular culture has not been studied often and well because of the eliteness of academic communities, whose members are usually repulsed by objects of mass culture, or at least pretend to be. As Lewis (1979, 35) wrote, only "recently, and grudgingly" have social scientists in the United States and Europe conceded that contemporary culture is worth studying. Popular culture has been dumped on the same academic trash heap that was occupied by mass communications and information a generation or more ago. Social scientists "discovered" the importance of mass communications in their studies only after governmental, business, and other interests put up the money for research.

Lewis (1979, 36) outlined the four major criticisms of popular culture used by the academic community as justifications for ignoring it: (1) the negative character of popular culture creation — undesirable because it is mass-produced by profit-motivated entrepreneurs for the gratification of a paying audience; (2) the negative effects on high culture of borrowing and eventual debasement; (3) the negative effects on the popular culture audience of spurious, and sometimes emotionally harmful, gratification; and (4) the negative effects on society of wide distribution channels that reduce the level of cultural quality.

Probably most detrimental has been the confusion associated with trying to define popular culture. Complaining that the term has too many meanings and too little theory and classification, Lewis (1979, 40) said, "Thus, one has labelled as popular culture peasant art in Yugoslavia, folk dance in Nigeria, working class culture in Elizabethan England, Pompeian graffiti, contemporary rock music, Mexican-American barrio wall murals, and the products of Walt Disney."

In his own efforts to delineate the field, Lewis used the subcategories of mass, folk, and elite cultures. He believed popular culture should not be limited to the study of industrialized societies but also should include folk-based, traditional ones. Elite culture, he said, is usually not part of popular culture but is defined within the popular culture context (Lewis 1979, 41). Popular culture in the Caribbean will be broadly categorized because of these unclear and inconsistent definitions.

A number of questions about Caribbean popular culture are left unanswered. How does one categorize Caribbean folk forms that have become popular? With all the superimpositions of cultures in the region, what is Caribbean popular culture as distinguished from United States, British, French, Dutch, or Spanish popular culture? Where is the cutoff point between mass communications and popular culture, or is there one?

In this literature review, advertising, television, and magazines, although they play large roles in Caribbean popular culture, will be omitted. Studies of these and other mass communication forms can be found in abundance elsewhere. Film and comic art, however, are included because they are such integral parts of popular culture. Also included are music, Carnival, and sports. This review is not meant to be exhaustive but rather to be representative.

GENERAL RESOURCES

Besides sources on Caribbean mass communications (Lent, 1977b, 1981a; Cuthbert and Pidgeon 1981; Brown and Sanatan 1987; Soderlund and Surlin 1985) that are very useful to the study of popular culture, other more specific materials also exist.

Much appears in the periodical literature, including an annual dealing with popular culture in Latin America and the Caribbean. Initiated at the beginning of the 1980s, the well-edited *Studies in Latin American Popular Culture* is thick with articles of relevance. Other popular culture journals, including the *Journal of Popular Culture* and other periodicals of Bowling Green University's Popular Press and the now-defunct *International Popular Culture,* have carried occasional articles, as have area studies periodicals such as *Caribbean Review, Caribbean Quarterly, Jamaica Journal, Caribbean Contact,* and the many periodicals of Cuba and the Dominican Republic.

Cuba is the most developed of Caribbean nations in the production of periodical literature on popular culture. *Cine cubano,* in more than 115 issues since it was started in 1960, has done a splendid job of documenting Cuban and, to a lesser extent, Latin American film. It has had scores of interviews with prominent directors, such as Alvarez, Solás, García Espinosa, Gutiérrez Aléa, and Gómez, as well as reviews and essays on films. Photography is discussed in *Fototécnica,* journalism in *UPEC* and *CEMEDIM,* and sports in *Semanario deportivo LPV,* which dates to the 1960s. Additionally, Cuban institutions regularly publish journals for literature, theater, and dance.

In Jamaica, the *Journal of West Indian Literature* was initiated in 1987 by the University of the West Indies (see review in *Caribbean Contact,* June 1987, 10–11).

Longer treatments discussing Caribbean culture in general terms include Nettleford (1979) and two in a UNESCO series, "Studies and Documents on Cultural Policies." Nettleford covered all popular cultural genres, including theater, dance, music, film, painting, mass media, and sports, placing them in the context of their use for development and social change. The UNESCO documents dealt with Cuba and Jamaica and were published in the late 1970s. They discussed cultural associations, their objectives and budgets, and other information in light of national cultural policy. I have also edited a forthcoming volume that includes Carnival overseas, in Antigua, and in the Virgin Islands; *zouk;* reggae and youth; music and elections; basketball; radio in Guadeloupe; and radio drama.

CARNIVAL

A number of popular culture forms are identified with Carnival; among these are calypso, mas' (masquerade bands), and steel bands. A product of Trinidad, Carnival in recent times has been exported as one of that country's major products to smaller Caribbean countries, Canada, England, and the United States. At the same time, it has become highly commercialized.

Relative to its significance, Carnival has not been researched extensively. Hill (1972) and Boyke (1973) wrote books on Carnival in Trinidad and Tobago; the latter featured among other essays one by the calypsonian, "The Mighty Sparrow." Others have explored smaller-island carnivals: Abrahams (1970) focused on Tobago, Crowley (1955) on St. Lucia, and Abrahams and Bauman (1978) on St. Vincent. St. Vincent was also featured in *Carnival: St. Vincent and the Grenadines* (n.d.). *Caribbean Quarterly* devoted its fourth issue of 1956 to Carnival in Trinidad and the rest of the region. Crowley (1956) studied traditional Carnival masques, and Pearse (1956) did a historical appraisal of Trinidadian Carnival in the nineteenth century. Belizean Carnival was written about by Briceño (1981).

Manning (1978), who has written more on Caribbean popular culture than nearly any other scholar, observed Antiguan Carnival, showing how it differed from that of Trinidad. He said that Antigua's Carnival has more emblems of island identity, regional harmony, and themes of black identity and is held in August.

Some writers have concentrated on the overseas Carnival celebrations established by West Indians in New York, London, Toronto, Montreal, and, to a lesser degree, elsewhere in the United States. All described the difficulties in setting up Carnival because of class, race, and island differences. Manning (1983a) said that Toronto Carnival, a year-round affair whenever Caribbean people get together, has distinctly Canadian characteristics. Cohen (1980, 1982) found similar political splits associated with the creation of a London Carnival.

Discussing exportation of the Carnival industry, Manning (1983b) said it has moved from populist roots ("we ting") to the "Greatest Show on Earth," with significant changes in its artistic and commercial organization. For example, masquerade bands have become bigger, more spectacular, and more costly, making them a middle-class hobby that is out of the reach of many former participants. Steel bands no longer play a big role in island Carnival, according to Manning, because their music is inaudible in the streets since they lack modern sound systems. Calypso has been replaced by soca (simpler lyrics and heavier baseline rhythm) because it is more commercially marketable abroad. Placing some of the blame on the Trinidad Tourist Board, Manning (1983b, 13) said that Trinidad Carnival "has thus become less a popular festival and more a stage spectacle, media event, and tourist attraction."

MUSIC

Popular music in the Caribbean always has had an uphill climb, battling for a place with U.S. and European sounds. Radio stations for years played predominantly foreign music of the Billboard Top 20 or Top 40 variety. Since the 1970s, some stations in the British and Dutch islands have instituted policies requiring a percentage of broadcast time for Caribbean music.

Whether because of this policy or on its own merit, Caribbean music has caught on in the Caribbean, North America, and Europe. The region has become an exporter of music, such as *zouk* of Martinique and Guadeloupe and reggae of Jamaica.

Since the mid-1980s, *zouk,* a type of music relying on rhythm, participatory singing, and dance, has been number one on French Antilles radio charts; it has also sold better in the rest of the Caribbean, Africa, and Europe than any previous Creole music. Guilbault (1987b, 9) has written an interesting analysis of *zouk,* calling it Carnival music and "music of freedom." She said that the music, associated with the Kassav Group, is closely correlated with young people who are unemployed. In five years, the Kassav produced twenty *zouk* albums, several of which became gold platters. Others who have written about French Antilles music include Desroches (1985), who discussed traditional Martiniquan music, and Renard (1981), who focused on popular music of Creole Caribbean. Jallier and Lossen (1985) did an overview of Antillean music in their book, providing lyrics, interviews, and illustrations. The work dealt with the origins and outside influences upon the music, Antillean songs, and contemporary music. Guilbault, who has become one of the most prolific writers on music of Creole Caribbean, has also contributed a monograph on twenty-two musical instruments she identified on St. Lucia (Guilbault 1983).

Reggae is probably the best-known Caribbean music worldwide. Numerous writers have described its lyrics and musicians and its roots in Rastafarianism. Among books on reggae are those by Kallyndyr and Dalrymple (1973), Davis and Simon (1977) (considered the most useful analysis), and White (1983), a biography of the first reggae superstar, Bob Marley. Some periodicals have featured reggae music in articles;

among these are *Rolling Stone* (Thomas 1976; McCormack 1976; Cromelin 1975; Crowe 1977; Goodwin 1975), the *Village Voice* (Carr 1975; Cooper 1980; Fergusson 1982), *Black Echoes* (Griffith 1976, 1978), *Melody Maker* (Coleman 1976; Goldman 1979; Williams 1972), and *Time* (1976), to name a few.

Reggae, which evolved over fifteen years with African, Jamaican, and U.S. influences, is one of the very few distinctly Jamaican music forms. It developed when Jamaican artists combined rhythm and blues with their own "mento" to form the bluebeat, which was followed by "ska," then rock-steady, and finally, reggae. The music uses themes of ghetto protest, religious/philosophical expressions of Rastafarianism, black awareness, and freedom from oppression. Winders (1983, 67) labeled it Jamaican music produced in Jamaica, the music of the slums of Trenchtown, and Jamaica's major export, rivaling bauxite.

Hebdige (1977, 430), in a short but worthwhile history of reggae, discussed its use by Manley and other politicians, as well as its chances of survival. He believed reggae's form guaranteed autonomy and resistance to outside influences. Hebdige's description of reggae is worth quoting: "transmogrified American 'soul' music, with an overlay of salvaged African rhythms, and an undercurrent of pure Jamaican rebellion." Bilby (1977, 17), relating the reluctant interest of the United States in reggae, said a breakthrough occurred in 1977, when CBS Records bought Jamaica's Federal Records and, with other foreign record companies, promoted reggae as a way of life. He classified reggae as popular music and as urban folk music (Bilby 1977, 18).

Cuthbert (1985, 385) provided one of the few empirical studies on Caribbean music and its audience. Surveying three hundred Jamaican youth, she found that reggae was the favorite of only the lower-socioeconomic youth; that of the favorite singers of Jamaican youth, six were foreign and four local (three were reggae); and that upper-class teenagers preferred the imported music.

Because reggae calls attention to aspects of Jamaica the government is not proud of, reggae is banned from radio until after midnight and is not represented as a West Indian art form at the Caribbean Festival of the Arts. Jamaicans hear reggae at dance halls, where they tape the music; they also purchase records from independent recording studios that also own record shops. Thus, as Rastafarian psychologist Leachim Semaj said, reggae is part of Jamaican popular culture but not of the national culture.

Other sources on reggae and/or Rastafarianism are de Albuquerque (1979), Huey (1981), Gritter (1980), Farrell (1976), Reckford (1982), Spencer (1975, 1977), and Steffens (1981). On the broader topic of Jamaican music, Clarke (1980) wrote of its evolution in his book, *Jah*

Music, and Garth White did two long articles, one tracing traditional music and its influence upon popular music (1982), the other showing the merger of the two (1984). O'Gormon (1972) wrote about the study of Jamaican music, and a bibliography on Bob Marley was made available through the National Library of Jamaica.

A music form that has come under closer academic scrutiny is calypso, perhaps because of its political content and use. From at least 1898, when Calypsonian Richard Coeur de Leon attacked the British for wanting to abolish the Port of Spain City Council, the political content was present. Since then politicians, among them Maurice Bishop, Albert Gomes, and Eric Williams, recognized the clout of calypso. In recent years, calypso has been the subject of numerous articles and a 1986 seminar held in Trinidad (see Marshall 1986). There has also been a controversial debate about calypso's origins (one writer claiming it was created in Barbados in 1627).

At least one calypsonian, "The Mighty Sparrow," has put down some of his memoirs in a 1986 Inprint booklet for the occasion of his fiftieth birthday. Although it is a beginning, with reminiscences by other calypsonians, his teachers, and his wife, the booklet is poorly organized and lacks substantial content (see Sealy 1986). Perhaps more interesting is an article that was written after the Association for Caribbean Studies, at its 1985 meeting, invited "The Mighty Sparrow" (Slinger Francisco) and "Lord Kitchener" (Aldwin Roberts) to talk about calypso. Their insights on the meaning, purpose, and competition of calypso were presented in the *Journal of Caribbean Studies* (Dathorne 1985–1986). Earlier, another calypso singer, Raymond Quevedo ("Atilla the Hun") did an excellent study of calypso up to 1951 (Quevedo 1983), in which he discussed the music's development, his role, and the lyrics, many of which are included along with the musical scores and photographs. Lashley (1982) wrote his doctoral dissertation at Howard University on the topic of calypso, and the June 1985 issue of *Caribbean Quarterly* carried the theme of "Carnival Calypso and the Music of Confrontation."

Among periodical literature, works by Lewis, McLean, Manning, Elder, and Austin stand out. Lewis (1981) concentrated on the music of "The Mighty Shadow" (Winston Bailey), analyzing the lyrics, citing many verses, and meshing them all with what Bailey said in an interview. Lewis went further to describe calypso's occasional tendency toward violence, cruelty, and belligerence, to briefly trace the music's genesis, and to offer the following definition.

> One of the Caribbean's most outstanding art forms is the Trinidadian calypso. More than a "spontaneous typical West Indian song,"

the calypso has long since metamorphosed from earthy spontaneous outpourings to a sophisticated and profound socio-political and cultural medium of expression. Not only has the calypso matured in terms of its lyrical content, but also in terms of its ability to incorporate other musical sounds into its own, e.g., the creativity demonstrated in the attempt to combine North American Soul and Disco music with the calypso. These attempts are evident in Lord Beckette's (Alston Cyrus Beckette) Discocalypsoes and the popular Soca (soul and calypso) music originated by Lord Shortie (Garfield Blackmah) (Lewis 1981, 20).

Looking at the use and impact of calypso before and during Maurice Bishop's revolution on Grenada, McLean (1986) studied the work of Cecil Belfon ("Flying Turkey"). She said that in 1976, Belfon talked to Bishop about a breakaway calypso tent (organization), called "We Tent," which opened a year later and was useful to Bishop's New Jewel Movement, otherwise shut out of the formal media. After the 1979 revolution, Belfon, with other progressive calypsonians, pushed the revolution's idealism, education, and political aims, in the process "bridging the gap between the content of the song and the Party's policies" (McLean 1986, 92).

McLean (1986, 87) also provided a compact list of uses for calypso: (1) a vehicle of social and political protest, (2) a device to analyze male-female relationships, (3) a medium of information and agitation, (4) a means of highlighting a country's economic dilemma and internal contradictions, (5) an exercise in institutional abuse, (6) an avenue to explore imbalances between the haves and the have-nots, and (7) a part of the cultural heritage of the region.

Calypso and politics in Trinidad and Tobago, St. Vincent, and Barbados are the subjects of Manning's article. Showing how smaller islands now claim some of the best calypsonians, Manning said that these men are also among the region's most volatile political personalities. He described the devastating effects Becket's "Horn for Them" had upon the bid of the ruling party in St. Vincent's 1984 election and the role of "The Mighty Gabby" as a thorn in the side of the Barbados prime minister, the late Tom Adams. Gabby's songs, most of which were banned from radio, included the popular "Boots," against Barbados militarization; "Mr. T," about stealing votes; "Jack," against an official who wanted to keep Barbadians off the beaches; and "Culture," on the U.S. cultural invasion of the Caribbean. Richards (1986), who portrayed Gabby in some detail, attributed revolutionary and radical qualities to his music. Hylton (1975) also looked at the political role of calypso, while Roberts (1972) discussed calypso as one aspect of black music.

One of the first Caribbean academicians to carry out in-depth research on calypso was Jacob Elder, who wrote about male-female relationships in the music (1968) and, later, about calypso's morphology (1973). Elder, in a content analysis of 107 calypsos, reported that there were more aggressive than nonaggressive songs, that the female theme predominated over that of the male, and that aggressiveness towards males in songs decreased over the years. In his psychoanalysis of calypso, the author probed the male's hostility to the mother in West Indian society (Elder 1968).

Critiquing Elder's work, Austin (1976, 76) stated that the aggression in calypso toward the mother cannot be inferred from aggressive remarks made about women. In a rambling essay that had much more to say about male-female relationships than about calypso, Austin said calypsonians sing about sex because their lower-class audiences traditionally appreciated boasting about sexual feats. Modern audiences, according to Austin, are better educated, and thus calypsos developed more varied lyrics with less focus on the negative aspects of women (Austin 1976, 80–81).

In a different type of study, Malm and Wallis (1985) compared Trinidad's calypso with Sri Lanka's *baila*.

Another Carnival derivative, steel band, was featured in a book by Bartholomew (1980). Many types of Caribbean music (ska, calypso, reggae, etc.) will be discussed in a forthcoming book by Hebdige; he plans to trace the roots of the music and describe its style and the sense of cultural identity that developed alongside it. Pearse (1978–1979) also scanned the spectrum of Caribbean music and related it to popular culture, while Thompson (1980) analyzed the music content of Puerto Rican newspapers during the Spanish colonial period. Jenkins and Jenkins (1982) and Hadel (1973) wrote about Garifuna and Carib music, respectively, in Belize.

FILM

As we have seen, the Caribbean country with the most established and competitive film is Cuba, where international film festivals and training schemes are regularly offered (see chapter 12). Cuban film is very well documented in the regularly published, quality periodical *Cine cubano* and in many books and articles. Indices to *Cine cubano* and filmographies have been compiled by Douglas (1980), Esquieu (1979), and García Mesa (1977). The famous documentary director, Santiago Alvarez (1975), wrote a book on cinema and the Revolution, and Fanshel (1982) compiled interviews with seven famous directors and critiques of twenty films into a volume. Other books were written by Fornet (1982) and Chanan (1985).

Julianne Burton (1977, 1978) has written profusely on Cuban popular culture and film; usually her work takes the form of interviews. Her interview with Manuel Octavio Gómez on popular culture appeared in *Jump/Cut* (1979), and her valuable interviews with Julio García Espinosa on theory and practice of film and popular culture were published in *Studies in Latin American Popular Culture* (1982a) and *Quarterly Review of Film Studies* (1982b). Besides these, other periodicals that have had occasional articles are *Afterimage, Film Quarterly, Cineaste, Pensamiento crítico, Arte, Granma Weekly Review,* and *Sight and Sound* (see Lent 1981a, Lent forthcoming).

The literature on film in the rest of the Caribbean is made up of scattered articles that discuss local films in the few producing countries and audiences and locations for foreign films. Concerning the Netherlands Antilles, van Gorkom (1959) and Swindels (1977) wrote on film in Suriname. Commonwealth Caribbean film is served with occasional articles, one of the oldest being Sellers (1951), as well as with reviews of the few locally produced films, such as "The Harder They Come" and "Countryman," both from Jamaica. Sierra (1980) wrote a thirty-page piece on Dominican Republic film. *Variety,* especially in its special editions or sections on Latin America, carries up-to-date journalistic accounts of film businesses in the islands.

SPORTS

Sports perform a very important role in Caribbean popular culture, with cricket, soccer, and baseball traditionally being the most popular. However, the Mandles (1988) showed that, in the 1980s, basketball has increased in popularity, partly because of the televised National Basketball Association games received from the United States via satellite overspill and/or cable. Using participation/observation techniques, they studied many basketball players in Trinidad and Tobago, where Jay, a referee, gave clinics.

Cricket's significance in the Commonwealth Caribbean is attested to by the festivals built around it. Manning (1981) examined the festival in Bermuda, which, he said, is next to Christmas as the major celebration. After discussing the festival's social history, its carnivalesque character, and the ancillary activity of gambling, Manning took the reader on tour of a cricket festival. He proposed that the festivals symbolically depicted a "reflexive, assertive sense of black culture and a stark awareness of black economic dependency on whites." In an earlier article, Manning (1973) did the same type of analysis of the cricket clubs of black Bermudians, reporting that they had evolved into major centers of sport, entertainment, and sociability. St. Pierre (1973) also wrote about West Indian cricket, as did C. L. R. James (1963), the noted historian, teacher, and journalist, who analyzed the game in his autobiography.

In Cuba and the Dominican Republic, baseball is favored. The history of Cuban baseball has been well studied in books by Hernández (1969), Enríquez (1968), and Capteillo (1971). Pickering (1978) treated Cuban baseball as part of his volume on sports in Communist countries.

Fimrite (1977) provided empirical evidence about baseball's popularity among Cubans. He analyzed the content of *Semanario deportivo LPV,* the leading Cuban sports periodical, from 1969 through 1972. He said that the periodical usually devoted seven of its thirty-six pages to baseball, and that thirty of 127 covers featured this sport. Wagner (1982) compared baseball in Cuba and Nicaragua, two Latin American countries in the throes of revolution. He provided an overview of the sport's development, role, and success in Cuba. Fidel's philosophy concerning this U.S. import is that sport is the right of the people, integrated into the Revolution. According to Wagner, baseball came to Cuba in 1864, and when the popular classes assumed power in 1959, the sport came with them.

COMIC ART

Although cartoonists exist throughout the Caribbean, only in Cuba are cartoons and comics an established popular art. The Cubans sponsor international humor festivals at least yearly and publish humor magazines. *De De Té,* published as a weekly supplement of *Juventud rebelde,* consists mainly of the work of Cuba's famous gag and political cartoonists.

Reporting regularly upon Cuban cartoonists and other graphic artists are the *Granma Weekly Review,* in its English-language overseas edition of the national daily,[1] *CEMEDIM,* and *UPEC,* the latter two published for journalists in Havana.

In the Commonwealth Caribbean, the literature on comic art is very sparse; thus, when journalistic treatments appear, such as those in *Caribbean Contact* (1975a, 1975b), they become very useful. Anthologies of political cartoons have been published in at least Trinidad and Guyana. Hitchins (1959) collected political cartoons that appeared in the *Trinidad*

Guardian and the *Sunday Guardian* from 1954 to 1959, while the *Mirror,* the opposition newspaper of the Jagans in Guyana, pulled together a number of its cartoons that attacked the Forbes Burnham government. Tarter (1985), in his University of Washington thesis on Haiti, devoted some attention to cartoons.

CONCLUSION

Other aspects of Caribbean popular culture have been dealt with, such as satire and literature (Crowley 1977), funeral wakes and their music in St. Lucia (Guilbault 1987a), nicknames and license plates as identification and cultural placement (Manning 1974), and the internationally known posters (Goldman 1984) and public graphics of Cuba (Kunzle 1975). Popular drama has been studied in journals on theater in Cuba and literature in the West Indies, in a larger manuscript by Ford-Smith (1980), and in many articles, including those that made up a special issue of *Carib* (1986) on "Caribbean Theatre." That issue had articles on theater in Jamaica and the French West Indies. The latter country is covered in works by Jeanne (1980) and Zobdar Quitman (1981). Cornevin (1973) wrote about Haitian theater.

Much remains to be accomplished. On a general level, there is a need for a center that would integrate into a whole the various aspects of popular culture, preserve its artifacts, and record its traditions through oral histories with pioneering artists. This work should not be isolated to one island or island group but rather should include the entire region. A university curriculum on popular culture, eventually leading to a diploma or degree, would help legitimize the field of study.

Specifically, some popular culture genres have received less attention than others. More study of topics such as comic art, steel band, or various popular sports would be appropriate, as would studies of the culture policies of various governments.

27

Overall Trends and Developments

Colonialists brought printing and journalism to the Caribbean relatively late compared with other areas where they launched presses, such as Latin American or Asia. The first press in the English-settled islands was in 1716; in the French region, probably 1725; in the Dutch region, 1790 to 1793; and in the Danish region, 1770. Even the Spanish, noted for setting up presses in their settlements much earlier, did not establish presses in Cuba until 1723 and in Puerto Rico until 1806.

A few aspects of the colonial experience in journalism are interesting sidelights to the history of the Caribbean. For example, some of the independence movements of the region were led by journalist-nationalists, such as Inniss and Wickham of Barbados, Marryshow of Grenada, Martí of Cuba, or Nuñez de Caceras of the Dominican Republic. Women played an early role in journalism, with the three Stockdale sisters running the *Bermuda Gazette* at the beginning of the nineteenth century, Mary Baldwin operating the *Weekly Jamaica Courant* in 1722, Mrs. Browne doing her *Mrs. Browne's Roseau Gazette and Dominica Chronicle* in 1791, and the widows of William Lee, Richard Hatchett, and Jean Bénard publishing newspapers in Curaçao, St. Croix, and Guadeloupe, respectively.

Lingering traits of colonialism that have not been obliterated relate to cultural and media dependency and governmental control. The first newspapers often were started by colonialists, or sympathetic members of the elite, who gathered and wrote news as if the masses did not matter. Much of the content of the early newspapers rehashed, months late, news of the metropolitan country in Europe, and in some colonies, editors were on temporary loan — on secondment from their positions in Europe. When broadcasting was introduced much later, its backers were

Rediffusion or Thomson of England and United States, French, or Dutch networks or companies. Much of broadcasting's news and entertainment programming emanated from outside the region.

Although changes have been made — editors are not on secondment any longer, and most media are locally owned — foreign influences are still prominent in the Caribbean's mass media.

In at least Puerto Rico, the U.S. Virgin Islands, Guadeloupe, Martinique, French Guiana, and various parts of the Commonwealth Caribbean, outside entities own newspapers and broadcasting stations. Among the current foreign owners are Worrell Newspapers, Gannett, Hersant, Hallmark, Harris Cable, Columbia Broadcasting System, Scripps-Howard, Rediffusion, and Pegasus. Additionally, television channels in the U.S. Virgin Islands are affiliates of mainland U.S. networks. Others that had interests in the past were Cowles, Knight-Ridder, Thomson, King, the American Broadcasting Company, Western Broadcasting, and Columbia Pictures. Cuba and the Netherlands Antilles do not have outside ownership of mass media.

The contents of the electronic media and, to a lesser degree, newspapers and magazines, reflect a world outside the Caribbean. In many cases, the percentage of television time devoted to foreign programs has increased during the past decade, whereas comparable figures for other parts of the world have shown a decline. Both national and private television systems receive U.S. or European shows via satellite, and they are then retransmitted either over the air or by cable. This type of hookup is very popular in the Commonwealth Caribbean, threatening the very existence of national broadcasting services, such as those of the Leewards and Windwards. In Belize, the creation of a national service was bypassed as eighteen privately owned television and cable services were established since 1980 to rebroadcast U.S. satellite-relayed programming. Belizeans, who have a television outlet for every nine thousand or fewer people, see virtually no local programming. A ruling that 1 percent of the shows be local has never been met.

Similarly, the French-speaking islands have very little local television; Guadeloupe carries four hours monthly. The U.S. Virgin Islands channels use mainland U.S. network materials, some of which are not relevant or popular. When Caribbean television shows are produced, they usually are very close copies of U.S. or Western European prototypes.

Along the same lines, Caribbean radio has been called the jukebox for the top twenty to forty popular songs of the United States or England, and this situation is not limited to only the English-speaking territories. The U.S. gospel stations that have been set up on many islands bring in other messages, some of which have been criticized by the region's clerics as inimical to Caribbean churches.

Some attempts have been made to reverse the dependency upon Western programs. In Trinidad, the Banyan group has done interesting drama, and a few years ago, Barbados' Caribbean Broadcasting flirted with experimental television shows. Some Commonwealth Caribbean and Netherlands Antilles stations have adjusted their schedules to include more local music, sometimes with prodding from the government. In the French Antilles, local music has become number one on radio naturally, as the population is captivated by *zouk*. Guadeloupe's Radyo Tanbou and Haiti's Radio Lumiére also have worked toward indigenization. As local music became popular in some Caribbean cultures, partly through radio, it was repackaged and sold on the international market, often to the dismay of some purists of popular culture.

During the past generation, some efforts have been made to replace metropolitan languages with local ones. Most successful has been the experience of the Netherlands Antilles, where since the 1970s Papiamento has become the favorite broadcast and print media language. In the Commonwealth Caribbean Windward Islands, Creole is used in some radio broadcasting, as it is on Haiti's Radio Soleil and Guadeloupe's Radyo Tanbou, among a few others.

However, most of these efforts are either too miniscule or too slow to stem the flow of foreign media contents into the Caribbean. Although significant structural changes have been made to some media systems, they fall far short of solving the problem of media dependency. The privatization of Jamaican broadcasting proposed by former Prime Minister Edward Seaga is likely to increase foreign usage, as more stations vie for the limited local talent pool. The restructuring of Guyana's media in the 1970s may have temporarily slowed outside influences but created an authoritarian atmosphere with the government owning all the major media. Cuba alone has developed a national communications policy, having organized the mass media structurally and functionally and having established strong professional organizations for each medium.

Besides the media contents, the other area where there is a deepening dependency upon foreign companies is in communications technology. Multinational corporations, such as Cable and Wireless, RCA Global Communications, ITT, MCI International, and Philips, among others, have teamed up with local governments to inundate the smallest of islands with the sophisticated technology of fiber optics, satellites, cable, or digitalization. Equipment supply lines for such systems normally follow old colonial links. Despite all the benefits governmental officials and the giant corporations claim they provide, the ultramodernization of Caribbean telematics has had debilitating effects upon national economies, which have continued to borrow at high interest rates in order to handle the strain.

Another strong holdover from the colonial period is the manner in which mass media and governments interact. For years, the media laws of European countries were in force in the Caribbean. Strict Danish regulations controlled the media in the Virgin Islands, and they were replaced after 1917 by the regulations of the United States. At other times, during periods of occupation, U.S. governance permeated Caribbean media—in the Dominican Republic for a period beginning in 1916; in Haiti from 1915 to 1934 and in Grenada from 1983 to 1984. Of course, the French legal hand is still very much evident in media control in Martinique and Guadeloupe. Similarly, the Dutch influence is felt in the Netherlands Antilles and the British in the Commonwealth Caribbean.

During the colonial era, governments and political parties often owned the mass media. Despite some attempts at privatization, much of Caribbean broadcasting is still government owned. In the cases of Antigua and Guyana, almost all the media are government owned, while in Cuba they are the properties of the state and the Communist party. In the Commonwealth Caribbean and the French and Netherlands Antilles, many newspapers are owned by political parties. This factor often makes for a lively and irresponsible type of journalism, as editors and politicians fling insults at one another much in the tradition of the partisan press era of the United States in the late 1700s.

It is difficult to generalize about limitations on freedom of expression in the Caribbean because, although some carryover restrictions may be in the books and editors continually scream "foul play," the mass media (especially newspapers) are relatively freer than those of many parts of the world.

Some long-tenured, one-man governments have ruled in the Caribbean, and though this normally creates less-than-ideal press conditions, they cannot all be given a blanket label and be considered detrimental. Sharp differences can be seen between the long but generally democratic reign of Eric Williams in Trinidad and the harsh dictatorships of the Duvaliers in Haiti or Trujillo in the Dominican Republic. In each of a number of other countries—Antigua, Belize, Grenada, Guyana, and St. Lucia for example—a strong leader ruled for over a decade but with varying degrees of press control. For instance, many more restraints were placed upon the media by Grenada's Eric Gairy and Guyana's Forbes Burnham than by St. Lucia's John Compton or Belize's George Price. In Cuba, where Fidel Castro has ruled for more than thirty years, the Latino flavor of communism allows for a freer press than in countries such as North Korea, Mongolia, or Albania. Cuban journalists have been assured of "complete freedom" if they remain within the spirit and policies of the Revolution.

A potential infringement upon press freedom in the Caribbean is caused by ownership of the media by conglomerates and by the close alignments of newspapers and broadcasting with other big business interests. In some countries, the media have become large enough to attract impressive local and foreign entrepreneurs. The Trinidad and Barbados presses, the former accused of doing the will of the business community, are owned by local conglomerates; the Jamaica *Gleaner* is glued to the big-business class, to the exclusion of other viewpoints; and in Puerto Rico and the Dominican Republic, the mass media are part of group or cross-channel operations, some of which are foreign.

However, in far more instances, the mass media are small concerns struggling for survival in very glutted markets. For example, Martinique, Guadeloupe, and Haiti each have about three dozen radio stations, while Belize supports eighteen television and cable stations; the U.S. Virgin Islands operates three television and nine radio stations, two daily newspapers, and cable systems. All of these countries are rich in media with limited commercial sectors. One of the most saturated media markets is Puerto Rico, with four dailies, forty weeklies, ten television channels, more than thirty cable systems, and 110 radio stations.

Some Caribbean mass media set out to accomplish something more than – or other than – making a profit. Development communication has been practiced in the region since at least the mid-1970s, when UNESCO sponsored a seminar on the topic in Guyana and other groups dealt with specific topics, such as nutrition, education, or literacy. The Cuban mass media have been effectively geared to developmental projects, especially those dealing with education and literacy. In the Dominican Republic, a few projects have been underway to use radio for community basic education, and in Haiti, Radio Soleil and Radio Lumiére regularly promote developmental projects. The latter station strives to be appropriate for Haitians' needs, especially through indigenization of staff and programming. Radyo Tanbou of Guadeloupe, while using intellectual and stimulating shows, backs a number of causes on behalf of the masses. Communication for development has been a chief aim of Stichting Grafische Communicatie (SGC) in Curaçao, which sponsors seminars, publishes local books, and carries out a newspaper classroom project.

SGC also trains journalists and promotes mass communications research, neither of which has been very pronounced in the Caribbean; for example, only eight official schools or programs of communications exist. Cuba has the most sophisticated and organized training and education schemes in mass communications. In recent years, Cuban authorities have established international training schools in journalism and film in Havana. Additionally, groups such as UPEC and ICAIC offer training, promote professionalization through publication of books and periodicals, and generally look after the welfare of their members. Besides Cuba, the only other countries or territories with full-scale mass communications programs are the Dominican Republic, Jamaica, and Puerto Rico.

Very little research results from the journalism or mass communications schools, but West Indians studying in the United States and Europe, a few local and foreign scholars, and some governmental bodies have carried out studies. Wide gaps exist in the research. Most of the best historical work was written before World War II. Few content analyses have been completed, and most of the limited number of audience studies used only market-oriented approaches.

A Press in St. Bartholomew

A historical sweep of the Caribbean region uncovers obscure presses in the most unlikely places. For example, as chapter 16 notes, the first press in the Netherlands Antilles was set up in St. Eustatius.

For a brief time between 1799 and 1819, St. Bartholomew, in what was then the Swedish West Indies, possessed a printing press and brought out a regular publication. Like St. Eustatius, the island was important to shippers in the latter eighteenth century.

Apparently, a printing press existed in 1799, for a mention in the first newspaper five years later reported that on 15 March 1799, the Free Builders Lodge "issued a publication *which was afterwards printed and distributed round the town,* stating that the institution had been sanctioned by the King" (Cave 1978b, 214). An *Avertissement* appeared in 1804 before the first and probably only periodical, the *Report of St. Bartholomew,* was launched on 2 April. Andrew Berstedt, Justiciarius of St. Bartholomew, ran the newspaper, which appeared in English. The first issue contained an unusual prospectus in the form of a "Dialogue between one of the *Editors* and a *Reader* to serve as *Prospectus*":

Editor. —Shortly my Report will contain all matters within my reach consistent with Laws, Morals, and Decorum, and for the rest usefull or amusing.

Reader. Aye, Aye! We will hear of Balls, Marooning Parties, Cavalcades, Lectures on Heads, Pantomines breaking the Ears of the Spectators, Run aways and so forth.

Editor. Pray! What else do you read in the best papers of Europe.

Reader. And the important_____.

Editor. "Accounts you mean, of Ministerial and Military differences, Extra ordinary accidents, cases of law, Matters of Police" oh! my Report shall mind all these matters: J'll tell you for instance, How Sweden is at war and at Peace again with the Belligerent Powers twice a day; How St. Martins has been taken and retaken in one day by Capitulation and Recapitulation between no parties at all . . . (in Cave 1978b, 207).

Besides these contents, the *Report* also carried literary fare, articles on the history and geography of Sweden, and four slave songs collected by an islander (Cave 1979, 85–90).

The paper suffered numerous setbacks, appearing late by weeks or suspending publication temporarily because of the "unwarranted neglect" of a printer or a printer who "had just turned Merchant." Advertising was very limited (to about one-half column per issue), as was circulation (forty-three subscribers in 1814, sixteen in 1817).

Berstedt seemed to lose control of the *Report* for a brief time in 1811. Later that year, after a trip to Boston, he was denied re-entry by St. Bartholomew's governor, who said he could not guarantee his safety. The *Report* was resumed in November 1811 by John Allan, but by the following year it was suspended for lack of subscriptions. In 1814, Allan revived the *Report*. After three months, he lamented that the paper had received only $151 from all sources during the previous quarter, and, carefully adding up his expenses, Allan said that $1.50 was his quarterly salary (in Cave 1978b, 211).

The Report of St. Bartholomew ceased publication with issue 368 on 28 October 1819. One other newspaper, the *St. Bartholomew Chronicle* of 1828, is thought to have appeared on the island.

N O T E S

1. Perhaps the more useful results of their study were the data on media preferences. Of teenagers (fifteen was the average age) in the sample, 96 percent had been exposed to Belizean newspapers and 39 percent to U.S. papers; 98 percent to Belizean radio, 7 percent to U.S. radio, and 10 percent to other; 68 percent to U.S. television, 10 percent to Mexican, 13 percent to Guatemalan, and 5 percent to Honduran television. They also found that 95 percent of the houses had radio receivers. Sixty percent of the teenagers preferred soul and disco music, 14 percent reggae and calypso, 13 percent rock, and 10 percent country and western.

CHAPTER 10

1. Thompson (1962, 95) and Otero (1953, 295) agree that *Gazeta* first appeared in 1782. Contemporary Cuban writers list the date as 1764. An International Organization of Journalists (1976, 159) publication reported that the Count of Ricla, then colonial governor of Cuba, ran *Gazeta* from 1764 to 1766; Vera (1979, 13) also listed the date as 1764. This author tried unsuccessfully to verify the date while in Cuba in 1982.

2. The same tendency was evident in 1955: 12.3 percent national news, 4 percent international news, 41.2 percent advertising, 1.5 percent culture, etc.

3. Another source listed more than fifty dailies in Cuba in 1953 with a total circulation of 610,340. The largest paper was *Prensa libre,* founded in 1941, with more than one hundred thousand.

4. Carty (1978a) said that journalists under Batista were the most bribe-prone in the hemisphere, and that *la mordida* (the bite) prevailed. Under the weekly *botella* (bottle system), journalists received handouts (at first, bottles of rum) that eventually ran into millions of dollars. Nichols (1982a, 258) said that Batista paid the press about U.S. $450,000 monthly in bribes, allowing some prominent journalists to pocket tens of thousands of dollars monthly.

5. Other specialized periodicals published by PSP, including a theoretical journal, were successful. In May 1959, the PSP's weekly radio hour became a daily program.

6. Nichols (1982a, 257) stated, "When he [Castro] came to power in 1959, Cuba's broadcast media were among the few useful assets in that extremely poor

country. Most homes outside of Havana lacked running water but not a radio receiver." In 1959, Cuba had more television sets per capita than any Latin American nation and ranked eighth in the world in numbers of TV sets per capita (Wiarda 1968, 188). Vera (1979, 14) reported that in 1959, Cuba had five national radio networks (CMQ; Cuban National Circuit, or CMW; Radio Progress, CMBC; Union Radio, CMCF; and Oriente Radio Network, CMCI) of 260.5 kilowatts and a total of 156 radio stations (including repeating stations) for 348.1 kilowatts of power. Five privately owned television channels functioned.

7. For example, animated film for television was attempted at the Cuban Broadcast Institute between 1959 and 1967. The efforts, however, were not very successful, and in 1968, a separate branch of the institute, Animated Film Studios, was set up. It had produced 349 films by 1971 (*OIRT Information,* 1972, 5).

8. There is a question about when this school started. The chief of the University of Havana School of Journalism said that their work was fifteen years old in 1982 (Interview, Trelles 1982).

CHAPTER 12

1. During Castro's guerrilla war of the 1950s, the insurgents had a film unit, Cine Rebelde, headed by Julio García Espinosa.

CHAPTER 13

1. I scanned the following newspapers at the Archivo Nacional in Santo Domingo in May 1983: *El telégrafo constitucional de Santo Domingo,* 5 April, 12 April, 19 April, 26 April, 7 June, 14 June, 21 June, 28 June, 5 July, 12 July, 19 July, and 26 July, all in 1821; *El duende,* 15 April, 22 April, 29 April, 3 June, 17 June, 24 June, 1 July, 8 July, and 15 July, all in 1821; and *El eco del pueblo,* 27 July, 19 October, 26 October, 14 December, and 21 December, all in 1856, and 25 January, 5 April, 10 May, all in 1857.

2. According to various reports in the *New York Times* and *Editor and Publisher,* Ornes himself was won over to Trujillo's side.

CHAPTER 14

1. For example, Cave (1974–1975, 13–14) said that he found no imprints in the islands predating the 1760s.

2. I read these works at the Archives Departementales de la Martinique, Fort-de-France.

3. I am indebted to Alvina Ruprecht, who provided the translation of Ollivrin's comments.

4. Numbers 971 and 972 are the department numbers for Guadelope and Martinique, respectively, in France's administrative apparatus.

5. I read the papers during the last week of May 1979 in Martinique and the last week of May 1988 in Guadeloupe.

CHAPTER 15

1. I saw copies of *Affiches américaines* at Philadelphia's Library Company. Deposited there are the issues for: 13 February, 20 February, 24 July, 14 August, 11 September, 2 October, and 23 October, all in 1782; 29 January, 5 February, 21 February, 5 March, 12 March, 26 March, 9 April, 23 April, 7 May, 21 May, 11 June, 9 July, 23 July, and 27 August, all in 1783, plus extras and supplements for 30 January and 6 February of 1782, and 18 January, 9 April, 23 April, 28 May, 11 June, 16 July, and 27 August of 1783. Also at the same library are issues of the *Gazette royale d'Hayti* for 17 April, 13 June, 29 June, and 19 July, all in 1815.

2. Gropp (1941, 473) said that among those papers was *Le telégraphe,* published first in January 1832. According to him, "This was the first official newspaper of the Republic. In 1842, it was replaced by *Feuille de commerce,* which remained the official newspaper only until 1845, but continued publication until 1860."

CHAPTER 16

1. Gene is a language that existed side by side with Papiamento. It was a secret language used by the slaves among themselves. "Though the slaves were not allowed to speak to each other in the presence of the master, singing was a different matter, since it increased their working capacity. And so the cunning slaves were able to improvise quasi-working songs, in which they mocked their masters." The language did not survive (Hartog 1968, 158).

CHAPTER 19

1. The confusion was serious enough that Pedreira (1970) spent considerable effort showing numerous errors in the listings of early newspapers by Coll and Toste and Miller.

2. Actually, in 1983, Lorimar-Telepictures agreed to buy one-half interests in WKBM-TV of Caguas-San Juan and WSUR-TV of Ponce. Neither was on the air at the time, as their parent company, American Colonial Broadcasting Corporation, had filed for bankruptcy.

3. Malrite owned sixteen broadcasting properties at the time, eleven radio and five television stations.

4. Most of WKAQ's programming does not go on network to other Telemundo stations on the mainland, such as WNJU (New York), WSCV (Miami), KVEA (Los Angeles), KSTS (San Francisco), and others in Houston and San Antonio-Phoenix.

CHAPTER 21

1. Although this section deals with the U.S. Caribbean, the British Virgin Island of Tortola is included because its media are closely tied to those of its U.S. neighbors.

CHAPTER 24

1. Directories such as Sell's and Hubbard's reported upon the West Indies in the 1880s.

2. See *Caribbean Quarterly,* December 1976, 90–106; *Gazette,* 19(1973): 91–106; *Caribbean Monthly Bulletin,* February 1977, 21–26; *Caribbean Studies,* July 1976, 184–218; *Journal of Communications,* Spring 1975, 128–35; *Jamaica Daily News,* 6–9 March 1976; *Democratic Journalist* 10(1976): 8–11; *Journalism History,* Summer 1975, 58–60; *Times of the Americas,* 3 March 1976, 2; *Journalism Quarterly,* Spring 1975, 114–17; *Revista Interamericana,* Spring 1976, 78–86, and Summer 1977, 260–75; *IPI Report,* September 1976, 1–4; *IPI Report,* October 1977, 12–13; *IPI Report,* November 1977, 13–14; and *Index on Censorship,* Autumn 1973, 55–70; plus items in this book.

3. Hosein's study was controversial because the Guyanese officials disagreed with his findings that freedom of the press was in trouble in Guyana.

CHAPTER 26

1. See (at least) issues dated 27 February and 19 June 1983; 5 August 1984; 19 May, 9 June, 14 July, 22 September, and 27 October, all in 1985; 15 June, 22 June, 21 September, 28 September, and 2 November, all in 1986; 22 February, 19 April, 7 June, 5 July, and 13 September, all in 1987; and 31 January 1988.

BIBLIOGRAPHY

BOOKS AND ARTICLES

Abrahams, Roger. 1970. "Patterns of Performance in the British West Indies." In *Afro-American Anthropology: Contemporary Perspectives,* ed. Norman Whitten, Jr. and John Szwed, 163–79. New York: The Free Press.

Abrahams, Roger, and Richard Bauman. 1978. "Ranges of Festival Behaviour." In *The Reversible World: Symbolic Inversion in Art and Society,* ed. Barbara Babcock, 193–208. Ithaca, N.Y.: Cornell University Press.

Action. 1980. "Guyana Paper Struggles." December, 7.

Agramonte, Arturo. 1966. *Cronología del cine cubano.* La Habana: Ediciones ICAIC.

Ahmed Rajab. 1979. "The Hushed Voice of Haiti." *Index on Censorship,* November–December, 50–53.

Ainslie, Rosalynde. 1968. *The Press in Africa: Communications Past and Present.* New York: Walker.

Algería, José S. 1960. *El periodismo puertorriqueño desde su aparición hasta los comienzos del siglo XX.* Barcelona: M. Pareja, for Instituto de Cultura Puertorriqueña, San Juan.

Alisky, Marvin. 1981. *Latin American Media: Guidance and Censorship.* Ames: Iowa State University Press.

Alleyne, Mervin. n.d. "Communications and Politics in Jamaica." *Caribbean Studies* 3(2):22–61.

Almeyda, Vincentita C. 1965. "Pointers for the Development of an Educational Home Economics Program Through Television in Puerto Rico." Master's thesis, Michigan State University.

Alvarez, Santiago, et al. 1975. *Cine y revolución en Cuba.* Barcelona: Editorial Fontamara.

Americas Watch and CPJ. 1984. "Journalists in Jeopardy: The Haitian Reality." New York: Americas Watch and Committee to Protect Journalists. Mimeo.

Amiama, Manuel A. 1933. *El periodismo en la República Dominicana; Notas para la historia crítico-narrativa del periodisma [sic] nacional, desde sus orígenes hasta nuestros días.* Santo Domingo: Talleres Tipográficos "La nación."

Anderson, Robert. 1977. *La prensa en Puerto Rico.* San Juan: Comisión de Derechos Civiles.

Andújar, Sonia. 1982. "Mujer-Tec: An Appropriate Intervention." *Development Communication Report,* June, 15.

Antillen Review. 1981. "Journalism Training to Get International Dimension." June–July, 39–40.

Archer, Horace. 1976. "Food and Nutrition Content and Approaches in CARICOM Media." Paper read at Nutrition and Mass Media Symposium, September, St. Catherine's, Jamaica.

Archer, Thomas A. 1964. "Radio in Barbados." *The Bajan,* March, 29.

Astroff, Roberta. 1983. "Communication and Contemporary Colonialism: Television in Puerto Rico." Paper read at Conference on Culture and Communication, March, Temple University, Philadelphia, Pa. Mimeo.

―――. 1987. "Communication and Contemporary Colonialism: Broadcast Television in Puerto Rico." *Studies in Latin American Popular Culture* 6:11–26.

Aufderheide, Pat. 1979. "Latins, Exiles, U.S. Chicanos Attend Havana's Filmfest." *Variety,* 19 December, 22.

―――. 1984. "Red Harvest." *American Film,* March, 28–34.

Austin, Roy. 1976. "Understanding Calypso Content: A Critique and an Alternative." *Caribbean Quarterly,* June–September, 74–89.

Ayeast, Morley, 1960. *The British West Indies: The Search for Self Government.* London: George Allen and Unwin.

Balch, E. G. 1972. *Occupied Haiti.* New York: Garland.

Barrett, A. E. 1945. "Broadcasting Survey of the British West Indian Colonies in Connection with the Establishment of a Commonwealth Relay Station and Caribbean Area Station." London: British Broadcasting Corporation.

Barry, Jessica. 1984. "The Belize Dilemma." *Media in Education and Development,* March, 11–13.

Bartholomew, John. 1980. *The Steel Pan.* London: Oxford University Press.

Belize Today. 1987a. "Personality of the Month." April, 10, 16.

―――. 1987b. "Talking to Mr. Thompson." April, 6–7, 13.

Benjamins, H. D., and Joh. F. Snelleman. 1914–1917. *Encyclopaedie van Nederlandsche West-Indie.* Leiden: E. J. Brill.

Berges Rib, Virginia. 1988. "RADECO: A Precedent in Education." *Development Communication Report* 1:7.

Besas, Peter. 1978. "Cuba Breaks Yank Film Blockade." *Variety,* 4 October, 1.

―――. 1986. "Puerto Rico TV Mart Exploding." *Variety,* 12 March, 1, 98.

Bilby, Kenneth. 1977. "The Impact of Reggae in the United States." *Popular Music in Society* 5(5):17–22.

Bishop, Maurice. 1981. "Feature Address." Presented at official launching of Media Workers Association of Free Grenada, 11 July, St. George's, Grenada.

―――. 1982. "Address." Presented at First Conference of Journalists from the Caribbean Area, 17–19 April, St. George's, Grenada.

Black, Jan Knippers. 1976. *Area Handbook for Cuba.* Washington: U.S. Government Printing Office.

Blanche, Lénis. 1935. *Contribution à l'histoire de la presse à la Guadeloupe.* Point-a-Pitre: Government of Guadeloupe.

―――. 1938. *Histoire de la Guadeloupe.* Paris: M. Lavergne.

Bohning, Don. 1981. "Grenada Stifles Newspaper as Intimidation Continues." *Miami Herald,* 19 July.

Bousquet, Earl. 1986. "TV Poison in St. Lucia." *Caribbean Contact,* December, 7.

Bovenkerk, Frank, and L. M. Bovenkerk-Teerink. 1972. *Surinamers en Antillianen in de Nederlandse pers.* Amsterdam: Universiteit van Amsterdam, Antropologisch-Sociologisch Centrum, Afdeling Culturele Antropologie.

Boyke, Roy, ed. 1973. *Trinidad Carnival: The Greatest Spectacle on Earth.* Port of Spain, Trinidad: Kepy Caribbean Publication.

Briceño, Jaime. 1981. "Carnival in Northern Belize." *Belizean Studies,* May.

Brigham, C. S. 1940. *Cabon's History of Haiti Journalism.* Worcester, Mass.: American Antiquarian Society.

Broadcast Communications. 1978. "Changing to FM." October, 21.

Broadcasting and Television Act. 1983. Belize City: Government of Belize.

Brown, Aggrey. 1986. "The Caribbean Institute of Mass Communications." *COMBROAD,* April–June, 13–18.

––––––. 1987. "The Electronic Re-colonisation of the Caribbean." *Media Development,* No. 1, 20–22.

Brown, Aggrey, and Roderick Sanatan. 1987. *Talking with Whom? A Report on the State of the Media in the Caribbean.* Mona, Jamaica: CARIMAC, University of the West Indies.

Brown, Robert U. 1960. "IAPA Urges Castigation of Cuba's Press Seizure." *Editor and Publisher,* 26 March, 10.

Browne, Donald R. 1982. *International Radio Broadcasting: The Limits of the Limitless Medium.* New York: Praeger.

Bruijning, C. F. A., and J. Voorhoeve. 1977. *Encyclopedie van Suriname.* Amsterdam: B. V. Uitgeversmaatschappij Argus Elsevier.

Brutus, Fred, ed. 1982. *Haiti Presse 82.* Port-au-Prince: Imprimerie Henri Deschamps.

Burke, Charles. 1981. "The Caribbean News Agency (CANA): Perceptions and Usage of a Regional News Agency in the Third World." Ph.D. dissertation, University of Missouri.

Burton, Julianne. 1977. "Film: Revolutionary Cuban Cinema." *Handbook for Latin American Studies,* No. 39, 425–34.

––––––. 1978. "The Camera As 'Gun': Two Decades of Culture and Resistance in Latin America." *Latin American Perspectives,* Winter, 49–76.

––––––. 1979. "Popular Culture and Perpetual Quest: An Interview with Manuel Octavio Gómez." *Jump/Cut,* May, 17–20.

––––––. 1982a. "Folk Music, Circuses, Variety Shows and Other Endangered Species: A Conversation with Julio García Espinosa on the Preservation of Popular Culture in Cuba." *Studies in Latin American Popular Culture* 1:216–24.

––––––. 1982b. "Theory and Practice of Film and Popular Culture in Cuba: A Conversation with Julio García Espinosa." *Quarterly Review of Film Studies,* Fall, 341–51.

Butcher, Pablo. 1988. "Haiti: The Message on the Wall." *Index on Censorship* 3:10–13.

Camarena, Perdomo. 1927. *La libertad de prensa.* (Trabajo premiado por el jurado de la Exposicíon Nacional de Santiago de los Caballeros 1927). Santo Domingo: Imprenta J. R. Viudo García Sues.

Campbell, Averille E. 1978. "A Content Analysis of the Trinidad and Tobago Weekly *Sunday Guardian* for the Time Periods—1947, 1957, 1962, and 1976." Master's thesis, Iowa State University.

Canadian Foundation for Caribbean Development and Cooperation. 1984. *De-

velopment Communication in the Commonwealth Caribbean. Ottawa.

Capteillo, Enrique. 1971. "103 años de lucha, 105 años de beísbol." *Semanario deportivo LPV,* 30 November, 14–17.

Carib. 1986. "Caribbean Theatre." No. 4, 1–78.

Caribbeana. 1741. London: Printed for T. Osborne and W. Smith.

Caribbean Contact. 1975a. "Cartoon—As an Instrument of Development." February, 16.

_____. 1975b. "Cartoonists at Work." April, 4.

_____. 1979. "CCC's Cable to Grenada." November, 20.

_____. 1981a. "A Clumsy and Blatant Fraud—Reports Lord Avebury." January, 1.

_____. 1981b. "JLP Govt's Squeeze on Journalists." February, 16.

_____. 1981c. "Why PRG Banned the 'Grenadian Voice.'" July, 3.

_____. 1982. "Battles of Burnham's Government and the *Catholic Standard.*" October, 11.

_____. 1984. "Decolonising the Region." September, 3.

_____. 1985. "Tougher Antiguan Gov't Stance as Opposition Forms." August, 2.

_____. 1986a. "Hector Vindicated." June, 2.

_____. 1986b. "J'can Human Rights Infringed." April, 16.

_____. 1987a. "Guyana Government Dismisses Reporters." January, 2.

_____. 1987b. "Literature and Theatre in the C'bean." June, 7.

_____. 1987c. "New Status for Singh in Barbados." February, 16.

_____. 1988. "Storm Breaks over Swaggart." February, 1, 10.

Caribbean Council of Churches. 1986. "Draft Reports and Proposals: CCC-Intermedia Cooperation on Communication for Human Development." Barbados.

Caribbean Monthly Bulletin. 1977. March, 12–13.

_____. 1979. May, 16.

Carmichael, Gertrude. 1961. *The History of the West Indian Islands of Trinidad and Tobago, 1498–1900.* London: Alvin Redman.

Carnival: St. Vincent and the Grenadines. n.d. Kingstown, St. Vincent: NMM Associates.

Caroit, Jean-Michel. 1987. "'Our Radio Echos What the People Say and Think.'" *IPI Report,* September, 29.

Carr, Patrick. 1975. "Bob Marley Is the Jagger of Reggae." *Village Voice,* 30 June.

Cartoons from the Mirror. 1974. Georgetown: New Guyana Co., Ltd.

Carty, James W., Jr. 1975. "In the U.S. Virgin Islands, Press Has Lively and Varied History." *Times of the Americas,* 5 March.

_____. 1978a. *Cuban Communications.* Bethany, W. Va.: Bethany College.

_____. 1978b. "Communist Ideology Basic to J-Education in Cuba." *Journalism Educator,* October.

_____. 1980. "Press Seen As Tool for Cubans' Self-Evaluation." *Times of the Americas,* 9 April, 6.

_____. 1981. "Prensa Latina and Noticias Aliadas: Different Models." *Media Development,* No. 1, 25–27.

_____. 1987. "Alternative Newspaper in Puerto Rico." *Media Development* 3:34–35.

Castañeda, Mireya. 1987. "Proposal That Grows Like Caribbean Flora." *Granma Weekly Review,* 9 August, 7.

Cave, Roderick. 1974–75. *Working Papers on West Indian Printing.* Series 1. Mona, Jamaica: Department of Library Sciences, University of the West Indies.

_____. 1976. *Working Papers on West Indian Printing.* Series 2. Mona, Jamaica: Department of Library Sciences, University of the West Indies.

_____. 1978a. "Early Printing and the Book Trade in the West Indies." *Library Quarterly* 48(2):163–92.

_____. 1978b. "Printing in the Swedish West Indies." *Libri,* September, 205–14.

_____. 1979. "Four Slave Songs from St. Bartholomew." *Caribbean Quarterly,* March–June, 85–90.

_____. 1985. "The Jamaican Press Viewed from King's House: Governor Darling's Report to the Colonial Office, 1861." *Journal of Newspaper and Periodical History,* Winter, 10–16.

Central Rediffusion Services Ltd. 1956. *Commercial Broadcasting in the British West Indies.* London: Butterworth's Scientific Publications.

CETTEM Newsletter. 1982. "Telecommunications in Latin America." December, 4–5.

Chamberlain, Greg. 1984. "Gagging the Press." *Index on Censorship* 6:34–36.

_____. 1986. "Haitian Media Contribute to Duvalier's Downfall." *Media Development* 4:35–37.

Chanan, Michael. 1985. *The Cuban Image: Cinema and Cultural Politics in Cuba.* Bloomington: Indiana University Press.

Charles, Jefferson Oliver. 1981. "Satellite Use in the English-Speaking Caribbean: Towards a More Integrated Model." Ph.D. dissertation, Stanford University.

Chilcote, R.H. 1963. "The Press in Latin America, Spain and Portugal." Special number, *Hispanic American Report,* August.

Chiles, Paul Nelson. 1975. *The Puerto Rican Press Reaction to the United States, 1888–1898.* New York: Arno.

Cholmondeley, Hugh. 1984. "Communications in the Caribbean." *COMBROAD,* January–March, 12–16.

Cintron, Isabel. 1983. "Get That Journalist!" *Caribbean Contact,* August, 7.

Clarke, Sebastian. 1980. *Jah Music—The Evolution of Popular Jamaican Song.* London: Heinemann.

Cohen, Abner. 1980. "Drama and Politics in the Development of a London Carnival." *Man*(n.s.)15:65–87.

_____. 1982. "A Polyethnic London Carnival as a Contested Cultural Performance." *Ethnic and Racial Studies* 5(1):23–41.

Coleman, Ray. 1976. "Root Strong in Funky Kingston." *Melody Maker,* 12 June.

Colli, Claudia. 1979. "Will ZBTV Make It This Time?" *Virgin Islander,* March–April, 25, 27–28.

COMBROAD. 1986. "Restructuring Broadcasting in Jamaica." July–September, 12–16.

Comitas, Lambros. 1968. *Caribbeana 1900–1965: A Topical Bibliography.* Seattle: University of Washington Press.

_____. 1977. *The Complete Caribbeana 1900–1975: A Bibliographic Guide to the Scholarly Literature.* 4 vols. Millwood, N.Y.: KTO Press.

Communist Party, Cuba. 1981. *Statutes of the Communist Party of Cuba. Adopted by the First Congress, with the Modifications Agreed by the Second Congress.* Havana: Political Publishing House.

Condero, Walter, et al. 1976. *Actitudes de los directores de los medios de comunicación de masas frente a la planificación familiar.* Santo Domingo: Consejo Nacional de Población y Familia.

Constitution of the Republic of Cuba. n.d. New York: Center for Cuban Studies.

Cooper, Carol. 1980. "Tuff Gong: Bob Marley's Unsung Story." *Village Voice,* 10 September.

Cornevin, Robert. 1973. *Le theatre haitien des origines a nos jours.* Montreal.

Costa Gómez, Moises Frumencio da. 1957. *De vrijheiderechten van de mens in de Nederlandse Antillen.* Curaçao: Augustus.

Cozier, Jimmy. 1970. "Barbadian Representatives of the Fourth Estate." *Barbados Advocate-News,* 1 October, 3.

Cozier, Tony. 1986. "Cable TV Bombards Caribbean Culture." *Action,* February, 5.

CPJ Update. 1984. "Grenada." January–February, 7.

CRAM International (WI) Ltd. 1971. "National Television Audience Survey Jamaica 1971." Mimeo.

Cromelin, Richard. 1975. "An Herbal Meditation with Bob Marley." *Rolling Stone,* 11 September.

Crowe, Cameron. 1977. "Bob Marley: The Shooting of a Wailer." *Rolling Stone,* 11 January.

Crowley, Daniel. 1955. "Festivals of the Calendar in St. Lucia." *Caribbean Quarterly* 4:99–121.

———. 1956. "The Traditional Masques of Carnival." *Caribbean Quarterly* 4:194–223.

———, ed. 1977. *African Folklores in the New World.* Austin: University of Texas Press.

Cundall, Frank. 1916. "The Press and Printers of Jamaica Prior to 1820." *Proceedings of the American Antiquarian Society* 26:290–412.

———. 1935. *A History of Printing in Jamaica from 1717 to 1834.* Kingston: Institute of Jamaica.

Cuthbert, Marlene, ed. 1975. *Caribbean Women in Communication for Development.* Bridgetown, Barbados: Cedar Press.

———. 1976. "Some Observations on the Role of the Mass Media in the Recent Socio-Political Development of Jamaica." *Caribbean Quarterly,* December, 50–57.

———. 1979. "The Caribbean News Agency: Genesis of an Indigenous News Agency in a Developing Region." Ph.D. dissertation, Syracuse University.

———. 1981. "The First Five Years of the Caribbean News Agency." *Gazette* 28:3–15.

———. 1985. "Cultural Autonomy and Popular Music: A Survey of Jamaican Youth." *Communication Research,* July, 381–93.

Cuthbert, Marlene, and Michael W. Pidgeon, eds. 1981. *Language and Communication in the Caribbean.* Bridgetown, Barbados: Cedar Press.

Cuthbertson, Clarence. 1981. "Ariel Melchior—Fulfilling a Journalistic Mission." *Virgin Islander,* January, 16–17, 30.

Darville, Vernon M. 1972. "The Bahamas Press: A Study of the Editorial Coverage of the 1967–1968 General Election by the Two Nassau Dailies, the Nassau *Guardian* and the Nassau *Tribune.*" Master's thesis, University of Florida.

Dathorne, O. R. 1985–86. "A Kind of Picong: A Dialogue Between Lord Kitchener and the Mighty Sparrow." *Journal of Caribbean Studies,* Fall/Spring, 57–58.

Davey, William G. 1979. "A Situational Approach to Criticism of Intercultural Discourse: An Analysis of the Puerto Rican Campaign of 1940." In *International and Intercultural Communication Annual,* 59–70. Beverly Hills: Sage.

David, Peter. 1982. "More Power to RFG." *Media Worker,* April, 7.

Davies, Gwenllian. 1984. *Extracts from the Bermuda Gazette.* Hamilton: Privately printed. (Available through Bermuda Archives.)

Davis, Stephen. 1975. "Reggae – Jamaica's Inside-Out Rock and Roll." *New York Times,* 30 November.

Davis, Stephen, and Peter Simon. 1977. *Reggae Bloodliness: In Search of the Music and Culture of Jamaica.* Garden City, N.Y.: Anchor.

de Albuquerque, Klaus. 1979. "The Future of the Rastafarian Movement." *Caribbean Review* 8(4):22–25, 44–46.

de Freitas, G. V. 1956. "Press and Radio." *The Statist,* September, 69.

DeLor, Sonia. 1970. "La presse en Martinique et l'evolution du statut politique de 1945 á 1958." Travail d'Etude et de Recherche pour la Maitrise d'Histoire, Université de Toulouse.

Democratic Journalist. 1967. "Endeavours To Raise the Professional Qualifications of Cuban Journalists." July–August, 80–81.

_____. 1978. "The Mirror and Press Freedom in Guyana." No. 3, 18.

_____. 1982. "Caribbean Journalists Meet in Grenada." Nos. 7/8, 14.

Despradel, A., and R. Mata Diaz. 1937. *La imprenta y sus beneficios en la Republica Dominicana.* Mexico: Congreso Bibliográfico Mexicano.

Desquiron, Jean. 1988. "Try To Write . . . and You Will See What Happens." *Caribbean Review,* Winter, 13, 36.

Desroches, Monique. 1985. *La musique traditionelle de la Martinique.* Montreal: Centre de Recherches Caräibes de l'Universite de Montreal.

Devaux, Robert. ca. 1970. "History of Newspapers in St. Lucia, 1788–1970." Prepared as publication of St. Lucia Archeological and Historical Society. Mimeo.

DeVoss, David. 1977. "The Reggae Message." *Human Behavior,* January, 64–69.

Diederich, Bernard. 1988. "A Poor King without a Crown: A Review of the Haitian Press During the Manigat Months." *Caribbean Review,* Winter, 10–12, 35.

Diederich, Bernard, and Al Burt. 1969. *Papa Doc: The Truth About Haiti Today.* New York: McGraw-Hill.

Dinhofer, Al. 1983. "Cable Boom in Puerto Rico." *Variety,* 17 August, 55.

Dobson, Narda. 1973. *A History of Belize.* London: Longman Caribbean.

Dodge, Steve. 1987. *The Bahamas Index: 1986.* Decatur, Ill.: White Sound Press.

Dookhan, Isaac. 1974. *A History of the Virgin Islands of the United States.* St. Thomas: Caribbean Universities Press, in association with Bowker.

Douglas, Maria E. 1980. *Filmografía del cine cubano, 1959–Julio, 1980.* Havana: Cinemática de Cuba, Sección de Cine Cubano.

"Draft Proposal for a Constitution for MWAFG." 1981. St. George's, Grenada.

Draper, Gordon. 1977. "The Media in the Caribbean—The Perspective of Management." *COMBROAD.* January–March, 17.

Drop, Edward Nearen. 1982. "The Situation in Suriname." *Democratic Journalist,* July–August.

Dunn, Hopeton. 1978. "Lessons of the DN Struggle." *PAJ News,* January, 5.

Dupuch, Etienne. 1967. *Tribune Story.* London: Ernest Benn Ltd.

Dupuy, Ben. 1982. "The Role of Journalists in the Struggle for Freedom of the Press in Haiti." In *First Conference of Journalists from the Caribbean Area, St. George's, Grenada, April 1982,* 97–103. Prague: International Organization of Journalists.

Duvivier, Ulrick. 1941. *Bibliographie generale et methodique d'Haiti.* 2 vols. Port-au-Prince, Haiti.

Eames, Wilberforce. 1928. "The Antigua Press and Benjamin Mecom, 1748–1765." *Proceedings of the American Antiquarian Society* 38:303–48.

Editor and Publisher. 1968. "Virgin Islands Press Control Bill Scored." 25 May, 12.

———. 1969. "St. Croix Paper 125 Years Old." 26 July, 18.

Elder, Jacob D. 1968. "The Male-Female Conflict in Calypso." *Caribbean Quarterly,* September, 23–41.

———. 1973. *The Calypso and Its Morphology.* Port of Spain, Trinidad: National Cultural Council.

Enríquez, Celso. 1968. *Sports in Pre-Hispanic America.* Mexico, D.F.: Litográfica Machado, S.A.

EPICA. 1982. *Grenada: The Peaceful Revolution.* Washington, D.C.

Esquieu, Gloria. 1979. *Indice de la revista cine cubano, 1960–1974.* Havana: Biblioteca Nacional José Martí.

Esterquest, Ralph T. 1940. "L'Imprimerie Royale d' Hayti (1817–1819): A Little Known Royal Press of the Western Hemisphere." *Papers of the Bibliographical Society of America,* 2nd Quarter, 171–84.

Ettlinger, Pauline. 1970. "Ten-Year-Old San Juan Star Shines Brightly over the Caribbean." *Editor and Publisher,* 14 February, 12–13.

Extraits de presse. n.d. Fort-de-France: Archives Nationales.

Fagen, Richard. 1969. *The Transformation of Political Culture in Cuba.* Stanford: Stanford University Press.

Fanon, Frantz. 1965. *Studies in a Dying Colonialism.* New York: Monthly Review Press.

Fanshel, Susan. 1982. *A Decade of Cuban Documentary Film, 1972–1982.* New York: Young Filmmakers.

Farace, R. Vincent. 1968. "Local News Channel Preferences in Puerto Rico." *Journalism Quarterly,* Winter, 692–97.

Farber, Samuel. 1983. "The Cuban Communists in the Early Stages of the Cuban Revolution: Revolutionaries or Reformists?" *Latin American Research Review* 18:59–83.

Farrell, Barry. 1976. "Bob Marley—The Visionary as Sex Symbol." *Chic,* November.

Ferguson, Erna. 1946. *Cuba.* New York: Alfred A. Knopf.

Fergusson, Isaac. 1982. " 'So Much Things To Say'—The Journey of Bob Marley." *Village Voice,* 18 May.

Fimrite, Ron. 1977. "In Cuba, It's Viva El Grand Old Game." *Sports Illustrated,* 6 June, 68–80.

Findley, Eleanor Elizabeth. 1969. "A Content Analysis Comparing Symbols of Nationalism, Socialism, and Scientism As Found in the Jamaica *Daily Gleaner* in 1954, 1960, and 1966." Master's thesis, University of Washington.

Flores-Caraballo, Eliut D. 1988. "The Role of New Communication Technologies in the Cultural and Political Process of Puerto Rico." Paper read at International Association of Mass Communication Research, July, Barcelona, Spain.

Ford-Smith, Honor. 1980. *SISTREN: Women's Theatre and Community Education.* Kingston: Jamaica School of Drama, Cultural Training Centre. Unpublished manuscript.

Foreign Broadcast Information Service (FBIS). 1975. *Broadcasting Stations of the World.* Washington, D.C.: Government Printing Office.

Fornet, Ambrosio. 1982. *Cine, literatura, sociedad.* Habana: Editorial Letras Cubanas.

Forsythe, Victor L. C. 1983. "Guyana: Video Parties – and Fewer Cars Stolen." *Intermedia,* July–September, 52–53.

Fowler, Carolyn. 1981. "The Rise – and Fall – of Haiti's Press." *Christian Science Monitor,* 6 February, 23.

Frederick, Howard. 1982. "La Guerra Radial: Radio Wars Between Cuba and the United States." In *Critical Communication Review, Vol. II,* eds. Vincent Mosco and Janet Wasko. Norwood, N.J.: Ablex.

———. 1986. *Cuban-American Radio Wars: Ideology in International Telecommunications.* Norwood, N.J.: Ablex.

Frost, J. M. 1947 to date. *World Radio TV Handbook.* Hvidovre, Denmark: WRTH.

García, Magaly. 1967. "Cuba's Press: Past and Present." *Granma Weekly Review,* 16 July, 2.

García Mesa, Hector. 1977. *Catálogo general del cine cubano, 1897–1975.* 2 vols. Havana: Instituto del Libro y Cinemateca de Cuba.

Goldman, Shifra M. 1984. "Painters into Poster Makers: Two Views Concerning the History, Aesthetics and Ideology of the Cuban Poster Movement." *Studies in Latin American Popular Culture* 3:162–173.

Goldman, Vivien. 1979. "Bob Marley in His Own Backyard." *Melody Maker,* 11 August.

González-Manet, Enrique. 1982. "Cultural Policy and Audiovisual Media in Cuba. A Case Study." Havana: Cuban National Commission for UNESCO, Center for the Study of Mass Diffusion Media.

Goodwin, Michael. 1975. "Marley, The Maytals and the Reggae Armageddon." *Rolling Stone,* 11 September.

Granma Weekly Review. 1982. "Publishing Industry To Diversify." 21 November, 13.

Green, Harvey. 1951. "The Use and Limitation of Communication by the Dominican Republic." Master's thesis, American University.

Green, Timothy. 1972. *The Universal Eye: World Television in the Seventies.* London: The Bodley Head.

Grenada Newsletter. 1979. October, 5–6.

Griffith, Pat. 1976. "Shanker in Action." *Black Echoes,* August.
_____. 1978. "The Drug in Reggae." *Black Echoes,* January.
Gritter, Headley. 1980. "The Magic of Bob Marley." *Record Review,* April.
Gropp, Arthur. 1941. *Guide to Libraries and Archives in Central America and the West Indies, Panama, Bermuda, and British Guiana.* New Orleans: Tulane University.
Guérin, Daniel. 1961. *The West Indies and Their Future.* London: Dennis Dobson.
Guilbault, Jocelyne. 1983. *Instruments musicaux à Sainte-Lucie.* Paris: Agence de Coopération Culturelle et Technique.
_____. 1987a. "Fitness and Flexibility: Funeral Wakes in St. Lucia, West Indies." *Ethnomusicology* 3(2):273–99.
_____. 1987b. "When a Third World Music Becomes a World-Wide Hit." Paper read at American Musicological Society, 26 September, Ottawa, Canada. Mimeo.
_____. n.d. "La musique créole: Dynamisme et authenticité." *Francophonie,* forthcoming.
Hadel, Richard. 1973. "Carib Dance Music and Dance." *Belizean Studies,* November.
Hague, Carter. 1980. "V.I. Newspapers—210 Years Old." *Daily News,* 1 August, 13-A, 96-A.
Haiti-Progrès. 1988. "Qui défend la liberté de la presse?" 8–14 June, 6, 22–24.
Hallett, A. C. Hollis. 1985. *Bermuda in Print.* Hamilton.
Hallett, Robert. 1957. "Newspaper Growing Pains in New Nation." *IPI Report,* November, 3.
Hamelink, Cees, ed. 1985. *Telecommunications Policy in the Caribbean Region.* The Hague: Institute of Social Studies, in collaboration with Caribbean Institute of Mass Communication, Mona, Jamaica.
Haniff, Neshaz. 1988. *Blaze a Fire.* Toronto: Sister Vision.
Haniff, Yussuff. 1987. "Controversy at NBC in St. Vincent." *Caribbean Contact,* June, 14.
Hanssen, Andrew, Steven Kozlow, and Anne Olsen. 1983. "RADECO: Radio-Based Primary Education in the Dominican Republic." *Development Communication Report,* June, 1, 11, 15.
Hart Davalos, Armando. 1982. "Our Cultural Policy . . ." *Granma Weekly Review,* 25 July, 4–5.
Hartog, Johan. 1944. *Journalistiek leven in Curaçao.* Utrecht: Dekker and van der Vegt N.V.
_____. 1948. "Oud nummer van de 'St. Eustatius Gazette.' " *West Indische gids* 29:161–74.
_____. 1961. *Aruba: Past and Present.* Oranjestad: D. J. De Wit.
_____. 1968. *Curaçao from Colonial Dependence to Autonomy.* Oranjestad: De Wit Inc.
_____. 1984. "Life on St. Eustatius in 1790–1794, as Portrayed by Rediscovered Local Newspapers." *Gazette* 34:137–58.
Hebdige, Dick. 1977. "Reggae, Rastas and Rudies." In *Mass Communication and Society,* eds. James Curran et al. 426–39. London: Edward Arnold.
_____. n.d. *Culture, Identity and Caribbean Music.* London: Methuen/Comedia, forthcoming.
Helwig, John F., and Jamesine Friend. 1985. "Teaching Where There Are No Schools." *Development Communication Report,* Spring, 11–12.

Hernández, Andres R. 1976. "Cinema and Revolution in Cuba in the 1970s." Paper read at Latin American Studies Association, 24–27 March, Atlanta, Georgia.

Hernández, Luis. 1969. "Un siglo de beísbol en Cuba." *Semanario deportivo LPV,* 2 December, 8–9.

Hill, Errol. 1972. *The Trinidad Carnival: Mandate for a National Theatre.* Austin: University of Texas Press.

Hill, Valdemar A., Sr. 1971. *Rise to Recognition (An Account of Virgin Islanders from Slavery to Self-Government).* St. Thomas.

Hilton, Ronald. 1963. "The Press in Latin America, Spain, and Portugal." *Hispanic American Report,* Special Issue, 1–48.

Hitchins, William E. 1959. *J.M. and Other Cartoonists from the Trinidad Guardian.* Port of Spain: Trinidad Publishing Co. Ltd.

Hofmann, Paul. 1965. "Dominican Leader Silences Radio Controversy." *New York Times,* 7 September.

Hoover, Stewart M. 1986. "Report of the Special Study Committee on Emerging Communication Technologies in National Development." New York: Intermedia. Mimeo.

Hosein, Everold. 1975a. "Mass Media Preferences, Media Credibility and CARICOM Awareness in Urban St. Lucia." *Caribbean Monthly Bulletin,* July, 14–20.

_____. 1975b. "The Implications of Expanded Government Ownership of the Mass Media for Freedom of the Press in Guyana." *Caribbean Monthly Bulletin,* April, 18–22.

Hoyos, F. A. 1953. *Our Common Heritage.* Bridgetown, Barbados: Advocate Press.

Hubbard's Newspaper and Book Directory of the World. 1882. New Haven: H. P. Hubbard.

Hubbard's Right Hand Record and Newspaper Directory. 1880. New Haven: H. P. Hubbard.

Huey, John. 1980. "In Jamaica, the *Gleaner* Fights the Government and Is an Election Issue." *Wall Street Journal,* 23 October, 1.

_____. 1981. "Hypnotic Sound of Reggae Floats Far From the Slums of Jamaica." *Wall Street Journal,* 10 August.

Hughes, Alister. 1980. "Mixed Score for the PRG." News release, 18 March. Mimeo.

Hunt, L. 1967. "Mass Media in the West Indies." *Democratic Journalist,* April, 52–54.

Hylton, Patrick. 1975. "The Politics of Caribbean Music." *The Black Scholar,* September, 23–29.

Index on Censorship. 1987. "Jamaican Press Negligent over Police Killings." November–December, 5.

Information Department of Colonial Office. 1956. *Handbook on Broadcasting Services in the Colonies Etc. 1956.* London: Information Department of Colonial Office.

Inter American Press Association (IAPA). 1970. "Report by the Committee on Freedom of the Press." Presented at IAPA meeting, April, at Montego Bay, Jamaica.

Inter American Press Association News. 1988. "Dominican Press Free and Open." April, 14.

International Broadcasting Institute (IBI). 1975. "Communications and Information for Development Purposes in the Caribbean Area." London: IBI.

International Christian Broadcasters (ICB). 1966. "Audience Research in Aruba with Particular Reference to Radio Station PJA-6." Downers Grove, Illinois: ICB. Mimeo.

International Organization of Journalists (IOJ). 1976. "Republic of Cuba." In *Mass Media in C.M.E.A. Countries,* 159–74. Prague: IOJ.

_____. 1982. *First Conference of Journalists from the Caribbean Area, St. George's, Grenada, April 1982.* Prague: IOJ.

IOJ Newsletter. 1987. "IOJ Delegation in the Dominican Republic." July, 1–2.

IPI Report. 1979. "A Journalist Is Being Murdered . . . and the Police Do Nothing." October, 3.

Jagan, Cheddi, and Moses Nagamootoo. 1980. *The State of the Free Press in Guyana.* Georgetown: New Guyana Co. Ltd.

Jallier, Maurice, and Yollen Lossen. 1985. *Musique aux Antilles. Mizak bo Kay.* Paris: Editions Caribeennes.

James, C. L. R. 1963. *Beyond a Boundary.* London: Hutchinson.

Jarvis, J. Antonio. 1938. *Brief History of the Virgin Islands.* St. Thomas: The Art Shop.

Jeanne, Max. 1980. "Sociologie du theatre antillais." *CARE.* May.

Jenkins, Carol, and Travis Jenkins. 1982. "Garifuna Musical Style and Culture History." *Belizean Studies* 10(3/4).

Jordan, Octavio. 1952. "Cuba's Right-of-Reply Law in Radio Broadcasting." *Journalism Quarterly* 28:358–364.

Joseph, Leo. 1981. " 'Baby Doc' Abruptly Ends Free Speech in Haiti." *The Press,* February, 8–9.

Journal of the Barbados Museum and Historical Society. 1958. "Extracts from the Liberal Newspaper." Pp. 9–19, 56–162.

Kalff, S. 1923–24. "Surinaamsche journalistiek." *West Indische gids,* 5, 463–74.

Kallyndyr, Rolston, and Henderson Dalrymple. 1973. *Reggae: A People's Music.* London: Carib-Arawak Publications.

Kay, Frances. 1966. *This—Is Grenada.* Trinidad: Caribbean Printers.

Kershen, Albert S. 1953a. "Puerto Rico Tabloid Plays Sports Coverage." *Editor and Publisher,* 28 February.

_____. 1953b. "Virgin Island Papers Must Rely on Side-Lines." *Editor and Publisher,* 16 May.

Kingson, Walter K., and Rome Cowgill. 1951. "Radio in Puerto Rico." *The Quarterly of Film, Radio and Television,* Winter, 154–72.

Kittross, J. M. 1978. *A Bibliography of Theses and Dissertations in Broadcasting, 1920–1973.* Washington, D.C.: Broadcast Education Association.

Kopkind, Andrew. 1980. "Trouble in Paradise." *Columbia Journalism Review,* March–April, 41.

Krohn, Stewart. 1979. "Television for Belize: Down This Road Lies Madness!" *Brukdown,* No. 10, 11–13.

_____. 1981. "Television Mania! The Stations Turn On, the Nation Tunes In, Will Government Freak Out?" *Brukdown,* No. 6, 15–21.

Kunzle, David. 1975. "Public Graphics in Cuba: A Very Cuban Form of International Art." *Latin American Perspectives* 2(4):91.

Labour Spokesman. 1984. "TV—So Many Questions." 16 May, 2.

Lapper, Richard. 1984. "From Pirate to Private—with Government Approval." *TV World,* November, 16–17.

Lashley, Leroy L. G. 1982. "An Analysis of the Calypso As a Mass Communication Medium: The Social and Political Uses (Trinidad)." Ph.D. dissertation, Howard University.

LeMoyne, James. 1983. "Suriname's New Press: Unesco's Disciple." *New York Times,* 29 December, A-3.

Lent, John A. 1971a. "Mass Media in the Netherlands Antilles." *Gazette* 17(2):51–73.

———. 1971b. "Smallness Is a Problem of Antillean Press." *The Democratic Journalist,* No. 2, 15–17.

———. 1972. "Commonwealth Caribbean Mass Media: Historical, Cultural, Economic and Political Aspects." Ph.D. dissertation, University of Iowa.

———. 1974. "Mass Communications Bibliography of the English-Speaking Caribbean." *Caribbean Studies,* July, 159–202.

———. 1975. "English-Speaking Caribbean Media History: Bibliographic References and Research Sources." *Journalism History,* Summer, 58–60.

———. 1976a. "Caribbean Mass Communications: Selected Information Sources." *Journal of Broadcasting,* Winter, 111–26.

———. 1976b. *Mass Media in the Commonwealth Caribbean: Recent Bibliographic Sources.* Philadelphia: Temple University, School of Communications and Theatre.

———. 1977a. "The Long, Long Case of the State Versus Dayclean." *IPI Report,* October, 12–13.

——— 1977b. *Third World Mass Media and Their Search for Modernity: The Case of Commonwealth Caribbean, 1717–1976.* Cranbury, N.J.: Associated University Presses.

———. 1977c. "Why Editors Feared a Phone Call from Mr. Manley." *IPI Report,* November, 13–14.

———. 1980. "The Press of the French Antilles: A History and Listing of Periodicals." *Publishing History,* No. 8, 45–64.

———. 1981a. *Caribbean Mass Communications: A Comprehensive Bibliography.* Waltham, Mass.: Crossroads Press.

———. 1981b. "Mass Communications in the Netherlands Antilles: What a Difference a Decade Makes." *Gazette* 28(3):141–55.

———. 1985. "Mass Media in Grenada: Three Lives in a Decade." *Journalism Quarterly,* Winter, 755–62.

———. 1986. "Mass media aux Iles Vierges: Une perspective contemporaire." In *Annales des pays d'Amèrique Centrale et des Caraibes* 5:107–21. Aix-en-Provence: Université d'Aix-Marseille III.

———. 1987. "Caribbean." In *Global Guide to Media and Communications,* ed. John A. Lent, 57–64. Munich: K. G. Saur for George Kurian Reference Books.

———. *Bibliographic Guide to Caribbean Mass Communications.* Unpublished manuscript.

———. n.d. *Caribbean Popular Culture.* Bowling Green, Ohio: Popular Press, forthcoming.

Lenti, Paul. 1988. "Tax Exemption Helps Industry Get a Foothold in Puerto Rico." *Variety,* 16 November, 5.

Leon Enrique, Roberto. 1975. *Ultimo edición. Bosquejo Histórico de la prensa cubana en la lucha de clases.* Havana: Editorial Arte y Literatura.

Leslie, Vernon. 1978. "Books in 19th Century Belize." *Belizean Studies,* September, 25–33.

Lett, Leslie. 1982. "Antigua—Trial by Satire." *Caribbean Contact,* August, 11.

Lewis, George H. 1979. "Mass, Popular, Folk and Elite Cultures: Webs of Significance." *Media Asia* 6(1):34–43.

Lewis, Gordon K. 1968. *The Growth of the Modern West Indies.* London: Macgibbon and Kee.

———. 1972. *The Virgin Islands. A Caribbean Lilliput.* Evanston: Northwestern University Press.

Lewis, Linden. 1981. "The Mighty Shadow." *Caribbean Review,* February, 20–23, 49–50.

Lewisohn, Florence. 1970. *St. Croix Under Seven Flags.* Hollywood, Fla.: Dukane Press.

"Liberty Day Nov. 1." n.d. St. Thomas: Public Library. Brochure.

Liebling, A. J. 1948. "The Wayward Press: Caribbean Excursion." *New Yorker,* 10 April, 60–62, 64–68.

Lincoln, Waldo. 1913. "Account of a Visit to the West Indies in Search of Files of Old Newspapers." *Proceedings of the American Antiquarian Society.* October.

———. 1924. "Report of the Council." *Proceedings of the American Antiquarian Society.* October, 136–47.

———. 1925. "History of Bermuda Newspapers." Worcester, Mass.: American Antiquarian Society.

———. 1926. "List of Newspapers of the West Indies and Bermuda in the Library of the American Antiquarian Society." *Proceedings of the American Antiquarian Society,* April, 130–55.

Lionarons, Wilfred. 1985. "No Criticism Possible." *Index on Censorship* 5:15–16.

Logan, Rayford W. 1968. *Haiti and the Dominican Republic.* New York: Oxford University Press.

López, Oscar Luis. 1981. *La radio en Cuba: Estudio de su desarrollo en la sociedad neocolonial.* Havana: Editorial Letras Cubanas.

López Virgil, José Ignacio. 1983. "Escribiendo para la radio local." *Media Development* 3:18–21.

Louison, Lucien. 1971. "Eléments d'une histoire de la presse à la Martinique (1920–1939)." Toulouse: Université de Toulouse–Le Mirail.

Lowe, Kathy. 1983. "How Communities Run Radio Stations in Italy and the Dominican Republic." *Media Development* 3:14–17.

Lynn, Wilma H. 1981. "Towards an Integrated Communication Strategy in Support of National Development Community Media: A Jamaican Case Study." Master's thesis, American University.

Maddison, John. 1971. "Radio and Television in Literacy: A Survey of the Use of the Broadcasting Media in Combating Illiteracy Among Adults." Paris UNESCO.

Malik, Rex. 1987. "In Conversation with Edward Seaga." *Intermedia,* July–September, 3–4.

Malm, Krister, and Roger Wallis. 1985. "The *Baila* of Sri Lanka and the Calypso of Trinidad." *Communication Research,* July, 227–300.

Mandle, Jay R., and Joan D. Mandle. 1988. "Grassroots Commitment: Dependency and Creativity in Trinidad and Tobago Basketball." Paper read at Caribbean Studies Association, 25 May, Pointe-à-Pitre, Guadeloupe. Mimeo.

Manléon de Benítez, Carmen. 1978. *Estudio sobre la televisión en Puerto Rico.*

Río Piedras: Instituto de Investigaciones de Problemas del Consumidor, Universidad de Puerto Rico.

Manning, Frank. 1973. *Black Clubs in Bermuda: Ethnography of a Play World.* Ithaca, N.Y.: Cornell University Press.

———. 1974. "Nicknames and Number Plates in the British West Indies." *Journal of American Folklore,* April–June, 123–32.

———. 1978. "Carnival in Antigua: An Indigenous Festival in a Tourist Economy." *Anthropos* 73:191–204.

———. 1981. "Celebrating Cricket: The Symbolic Construction of Caribbean Politics." *American Ethnologist,* 616–32.

———. 1983a. "Carnival in the West Indian Diaspora." *The Round Table* 286:186–96.

———. 1983b. "The Carnival Industry." *The Caribbean and West Indies Chronicle,* April–May, 12–13.

———. 1984. "The Performance of Politics: Caribbean Music and the Anthropology of Victor Turner." *Antropológica* 26:1.

———. 1986. "Challenging Authority: Calypso and Politics in the Caribbean." In *The Frailty of Authority,* ed. Myron J. Aronoff, 167–79. New Brunswick, N.J.: Transaction Books.

Marketing Advisory Service Ltd. 1965. "Jamaica '65, the Third Comprehensive Survey of Radio Listening." London: Metropolis Press.

Market Research Ltd. 1973. "1973 Jamaica Radio Survey." Kingston: Montrose Printery Ltd.

Marshall, Trevor. 1985. "Media Technologies Seriously Affect C'bean Cultures." *Caribbean Contact,* October, 8–9.

———. 1986. "Calypso—A Caribbean Journey." *Caribbean Contact,* February, 12.

Martí, Jorge L. 1946. "The P ess in Cuba: Its 'Rebirth' Since 1939." *Journalism Quarterly* 22:124–29.

Martínez, Héctor. 1978. *La prensa clandestina.* Santo Domingo: Universidad Autónoma de Santo Domingo.

Martínez Paulino, Marcos A. 1973. *Publicaciones dominicanas desde la colonia.* Santo Domingo: Editoria del Caribe.

Martínez Victores, Ricardo. 1978. *7RR La historia de Radio Rebelde.* Havana: Editorial de Ciencias Sociales.

Massey, Hector John. 1972. "The Jamaican Press and Federalism." Ph.D. dissertation, University of Toronto.

Matéo-Nin, Milcíades. 1974. *Evolución de la prensa en Santo Domingo: Estructura de poder en la comunicación colectiva.* Santo Domingo.

Maxwell, John. 1958. "Towards Good Radio." *Public Opinion,* 8 February.

McCormack, Ed. 1976. "Bob Marley with a Bullet." *Rolling Stone,* 12 August, 37–41.

McCulloch, William. 1921. "Additions to History of Printing." *Proceedings of the American Antiquarian Society,* April, 243–47.

McFarlane, Basil. 1963. "The Rise and Fall of 'The Times.'" *The Welfare Reporter,* February, 26.

McLean, Polly E. 1986. "Calypso and Revolution in Grenada." *Popular Music and Society* 10(4):87–99.

McMurtrie, Douglas C. 1928. "A Project for Printing in Bermuda, 1772." Chicago: Privately printed.

_____. 1932. "The First Printing in Dominica." London: Privately printed.

_____. 1933. "Early Printing in Barbados; Being an Account of the Establishment of the Press on that Island and of the Known Works of David Harry, Samuel Keimer, William Beebe, William Brown, G. Esmand, John Orderson, Thomas W. Perch, Isaac W. Orderson and W. Walker." London: Privately Printed.

_____. 1934a. "The Early Press of Jamaica." Metuchen, N.J.: Privately printed.

_____. 1934b. "The First Printing on the Island of Jamaica." Metuchen, N.J.: Privately printed.

_____. 1936. "A Broadside Issued at Mobile (Now in Alabama) in 1763, But Printed on the Island of Jamaica in the Same Year." Chicago: Chicago School of Printing.

_____. 1942a. "A Preliminary Check List of Published Materials Relating to the History of Printing in Dominican Republic." Chicago: Committee on Invention of Printing.

_____. 1942b. "The First Printing in Jamaica, with a Discussion of the Date of the First Establishment of a Press on that Island by Robert Baldwin. . . ." Evanston, Ill.: Privately printed.

_____. 1943a. "Early Printing on the Island of Antigua." Evanston, Ill.: Privately printed.

_____. 1943b. "The First Printing Press on the Island of Tobago." *National Printing Education Journal,* April.

_____. 1943c. "Notes on the Beginning of Printing on the Island of Trinidad." Fort Worth: National Association for Printing Education.

McReynolds, Martin. 1965. "Dominican Papers Silenced in Crisis." *Editor and Publisher.* 4 September, p. 26.

Media Worker, September 1981, 2.

Media Worker, April 1982, 7.

Medina, Jose T. 1904. *La imprenta en la Habana 1707–1810.* Santiago de Chile: Imprenta Elzeviriana.

Melchior, Ariel, Sr. 1980. "The Birth and Growth of the Daily News." *Daily News,* 1 August, A-8, A-9.

_____. 1981. *Thoughts Along the Way: An Anthology of Editorials from the Virgin Islands Daily News, 1930–78.* St. Thomas: Privately printed.

Meyerson, Michael. 1973. *Memories of Underdevelopment: The Revolutionary Films of Cuba.* New York: Grossman Publishers.

Micklewright, Barry. 1980. "From Morse Code to Videotape." *Daily News,* 1 August, B-68.

Milner, Judy Oliver. 1979. "Fidel Castro and the Cuban Media." In *Mass Media in/on Cuba and the Caribbean Area: The Role of the Television, Radio and the Press,* ed. Jan Herd, 18–21. Erie: Northwestern Pennsylvania Institute for Latin American Studies, Mercyhurst College.

Mitchell, Harold. 1968. *Contemporary Politics and Economics in the Caribbean.* Athens: Ohio University Press.

Morales, Cecilio J., Jr. 1983. *A Survey of Press Freedom in Latin America.* Washington, D.C.: Council on Hemispheric Affairs and the Newspaper Guild.

_____. 1984. *A Survey of Press Freedom in Latin America 1983/84.* Washington, D.C.: Council on Hemispheric Affairs and the Newspaper Guild.

Morales, Cecilio J., Jr., and Meghan Ballard. 1985. *Survey of Press Freedom in Latin America 1984/85.* Washington, D.C.: Council on Hemispheric Affairs and the Newspaper Guild.

Mota, Francisco. 1985. *Para la historia del periodismo en Cuba: Un aporte bibliográfico.* Santiago de Cuba: Editorial Oriente.

Mydans, Seth. 1984. "Grenada Can Sound Off Again in Revived Paper." *New York Times,* 5 January, 6.

Nascimento, Christopher A. 1974. "The Transferability of the Concepts of Media Ownership and Freedom." Paper presented at "Communications and Information for Development Purposes in the Caribbean Area," Georgetown, Guyana. Mimeo.

Nation, The. 1927a. "A Voice from a Haitian Jail." 17 August, 168.

———. 1927b. "The Press in Haiti." 17 August, 166, 168.

Nation, Fitzroy. 1987. "Gleaner's Monopoly Ended." *Caribbean Contact,* December, 11.

Negron-Portillo, Mariano. 1980. "A Study of the Newspaper 'La Democracia,' Puerto Rico, 1895–1914: A Historical Analysis." Ph.D. dissertation, State University of New York at Stony Brook.

Neita, Clifton. 1953. *One Hundred Years of Famous Pages from the Press of Jamaica, 1853–1953.* Kingston: Gleaner Co.

———. 1979. "The *Daily Gleaner*'s Lonely Battle." *Wall Street Journal,* 19 March.

Nettleford, Rex M. 1979. *Cultural Action and Social Change: The Case of Jamaica. An Essay in Caribbean Cultural Identity.* Ottawa: International Development Research Centre.

New Jewel. 1981. "Defiant Move by Workers." 21 August.

New Jewel Movement. 1981. "The Revolution Must Be Respected."

News Front. 1981. "CNN Opens a New World in the Virgin Islands." May.

Nichols, John Spicer. 1979. "The Havana Hustle: A New Phase in Cuba's International Communication Activities." In *Case Studies of Mass Media in the Third World.* Special edition of *Studies in Third World Societies,* ed. John A. Lent. Williamsburg, Va.: College of William and Mary.

———. 1982a. "Cuba." *World Press Encyclopedia,* ed. George Thomas Kurian, 257–71. New York: Facts on File.

———. 1982b. "Cuban Mass Media: Organization, Control and Functions." *Journalism Monographs,* November.

———. 1982c. "Functions of the Cuban Mass Media in Social Conflict: Prospects of the 80s." In *Cuba: Internal and International Affairs,* ed. Jorge Domínguez. Beverly Hills: Sage.

Nicolini, Pia. 1987. "Puerto Rican Leaders' Views of English-Language Media." *Journalism Quarterly,* Summer/Autumn, 597–601.

Nippon Hoso Kyokai. 1977. *World Radio and TV 1977.* Tokyo: Radio and TV Culture Research Institute.

Nixon, Raymond B. 1981. *Education for Journalism in Latin America: A Report of Progress.* Minneapolis: Minnesota Journalism Center.

O'Gorman, Pam. 1972. "An Approach to the Study of Jamaican Popular Music." *Jamaica Journal,* December, 51.

OIRT Information. 1972. "Cuban Radio and Television." Nos. 10–11, 5–6.

Okinshevich, Leo. 1966. *Latin America in Soviet Writings: A Bibliography.* Vol. 1 (1917–1958), Vol. 2 (1959–1964). Baltimore: Johns Hopkins Press.

Oliveira, Omar Souki. 1986a. "Effects of Transborder Television in Corozal Town and Surrounding Villages." *Belizean Studies* 14:31–51.

———. 1986b. "Satellite TV Dependency: An Empirical Approach." *Gazette* 38:127–45.

Oltheten, Th. H. 1977. *Communicatie in de Nederlandse Antillen.* Achtergronden voor een Media-beleid.

Ornes, German. 1958. *Trujillo: Little Caesar of the Caribbean.* New York: Thomas Nelson and Sons.

Oswald, John Clyde. 1968. *Printing in the Americas.* New York: Hacker Art Books.

Otero, Gustavo Adolfo. 1953. *La cultura y el periodismo en América.* Quito: Casa Editora Liebmann.

Otero, Rafael Lechuga. 1980. *La información en televisión.* Santiago de Cuba: Editorial Oriente.

Oudschans Dentz, Fred. 1933. "Surinaamsche journalistiek." *West Indische gids* 20:33–44, 65–76, 289–90.

Pactor, Howard S. 1988. "VIBAX: Nassau's Forgotten Radio Station." *Journalism Quarterly,* Winter, 1000–3.

PAJ News. 1978. "The North Street Scene." March–April, 9.

———. 1979a. *"Gleaner"* under Fire. October, 8–9.

———. 1979b. "Torchlight Put Out." October, 5.

Paláu, Awilda. 1979. *Prensa comercial. Posiciones de clase ante la situación laboral.* Guaynabo: Editorial Sagita.

Pearse, Andrew. 1955. "Aspects of Change in Caribbean Folk Music." *Journal of the International Folk Music Council* 7:29–36.

———. 1956. "Carnival in Nineteenth Century Trinidad." *Caribbean Quarterly* 4:176–93.

———. 1969. "Mitto Sampson on Calypso Legends of the Nineteenth Century." *Caribbean Quarterly* 15:2–3.

———. 1978–79. "Music in Caribbean Popular Culture." *Revista interamericana,* Winter, 629–39.

Pedreira, Antonio S. 1941. *El periodismo en Puerto Rico; bosquejo histórico desde su iniciación hasta el 1930.* La Habana: Imp. Ucar, García y Cía.

———. 1970. *Obras de Antonio S. Pedreira II.* San Juan: Instituto de Cultura Puertorriqueña.

Penn, V. E., and E. R. Penn. 1968. *Tortolana: A Bibliography.* Tortola: Public Library.

People's Law No. 18. 1981. "Proclamation by the People's Revolution Government. A Law To Make Certain Temporary Provisions Concerning Publications Until the Formulation of a National Media Code." Gazetted 19 June.

Petch. Trevor. 1987. "Television and Video Ownership in Belize." *Belizean Studies* 15:12–14.

Phillips, R. Hart. 1959a. "Castro Methods Hurt Cuba Press." *New York Times,* 24 August.

———. 1959b. "Society News Tax is Dropped in Cuba." *New York Times,* 5 June.

———. 1959c. "Tax Society News? Cuban Editors Aghast." *New York Times,* 2 June, 21.

———. 1961a. "Castro Controls Cubans by His Oratory and Arms." *New York Times,* 13 June, 1, 18.

_____. 1961b. "Cuban TV: The Fidel Show." *New York Times,* 23 July.

Pickering, R. J. 1978. "Cuba." In *Sport Under Communism,* ed. James Riordan, 148–49. London: C. Hurst.

Piedra, Armando Jorge. 1972. "The Development of Advertising in Puerto Rico." Master's thesis, University of Florida.

Pierce, Robert N. 1982a. "Dominican Republic." In *World Press Encyclopedia,* ed. George Thomas Kurian, 295–301. New York: Facts on File.

_____. 1982b. "Haiti." In *World Press Encyclopedia,* ed. George Thomas Kurian, 429–36. New York: Facts on File.

Prida, Dolores. 1980. "Cuban TV: Worthy But Too Often Dull." *World Broadcast News,* September, 10–11.

Pritchard, Bill. 1987. "Guyanese Catholic Newspaper Suspends Publication." *Editor and Publisher,* 12 September, 22, 62.

Procope, Stanley. n.d. "History of the Press (of St. Kitts)." Unpublished manuscript.

Quesada, Vicente G. 1917. "Legislation in Old Spain and the Indies on Printing and the Book Trade." In *La vida intelectual en la Américas española.* Buenos Aires.

Quevedo, Raymond. 1983. *Atilla's Kaiso: A Short History of Trinidad Calypso.* St. Augustine, Trinidad: University of the West Indies.

Radio Havana Cuba. 1982. *XX Aniversario de Radio Habana Cuba.* Havana: Editora Política.

Radio Hoyer. 1959? *Gedenkboek 5 jaar Radio Hoyer: 10 Maart 1954–10 Maart 1959.* Oranjestad: Radio Hoyer.

Radio Jamaica. 1965. "Jamaica Market Profile 1965." London.

_____. 1969. "Jamaica Survey No. 6. Audience Research in Jamaica." Kingston: Radio Jamaica.

Radio Jamaica and Rediffusion. 1956. "A Guide to Mass Information in Jamaica: A Report on a Survey of Listening Habits." Kingston.

Radio Trinidad. 1967. "Market Profile Trinidad." Port of Spain: Radio Trinidad.

_____. 1969. "Market Profile Trinidad." Port of Spain: Radio Trinidad.

Ratliff, William A. 1987. *The Selling of Fidel Castro: The Media and the Cuban Revolution.* New Brunswick, N.J.: Transaction Books.

Ray, Ellen, and Bill Schaap. 1980. "Massive Destabilization in Jamaica: 1976 with a New Twist." *Covert Action,* August–September, 7–17.

Reckford, V. 1982. "Reggae Rastafarianism and Cultural Identity." *Jamaica Journal* 46:69–79.

Redding, Jerry. 1971. " 'Castro-ating' the Media." *Educational Broadcasting Review,* June, 35–42.

Renalls, Martin A. 1968. "Development of the Documentary Film in Jamaica." Master's thesis, Boston University.

Renard, Yves. 1981. "Kadans: Musique populaire de la Caraibe créolophone, Facteur d' intégration régionale?" Paper read at Troisième Colloque International des Etudes Créoles, 3–9 May, St. Lucia. Mimeo.

Richards, Michael. 1986. "Mighty Calypsonian: Controversial Gabby." *Caribbean Contact,* January, 12.

Richards, Novelle H. 1964. *The Struggle and the Conquest.* St. John's, Antigua: Workers Voice Printery.

Rivera de Otero, Consuelo. 1973. "An Examination of Selected Puerto Rican Communications Divisions with a View to the Development of Guidelines for the Establishment of a Communications Media Center." Ph.D. dissertation, New York University.

Roberts, John S. 1972. *Black Music of Two Worlds.* New York: Praeger.

Rodman, Selden. 1961. *Haiti: The Black Republic.* New York: The Devin-Adair Co.

Rodríguez, Ernesto E. 1978. "Public Opinion and the Press in Cuba." *Cuban Studies,* July, 51–65.

Rodríguez, Rodrigo. 1967. "Mass Media Exposure and the Adoption of Farm Practices: A Study of Puerto Rican Tobacco Farmers." Master's thesis, Michigan State University.

Rodríguez-Betancourt, Miriam. 1980. "Cuban Media Yesterday and Today." *Democratic Journalist,* December, 17–19.

Rodríguez-Demorizi, Emilio. 1944. *La imprenta y los primeros periódicos de Santo Domingo.* Ciudad Trujillo: Imp. San Francisco.

Rodríguez Méndez, José. 1976. *La especialización periodista: Algunos métodos.* Havana: Serie Literatura y Arte.

Rodway, James. 1918. "The Press in British Guiana." *Proceedings of the American Antiquarian Society,* October.

Rohlehr, Gordon. 1972. "Forty Years of Calypso." *Tapia* 2:3–16.

Roosberg, Leslie. 1977. *De Curacaose dagbladpers en omroep in maatschappelijk perspektief; stageverslag.* Nijmegen: Sociologisch Institut.

Roppa, Guy, and Neville Clarke. 1969. *The Commonwealth Caribbean: Regional Cooperation in News and Broadcasting Exchanges.* Paris: UNESCO.

Rosario Adames, Fausto. 1987. "Radio Journalism: Problems and Perspectives." *Democratic Journalist,* November, 21–22.

Roser, Connie, Leslie B. Snyder, and Steven H. Chaffee. 1986. "Belize Release Me, Let Me Go: The Impact of U.S. Mass Media on Emigration in Belize." *Belizean Studies* 14:1–30.

Ross, Joan. 1979. "Citizens To Probe *Gleaner.*" *PAJ News,* October, 10.

_____. 1982. "One Year Later, A Brief History of TFG." *Media Worker,* April, 6.

Rotberg, Robert I. 1971. *Haiti: The Politics of Squalor.* Boston: Houghton Mifflin.

Royes, Heather. 1987. "Jamaica: Trembling on the Brink." *Intermedia,* July–September, 54–55.

Rudder, Michael. 1985. "Broadcasting in the Caribbean: A Unique Experience." *The Third Channel* 1:125–35.

_____. 1986. "Broadcasting, Step-Child or Blood Relative?" In *Telecommunications for Development. Exploring New Strategies. An International Forum,* 121–27. Washington, D.C.: INTELSAT.

Ruprecht, Alvina. 1988. "Radyo Tanbou: The Function of the Popular Media in Guadeloupe." Paper read at conference of Caribbean Studies Association, 27 May, Pointe-à-Pitre, Guadeloupe.

Samson, Ph. A. 1950. "De Surinaamse pers gedurende het engelse tussenbestuur." *West Indische gids* 31:80–92.

_____. 1952. "Preventieve maatregelen tegen de pers in Suriname." *West Indische gids* 33:222–28.

Sánchez Betances, Luis. 1976. *Estudio sobre la televisión en Puerto Rico.* Río

Piedras: University of Puerto Rico.

Sanders, Ron. 1978a. *Broadcasting in Guyana.* London: Routledge and Kegan Paul.

_____. 1978b. "Stagnation in Guyana." *Intermedia,* June, 12–13.

Sanger, Jesse William. 1919. *Advertising Methods in Cuba.* Washington, D.C.: Government Printing Office.

Sargent, Leslie. 1979. "Information and Change in the Caribbean: Problems and Prospects for the Media." In *Caribbean Media in Transition.* Kingston: Institute of Mass Communication, University of the West Indies.

Sealy, Clifford. 1986. "Unjust to a Genius." *Caribbean Contact,* May, 15.

Sellers, W. 1951. "Film Production in the West Indies." *Colonial Cinema,* December, 91–92.

Shaw, Audley Fitz-Albert. 1981. "Multinational Enterprises and Public Relations: A Study of the Bauxite/Alumina Companies in Jamaica." Master's thesis, Northern Illinois University.

Shearman, Montague, and O. T. Rayner, eds. 1926. *The Press Laws of Foreign Countries.* London: His Majesty's Stationery Office.

Sherlock, Philip. 1966. *West Indies.* London: Thames and Hudson, Ltd.

Shilstone, E. M. 1958. "Some Notes on Early Printing Presses and Newspapers in Barbados." *The Journal of the Barbados Museum and Historical Society,* November, 24.

Sierra, Julio. 1980. *Cine en Santo Domingo.* Santo Domingo: Comité por Instituto Nacional de Estudios Cinematográficos.

Simmonds, Peter Lund. 1841. "Statistics of Newspapers in Various Countries." *Statistical Society of London Journal,* July, 123.

Singh, Rickey. 1981. "Our Stand on Bishop's Grenada." *Caribbean Contact,* January–February, 1, 3.

_____. 1984a. "Caribbean Media and the Grenada Affair." *Caribbean Contact,* January–February, 14.

_____. 1984b. "The Right to Choose." *Caribbean Contact,* June, 5.

Singham, A. W. 1968. *The Hero and the Crowd in a Colonial Polity.* New Haven: Yale University Press.

Skinner, Ewart C. 1984. "Foreign TV Program Viewing and Dependency: A Case Study of U.S. Television Viewing in Trinidad & Tobago." Ph.D. dissertation, Michigan State University.

_____. 1987. "Use of United States Produced Media in Caribbean Society: Exposure and Impact." *Studies in Latin American Popular Culture* 6:183–95.

Smeyak, Gerald P. 1973. "The History and Development of Broadcasting in Guyana, South America." Ph.D. dissertation, Ohio State University.

Smikle, Patrick. 1979. "Reflections on a Closure." *PAJ News,* October, 5–7.

Snitkey, Richard N. 1974. "A Content Analysis of the Newscasts of Radio Habana Cuba." Master's thesis, University of Minnesota.

Snow, R. F. 1977. "Nota betreffende de grafische communicatie in het algemeen en de dagbladpers in het bijzonder op de Nederlandse Antillen." Curaçao: Stichting Grafische Communicatie.

Snyder, Donald. 1983. "Cable Television in the Caribbean: The Case of Jamaica." Paper read at conference of Caribbean Studies Association, May, Santo Domingo, Dominican Republic.

Soderlund, Walter C., and Stuart H. Surlin, eds. 1985. *Media in Latin America and the Caribbean: Domestic and International Perspectives.* Windsor: University of Windsor.

Spencer, Neil. 1975. "Me Just Wanna Live, Y'unnerstan?" *New Musical Express,* 19 July.

———. 1977. " 'Me No Political Man'—Inside Bob Marley's UK Hideaway." *New Musical Express,* 23 April.

Spotlight. 1964. "Recollections of Evon Blake." December, 7–8.

St. Croix Avis. 1969. "125th Anniversary Issue." May.

St. Pierre, Maurice. 1973. "West Indian Cricket: A Sociohistorical Appraisal." *Caribbean Quarterly* 19:7–27.

Steffens, Roger. 1981. "Dreadlocks Forever—The Life and Death of Bob Marley." *Los Angeles Reader,* 22 May.

Stichting Grafische Communicatie (SGC). 1979? "De krant op school." Curaçao.

Stivers, Mark. 1981. "Radio Antilles." *WXPN Express,* August, 1.

Stix, Gary. 1984. "Press Hit by Harsh Response to Dominican Riots." *CPJ Update,* May–June, 3–4.

Straubhaar, Joseph Dean. 1986. "The Impact of Videocassette Recorders on Broadcasting in Brazil, Colombia, Dominican Republic and Venezuela." Paper read at Studies in Latin American Popular Culture conference, 10–12 April, New Orleans, La.

Suárez-Murias, Marguerite C. 1980. "Cuba Painted by Cubans: The Nineteenth Century Journalistic Essay." *Revista interamericano de bibliografía.* 30:375–86.

Surlin, Stuart. 1986. "Uses of Jamaican Talk Radio." *Journal of Broadcasting and Electronic Media,* Fall, 459–66.

Swan, Bradford. 1956. "A Checklist of Early Printing on the Island of Antigua (1748–1800)." *Papers of Bibliographical Society of America* 50:285–92.

———. 1970. *The Spread of Printing. Western Hemisphere. The Caribbean Area.* Amsterdam: Vangendt and Co.

Swindels, J. 1977. "Filmkunst." In *Cultureel mosaiek van Suriname. Bijdrage tot onderling begrip,* ed. Albert Helman, 407–11. De Walburg Pers Zutphen, C. F. J. Schriks.

Szulc, Tad. 1959. "A Year of Castro Rule in Cuba: Leftists Speeding Vast Reforms." *New York Times,* 17 December, 4.

———. 1960. "Red Influence Growing in Cuba Behind Facade of the Revolution." *New York Times,* 2 August, 1,4.

Taitt, Sam. 1987. "New Developments in CaBC in Barbados." *COMBROAD,* July–September, 25–32.

Tarter, William V. 1978. "Many Hands Make Light Work: Audience Participation Programming by Cassette in the Plaisance Valley IRD Project, S. Haiti." Unpublished report.

———. 1985. " 'Many Hands—Load Not Heavy' (Min Anpil—Chay Pa Lou): A Study of Participatory Communication in Rural Haiti." Master's thesis, University of Washington.

Taylor, Douglas. 1970. "New Languages for Old in the West Indies." In *Readings in the Sociology of Language,* ed. Joshua A. Fishman, 609–19. The Hague: Mouton.

Taylor, Jeremy. 1976. "The Banyan Experiment." *People,* November–December, 43, 45, 57.

_____. 1982. "Drama on a Dime: Trinidad Producers' Specialty." *World Broadcast News,* February, 32, 34.

Thatcher, Bill, and Bill Tarter. 1983. "How Local Radio Became Community Radio in Haiti — The Story of Radio Lumière." *Media Development,* No. 3, 34–36.

Thomas, Erwin K. 1972. "The Republic of Guyana: Background Study for the Development of a Television Schedule." Master's thesis, Brooklyn College.

_____. 1978. "The Beginnings of Broadcasting in the West Indies, 1920–1949 (Barbados, British Guiana, Jamaica, and Trinidad and Tobago)." Ph. D. dissertation, University of Missouri.

Thomas, Isaiah. 1874. *The History of Printing in America with a Biography of Printers and an Account of Newspapers.* Albany: Joel Munsell.

Thomas, Jo. 1981. "Small Paper Creates Big Stir in the Virgin Islands." *New York Times,* 26 April, 25.

Thomas, Michael. 1976. "The Rastas Are Coming! The Rastas Are Coming!" *Rolling Stone,* 12 August, 34.

Thomas, Tess. 1983. "Jamaica: The Miami Connection." *Intermedia,* July–September, 57.

Thompson, Annie F. 1980. "Puerto Rican Newspapers and Journals of the Spanish Colonial Period as Source Materials for Musicological Research: An Analysis of Their Musical Content." Ph.D. dissertation, Florida State University.

Thompson, Lawrence S. 1962. *Printing in Colonial Spanish America.* London: Archon Books.

Time. 1976. "Singing Them a Message." 22 March, 83–84.

Tiquamt, Alain. 1982. "Address." In *First Conference of Journalists from the Caribbean Area, St. George's, Grenada, April 1982,* 111–14. Prague: IOJ.

"Torchlight Workers: Why We Took Control." 1981. Newsletter. August.

Torres-Ramos, Clara Maria. 1974. "A History of the Development of Instructional Television in Puerto Rico from 1958 to 1970." Ph.D. dissertation, New York University.

Treaster, Joseph B. 1986a. "Free Press Can Flower: Haiti's Press Now 'Has No Reins.'" *Presstime,* August, 20.

_____. 1986b. "Haiti's Press is Unshackled, and Unbridled, Too." *New York Times,* 25 August, A-2.

Treffkorn, Hans. 1982. *Budapest, Berlin, Sophia and Other Training Centers: A World Directory 1982.* Prague: IOJ.

UNESCO. 1947–51. *Press, Radio, Film.* Reports on the Facilities of Mass Communications. Paris: UNESCO.

_____. 1964. *World Communications: Press, Radio, Television, Film.* Paris: UNESCO.

_____. 1965. *World Radio and Television.* Paris: UNESCO.

_____. 1975. *World Communications: A 200 Country Survey of Press, Radio, Television, Film.* Paris: UNESCO.

United States Information Agency. "Listing of Research Reports, 1967–1978." Washington, D.C.: USIA.

_____. *Research Reports. Communication Fact Books.* Washington, D.C.: USIA.

Urivazo, Renaldo Infante. 1982. "Introducing Students to Mass Media: Radio Victoria de Girón." *Prospects* 12:387–94.

Valdez Rodríguez, J. M. 1963. *Ojeada al cine cubano, 1906–1958.* La Habana:

Comisión de Extensión Universitaria.

Valdor, Marie-Louise. 1973. "La presse en Martinique et l'evolution du statut politique de la Martinique de 1958 à 1970." Travail d'Etudes et de Recherches, Université de Toulouse–Le Mirail.

Valenzuela, Lídice. 1986. "The Havana School Will Be Anti-Academic." *Granma Weekly Review,* 26 October, 7.

van Gorkom, J. A. J. 1957. "De filmkunst in Suriname." *Culturele activiteit in Suriname,* 76–83.

———. 1959. "Filmkunst in Suriname." *Wikor* 7(3):104–6.

Variety. 1978. "WTJX Satellite in Virgin Islands." 20 December, 62.

Varlack, Pearl, and Norwell Harrigan. 1977. *The Virgins: A Descriptive and Historical Profile.* St. Thomas: Caribbean Research Institute, College of the Virgin Islands.

Vaughan, H. A. 1966–67. "Samuel Prescod: The Birth of a Hero." *New World,* 60.

Vaughn, Robert V. 1981. "Virgin Islands Mass Communications 1981 – A Survey." Frederikstad: Aye-Aye Press.

Vélez, Héctor. 1983. "Television and Culture: The Case of Puerto Rico." Ph.D. dissertation, Cornell University.

Vélez Aquino, Luis Antonio. 1968. "Puerto Rican Press Reaction to the Shift from Spanish to United States Sovereignty, 1898–1917." Ed.D. dissertation, Columbia University.

Vera, Ernesto. 1978. "The Press and the Ideological Struggle in Cuba." *Democratic Journalist,* November–December, 18–23.

———. 1979. "Mass Media in Cuba." *Democratic Journalist,* November, 12–16.

Vitez, Michael. 1988. "The Shattered Dream of Haiti." (Philadelphia) *Inquirer Magazine,* 3 April, 21–32.

Waggoner, Barbara A. 1967. "News and the Mass Media in the Dominican Republic." *Journalism Quarterly,* Autumn, 533–39.

Wagner, Eric. 1982. "Sport After Revolution: A Comparative Study of Cuba and Nicaragua." *Studies in Latin American Popular Culture* 1:65–73.

———. 1984. "Baseball in Cuba." *Journal of Popular Culture,* Summer, 113–20.

Walters, Ewart. 1979. "Freedom of the Press and Political Change: The Case of Jamaica and the *Daily News.*" Master's thesis, Carlton University.

Warner, Keith Q. 1982. *Kaiso! The Trinidad Calypso: A Study of the Calypso as Oral Literature.* Washington, D.C.: Three Continents Press.

Werker, H. N. 1974. *Funkties van de massamedia in Suriname.* Amsterdam: Universiteit van Amsterdam, Sociografisch Instituut FSW.

Wertheim, Jorge Ricardo. 1977. "A Comparative Analysis of Educational Television in El Salvador and Cuba." Ph.D. dissertation, Stanford University.

Westergaard, Waldemar. 1917. *The Danish West Indies Under Company Rule (1671–1754). With Supplementary Chapter, 1755–1917.* New York: Macmillan.

Wetzel, Hayden. 1986. "Telecommunications Equipment Markets in the Caribbean/Central American Area." Washington, D.C.: U.S. Department of Commerce.

White, Dorcas. 1977. *The Press and the Law in the Caribbean.* Bridgetown, Barbados: Cedar Press.

White, Garth. 1982. "Traditional Musical Practice in Jamaica and Its Influence on the Birth of Modern Jamaican Popular Music." *ACIJ Newsletter,* No. 7, March, 41–67.

———. 1984. "The Development of Jamaican Popular Music—Pt. 2. Urbanisation of the Folk: The Merger of the Traditional and the Popular in Jamaican Music." *ACIJ Research Review,* No. 1, 47–80.

White, Timothy. 1983. *Catch a Fire: The Life of Bob Marley.*

Wiarda, Howard J. 1968. "Cuba." In *Political Forces in Latin America: Dimensions of the Quest for Stability,* eds. Ben Burnett and Kenneth Johnson. Belmont, Ca.: Wadsworth.

———. 1969. *The Dominican Republic: Nation in Transition.* New York: Frederick A. Praeger.

Williams, Richard. 1972. "The Facts of Reggae." *Melody Maker,* 19 February.

Wilson, Gladstone. 1985. "Dependence on External Media." *Caribbean Contact,* November, 7.

———. 1987. "Address." Paper read at OCPLACS/CALACS Conference, 10 October, Windsor, Canada. Mimeo.

Winders, James A. 1983. "Reggae, Rastafarians and Revolution: Rock Music in the Third World." *Journal of Popular Culture,* Summer, 61–73.

Wood, Donald. 1968. *Trinidad in Transition.* London: Oxford University Press.

World Broadcast News. 1981. "Trinidad Banyan Group: Prize-Winning Video from a Garage Studio." January, 8–9.

Zabriskie, Luther K. 1918. *The Virgin Islands of the United States of America.* New York: G. P. Putnam's Sons.

Zandronis, Dannyck. 1979. "La presse Guadeloupéenne." *Le naif qui va plus loin,* April, 11–13.

Zimmerman, Irene. 1961. *A Guide to Current Latin American Periodicals. Humanities and Social Sciences.* Gainesville: Kallman Publishing.

Zobdar-Quitman, Soniar. 1981. *Culture et politique en Guadeloupe et Martinique.* Paris: Editions Alizés-Karthala.

INTERVIEWS

Transcripts of these interviews are in the author's possession and will eventually form part of the John A. Lent Collection to be housed at the Alden Library, Ohio University, Athens, Ohio.

Allfrey, Phyllis and Robert, editors, *Dominica Star,* Roseau, Dominica, 6 May 1971.

Alvarez, Santiago, film director, talk to and interview by Media Study Tour, Havana, Cuba, 6 May 1982. (Tour led by John A. Lent and Howard Frederick.)

Bain, James, chairman of boards, Trinidad and Tobago Television and National Broadcasting Service, Port of Spain, Trinidad, 14 January 1977.

Benitez, José Antonio, vice president, UPEC, and editor, *Granma Weekly Review,* talk to and interview by Media Study Tour, Havana, Cuba, 4 May 1982.

Bird, Ivor, general manager, ZDK, St. John's, Antigua, 28 May 1984.

Boyd, S. A. W., editor, *Dominica Chronicle,* Roseau, Dominica, 5 May 1971.

Bramble, Howell, editor, *Montserrat Times,* Plymouth Montserrat, 29 May 1984.

Brewley, E. Walwyn, general manager, ZBVI, Tortola, British Virgin Islands, 25 May 1981.

Brown, Aggrey, director, CARIMAC of University of the West Indies, in Miami, Florida, 10 March 1984.

Browne, Whit, editor, *Opron Star,* Basseterre, St. Kitts, 31 May 1984.

Caines, G. O., general manager, ZIZ radio and television, Basseterre, St. Kitts, 1 June 1984.

Chongsing, Lenn, editor, *Guardian,* Port of Spain, Trinidad, 1 September 1970.

Christensen, Dennis, program director, Radio Victoria, Oranjestad, Aruba, 29 August 1968.

Clyne, Reggie, editor, *West Indian,* St. George's, Grenada, 12 May 1971.

Collins, John, UPI correspondent, Charlotte Amalie, St. Thomas, U.S. Virgin Islands, 30 May 1981.

Collymore, Frank, editor, *Bim,* Bridgetown, Barbados, 14 May 1971.

Conyers, M. A., general manager, Trinidad Publishing Company, Port of Spain, Trinidad, 14 January 1977.

Coro Antich, Arnoldo, master technician, ICRT, Havana, Cuba, 5 May, 7 May, and 13 July 1982.

Cruickshank, A. M., editor, *Vanguard,* St. George's, Grenada, 12 May 1971.

Cuales, Orlando, general manager, Radio Curom, Willemstad, Curaçao, 9 May 1980.

Daantje, Carlos, editor, *Nobo,* Willemstad, Curaçao, 9 May 1980.

Delph, Compton, editor, *Evening News,* Port of Spain, Trinidad, 1 September, 1970.

Diefenthaler, Albert R., president-director, Radio Carina FM, Oranjestad, Aruba, 6 May 1980.

Downing, Carlos, editor-publisher, *The Island Sun,* Roadtown, Tortola, British Virgin Islands, 25 May 1981.

Dunlop, Roy, director, Radio Anguilla, The Valley, Anguilla, 29 April 1971.

Ewing, Agnes, secretary, Belize Broadcasting Authority, Belize City, Belize, 29 May 1987.

Faux, William, official, Radio Belize, in St. Catherine, Jamaica, 16 September 1976.

France, J. N., editor, *Labour Spokesman;* secretary of Labour Party; general secretary of St. Kitts-Nevis Trades and Labour Union, Basseterre, St. Kitts, 31 May 1984.

Gómez-Lampkin, Jane, news director, Radio Carina FM, Oranjestad, Aruba, 6 May 1980.

González-Manet, Enrique, communications advisor, Ministry of Foreign Affairs, Havana, Cuba, 15 July 1982.

Gordon, Ken, general manager, *Express,* Port of Spain, Trinidad, 2 September 1970.

Grande, Jacinto, director, *Juventud Rebelde,* talk to and interview by Media Study Tour, Havana, Cuba, 5 May 1982.

Grosvenor, Neville, general manager, *Advocate-News,* Bridgetown, Barbados, 7 September 1970.

Hartog, Johan, librarian and historian, Aruba Public Library, Oranjestad, Aruba, 29 August 1968.

Hector, Tim, editor, *Outlet,* St. John's, Antigua, 28 May 1984.

Heiligers, Frans, editor, *Amigoe,* Willemstad, Curaçao, 9 May 1980.

Hermelijn, Jacques A., director, Curaçao Government Information Office, Willemstad, Curaçao, 2 September 1968.

Hernàndez, Eitel, manager-director, TELECURAÇAO, Willemstad, Curaçao, 3 September 1968.

Hoyer, Horacio, proprietor, Hoyer Stations, Willemstad, Curaçao, 3 September 1968.

Hughes, Alister, editor, *Grenada Newsletter,* in Philadelphia, Pa., 11 November 1984.

Ince, Johnson, editor, *Sunday Guardian,* Port of Spain, Trinidad, 13 January 1977.

Jagan, Cheddi, former prime minister and leader of opposition People's Progressive Party, in Willemstad, Curaçao, 8 May 1980.

Jones, Fitzroy, editor, *The Democrat,* Basseterre, St. Kitts, 1 June 1984.

King, Emory, former owner, Tropical Vision, Belize City, Belize, 29 May 1987.

Krohn, Stewart, producer, Great Belize Productions, Belize City, Belize, 29 May 1987.

Llauradó, Adolfo, film actor, Havana, Cuba, 5 May 1982.

Maas, J. C., head editor, *Amigoe di Curaçao,* Willemstad, Curaçao, 2 September 1968.

Maduro, Audrey, manager, TELEARUBA, Oranjestad, Aruba, 27 August 1968.

Mai, Amalia, editor, *Belize Times,* Belize City, Belize, 29 May 1987.

Manley, Michael, former prime minister and leader, People's National Party of Jamaica, in Philadelphia, Pa., 2 November 1981.

Margolles Villanueva, Pedro, chief, International Information, Department of Revolutionary Orientation, Central Committee, Communist Party, talk to and interview by Media Study Tour, Havana, Cuba, 6 May 1982.

Martínez Pirez, Pedro, director of information, Radio Habana Cuba, talk to and interview by Media Study Tour, Havana, Cuba, 4 May 1982.

Mason, Elcon, editor, *Torchlight,* St. George's, Grenada, 12 May 1971.

Mekel, Alexyma, editor and member, board of directors, Radyo Tanbou, Point-à-Pitre, Guadeloupe, 27 May 1988.

Melchior, Ariel, Jr., publisher editor, *Daily News,* Charlotte Amalie, St. Thomas, U.S. Virgin Islands, 29 May 1981.

Miller, Robert, vice president, WSTX, Christiansted, St. Croix, 22 May 1981.

Ollivrin, Alfred, directeur, editor-in-chief, *France-Antilles,* Point-à-Pitre, Guadeloupe, 26 May 1988.

Panneflek, A. E., editor, *La cruz,* Willemstad, Curaçao, 2 September and 3 September 1968.

Pitsch, Jim, station manager, Radio Victoria, Oranjestad, Aruba, 29 August 1968.

Potter, Joe, general manager, WBNB, Charlotte Amalie, St. Thomas, U.S. Virgin Islands, 29 May 1981.

Prado, José, general vice director, Radio Habana Cuba, talk to and interview by Media Study Tour, Havana, Cuba, 4 May 1982.

Pringle, Peter, director, Caribbean Institute of Mass Communications, Kingston, Jamaica, 15 January 1976.

Ramírez-Corría, Mariana, television actress and program hostess, Havana, Cuba, 5 May 1982.

Reid, Stanley, editor, *Crusader,* Castries, St. Lucia, 8 May 1971.

Ricardo, Lawrence (Ric), vice president and station manager, WVWI, Charlotte Amalie, St. Thomas, U.S. Virgin Islands, 29 May 1981.

Roosberg, Leslie, publisher-editor, *Tempu,* Willemstad, Curaçao, 9 May 1980.

Rosario, Guillermo, editor, *Opinion,* Willemstad, Curaçao, 3 September and 4 September 1968.

Ruprecht, Alvina, professor and French Caribbean researcher, Carlton University, Ottawa, in Pointe-à-Pitre, Guadeloupe, 26 May and 27 May 1988.

Salsbach, Goretti, editor, *Amigoe,* Willemstad, Curaçao, 9 May 1980.

Schouten, G. J., director, *The News* and *Chuchubi,* Oranjestad, Aruba, 29 August 1968 and 5 May 1980.

Scobie, Edward, former editor, *Herald,* Castries, St. Lucia, 9 January 1976.

Seon, Leslie, former WIBS program director and former GIS director, St. George's, Grenada, 13 May 1971.

Simo, Luis, reporter, *News,* Santo Domingo, Dominican Republic, 27 May 1983.

Singh, Rickey, editor, *Caribbean Contact,* Port of Spain, Trinidad, 13 January 1977.

Smith, Ray, director, WIBS, St. George's, Grenada, 12 May 1971.

Snow, Roger, director, Stichting Grafische Comunicatie, Willemstad, Curaçao, 8 May 1980.

Suares, Hector, government public relations, Government Building, Willemstad, Curaçao, 4 September 1968.

Theobalds, Claude, chief program officer, WIBS, Kingstown, St. Vincent, 11 May 1971.

Torres, Ernesto, manager designate, international services, Belize Telecommunications Authority, Belize City, Belize, 29 May 1987.

Trelles, Irena, chief, University of Havana School of Journalism, Havana, Cuba, 5 May 1982.

van der Schoot, J. A., editor, *Amigoe,* Oranjestad, Aruba, 5 May 1980.

van Dongen, Toon, acting publisher, *Amigoe di Aruba,* Oranjestad, Aruba, 27 August 1968.

van Goens, R., veteran staffer, *Beurs en Nieuws-berichten,* Willemstad, Curaçao, 3 September 1968.

Vásquez, Nestor C. A., chairman, BTA, owner of Tropical Vision and Channel 7, Belize City, Belize, 28 May 1987.

Veeris, Jacques, minister of education, culture, social welfare, and sports of Netherlands Antilles, Willemstad, Curaçao, 8 May 1980.

White, Wilsie, general manager, ZJB; chief information officer, Government Information Unit, Plymouth, Montserrat, 29 May 1984.

Whitmarsh, John, station manager, Radio Caribbean, Castries, St. Lucia, 7 May 1971.

Whylie, Dwight, general manager, Jamaica Broadcasting Corporation, Kingston, Jamaica, 14 January 1976.

Wickham, John, editor, *Bim* and *The Bajan,* Bridgetown, Barbados, 14 May 1971.

Willock, Rose, program director, Radio Antilles, Plymouth, Montserrat, 29 May 1984.

York, Ed., programme organizer, Radio One, Belize City, Belize, 29 May 1987.

CORRESPONDENCE

Copies of all correspondence are in the author's possession and will eventually form part of the John A. Lent Collection to be housed at the Alden Library, Ohio University, Athens, Ohio.

Bennett, Wycliffe, to deputy general manager, Jamaica Broadcasting Corporation, 11 December 1980.

Brodie, Ben, to "interested individuals and groups," 1 March 1981.

Brodie, Ben, PAJ president, to Jamaica Broadcasting Corporation staff, 9 March 1981.

Krohn, Stewart, to Curt Thompson, minister of home affairs, Belize, 28 May 1987.

Persaud, Nerbada, general manager, New Guyana Company Ltd., and member of Parliament, to Curl Blackman, managing editor, *Chronicle,* 20 October 1977.

Persaud, Nerbada, to John A. Lent, 1 November 1977.

INDEX